LEARNING TO TEACH HIST
IN THE SECONDARY SCHO

Praise for previous editions...

'This book is without question the standard text for the history PGCE market.' – *Dr Ian Davies, University of York, UK*

'Full of good ideas and better advice ... Mentors will certainly want to use it, and so, I'm sure, will the rest of the history department ... Make sure they buy one, and keep your copy under lock and key.' – *Michael Duffy*, Times Educational Supplement

'A very well-written and readable book. Overall, this is an excellent book and one which students and teachers outwith England would find a valuable addition to their library.' – *Scottish Association of Teachers of History, Resources Review*

In some hands, history can be an inspirational and rewarding subject, yet in others it can seem dry and of little relevance. *Learning to Teach History in the Secondary School*, now in its fourth edition and established as the leading text for all training teachers, enables you to learn to teach history in a way that pupils will find interesting, enjoyable and purposeful. It incorporates a wide range of ideas about the teaching of history with practical suggestions for classroom practice.

The fourth edition has been thoroughly updated in light of the latest curriculum and policy changes, and offers a new chapter exploring subject knowledge for effective teaching and learning. Key topics covered include:

- purposes and benefits of school history
- planning strategies
- teaching approaches and methods
- developing pupils' historical understanding
- ensuring inclusion
- new technologies in the history classroom
- assessment and examinations
- your own continuing professional development.

Each chapter includes suggestions for further reading, weblinks to useful resources and a range of tasks enabling you to put learning into practice in the classroom. Written by experts in the field, *Learning to Teach History in the Secondary School* offers all training and newly qualified teachers comprehensive and accessible guidance to support the journey towards becoming an inspirational and engaging history teacher.

Terry Haydn is Professor of Education at the University of East Anglia. Before working in teacher education, he worked at an inner-city comprehensive in Manchester.

Alison Stephen is Head of History at Abraham Moss Community School, Manchester, and has written articles on history teaching for *Teaching History*.

James Arthur is Professor in Education and Head of School at the University of Birmingham, and has published widely in the areas of history and citizenship education.

Martin Hunt was formerly PGCE Course Leader and Principal Lecturer in Education at Manchester Metropolitan University. He was lead author of *A Practical Guide to Teaching History in the Secondary School* (Routledge 2006).

LEARNING TO TEACH SUBJECTS IN THE SECONDARY SCHOOL SERIES

Series Editors: Susan Capel and Marilyn Leask

Designed for all students learning to teach in secondary schools, and particularly those on school-based initial teacher training courses, the books in this series complement *Learning to Teach in the Secondary School* and its companion, *Starting to Teach in the Secondary School*. Each book in the series applies underpinning theory and addresses practical issues to support student teachers in school and in the training institution in learning how to teach a particular subject.

Learning to Teach in the Secondary School, 6ᵗʰ edition
Edited by Susan Capel, Marilyn Leask and Tony Turner

Learning to Teach Art and Design in the Secondary School, 3rd edition
Edited by Nicholas Addison and Lesley Burgess

Learning to Teach Citizenship in the Secondary School, 2nd edition
Edited by Liam Gearon

Learning to Teach Design and Technology in the Secondary School, 2nd edition
Edited by Gwyneth Owen-Jackson

Learning to Teach English in the Secondary School, 3rd edition
Edited by Jon Davison and Jane Dowson

Learning to Teach Geography in the Secondary School, 2nd edition
David Lambert and David Balderstone

Learning to Teach History in the Secondary School, 4th edition
Edited by Terry Haydn, James Arthur, Martin Hunt and Alison Stephen

Learning to Teach ICT in the Secondary School
Edited by Steve Kennewell, John Parkinson and Howard Tanner

Learning to Teach Mathematics in the Secondary School, 3rd edition
Edited by Sue Johnston-Wilder, Peter Johnston-Wilder, David Pimm and Clare Lee

Learning to Teach Modern Foreign Languages in the Secondary School, 3rd edition
Norbert Pachler, Ann Barnes and Kit Field

Learning to Teach Music in the Secondary School, 2nd edition
Edited by Chris Philpott and Gary Spruce

Learning to Teach Physical Education in the Secondary School, 3rd edition
Edited by Susan Capel

Learning to Teach Religious Education in the Secondary School, 2nd edition
Edited by L. Philip Barnes, Andrew Wright and Ann-Marie Brandom

Learning to Teach Science in the Secondary School, 3rd edition
Edited by Jenny Frost

Learning to Teach Using ICT in the Secondary School, 3rd edition
Edited by Marilyn Leask and Norbert Pachler

Starting to Teach in the Secondary School, 2nd edition
Edited by Susan Capel, Ruth Heilbronn, Marilyn Leask and Tony Turner

LEARNING TO TEACH HISTORY IN THE SECONDARY SCHOOL

A companion to school experience

Fourth edition

Terry Haydn, Alison Stephen, James Arthur and Martin Hunt

Routledge
Taylor & Francis Group

LONDON AND NEW YORK

Fourth edition published 2015
by Routledge
2 Park Square, Milton Park, Abingdon, Oxon OX14 4RN

and by Routledge
711 Third Avenue, New York, NY 10017

Routledge is an imprint of the Taylor & Francis Group, an informa business

First edition published 1997 by RoutledgeFalmer
Third edition published 2008 by Routledge

British Library Cataloguing in Publication Data
A catalogue record for this book is available from the British Library

Library of Congress Cataloging in Publication Data
Learning to teach history in the secondary school : a companion to school experience / Terry Haydn, Alison Stephen, James Arthur and Martin Hunt. -- 4th Edition.
pages cm
Includes bibliographical references and index.
1. History--Study and teaching (Secondary) I. Haydn, Terry, 1951- II. Stephen, Alison. III. Arthur, James, 1957- IV. Hunt, Martin, 1936-
D16.25.H38 2015
907.1'2--dc23
2014017195

ISBN: 978-0-415-86979-9 (hbk)
ISBN: 978-0-415-86981-2 (pbk)
ISBN: 978-0-203-79641-2 (ebk)

Typeset in Interstate
by Saxon Graphics Ltd, Derby

Printed and bound in Great Britain by
TJ International Ltd, Padstow, Cornwall

This book is dedicated to Martin Hunt, who inspired several generations of history teachers.

CONTENTS

FIGURES

TASKS

WEBSITE LINKED TO THIS BOOK

The book contains links to the website for the history PGCE course at the University of East Anglia. These links enable us to provide additional material and examples for classroom use, which enables us to update the book to keep abreast of ongoing development and new ideas in the field of history education.

http://terryhaydn.wordpress.com/pgce-history-at-uea

An alternative link to an earlier version of the site can be found at www.uea.ac.uk/~m242/historypgce/welcome.htm

ACKNOWLEDGEMENTS

The authors would like to acknowledge with thanks the contributions of Joe Haydn, (www.jingjongdoodles.weebly.com) who did the illustrations for the book and to mentors and students who have been so unfailingly helpful and such a pleasure to work with. Thanks also, to KH.

1 Introduction

I've come to a frightening conclusion that I am the decisive element in the classroom. It's my personal approach that creates the climate. It's my daily mood that makes the weather. As a teacher, I possess a tremendous power to make a child's life miserable or joyous. I can be a tool of torture or an instrument of inspiration. I can humiliate or heal. In all situations, it is my response that decides whether a crisis will be escalated or de-escalated and a child humanised or dehumanised. (Ginott, 1972: 15-16)

The aim of this book

The aim of this book is to provide practical guidance on how to become an effective and successful history teacher. This involves the development of insights into the factors which influence the extent to which pupils learn what we are trying to teach and a clear grasp of the wide range of ways in which young people can benefit from learning about the past. As the opening quotation indicates, we will argue that it is also important to teach history in a way that elicits the interest and enthusiasm of pupils. Almost every person who reads this book will have studied history as a school subject and will be aware of the difference the teacher can make to the experience of learning about the past. In some hands, school history can seem a boring subject, of dubious relevance or purpose; in others it can seem inspirational, important and rewarding. Research in English schools suggests that pupils believe that it is not the topic, the syllabus, the teaching approach, or even the subject itself which is the main determinant of how interesting and worthwhile history lessons will be, but the knowledge, skills and persona of the teacher (Harris and Haydn, 2006, 2012; QCA, 2005).

But it is not just a question of making lessons interesting or 'entertaining' for pupils, or 'getting bums on seats' after history becomes optional as a school subject. It is important that the subject is taught in a way which brings about positive outcomes for pupils, and for society. There is no shortage of evidence to suggest that school history has sometimes been used for ethically dubious purposes (Ferro, 1984; Foster and Crawford, 2006; Macmillan, 2009; Nakou and Barca, 2010; Tosh, 2008). As Chapter 2 will indicate, there are ethical dimensions of teaching history as a school subject, and it is important that history student teachers are aware of the ethical dimensions of their work. The experience of school history can change pupils' lives, not just in terms of which direction they take at Key Stage 4 and beyond (in England, under current arrangements, pupils can drop history at the end of 'Key

Stage 3', aged 13 or 14), but in terms of what they will be like as adults. In the words of historian Christopher Hill, 'History, properly taught, can help men to become critical and humane, just as wrongly taught it can turn them into bigots and fanatics' (Hill, 1953: 9). It is not surprising that politicians in the UK and elsewhere have taken a keen interest in the way that history should be taught in schools.

What is involved in becoming an effective and accomplished history teacher?

Most people acknowledge that although subject knowledge is important, it is not the only factor involved in becoming a good history teacher. There is no *necessary* correlation between how well you did in your history exams and how good you will be at teaching history to children, although it is difficult to envisage how to teach history without a sound grasp of the topics you are required to teach. Good subject knowledge is a necessary, but not sufficient prerequisite for effective teaching. Having degree level knowledge of the English Civil War does not in itself guarantee that you will be able to teach it in a way that makes sense to 12 year olds.

What are the other factors involved in teaching history, and how are the knowledge and skills involved best acquired? Practical guidance on these questions includes the question of how to bring together theory (ideas about teaching) and your own developing classroom practice. Teaching is not 'just a trade', that you can simply 'pick up on the job', with a bit of practice and experience of working with anyone who happens to have done it for a while. There is a substantial body of knowledge about effective teaching in history and it is helpful to try and learn from this body of knowledge. Reading is one of the ways that teachers get better at what they do. This book does not offer 'a one stop-shop' for becoming a history teacher. You will have to become acquainted with many other texts in the course of your training. Learning to become an expert and comprehensively accomplished history teacher is a complex (and long and ongoing) process. Even a book of over 300 pages cannot cover *in depth* every facet of 'what you need to become good at', although we do hope it will indicate the range of issues which you need to learn about, provide an effective introduction to these agendas, and guidance as to where to look for further development of your expertise in these areas. Many of the resources which we will suggest are freely available on the internet, and most of the books and history magazines/journals which we mention should be available from the institution which is providing your training, but there are some resources and websites where you have to pay for access (see Chapters 9 and 13), and there are obviously difficult judgement calls about what choices you make here, according to your priorities and the state of your finances.

There is more to it than some commentators imagine (it is said that one eminent academic historian once argued that teaching history was very easy and straightforward, 'You tell people things and they write them down'). You will find that it is more complicated than this. There are lots of things to learn about teaching history; more than can be encompassed in a single text. We will however try to provide guidance and links to other resources which we believe are useful. Chapter 2 attempts to 'unpack' the wide range of knowledge and ideas that history teachers need to be aware of if they are to be able to teach any topic, to any group of pupils, in a way that maximises the potential benefits of learning about that aspect of the past for all pupils.

It can be salutary to think about what proportion of the history you were taught you can remember, understand, and could explain confidently to another person. As Chapter 3 will indicate, there are significant problems of knowledge retention and knowledge application in learning about the past.

Figure 1.1 To think about...

Working within frameworks

It is important to remember that in most education systems, teachers have a substantial degree of latitude in terms of the ways in which they approach the teaching of their subject, and the topics which are specified by the curriculum or examination specification. However, you are not a completely free agent, and that there are frameworks in place which you must take account of, if you are teaching history in a school where it is mandatory to teach the National Curriculum. Perhaps the most important of these is the National Curriculum (NC) for history. In spite of concerns that a NC would significantly erode the professional autonomy of history teachers, (Phillips, 1991; Thatcher, 1993) it should be remembered that the NC is a framework for the teaching of history, not a straightjacket (see Byrom and Riley, 2003; Lee and Shemilt, 2003; Riley, 2000). It requires initiative, imagination and interpretation, to transform curriculum specifications into something that engages pupils and which 'makes sense' to them.

We are aware that you are preparing to be a history teacher in different situations and contexts. We have tried to make the content of this book relevant to all student teachers of history, but when talking about the statutory requirements for history have, for ease of reference, referred to the NC for England. Those of you who are subject to other regulations should still find that much of what is said is of relevance.

Another essential document in your Initial Teacher Education (ITE) course, if you are learning to teach in England, is the framework of *The Teachers' Standards*, laid down by the Department for Education (DfE, 2012). Unless you have reached competence in all the areas of teaching expertise specified by this document, it will not be considered appropriate to unleash you on future generations of pupils. The statements of competence stipulated by *The Teachers' Standards* are at the heart of the development of teaching capability, and you should refer to them regularly throughout your course, remembering that in terms of all these areas of competence, there is a continuum between complete ignorance and inadequacy on the one hand, and the (in practice unattainable) mastery of a teaching competence on the other.

Other important frameworks involved in your development as a history teacher are the schools and the history departments with which you work. History departments are organic and co-operative enterprises, which have a collective responsibility for delivering the history curriculum effectively, and for contributing to whole school policies. You have to harness your own talents and ideas to those of the department you are working with, so as to optimise the quality of experience for you, the department, and the pupils in your care. At its best, it can be a mutually enriching and positive experience for both the department and for the student teacher, but it is not invariably thus, and you need to deploy personal and professional qualities in addition to technical competence in the classroom. Just as you have to learn to 'fit in' to the department you are working in, departments have to 'fit in' with the ethos and policies of the school as a whole. This can be particularly difficult in terms of whole school assessment policy, where there may be philosophical differences between a department and the senior management team of the school, about how best to monitor and report pupil progress (see Burnham and Brown, 2004; Ofsted, 2011 for further development of this point). However, although there will hopefully be constructive professional dialogue between departmental heads and senior management teams over such issues, just as student teachers have to 'fit in' to departmental policies and approaches, departments have to 'fit in' to whole school policies as laid down by senior management teams.

Personal and professional qualities and the development of teaching competence

Very few history student teachers start their course with expert levels of proficiency and knowledge of all aspects of their subject, and in all aspects of teaching. Most student teachers will have some knowledge and experience in certain areas, but are novices in other aspects of subject knowledge and teaching expertise. Acquiring expertise and teaching proficiency is not just a matter of being instructed into a body of professional knowledge, it requires the application of personal qualities, such as perseverance, resilience, initiative, determination, and perhaps above all, willingness and ability to learn from experience, observation and advice. The overarching importance of your professional attitude and approach can be gleaned from the fact that 'Personal and Professional Conduct' merits an entirely separate section within the *Teachers' Standards* which currently define the competences required to gain Qualified Teacher Status (QTS) in England (DfE, 2012 - online at www.gov.uk/government/publications/teachers-standards: see page 14 for the section on 'Personal and Professional Conduct'). One interesting facet of the 2012 version of the competence specifications to become a teacher is the inclusion of the requirement that teachers should not undermine 'fundamental British values, including democracy, the rule of law, individual liberty and mutual respect, and tolerance of those with different faiths and beliefs' (DfE, 2012: 14). The inclusion of the phrase 'British values' clearly has important implications for history student teachers (see Chapter 5).

What does it mean, 'to be professional', as a student teacher?

Experience of interviewing people for courses of initial teacher education suggests that some applicants construe professionalism primarily in terms of 'looking smart', not having time off, and being punctual. Important though these qualities are, it is important to realise that there is much more to professionalism than this.

There is a lot more to being professional than looking smart, being punctual, and not having time off. These qualities or attributes are just a small part of being professional as a student teacher.

Figure 1.2 The complete professional?

In addition to the obvious qualities of professional integrity, reliability, conscientiousness and commitment to the welfare of the pupils in your care, you need to exercise qualities of adaptability, tact, and a willingness to make the best of whatever situation and circumstances you find yourself in.

'Fitting in'

As a student teacher, you should always work within the aims, policies and practices of the department and the school you are a guest in. An important part of preparing to be a teacher is learning to work as part of a team, and 'fitting in' so that you are in effect a member of the history department, doing your best to make a full contribution to the work of the department in exchange for the time, care and guidance you receive. In Section 8 of the *Teachers' Standards*, which relates to the ability to 'fulfil wider professional responsibilities', this is defined as the ability to 'develop effective professional relationships with colleagues, knowing how and when to draw on advice and specialist support', and to be able to 'take responsibility for improving teaching through appropriate professional development, responding to advice and feedback from colleagues (DfE, 2012: 13). The relationship between the student teacher and the history department should be a symbiotic one, where the student teacher contributes time, energy, imagination and initiative, in terms of developing resources, helping with visits, field work, schemes of work, and display work, in exchange for the support and advice which the history department provides. There are many difficult continuums involved in mentoring – the changing balance between pressure and support, encouragement and criticism, direction and freedom to experiment – as your competence and confidence develops. Your task, as a student teacher, is to make best use of all the resources and support available. This sometimes means reconciling conflicting views and advice as to best practice, and tests your skills of tact and diplomacy, as well as your ability to be 'a good learner'.

Open mindedness, quickness to learn, and willingness to test ideas out

Stenhouse (1975) argued that the purpose of educational research was for teachers to test ideas against their own experience, but if student teachers are not willing to test out ideas in their practice, they are unlikely to benefit fully from their reading – it requires student teachers to be *genuinely* open-minded. (It is perhaps interesting that the International Baccalaureate (IB) requires pupils *to be taught* and to *learn* to be open-minded: 'They (learners) are accustomed to seeking and evaluating a range of points of view, and are willing to grow from the experience' (Cannon *et al.*, 2012: 4). The IB learning Profile, with its 10 characteristics or dispositions which are considered desirable for learners to possess are interesting to read and may give some pause for thought in terms of the implications for the sort of teacher you want to become (International Baccalaureate, 2010: 1–2). Some aspects of learning history, and learning to teach history effectively are counterintuitive (Lee and Shemilt, 2003; Wineburg, 2001), and there are times when you need to try things out in your teaching even if you are not sure they will work well. Beware of the danger of 'confirmation bias' (Kahneman, 2011); where people have a tendency to blinker their outlook by only looking for and considering information and evidence which conforms to their current beliefs and understandings. In the words of Andrew Miller (2001: 104), 'It's difficult to change the way you see the world. We take on a certain view when we are young then spend the rest of our lives collecting the evidence.' The idea of the reflective practitioner has perhaps become a bit of a cliché; reflection is something that you are 'supposed to do', to the extent that on some courses, you are required to keep a 'reflective diary' of your teaching experiences. Reflection is only useful if on at least some occasions, it alters your thinking about things. As Klapper puts it, 'If teachers are to aspire to be truly reflective practitioners, they need regularly to question their beliefs, intuitions and assumptions' (Klapper, 2003: 40). It is difficult to get better at teaching if your mind is closed to new ideas.

Humility

Becoming an accomplished teacher requires a broader range of abilities, attributes, personal qualities, competences and understandings than is required to gain a first degree. Even if you are a highly intelligent and well qualified history graduate with strong and varied previous experience of working as a cover supervisor or learning support assistant, there will be many facets of teaching history where you will have limited experience and capability. You will discover that there are some aspects of learning to teach history that are quite challenging. Part of the job of your mentor and tutor is to point out in as constructively critical a manner as possible that there are deficits in your performance which need to be addressed. Your job is partly to accept that for all your success in life thus far, you are an apprentice, you have a lot to learn. An important part of being professional is to accept criticism without rancour or defensiveness, and work as hard as you can to act on advice given.

Few things are more 'heart-sink' for mentors than students who have already made their minds up about 'what works', who lack self-awareness of their developing strengths and comparative weaknesses, and who are not open to ideas and advice.

Resilience

Another important facet of professionalism is application and determination to keep going and doing your best, even when things are difficult; 'not giving up'. Part of learning to teach, and 'being professional', is learning how to handle things when they are not perfect or as they should be. There will be an extensive *dramatis personae* in your experience of learning to teach – tutors, mentors, teaching groups, individual pupils, year heads, colleagues, peers. It will be unusual if everything is perfect and unproblematic in your dealings with all these people throughout your course of training. It is normal to have 'good days and bad days'. The ability to learn from mistakes and to display will and determination in getting better at aspects of teaching which you may not find easy are key qualities in being able to handle 'bad days' constructively.

In this blog post, Laura McInerney eloquently explains the importance of resilience in developing into an effective teacher.
How I Survived the First Year of Teaching
By miss mcinerney (March 23, 2013)
Online at http://bit.ly/1o6P2Uu

Figure 1.3 The importance of resilience

Another part of your professionalism should be to aspire to the highest levels of competence possible in all aspects of history teaching, and to make as much progress as possible towards expert levels of competence, as a student teacher, and throughout your professional career. Why is this important? Because a significant proportion of the pleasure of teaching derives from the feeling you get when it goes really well, when you have had a very good lesson, and you don't need a written evaluation and feedback form to know that the pupils enjoyed the lesson, and they go out of the room still discussing the issues and questions which the lesson has raised. What you want is the respect of the pupils you teach and the respect of the colleagues you work with, and the self-respect that derives from knowing that you are becoming better as a teacher, and are good and steadily improving and developing in the range and quality of what you can do as a teacher.

Citing a study by Klemp (1977), John Elliott argues that some professionals become more accomplished and effective than others because they develop better 'situational understanding' than others, in contexts which require 'problem solving and decision making in complex situations' (Elliott, 1991: 128). Because teaching situations are complex and multi-faceted, they are often not subject to simple 'rule of thumb' solutions. Some student teachers in the early stages of their practice are often looking for a rule or standard procedure to solve problems (a sort of 'just tell me what to do' mentality, or what has been termed 'Waiting for the answer lady to come round'). The reality is that often there is not a cellophane-wrapped standard strategy which is guaranteed to work perfectly with all pupils and teaching groups. The answer (frustratingly) is often, 'It depends...'. However helpful and experienced your mentor, there are many times when to at least some extent, you have to learn to work things out for yourself. The qualities which Klemp attributes to successful professionals include:

- the ability to discern what is important and what is less important;
- skill in accurately analysing and assessing one's own behaviour and performance in the context of interaction with others;

- strong interpersonal skills, including the ability to convey meaning and messages effectively to others and convey to others that you understand their feelings;
- well-judged and moderate risk taking in order to achieve something new and untested;
- intelligent target setting;
- the ability to elicit helpful feedback from co-workers;
- the ability to influence and share goals with others (i.e. pupils) in order to get the job done; and
- strong 'micro-political awareness' - the ability to work constructively with others to achieve the goals of the organisation.

(A more developed explanation of these qualities can be found on pages 128-30 of Elliott, 1991.)

All these attributes require intelligent reflection *and action* (Elliott, 2007); reflection *on its own*, not accompanied by an experimental change of approach, and a willingness to test out new ideas, will not necessarily provide paths to improvement. (Hamlet was good at reflecting on things, not as good on the 'action' part of the process.)

How do you get better at teaching history?

The following activities (Figure 1.4) are all areas of experience which you will encounter in the course of your ITE. Which do you feel will be most influential in enabling you to develop your teaching competences?

A) **'Doing it'** - your own experience of teaching history in the classroom.

B) **'Observing it'** - watching experienced and accomplished teachers teaching their history lessons.

C) **Advice** - Comments from, and conversations with your school tutor, and/or course tutors.

D) **Teaching sessions** - Formal seminars, lectures or workshops either in school or at your Institute of Higher Education (IHE).

E) **Reading** - Either prescribed reading, reading books like this, reading for assignments or casual reading of the *Times Educational Supplement* or articles in the newspapers.

F) **Talking about it** - with fellow student teachers, in school, at your IHE institution or socially.

Figure 1.4 How do you get better at teaching history?

All of these experiences *might* make a contribution to the development of your competence as a classroom teacher, but the extent to which they are helpful depends on your response to them. It is important to consider that the process of becoming a history teacher is not purely aggregative, in that the more you do of all the above things, the better you become. Some student teachers are dismissive of 'theory' and tend to believe that it is mainly about 'doing it' in the classroom, and learning from 'seasoned combat veterans'. They may well miss out on some of the ways in which teachers improve their practice (see Figure 1.4). Others do lots of reading, talking and reflecting, but do not necessarily use these experiences to change the way they do things. It is about getting the most out of the range of experiences listed in Figure 1.4 by being open minded, being prepared to 'take things on board', trying things out and experimenting, and cultivating a good sense of self-awareness of your developing strengths and weaknesses as a teacher.

One theory which has been influential in teacher education in recent years is that of 'the reflective practitioner' (Schon, 1983). This rests on the proposition that gains in competence and understanding are at least to some extent influenced by the quality of thinking and learning which accompanies the activities undertaken by the student teacher. At its most simple, this encompasses the cliché that 'a mistake is not a mistake as long as you learn from it', and the idea that you must develop the skill of profiting from experiences by reflecting on them and attempting to distil the benefits which might be derived from them into what Labbett has termed, 'Principles of Procedure' (Labbett, 1996) for future occasions; what have I learnt from this, what would I do differently next time, how will this affect the way I operate in future? In Labbett's words, 'How have I transformed these experiences into practical suggestions to myself, when planning my teaching during first teaching practice?' It is possible that the comparative utility of these experiences will fluctuate in the course of your development as a history teacher, and that reading about teaching history, for instance, is more helpful when you can place the ideas and suggestions it contains in the context of classroom experience.

It should be stressed that the idea of the 'reflective practitioner' is only one model about how to develop competence as a teacher, albeit one which has been influential in recent years (for more development on this theme, see Moore, 2004). Others maintain that the craft of the history teacher is best acquired by the apprenticeship model, of learning it 'on the job', or that academic historians are best placed to deliver the enthusiasm for subject, and expert subject knowledge which are at the heart of good history teaching (Lawlor, 1996).

As with all theories concerned with education, it is important to be aware that there are usually differing theories and schools of thought as to how education is most effectively delivered, and that these theories need to be tested against your own experience to see which ones appear to be most valid or helpful. Teaching is not like bricklaying, plumbing or learning to play a technically correct backhand drop shot on a squash court; there is no single way of doing it which will work best for all pupils, for all classes, in all schools. There are different views on why history should be taught in schools, and how to teach it most effectively, and although teachers retain the ultimate control of how history is taught in the classroom, it is part of their responsibility to be aware of the range of views on why and how history might be taught.

How to use this book

The book is set out in a way which attempts to provide a pragmatic introduction to teaching history in the secondary classroom. An important element of this is the bringing together of theory and practice, so that you are aware of some of the current thinking, problems and differing views on aspects of history teaching and can relate them to the situations you encounter in your classroom practice, and become aware of ideas about history teaching which you might *not* encounter directly in your school experience. The text is also interspersed with tasks or suggestions for points to discuss or reflect on with tutors or fellow student teachers. Where the tasks ask you to engage in activities that impinge upon other people, whether it be structured observation, or asking for information, it is important that you first seek the permission of the staff concerned, and that you exercise tact, sensitivity and good judgement in the timing of such requests.

In some sections of the book, there are also links to material on the internet, which provide further examples, references and ideas. The book provides examples of the sort of activities which might be attempted in your practical teaching. They do not come with a guarantee that they will work perfectly with all teaching groups, and you may well want to amend, adapt or discard them from your teaching repertoire in the light of your experience. While you should feel free to experiment with some of these suggestions, or variations on them, you must remember that in the long term, you have got to develop your own ideas for planning for learning in history. Student teachers often find that it takes an inordinate amount of time to plan lessons in the early stages of school experience. There is an understandable temptation to use the resources which have already been developed by the department you are working in, or some of the ideas in this book. There is nothing wrong with this in the short term, and in a sense, all history teachers have to be 'scavengers' for ideas, materials and activities. What is important is that you progress towards using your own ideas, or adapting some of the ideas you encounter in this or other books to other historical contexts, or developing extensions and variations to these suggestions and examples. Your short-term 'want' is sometimes anything that will get you through Friday afternoon with 9Z; your long-term 'need' is to be able to function autonomously, in generating your own ideas for effective teaching and learning in history – not just in terms of individual lessons, but in terms of planning your own route through topics, and into medium and long-term planning for learning in history.

Theory and practice

An important element of preparing to become a history teacher is the attempt to bring together theory and practice. 'Theory', might be regarded as *ideas* about history teaching. Sometimes theories claim to be 'evidence based', in the sense that they offer some form of empirical data or other substantiation that the idea 'works', sometimes theories are little more than tentative suggestions. Isaac Newton once said, 'If I have been able to see further than others, it is because I have been able to stand on the shoulders of giants.' Even the most creative and imaginative history teachers have augmented their teaching repertoire with things they have read about, as well as things that have evolved out of their own practice. There is something slightly arrogant about suggesting that you don't need anyone else's ideas to become a good teacher, you can work it all out for yourself, and a bit narrow minded about thinking that the only ideas you need are those of the small number of history teachers you will work with directly in the course of your training. Fordham (2012a, 2012b) explains how approaches to teaching historical topics were refined, developed and improved by reading about teachers' and historians' work in relation to those topics. Theories about how to teach history effectively constitute a potentially important resource in your development as a history teacher. The trouble with theories is that there are different ones, they don't always work, and sometimes they contradict each other. This doesn't mean that they are not worth bothering with. Millions of words have been written about teaching history. Some of them will be helpful and give you insight, understanding and ideas to improve your teaching. Theories that do not seem to be of use can be discarded.

History in school can be a dispiriting and seemingly pointless experience for the pupils on whom it is inflicted. A survey of 10,000 pupils by Barber found that 70 per cent regularly counted the minutes to the end of the lesson (Barber, 1994). How many of us have not done this at some point? But history can also be taught to pupils in a way which gives them knowledge and understanding of the past, insight into some of the most important and difficult questions of human existence, and in addition, gives them other educational skills and an enthusiasm to pursue history beyond the point when the study of the subject is compulsory. The aim of this book is to provide practical guidance, ideas, and recommendations for further reading which will help you to teach history in a way which is rewarding and fulfilling for you and your pupils. Effective teaching is not just 'common sense', and to regard it as such is to undervalue the skill and professional expertise of experienced teachers. Teaching is a complex and difficult activity. It is because it is so difficult that it is also interesting, rewarding and worthwhile. Much of the job satisfaction of being a teacher derives from getting better at what you do (it can be helpful for student teachers to reflect on how much better they are in the latter stages of their course compared to their early efforts in the classroom). You will be exceptional if you manage to develop to expert levels of competence in all facets of history teaching in the course of your training, but you will hopefully witness expert levels of practice which will make you aware of levels to aspire to. We hope that this book will serve as a useful foundation for your development as a history teacher. The Board of Education Report for 1910-11 advised that 'in the long run, success or failure in history teaching, perhaps more than in any other subject, depends on the ability and interest of the individual teacher' (quoted in Aldrich, 1991: 97). We believe that this advice still applies.

What can you usefully do before the start of the course?

1   Join the Historical Association and start reading *Teaching History*.
    Probably the single most important thing you should do is to subscribe to the main professional journal for history teachers in England, *Teaching History*. It is the equivalent of reading the *British Medical Journal* if you are a doctor - if you are a history teacher, you should read it. The journal is essential because it helps to bring together 'theory and practice', providing a rationale for, and insight into a wide range of teaching approaches focusing on different aspects of historical knowledge and understanding, combined with practical and well tested ideas for classroom activities, written by experts in the field of history education. (Many of the same claims could be made for Ian Dawson's website, www.thinkinghistory.co.uk.) Secondary membership gives you electronic access to back issues of the journal and to the Historical Association's website, which is becoming an increasingly valuable resource for history teachers, in terms of keeping up to date with developments in the subject (see www.history.org.uk). Your school or university should have a subscription to the journal, but if you can afford to join the Historical Association, electronic access will save considerable amounts of your time.
2   Develop a sound working knowledge of the National Curriculum for history.
    It is important that before the course starts, you familiarise yourself with the National Curriculum for history for secondary schools, or whatever official government specification for the subject applies where you are teaching.

It is also important to familiarise yourself with what history pupils are likely to have encountered *at primary school*, so that you have some sense of 'where they are coming from' in terms of their knowledge and understanding of the past.

National Curriculum for history – secondary schools
www.gov.uk/government/uploads/system/uploads/attachment_data/
file/239075/SECONDARY_national_curriculum_-_History.pdf
National Curriculum for history – primary schools
www.gov.uk/government/uploads/system/uploads/attachment_data/
file/239035/PRIMARY_national_curriculum_-_History.pdf

Figure 1.5 The National Curriculum for history (DfE, 2013)

3   Gain experience of working in secondary school contexts.

Try to gain as much experience as possible of working or observing in a secondary history department. This is invaluable in terms of developing your 'situational understanding' (Elliott, 1991) of the context in which history curriculum specifications are turned into practice, and the wide range of factors that influence teaching and learning in the history classroom. As well as gaining experience of teaching or observing in an 'ordinary' secondary school, it can be invaluable to gain some insight into the teaching of pupils with special education needs, and of Pupil Referral Units (PRUs), for pupils who have been excluded from 'mainstream' schools. It can be helpful to also try to spend some time working or observing in primary schools. Work as a learning support assistant or cover supervisor can be invaluable in terms of developing your insight into the nature and challenges of teaching.

4   Work hard to develop your subject content knowledge.

Reading is one of the ways in which teachers get better at what they do. Read as widely as possible – books, articles about history in the newspapers, reviews of new history books in the review sections of the weekend papers, television history – anything that develops your subject knowledge. You may also wish to look at or subscribe to some of the many history magazines which are available, such as the *BBC History Magazine*, or *History Today*. It is particularly important to ensure that before the course starts, you have a solid overview knowledge of British history from 1066 onwards, as this remains a major strand of the National Curriculum for history (DfE, 2013).

5   Look at GCSE and A level examination specifications and exam papers to familiarise yourself with what pupils have to do in history exams.

Web addresses of the three main examination boards in England:
www.aqa.org.uk/subjects/history
www.edexcel.com/subjects/History/Pages/default.aspx
www.ocr.org.uk/qualifications/by-subject/history/

6   Familiarise yourself with some of the main history education websites and Twitter feeds. You should find time to familiarise yourself with some of the many websites and Twitter feeds which are designed to support history teachers (see Chapter 9). The internet is now an invaluable resource for history teachers, and the sooner you learn to 'tap in' to this resource, the better.

7   It can be helpful to read a book about classroom management and learning before starting the course. There are few schools where pupil behaviour is not an issue (see Harris and Haydn, 2012), where you can just walk in to any teaching group and just teach, without having to think of control issues. Some further guidance and suggestions for reading are given in the class management section of the website (www.uea.ac.uk/~m242/historypgce).

8   Try to keep up to date with recent developments in history teaching. The Historical Association's website is very useful for this, particularly the 'History in the news' section (www.history.org.uk/resources/secondary_news_1724.html), and the *Times Educational Supplement* is also a useful resource, particularly the website and subject specific news feeds.

Three resources which students have found to be helpful for developing disciplinary understanding of the subject:

●   the 'webtrails' feature of the Historical Association's website, which links to articles referring to particular concepts in history teaching, such as interpretations, significance and citizenship (www.history.org.uk/resources/secondary_resources_61.html).

●   Harris, R., Burn, K. and Woolley, M. (Eds) (2014) *The guided reader to teaching and learning history*, London, Routledge. This contains extracts from recent research and writing which are recommended as being helpful to improve theoretical understandings.

●   Davies, I. (Ed.) *Debates in history teaching*, London, Routledge. Another collection by experts in the field of history education.

These last two books are influential and up-to-date works, and hopefully your training institution will have them as either an e-book, or at least one or more hard copies.

Task 1.1 *The overarching importance of your professional attitude and approach to learning to teach history*

It is impossible to overstate the importance of this facet of learning to teach. Two questions you might ask yourself, one at the end of your first visit to your placement school, and one at the end of the whole placement experience:

After your first visit: 'To what extent did I make a good general impression on the colleagues I will be working with? To what extent are they looking forward to working with me, feeling confident that I will be highly professional and a pleasure to work with?'

At the end of your placement: 'If there was a job going in the department, how strongly would the department want me to apply for and get the job, even though they know there are a lot of very good history student teachers out there?'

Many teachers would argue that it is as important to be a good colleague as to be a good classroom teacher. One of the main concerns that a Head of History has when interviewing for a new history teacher is whether that person will 'fit in' and work well within the department. Yes, they expect that teacher to be 'good with the kids', and a good classroom practitioner, able to teach the subject in a way that motivates and engages pupils. But if you are not accomplished in terms of the professional atributes detailed in the *Teachers' Standards* (DfE, 2012), you may well struggle to find employment even if you are strong in other areas of the Standards. Read through the sections on the website relating to mistakes that some history student teachers have made, as reported by history tutors (www.uea.ac. uk/~m242/historypgce/mistakes).

Some of these relate to 'technical' issues related to history teaching, but most refer to flaws in student teachers' overall professional attitude and approach.

If you have been working with a group of other history student teachers, towards the end of the course, (discreetly), think about which of your peers you would want to have working in your department if you were a Head of History, what are the personal and professional qualities which makes some people attactive or congenial to work with?

Summary and key points

If you are to be an effective teacher, you must be well prepared and well informed. You must quickly acquire a sound grasp of the requirements of the Standards for Qualified Teacher Status (for teachers in England, see DfE, 2012), the curriculum specifications for your subject, and the schemes of work of the history department you are working in. Your overall professional attitude and approach to the challenges of becoming a teacher are of overarching importance in making progress. Progress in this area underpins progress in all strands of the *Teachers' Standards*. Particularly important aspects of professionalism are quickness and willingness to learn from experience, advice and reading, conscientiousness and determination to try to work to the highest possible professional standards, and the resilience to keep working hard when things are difficult. Part of learning to teach is how you handle things when they are not going well, and situations are not ideal.

 Using this book: we have inserted many web references in the book, as this can often provide easy access to relevant resources, but web addresses can change, so you may find in some places you have to search within the relevant website to locate the relevant page where the website has been revised or updated.

There is a website to support this book which is linked to the history PGCE course at the University of East Anglia, but it should be stressed that this is a personal, 'home made' and basic site, and does not have the range depth and sophistication of many of the major history education websites detailed in Chapter 9.

http://terryhaydn.wordpress.com/pgce-history-at-uea

Figure 1.6 A (very basic) website to support this book

References

Aldrich, R. (ed.) (1991) *History in the NC*, London: Kogan Page.

Barber, M. (1994) *Guardian*, 23 August.

Burnham, S. and Brown, G. (2004) Assessment without level descriptions, *Teaching History*, 115: 5–15.

Burston, W.H. and Green, C.W. (eds) (1962) *Handbook for History Teachers*, London: Methuen.

Byrom, J. and Riley, M. (2003) Professional wrestling in the history department: a case study in planning and teaching the British Empire at Key Stage 3, *Teaching History*, 112: 6–14.

Cannon, M., Jones-Nerzic, R., Keys, D., Mamaux, A., Miller, M., Pope, G., Smith, D. and Williams, A. (2012) *20th Century World History*, Oxford: OUP.

Davies, I. (ed.) (2011) *Debates in History Teaching*, London: Routledge.

Department for Education (2012) *Teachers' Standards. Statutory guidance for school leaders, school staff and governing bodies*, London: DfE. Online at www.gov.uk/government/uploads/system/uploads/attachment_data/file/283198/Teachers__Standards.pdf, accessed 12 February 2014.

DfE (2013) *History programmes of study: key stage 3: National Curriculum in England*, London, DfE.

Elliott, J. (1991) *Action Research for Educational Change*, Buckingham: Open University Press.

Elliott, J. (2007) *Reflecting Where the Action Is: The Selected Works of John Elliott*, London: Routledge.

Ferro, M. (1984) *The Use and Abuse of History: Or how the past is taught to children*, London: Routledge and Kegan Paul.

Fordham, M. (2012a) Disciplinary knowledge and the situation of history teachers, Educational Sciences, 2: 242–53. Online at www.mdpi.com/2227-7102/2/4/242, accessed 23 March 2014.

Fordham, M. (2012b) Out went Caesar and in came the Conqueror, though I'm sure something happened in between…, A case study in professional thinking, *Teaching History*, 147: 38–46. Online at www.history.org.uk/resources/secondary_resource_5578_171.html, accessed 22 March 2014.

Foster, S. and Crawford, K. (eds) (2006) *What shall we tell the children? International perspectives on school history textbooks*, Greenwich CT: Information Age Publishing.

Harris, R., Burn, K. and Woolley, M. (eds) (2014) *The Guided Reader to Teaching and Learning History*, London: Routledge.

Harris, R. and Haydn, R. (2006) Pupils' enjoyment of history – what lessons can teachers learn from their pupils?, *Curriculum Journal*, 17 (4): 315–33.

Harris, R. and Haydn, T. (2012) What happens to a subject in a 'free market' curriculum? A study of secondary school history in the UK, *Research Papers in Education*, 27 (1): 81–101.

Ginott, H. (1972) *Teacher and Child*, New York: Macmillan: 15–16.

Hill, C. (1953) *Suggestions on the Teaching of History*, Paris: UNESCO.

International Baccalaureate (2010) *The IB learner profile*, online at www.ibo.org/myib/digitaltoolkit/ files/brochures/LearnerProfile-EN.pdf, accessed 23 March 2014.

Kahneman, D. (2011) *Thinking, Fast and Slow*, London: Allen Lane.

Klapper, J. (2003) Taking communication to task? A critical review of recent trends in language learning, *The Language Learning Journal, 27* (1): 33–42.

Klemp, G. (1977) Three Factors of Success, in D.W. Vermilye (ed.) *Relating Work and Education*, San Francisco: Jossey-Bass: 102–9.

Labbett, B. (1996) Principles of Procedure and the Expert Teacher, online at: www.enquirylearning.net/ ELU/Issues/Education/Ed4.html, accessed 9 October 2007.

Lawlor, S. (1996) *Times Educational Supplement*, 6 September.

Lee, P. and Shemilt, D. (2003) A scaffold, not a cage: progression and progression models in history, *Teaching History*, No. 113: 13–23.

MacMillan, M. (2009) *The Uses and Abuses of History*, New York: Random House.

Miller, A. (2001) *Oxygen*, London: Spectre.

Moore, A. (2004) *The Good Teacher: Dominant discourses in teaching and teacher education*, London: RoutledgeFalmer.

Nakou, I. and Barca, I. (eds) (2010) *Contemporary Public Debates over History Education*, Greenwich CT: Information Age Publishing.

Ofsted (2011) *History For All*, London: Ofsted.

Phillips, R. (1991) National Curriculum History and teacher autonomy, the Major challenge, *Teaching History*, No. 65, October: 21–4.

Qualifications and Curriculum Authority (2005) Pupil perceptions of history at Key Stage 3, London, QCA, online at www.uea.ac.uk/~m242/historypgce/qcafinalreport.pdf, accessed 12 March 2014.

Riley, M. (2000) Into the Key Stage 3 history garden: choosing and planting your enquiry questions, *Teaching History*, No. 99: 8–13.

Schon, D. (1983) *The Reflective Practitioner*, New York: Basic Books.

Stenhouse, L. (1975) *An Introduction to Curriculum Research and Development*, Oxford: Heinemann.

Thatcher, M. (1993) *The Downing Street Years*, London: Harper Collins.

Tosh, J. (2008) *Why History Matters*, Basingstoke: Palgrave Macmillan.

Wineburg. S. (2001) *Historical Thinking and Other Unnatural Acts*, Philadelphia: Temple Press.

2 Ideas about the purposes and benefits of school history

What does history contribute to social literacy? What ways of thinking, writing and questioning would be lost if we eliminated history from the curriculum? (Gaea Lienhardt, quoted in Wineburg, 2001: ix)

Why do all regimes make their young study some history in school? Not to understand society and how it changes, but to approve of it, to be proud of it, to be or become good citizens. (Hobsbawn, 1997)

From a transcript of a lesson on the Munich Crisis of 1938. (One of the aims of the lesson was to help pupils understand the concept of appeasement):

Tentative question from an intelligent, well motivated and polite pupil:

'I'm sorry Miss... I'm not meaning to be rude... please don't take this personally, and I'm not meaning to get at history teachers... but why are we doing this?'

Figure 2.1 Why are we doing this?

Introduction

One of the most common causes of poor history teaching is that student teachers have not thought through clearly the purposes of school history, and do not have a sound grasp of the full breadth of benefits that young people can derive from the study of the past. If you are going to dedicate your professional life to becoming a history teacher, you ought to be able to justify the worth of your subject's place on the school timetable, and understand why the study of history will be of use to your students.

Objectives

At the end of this chapter you should:

- be aware of the ongoing debate about the place of history in the school curriculum and have a sound grasp of the current NC for History;
- be aware that there are differing views as to why and how history should be taught in schools;
- be familiar with the rationales for the teaching and learning of history which have been advanced in recent years, providing a justification which you could articulate to others for its continuing place in schools; and
- have a critical perspective on the teaching and learning of history within current developments, policies, practices and debates.

Task 2.1 *Developing your understanding of the range of views about why pupils should study history at school*

You should try to read widely on the recent history of the history curriculum and the public debates about the purposes of history in recent years. This should help you to acquire a clear and well developed sense of *why* you are teaching history, and an awareness that there are very different views about why young people should study history.

Differing views on the purposes of school history

(The list is not an exhaustive one, and in some cases, it could be argued that they are 'phoney' arguments, or false dichotomies; it is a question of balance, rather than 'either-or').

School history should be about cultural transmission; passing on the best of what has been written and said, giving pupils a sense of identity, and developing the values and attitudes that will make them good citizens.	School history should be about teaching pupils to handle information critically and intelligently; it should be about helping pupils to think for themselves, rather than teaching them what to think.
There needs to be more emphasis on British history, as this is the country that pupils grow up in.	We need to move away from a narrow, Anglocentric model of school history.

Political and constitutional history – great events, great men and women – should be at the heart of school history.

There should be more to school history than 'the great tradition'. School history should reflect changes in academic history and the moves towards 'histories'.

Modern/contemporary history is most relevant and useful for pupils.

There is a worrying trend towards pupils receiving a diet of 'Hitler, Stalin and the World Wars' – and repeating the same topics at KS3, GCSE and 'A' level.

There should be a clear separation between history and current affairs – history teaching has become too 'political'.

It is important to link the past to the present if it is to be relevant and helpful to pupils.

School history should be about providing pupils with a body of knowledge about the past. Pupils need to be told what happened, and learn facts and dates. Recent trends, such as analysing 'dismembered gobbets' of history, have meant that pupils don't really know 'what happened'.

Pupils also need to understand the nature of historical knowledge, and history as a discipline, if they are to make sense of these facts and dates.

History teachers should tell pupils what happened in the past.

History teachers need to teach pupils about 'interpretations' of the past – and to understand that more than one account or explanation can be constructed from the record of the past.

Figure 2.2 A 'thumbnail' summary of some of the recent arguments about school history

Task 2.2 *Developing an understanding of the breadth of ideas about why young people should learn history in school*

Look at the list of quotations about the purposes of school history at: www.uea. ac.uk/~m242/historypgce/purposes/purpquotes.htm. The purpose of this sub-collection of quotes is to make student history teachers aware of the range of views which are held about the purposes and benefits of the study of history. Is it possible to classify them into 'schools of thought'? Can you draw up a concise list of the benefits bestowed by the study of history by reading through the quotes, avoiding repetition? Do views on the purposes of school history depend on one's perspective? Do politicians tend to want history to develop loyal, patriotic and compliant citizens, educationists want school history to develop independence of mind, informed scepticism and good judgement? Could you make an intelligent guess whether the quotes were uttered by politicians, historians or educationalists? Does the study of history give people the ability to make inferential judgements of this nature?

The URL http://terryhaydn.wordpress.com/pgce-history-at-uea/pgce-student-teacher/purpose-of-school-history also contains a link to a longer list of quotations about the purposes of school history which may be of interest or use when writing assignments in this area (or go to www.uea. ac.uk/~m242/historypgce/purposes/purposesquotesintro.htm).

The history of the history curriculum: how did we get to where we are now?

Do you really need to know about previous versions of school history? Isn't it enough to know about the stipulations of the current National Curriculum for history, and current examination specifications?

You do need to know about current specifications, but one of the ideas about the uses of the past is that of 'historical perspectives' (Aldrich, 1997). Is there any issue, problem, or question, into which we cannot gain more insight by looking at what has gone before? What messages do you send to your pupils about the study of the past, if you say (and think) that there is no point in looking at 'what happened before'? Gaining an understanding of how school history has developed and changed over the past century can provide insights into the challenges and complexities of teaching history to young people, and an understanding that there are very different views about why pupils should study history at school.

Figure 2.3 Do I need to know about 'What went before'?

a) School history 'BNC' (Before the National Curriculum)

For much of the time that history has been on the school curriculum, its prime aim was seen as providing moral exemplars. In 1905, the Board of Education's *Suggestions for the consideration of History teachers*, argued that 'The lives of great men and women, carefully selected from all stations of life, will furnish the most impressive examples of obedience, loyalty, courage, strenuous effort, serviceableness, indeed, all the qualities which make for good citizenship' (Board of Education, 1905). In similar vein, Willis Bund, chair of the Worcestershire Education Board, argued that the job of the history teacher was:

> To bring before the children the lives and work of English people who served God in church and state, to show that they did this by courage, endurance and self-sacrifice, that as a result the British Empire was founded and extended, and that it behoved every child to emulate them. (Willis Bund, 1908)

The rationale for school history was also based on the idea that the transmission of a positive story about the national past would inculcate in young people a sense of loyalty to the state, and a reassuring and positive sense of identity and belonging. Aldrich describes the history curriculum which pertained in England until the 1970s as 'cast in a broadly self-congratulatory and heroic, high-political mould' (Aldrich, 1991). Some of the key themes to be transmitted to pupils were the development of a beneficent system of parliamentary democracy, Britain's rise to great power status through the industrial revolution and the acquisition of a (benevolently administered) empire, and Britain's triumph in the two major conflicts of the twentieth century.

Another characteristic of what might be termed 'traditional' school history was that it was essentially a 'received' subject, in the sense that pupils were given a story or stories that were to be considered as factually correct, and not subject to controversies of interpretation. Aldrich (1991) argued that it was seen as the duty of the academic historian to establish the historical record, and the job of the school teacher to transmit this record to pupils in simplified form, and as 'fact'. The idea that 'more than one story might be told' from the remnants of the national past was not a feature of school history, or at least, not until Advanced level study. The historian Robert Conquest, writing in a series of 'Black Papers' on education, criticising progressive trends in education, made the case for education as the passing on to the next generation of a 'canon' of essential knowledge:

> An educated man must have a certain minimum of general knowledge. Even if he knows very little about science and cannot add or subtract, he must have heard of Mendel and Kepler. Even if he is tone deaf, he must know something about Debussy and Verdi, even if he is a pure sociologist, he must be aware of Circe and the Minotaur, of Kant and Montaigne, of Titus Oates and Tiberius Gracchus. (Conquest, 1969: 3)

Slater has argued that until the 1970s, the selection from the culture that formed the basis of school history was 'an inherited consensus, based largely on hidden assumptions, rarely identified, let alone publicly debated'. He parodied school history as:

> Largely British, or rather Southern English; Celts looked in to starve, emigrate or rebel; the North to invent looms or work in mills; abroad was of interest once it was part of the Empire; foreigners were either, sensibly, allies, or, rightly, defeated. Skills – did we even use the word? – were mainly those of recalling accepted facts about famous dead Englishmen, and communicated in a very eccentric literary form, the examination-length essay (Slater, 1989: 1).

However, the general consensus over the form which school history should take came under pressure from the 1970s onwards. Concern about the nature and *state of health* of history as a school subject can be dated from Mary Price's influential paper, *History in danger* (Price, 1968). History in schools, Price suggested, was unpopular, in decline, and often taught with pupils adopting a mainly passive role absorbing a body of knowledge or facts from the teacher. There was real concern that the subject could be marginalised as just one component in an 'integrated' humanities/social studies model. Partly in response to these concerns, The *Schools Council History Project* was established in the early 1970s and promoted new teaching methods in order to generate more active learning among pupils and placed greater emphasis on the use of resources in the classroom. The Project was designed to encourage understanding of the nature of history and its fundamental concepts. This process of change was controversial for it entailed making history less exclusively a body of knowledge to be learned, and placed more emphasis on pupils' understanding of history as a form of knowledge, with its particular procedures and conventions. The 'New

History', as it came to be known, focused on concepts such as evidence, empathy and cause, and used primary sources as evidence in a more pupil centred approach. Former HMI for history John Slater described the Schools History Project as 'the most significant and beneficent influence on the learning of history to emerge this century', arguing that this form of school history could give young people 'not just knowledge, but the tools to reflect on, critically to evaluate, and to *apply* that knowledge. It proclaims the crucial distinction between knowing the past and thinking historically' (1989: 2-3).

The project was not without its critics. Williams (1986) argued that whilst history had been liberated from the transmission of a corpus of information in a linear and chronological framework, it was also true that a sense of chronology had been sacrificed and that this was something that traditional history did much better. Even defenders of the project such as Slater acknowledged that there was a price to be paid in terms of the breadth of content which could be covered if time was also to be given to providing pupils with more insight into the nature of historical knowledge, and in terms of coherence, continuity and focus (Slater, 1989: 2).

Criticism began to emerge that history had gone full circle, from an excessive emphasis on content to an excessive emphasis on process or skills. Beattie highlighted two main criticisms from the political right. First, an increase in what was seen as corrosive and insidious moral relativism, and the contention that there were no 'facts' in history any more since empathy, evidence and imagination were to take on greater importance as the pupils themselves were asked to analyse and interpret the past. Second, that the demand for relevance in history was reducing history to current affairs.

The fact that the new GCSE examination in 1988 appeared to adopt many aspects of 'new' history served to polarise the debate still further. Other than the stipulation that each examination board should offer at least one examination based on the history of the United Kingdom, and that syllabuses must be of sufficient length, range and depth, deal with key issues and be 'coherent and balanced', there was no requirement to teach any particular areas of historical content. It seemed to many to be a denial of the existence or desirability of a historical 'canon' which all pupils should be taught. To some, it seemed tantamount to saying that the content of school history didn't matter - that it was acceptable for pupils to learn GCSE history through content that had little or nothing to do with British history.

Another important contribution to the debate on school history was made by the Secretary of State for Education, Sir Keith Joseph. He strongly advocated the teaching of history to all up to the age of 16 and his speech remains a benchmark for the place of history in the school curriculum. Joseph pointed to a key difference between the processes of reasoning which might be used in history as opposed to science, when he noted that one of the purposes of school history was to help pupils to 'use their reason as well as their memories, and to develop skills of analysis and criticism in a situation where there cannot be a right answer' (Joseph, 1984: 12).

School history ANC (After the National Curriculum)

The 1980s saw calls for the introduction of a National Curriculum (NC). The NC for England and Wales was a product of the Education Reform Act of 1988, and was first taught in schools in 1991, when it was envisaged that history would be a compulsory subject to the age of 16.

In terms of the purposes of school history, the NC Working Group which formulated the original NC for History identified nine purposes of school history:

1   To help understand the present in the context of the past.
2   To arouse interest in the past.
3   To help to give pupils a sense of identity.
4   To help give pupils an understanding of their own cultural roots and shared inheritance.
5   To contribute to the pupils' knowledge and understanding of other countries and other cultures in the modern world.
6   To train the mind by means of disciplined study.
7   To introduce pupils to the distinctive methodology of historians.
8   To enrich other areas of the curriculum.
9   To prepare pupils for adult life. (DES, 1990)

By the 1990s, different ideas were emerging about the ways in which school history might be used as a sort of 'social cement', to bind the population together (Aldrich and Dean, 1991: 102). Some metropolitan education authorities wanted to use school history to promote appreciation of cultural diversity, celebrate cultural pluralism, and combat racism (Haydn, 1992b, 1996). National politicians (of all parties) tended to continue to call for the teaching of a positive and celebratory rendering of 'Our island story' as a recipe for improving social cohesion. In 2007, Gordon Brown argued for a 'National Museum of History', which would foster national pride, and for the explicit teaching of 'Britishness' as part of the school curriculum (Brown, 2007), and more recently, Michael Gove argued that:

> There is no better way of building a modern, inclusive, patriotism than by teaching all British citizens to take pride in this country's historic achievements. Which is why the next Conservative Government will ensure the curriculum teaches the proper narrative of British History – so that every Briton can take pride in this nation. (Gove, 2010)

Others expressed reservations about the use of school history to 'demonstrate' any of these claims or values, arguing that school history was more useful in terms of helping pupils' understanding of the world and their place in it: 'The reason for teaching history is not that it changes society, but that it changes pupils, it changes what they see in the world, and how they see it' (Lee, 1992: 23). Whether school history should concern itself with the affective domain of values and attitudes is another contested area. Is school history to tell pupils what to think or to teach them to think for themselves?

The public debate which was unleashed by the decision to introduce a NC for History did however make it clear that once one got beyond very general statements of aims, there were very differing views on what historical content should be taught, and which of the aims of school history were most important. Successive Prime Ministers and Secretaries of State for Education made pronouncements on school history, and there were hundreds of newspaper articles about school history (see Haydn, 2012; Kitson *et al.*, 2011 for further detail). The national debate on school history helped to raise the profile of the subject. At least it seemed that there was a consensus that history was very important, and that the way in which it was taught would have a significant bearing on the sort of citizens who would emerge from schools.

The debate also raised the question of the connection between the uses of history in general, and history in schools. One view of the purpose of history is to record those things which have been selected as important in giving us a sense of identity and context. Issues such as 'identity' and 'Britishness' help to explain the controversial and contested nature of school history. In the words of Tate, 'A fundamental purpose of the school curriculum is to transmit an appreciation of and commitment to the best of the culture we have inherited' (Tate, 1996). Implicit in this statement is the reality that as the record of the human past is so vast, we cannot learn everything about it, and we must therefore make a selection from the past.

It is at this point – when the business of school history is seen to be one of cultural transmission, that the difficulties in achieving consensus on school history becomes more apparent. Who selects? What are their motives? Are they promoting any particular ideology, explicitly or covertly? Is there any significance in those topics which are not selected? What criteria are used for the selection of content?

In addition to these concerns, developments in academic history also percolated through to school level, with the idea of a range of histories, rather than one grand historical narrative, including 'history from below', women's history, and the history of minority cultures. Whereas some academic historians were arguing for a strong emphasis on political and constitutional history in school history (Abulafia *et al.*, 2012), others were making the point that 'national' history was over-represented in school history (Mandler, 2012).

There is also disagreement over whether pupils should be given a version of history which can be presented to pupils as a valid and authoritative account of the national past. Sheila Lawlor (1989), from the Centre for Policy Studies has argued that any other approach will result in pupils being 'confused by being given different versions (of the past), and might be better off to master the facts'. However, Peter Seixas (2002) argues that 'students need guided opportunities to confront conflicting accounts, various meanings and multiple interpretations of the past, because these are exactly what they will encounter outside of school, and they need to learn to deal with them'.

Another important point to note is the relation between history for academic purposes, and history in schools. An explanation of some of the differences between academic and school history is provided by Husbands:

> Where historians are engaged in an interpretative activity relating the current state of the discipline to new research findings, history teachers are largely concerned with their pupils' intellectual and personal development.... There is an academic discipline called 'history', a school subject called 'history', and a widespread popular interest in 'history'. There is no reason why all these pursuits should have the same label, nor why the label should have the same meaning in different contexts. (Husbands, 1996: 5)

Keeping in mind these distinctions is an important part of learning to teach history effectively. We teach it not simply as a preparation for the study of history at university – some of your pupils will not go to university – but because some aspects of the subject are useful to pupils in their lives after school. History is both a body of knowledge, and a form of knowledge, and some of the historian's rules of procedure may aid intelligent decision making in life beyond the classroom. Some aspects of the discipline help pupils to cope with the 'spin' which has become a pervasive part of modern life. In the words of HMI, 'A subject that insists on the critical evaluation of evidence… and encourages the analysis of problems and the communication of ideas, not only contributes to pupils' general education, but develops skills and perceptions that increase the employability of young people' (HMI, 1985: 12).

As history teachers, how do we handle the lack of consensus about the purposes of school history, and about which (if any) values and attitudes should be promoted through school history? One way forward is to consider Slater's suggestion that school history is where values and attitudes are *examined, discussed and debated*, rather than simply transmitted:

> (History) not only helps us to understand the identity of our communities, cultures, nations, by knowing something of their past, but also enables our loyalties to them to be moderated by informed and responsible scepticism. But we cannot expect too much. It cannot guarantee tolerance, though it can give it some intellectual weapons. It cannot keep open closed minds, although it may sometimes leave a nagging grain of doubt in them. Historical thinking is *primarily* mind-opening, *not* socialising. (Slater, 1989: 12)

Examining competing claims about the past, and making comparisons between the past and the present is a way of making history powerful, rigorous, relevant and interesting to pupils. As Arnold notes:

> If the past came without gaps and problems, there would be no task for the historian to complete. And if the past always spoke plainly, truthfully and clearly to us, not only would historians have no work to do, we would have no opportunity to argue with each other. History is above all else an argument. (Arnold, 2000: 13)

Some of the weaknesses and flaws in the current arrangements for the teaching of history in English schools have been well documented. These weaknesses include over-reliance and meretricious use of short 'snippets' from sources (sometimes termed 'Death by sources a-f' in the pages of *Teaching History*), failure to provide pupils with a coherent overview or 'usable mental map' of the past, a reduction in the time allocated to history in English schools, and unsatisfactory and ineffective forms of assessing pupil progress in history (see, for example, Burnham and Brown, 2009; Burn and Harris, 2010; Culpin, 2007; Hamer, 1997; Hake and Haydn, 1995; Ofsted, 2011). Former History HMI John Hamer points out the need for a sensible balance between 'stories and sources', and the importance of developing pupils' understanding of the relationships between them:

> Much is made of teachers focusing on the development of historical skills at the expense of what should be their proper concern: the imparting of historical content. Too often, discussion has been too strident and ill-informed. But there are issues about getting the balance right: about ensuring that pupils have a secure grasp of events, without being overloaded; that they are able to use the knowledge they have; and that they do not

spend time on mechanical tasks rehearsing formulaic responses to snippets from sources. (Hamer, 1997: 24)

In spite of these caveats, Ofsted reports suggests that overall, the picture of history teaching and history teachers which is presented by recent Ofsted reports on the teaching of history in English schools is a very positive and encouraging one (Maddison, 2013; Ofsted, 2011).

The 1991 version of the NC for history proved to be unwieldy and it was found that the amount of content to be covered was unrealistic. A revised version was introduced in 1995 which significantly slimmed down the content which had to be studied, and attempted to simplify assessment arrangements.

There have been three further revisions to the NC for History, in 2000, 2008, and the most recent revision, to be introduced in September 2014, so if you start your teaching at a school in England, you may be working with the 'Mark 5' version of the NC for History.

Task 2.3 *Familiarising yourself with the most recent version of the NC for History introduced in September 2014*

Access the current National Curriculum for history at: www.gov.uk/government/publications/national-curriculum-in-england-history-programmes-of-study/national-curriculum-in-england-history-programmes-of-study. (Web addresses sometimes change; if this link does not work, search for it under 'National curriculum in England: history programmes of study').

1   What does the new NC for History have to say about the purposes and benefits of school history? Does it talk about knowledge or skills/competences or both? Does it have anything to say about pupil *dispositions* towards history?
2   What are the seven areas of historical content which are compulsory at Key Stage 3 in the 2014 NC for history? (Look for the sections that say 'Pupils should be taught about...'). What is the balance between local, national and international history?
3   What does the new NC for history say about what pupils have to do at primary school (Key Stages 1 and 2)?

Task 2.4 *Justifying history to pupils and parents*

Your placement school is organising a year 9 options evening for pupils and parents, and you have been asked to help with a display which points out the benefits of taking history. How would you present the case for school history to a parent whose child 'enjoyed history but didn't think it would be very useful'.

You have stressed to a year 10 class the importance of arguing and debating issues in history in class. A pupil states that 'history is a waste of time because it won't help to get you a job when you leave'. What would you say in response to this question?

Implications for your practice

There continues to be much debate about the aims of school history. It is therefore important that you are aware of the differing views about the purposes of school history, and that in the light of this knowledge, you consider carefully what you are trying to achieve in your history lessons. With any area of historical content, and with regard to the discipline of history as a whole, you should be able to justify why it is worthwhile teaching it to young people.

It is important that you develop the ability to make clear to pupils the purposes of school history, and to persuade them that the study of history is useful, worthwhile and interesting. Some history teachers are able to convince pupils that in studying history, they are addressing some of the most important and difficult questions of human existence; like philosophy, history has its 'big questions' (see Swain, 2006). If you can ensure that you keep the purposes of school history clearly in mind in your teaching, and be explicit about them with your pupils, you are more likely to secure the positive engagement in learning that makes teaching a pleasure rather than a chore.

During school experience you should discuss with your mentor the department's policy and documentation which attempts to interpret the NC for History, and identify how the key aims in learning/teaching history are reflected in that documentation. You will generally find that history teachers do have views on the purposes of school history which influence the ways in which they teach their subject. Different teachers and departments see some purposes as more important than others.

Task 2.5 The aims of teaching history

As part of your school experience you are given a history departmental handbook which contains the stated aims of the history teaching in your school. You also have a number of opportunities to observe history teaching by qualified teachers in your subject prior to being responsible for planning and teaching history yourself. To what extent do the following aims feature in the practice and documentation of history teaching in your school? Use the four questions below to frame your answers.

- History taught 'for its own sake', because it is interesting.
- History taught to expand pupils' knowledge and understanding of their local, national, and international communities.
- History taught as a means of socialisation through the transmission of cultural norms and values to the next generation.
- History taught to introduce pupils to their heritage through monuments, historic buildings and towns, architecture, museums, and written sources which chronicle the events of the past.
- History taught to develop some of the skills of the historian, in a way which enriches the pupils' intellectual development.
- History taught to instil civic pride and patriotism.
- History taught to promote virtue and awareness of what is right and wrong.
- History to help people to handle information critically and intelligently.
- History to provide a sense of identity.

1   Which of these aims do you find in the department handbook?
2   Which of these aims did you observe being implemented in practice?
3   Which of these aims is your current teaching concerned with?
4   Which, if any, of the above aims of teaching history are problematic for your teaching of history to pupils and why would this be the case?

Describe any difficulty you might have with any of these aims; discuss these issues with your mentor.

Contrary to the assertions of the tabloid press, there are few history teachers who do not believe that it is important for pupils to develop knowledge and understanding of the past. Many also believe that it can be helpful if this is complemented by an understanding of the nature of history as a form of knowledge, and an academic discipline. If you think about the events of the twentieth century, the era of spin doctors, media manipulation, soundbite politics and information overload, 'it does require some little imagination to realise what the consequences will be of not educating our children to sort out the differences between essential and non-essential information, raw fact, prejudice, half-truth and untruth, so that they know when they are being manipulated, by whom, and for what purpose' (Longworth, 1981:1 9). It is difficult to think of another school subject which offers the potential to address this important issue as directly.

If you are going to develop into an effective and successful teacher, you need to read widely about what we are trying to achieve when we teach history to young people and how to teach these things effectively. It is also important, as noted in Chapter 1, to keep an open mind and be prepared to change your ideas and practice in the light of your developing knowledge and understanding. It is important to be sceptical of simplistic 'tabloid' caricatures of the way that history is currently taught in schools. As David Cannadine has noted, there is a tendency in modern society to reduce the past to crude Manichean stereotypes of good and evil, heroes and villains, and to eschew the complexities and difficulties of 'reading the past' (Cannadine, 2013; Lindmark, 2011). The same might be said of much of the public discourse about how history is taught in schools. You should be cautious about accepting claims that 'It's just about knowledge' (or 'It's just about skills'), or 'Groupwork is bad' (or 'Teacher instruction is bad').

There are interesting questions to be asked about the way in which the national past should be presented to young people, the proportion of school history that should focus on the national past, and the appropriate balance between teacher instruction and teacher directed enquiry. The answers to these questions are often nuanced and complex rather than simple and straightforward. Australian politician Kevin Rudd argued that it was time to abandon 'the polarisation that has begun to infect every discussion of our nation's past':

It's time we called a truce to the history wars between a straight narrative history that brooks no contradictions, and an extreme relativism that is only about interpretation and not about events; it is in fact unsustainable. In a liberal democratic society, we can agree that events happened while we agree to differ on how we interpret them. (quoted in Lindmark, 2011: 8)

If you read widely on the subject of how to teach history, you will find that the majority of experienced history teachers and teacher educators believe that history is useful to young people as a body of knowledge which helps to orient them in time and understand 'why things as they are' in today's society, and it is also useful to young people as a form of knowledge, which helps them to handle information intelligently.

In the words of Michael Fordham (2012, 244):

> The tired debate about 'knowledge' versus 'skills' is now well trodden, the debate itself increasingly seen as missing the point. Although the debate in the British media and amongst most politicians continues to take this form, history teachers and educationalists have since sought to move beyond this distracting dichotomy and to find some other basis on which an education in history might be based.

(For a more developed explanation of this point, see Counsell, 2000.)

If you are a student teacher, your time would be better spent thinking about how to get your pupils to develop a better understanding of the nature and status of historical knowledge. The phrase 'historical skills' is often used very loosely. As Lee (2000) has argued, 'It's not about skills, but understanding and often, there is only a loose link between skills and understanding.' History student teachers need to develop a clear and precise understanding of what is meant by 'skills' in history, and the difference between 'skills', understanding and dispositions in history education. Richards (1989) argues that the latter are often a neglected facet of school history, and that pupil attitudes to history are an important component of a historical education:

> History teaches many useful skills – information gathering, problem solving, the public presentation of arguments and assessments. But that should be secondary to the broader objective of discovering how we were and how we got to where we are. It is not my aim to turn out tunnel-visioned computer operators concerned only about where their next Porsche is coming from. I seek to awaken in my students an open minded broad-visioned humanity, informed by a love of learning, a love of ideas, a love of books, a love of argument and debate.

What should be the 'end-date' for the history which is taught in school?

In 1952, the Ministry of Education warned of the dangers of 'cordoning off' the past from the present in school history:

> The divorce between current affairs and history, so that they are regarded as two different subjects, gravely weakens both. It accentuates the natural tendency of children to regard history as something remote and irrelevant instead of something which has formed the world around them and which is continuously being formed by that world. And, it accentuates equally the tendency to look at contemporary questions as though they had no context in time, no parallels or precedents. (Ministry of Education, 1952: 32)

An important consideration in persuading pupils that the study of the past is of relevance to their lives is to clarify the relationship between historical knowledge and the present. There are many definitions of history, but Aldrich's is particularly helpful to the history teacher. 'History is about human activity with particular reference to the whole dimension of time - past, present and future' (Aldrich, 1997: 3). It is important to be explicit about the idea of historical perspectives as one of the ways of understanding how things are today, and how they might be in the future. Is there any present day problem or question where it might not be possible to glean some degree of further insight into that problem or question by considering what has gone before? Don't forget to look for opportunities to relate the past to the present and the future, in order to persuade pupils of the importance and relevance of history. HMI state that student teachers should demonstrate 'an ability to relate the present to the past' (Baker *et al.*, 2000: 219). Remember that not all your pupils have a clear idea about why historians bother 'to do history'. When asked to explain the success of a recent adaptation of Vanity Fair, Lisa Jardine commented, 'You need to generate a connection with today. That's how I teach' (Observer, 8 October 1998). When you think about the starting point for your lessons, remember that often the present, rather than the past, can be the best option.

A number of quotations which provide a 'warrant' for making connections over time, and linking the past to the present can be found at www.uea. ac.uk/~m242/historypgce/purposes/purpose_warrant_pastpresent.htm.

Understanding the full breadth of benefits which pupils can derive from being in your classroom

You need to be aware of the full breadth of benefits which pupils might derive from the study of your subject and from being in your classroom. All NC subjects provide opportunities to promote pupil learning in a range of areas beyond subject specific learning, e.g. to contribute to the development of what have been termed 'key skills'. These were defined in the 2008 version of the NC for England as communication, application of number, use of information communications technology (ICT), the ability to work with others, the ability to problem solve, and the ability to improve their own learning performance (QCA, 2008).

You should also teach history in a way that takes advantages of opportunities to develop pupils' spiritual, moral, social and cultural development, and history should also make an important contribution to education for citizenship (see the website for further development of these points: www.uea.ac.uk/~m242/historypgce/cit/welcome.htm.

What does history teach that other subjects don't?

To return to the question posed by Leinhardt at the start of this chapter; what is history's *unique* contribution to the school curriculum? If we attempt to justify it in terms of 'transferable skills', such as 'analysis', 'critical thinking', 'judgement', 'ability to formulate an argument', it could be argued that there are many other subjects which could perform this function. Below are four attempts to answer this question. They should not be regarded as definitive, but they might at least provide a starting point for your thinking.

- The complicated interplay of evidence which is itself not certain and subject to interpretation gives history a particularly valuable part in the development of an adult understanding. It helps pupils to understand that there is a range of questions – be they political, economic, social or cultural – on which there is no single right answer, where opinions have to be tolerated but need to be subjected to the test of evidence and argument. As the pupil progresses in this encounter with history, he should be helped to acquire a sense of the necessity for personal judgements in the light of facts – recognising that the facts often be far from easy to establish and far from conclusive. And it should equally awaken a recognition of the possible legitimacy of other points of view. In other words, it seems to be that the teaching of history has to take place in a spirit which takes seriously the need to pursue truth on the basis of evidence, and at the same time accepts the need for give and take in that pursuit and that teaching in that spirit should encourage pupils to take a similar approach (Joseph, 1984: 12).
- It is after all, the only subject in the school curriculum whose central preoccupation is the evidence of the behaviour, as it has changed through time, of human beings who actually lived. Those who wish to demolish its role in the curriculum must be prepared to defend a curriculum without that preoccupation (Slater, 1984: 16).
- In the study of history, and nowhere else, the chief objective is to enable pupils to gain some understanding of human activity in the past and its implications for the present. As part of that understanding they will be caused to think about continuity and change, similarity and differences, in a way and in a context quite different from their encounters with those concepts in other subjects, both within and outside the humanities (Joseph, 1984: 10).
- [History is...] the most sophisticated and rational way so far of handling life in the fourth dimension. (Lee, 2011: 64)

Figure 2.4 Some quotations about the particular contribution which school history can make to the education of young people

Further reading

Abulafia, D., Clark, J. and Tombs, R. (2012) *History in the new curriculum: 3 proposals*, London: Politeia, online at www.politeia.co.uk/sites/default/files/files/Final%20Appendix%20to%20Lessons%20from%20History.pdf, accessed 20 March 2014.

Byrom, J. (2013) Alive and kicking? Some personal reflections on the revised National Curriculum and what we might do with it, *Teaching History Curriculum Supplement*: 6-14. As well as a useful guide to thinking about the new NC for history, there is a useful one page 'thumbnail summary' of the new NC arrangements across all three Key Stages (page 7).

Culpin, C. (2007) What kind of history should school history be?, The Medlicott Medal Lecture, *The Historian*, Autumn: 6-13, online at www.history.org.uk/resources/he_resource_747_9.html, accessed 20 March 2014.

Evans, R. (2003) 'Our job is to explain' *Times Higher Education Supplement*, 13 June, online at www.timeshighereducation.co.uk/features/our-job-is-to-explain/177421.article, accessed 30 March 2014.

Haydn, T. (1994) 'Skeletons', *The Historian*, No. 44: 21-2. Focuses on how the national past should be presented to young people.

Joseph, K. (1984) 'Why teach history in school?', *The Historian*, No. 2: 10-12.

Lee, P. (1992) History in schools: aims, purposes and approaches. A reply to John White, in P. Lee, J. Slater, P. Walsh and J. White, *The aims of school history: the National Curriculum and beyond*, London: Tufnell Press: 20-34.

Lee, P. (2011) 'Historical education and historical literacy', in I. Davies (ed.) *Debates in history teaching*, London: Routledge: 63-72.

Slater, J. (1984) 'The case for history in school', *The Historian*, No. 2: 13-16.

A number of quotations about the purposes of school history can be accessed at www.uea.ac.uk/~m242/historypgce/purposes/purposesquotesintro.htm.

References

Abulafia, D., Clark, J. and Tombs, R. (2012) History in the new curriculum: 3 proposals, London, Politeia, online at www.politeia.co.uk/sites/default/files/files/Final%20Appendix%20to%20Lessons%20from%20History.pdf, accessed 20 March 2014.

Adey, K. and Biddulph, M. (2001) The influence of pupil perceptions on subject choice at 14+ in geography and history, *Educational Studies*, 27 (4): 439-51.

Aldrich, R. (1989) Class and gender in the study and teaching of history in England in the twentieth century, in *Historical Studies in Education*, i, No. 1, 119-35.

Aldrich, R. (ed.) (1991) *History in the National Curriculum*, London: Kogan Page.

Aldrich, R. and Dean, D. (1991) 'The historical dimension', in R. Aldrich (ed.) *History in the National Curriculum*, London: Kogan Page: 99-113.

Aldrich, R. (ed.) (1997) *The End of History and the Beginning of Education*, London: Institute of Education.

Arnold, J. (2000) *History: a very short introduction*, Oxford: Oxford University Press.

ATL (Association of Teachers and Lecturers) (2000) *Taking students off Site*, London, ATL.

Baker, K. (1988) Speech to the Conservative Party Conference.

Baker, L., Cohn, T. and McLaughlin, M. (2000) 'Inspecting subject knowledge', in J. Arthur, and R. Phillips (eds) *Issues in History Teaching*, London: Routledge.

Beattie, A. (1987) *History in Peril: May Parents Preserve It*, London: Centre for Policy Studies.

Board of Education (1905) *Suggestions for the Consideration of Teachers and Others Concerned with the Work of Public Elementary Schools*, London: HMSO.

Brown, G. (2007) 'Why I support a British history museum', *Daily Telegraph*, 12 December. Online at www.telegraph.co.uk/news/uknews/1572265/Brown-Why-I-support-British-history-museum.html, accessed 30 September 2012.

Burnham, S. and Brown, G. (2009) Assessment without level descriptions, *Teaching History*, No. 115: 5-15.

Burn, K. and Harris, R. (2010) *Historical Association Survey of history in English schools*, London: Historical Association.

Burston, W.H. and Green, C.W. (eds) (1962) *Handbook for History Teachers*, London: Methuen.

Cannadine, D. (2013) *The Undivided Past: History beyond our differences*, London, Allen Lane.

Counsell, C. (2000) 'Historical knowledge and historical skills: a distracting dichotomy', in J. Arthur, and Phillips, R. (eds) *Issues in History Teaching*, London: Routledge: 54-71.

Conquest, R. (1969) from Cox, C. and Dyson, A. 'Fight for education: a black paper', in *Critical Quarterly*, quoted in M. Ballard (ed.) (1970) *New Movements in the Study and Teaching of History*, London: Maurice Temple Smith.

Culpin, C. (2007) What kind of history should school history be?, The MedlicottMedal Lecture, *The Historian,* Autumn: 6-13, online at www.history.org.uk/resources/he_resource_747_9.html, accessed 20 March 2014.

Dean, J. (1995) *Teaching History at Key Stage 2*, Cambridge: Chris Kington.

DES (1988) *History from 5-16*, London: HMSO.

DES (1989) *Interim Report of the National Curriculum History Working Group*, London: HMSO.

DES (1990) *Final Report of the National Curriculum History Working Group*, London: HMSO.

DfEE (1999) *Health and Safety of Pupils on Educational Visits*, London: Department for Education and Employment.

DfEE/QCA (1999) *History: The National Curriculum for England*, London: DfEE/QCA.

DfES/QCA (2004) The National Curriculum, London: DfES/QCA.

DfE (2013) *National curriculum in England: history programmes of study*, London: DfE. Online at www.gov.uk/government/publications/national-curriculum-in-england-history-programmes-of-study, accessed 20 February 2014.

Fordham, M. (2012) Disciplinary History and the Situation of History Teachers, *Educational Sciences, 2* (4): 24253, online at www.mdpi.com/2227-7102/2/4/242, accessed 30 March 2014.

Gove, M. (2010) Speech to the Conservative Party Conference. Quoted online at www.matthewtaylorsblog.com/public-policy/michael-goves-response/, accessed 31 August 2012.

Hake, C. and Haydn, T. (1995) Stories or sources?, *Teaching History*, No. 78: 20-22.

Hamer, J. (1997) Ofsted and history in schools, *The Historian*, No. 53: 24-5.

Haydn, T. (1992a) History for ordinary children, *Teaching History*, No. 67, April, 8-11.

Haydn, T. (1992b) History reprieved?, *Teaching History*, No. 66, January, 17-20.

Haydn, T. (1996) Nationalism begins at home; the impact of national curriculum history on perceptions of national identity in Britain, 1987-1994, *History of Education Bulletin*, No. 57: 51-61.

Haydn, T. (2012) Longing for the past: politicians and the history curriculum in English schools, 1988-2010, *Journal of Education, Media, Memory and Society, 4* (1): 7-25.

Hallam, S. (1997) Unpublished lecture on Differentiation, Institute of Education, University of London, January.

Harris, R. and Haydn, R. (2006) Pupils' enjoyment of history – what lessons can teachers learn from their pupils?, *Curriculum Journal, 17* (4): 315-33.

Harris, R. and Haydn, T. (2012) What happens to a subject in a 'free market' curriculum? A study of secondary school history in the UK, *Research Papers in Education, 27* (1): 81-101.

Hill, C. (1953) *Suggestions on the Teaching of History*, Paris: UNESCO.

HMI (1985) *History in the Primary and Secondary Years*, London: HMSO.

Hobsbawn, E. (1997) 'To see the future, look at the past', *The Guardian*, 7 June.

Husbands, C. (1996) *What is History Teaching: Language, Ideas and Meaning in Learning about the Past,* Buckingham: Open University Press.

Johnson, P. (1994) *Daily Mail*, 30 April.

Joseph, K. (1984) 'Why teach history in school?', *The Historian*, No. 2: 10-12.

Kitson, A., Husbands, C. and Steward, S. (2011) *Teaching and learning history: understanding the past*, Maidenhead: Open University Press.

Lawlor, S. (1989) Quoted in *The Times*, 24 June 1989.

Lee, P. (1994) 'Historical knowledge and the National Curriculum', in H. Bourdillon (ed.) *Teaching History*, London: Routledge: 41-48.

Lee, P. (2000) Paper presented at the HTEN Conference, Homerton College Cambridge, 12 July.

Lee, P. (2011) 'Historical education and historical literacy', in I. Davies (ed.) *Debates in History Teaching*, London: Routledge: 63-72.

Lee, P. and Ashby, R. (2000) Progression in historical understanding among students ages 7-14, in P. Stearns, P. Seixas and S. Wineburg (eds) *Knowing, teaching and learning history*, New York: New York University Press.

Lee, P., Slater, J., Walsh, P. and White, J. (1992) *The Aims of Social History: The National Curriculum and Beyond*, London: Tufnell Press.

Leinhardt, G., quoted in Wineburg, S. (2001: ix) *Historical Thinking and Other Unnatural Acts*, Philadelphia: Temple Press.

Lindmark, D. (2011) 'The stolen generations and the Australian Curriculum: history education in a cultural war', paper presented at the ISHD Conference, University of Basel, 13 September.

Longworth, N. (1981) 'We're moving into the Information Society – what shall we tell the children?', *Computer Education*, June, 17-19.

MacBeath, J. (1998) *Observer*, 22 February.

Maddison, M. (2013) History in schools: learning from the past, planning for the future, Keynote address at the SHP November Conference, British Library, 30 November 2013, online at www.schoolshistoryproject. org.uk/Teaching/conferences/Index.htm, accessed 20 March 2014.

Mandler, P. (2012) *History, National Life and the New Curriculum*, keynote address at the SHP Conference, online at www.schoolshistoryproject.org.uk/ResourceBase/downloads/MandlerKeynote2013.pdf, accessed 20 March 2014.

Ministry of Education (1952) *Teaching History: Pamphlet No. 23*, London: HMSO.

NCC (1991) *History: Non-Statutory Guidance*, York: NCC.

Ofsted (1995) *History: A Review of Inspection Findings 1993/4*, London: HMSO.

Ofsted (2011) *History for all*, London, Ofsted, online at www.ofsted.gov.uk/resources/history-for-all, accessed 20 March 2014.

Phillips, R. (1997) *History Teaching, Nationhood and the State: A study in educational politics*, London: Cassell.

Price, M. (1968) History in danger, *History*, 53, 342-47.

Richards, J. (1989) Quoted in *The Independent*, 8 April.

Schick (1995) On being interactive: rethinking the learning equation, *History Microcomputer Review*, 11 (1), 9-25

Seixas, P. (2002) The Purposes of Teaching Canadian History, *Canadian Social Studies*, 36 (2). Online at www2.education.ualberta.ca/css/Css_36_2/ARpurposes_teaching_canadian_history.htm, accessed 19 August 2014.

Slater, J. (1984) The case for history in school, *The Historian*, No. 2.

Slater, J. (1989) *The Politics of History Teaching, a Humanity Dehumanised?*, London: ULIE.

Slater, J. (1991) 'History in the National Curriculum: the Final Report of the History Working Group', in Aldrich R. (ed.) *History in the National Curriculum*, London: Kogan Page: 8-38.

Swain, H. (2006) *Big Questions in History*, London: Vintage.

Tate, N. (1996) Address to the *SCAA Conference on Curriculum, Culture and Society, held at the Kensington Hilton Hotel, 7 February 1996*, School Curriculum and Assessment Authority.

Williams, N. (1986) 'The Schools council project: History 13-16, the first ten years of examinations', *Teaching History*, No. 46, October, 8-12.

Willis Bund, J. (1908) Quoted in G. Batho (1986) 'From a test of memory to a training for life', in M. Price, *The Development of the Secondary Curriculum*, London: Croom Helm: 212-26.

3 Subject knowledge

What do history teachers need to know?

At all stages, the subject expertise of the teacher is the most important factor determining the work of the teacher in the classroom. (Ofsted, 1995)

Research shows that there is a close relationship between teachers' subject knowledge and the quality and range of learning experiences in their classrooms. The message is, if you don't know it, you can't teach it. (Dean, 1995: 4)

Introduction

Although some challenges for the history teacher are perennial or longstanding ones (there have always been some pupils who 'can't see the point' of history – see Aldrich, 1987, and there have always been claims in newspapers that young people 'know nothing about history' – see Wineburg, 2000) – new ones are always emerging. There have been a number of innovations and changes in the areas of teaching methods, ideas about 'learning styles', curriculum specifications and educational technologies, all of which have impacted on pupils' learning in the history classroom, as have 'public' and political ideas about school history. It is an important part of your subject knowledge that you are aware of these issues and developments, and that you keep 'up to date' with your subject. It is your responsibility to be aware of the NC (or other appropriate) documentation pertaining to school history, and the general debate over the purposes of school history over the past decade or so. It can be immensely helpful to keep this debate in mind as you teach history in the classroom. As the non-statutory guidance to the original NC for History stated, 'a strong sense of why history is being taught should pervade all curriculum planning, influencing the selection of content and methods of teaching' (National Curriculum Council, 1991: 1). One of the most common mistakes made by student teachers when faced with unfamiliar or intractable areas of content is to resort to treating the topic as a slab of the past to be transmitted to pupils 'neat' or in simplistic form, without thinking about what questions it poses, or why it might be helpful to pupils to know about this facet of the past.

This chapter argues that there is more to teaching history than *just* possessing expert levels of subject content knowledge. Good knowledge of the topic you are teaching is a necessary but not sufficient condition for securing effective learning in history. The first section of the chapter focuses on the importance of good subject content knowledge, and how history student teachers can augment and develop their subject knowledge; later sections focus on other things that history student teachers need to know if they are to teach history effectively.

There is a tendency for those who have not had to teach children to underestimate the intellectual challenges involved. It might be quite difficult teaching the causes of the Wars of the Roses to undergraduate history students, but we would argue that it is even more difficult to teach this topic effectively, and in a way that 'makes sense' to 12 year olds, some of whom may not be driven scholars. If you are teaching 15 to 20 lessons a week, you are in effect devising and 'putting on' 15 to 20 new 'performances' a week, starting with a blank piece of paper, and functioning as screenwriter, directory, producer, props manager (and keeper of order). As Husbands has pointed out, 'To teach successfully, teachers must be intellectually capable, and well informed' (Husbands, 2011: 84). You are unlikely to inspire confidence in your pupils if you do not possess subject knowledge which is substantially beyond that which is available to them in textbooks.

- When you go in to teach a class, do you always have a sound grasp of the topic you are going to teach, so that you can teach it effectively, answer pupils' questions confidently, and retain the confidence of the pupils?
- Are you familiar with what history pupils will have studied at Key Stages 1 and 2?
- Are you familiar with safety regulations and guidance for working with pupils outside the classroom, for example, when undertaking field trips and visits to museums?
- Are you developing a sound basis of subject content knowledge across the compulsory elements of the NC, and in the examination syllabuses which the department enters pupils for?

Figure 3.1 To think about...

Objectives

At the end of the chapter you should:

- be aware of the importance of possessing good subject knowledge for any lesson and series of lessons that you are going to teach;
- know how to approach the development of your subject knowledge, both before the course starts and during your training;
- be aware of other aspects of knowledge that you need to know in order to be able to teach effectively.

Task 3.1 *Learning from your own experiences in a history classroom*

It is important not to make the assumption that because you probably enjoyed studying history at school, all pupils find history interesting and enjoyable. Several surveys over the past 50 years have found that many pupils think that school history is boring and useless (see Figures 3.6 and 3.7). You will have been 'the victim' of many history teachers. What were the characteristics and approaches which evinced your enthusiasm for the subject and made you want to learn and do well in history? And what were the activities and teacher characteristics which you found unhelpful in history lessons? (It is perhaps important to remember that this might be partly about what the teacher was like as a person, not just their pedagogical skills and teaching repertoire).

Knowledge and understanding of the substantive past

Providing feedback on their inspection of history teacher education courses, history HMIs reported that:

> First *and perhaps most importantly* (our italics), where trainees have high levels of subject knowledge they plan and teach confidently.... The contribution of substantial subject knowledge to effective teaching is very apparent when an inspector is able to observe a trainee teach two lessons, one where he or she has a mastery of subject content, and the other where he or she has read up on the topic only recently and briefly. The contrast, in terms of confidence, as well as skill, is usually marked. (Baker *et al.*, 2000: 217)

Before the course, you should familiarise yourself with the NC for history, and read widely, to develop a sound overview of the compulsory components of subject content which are specified which relate to British history ('pupils should be taught about...'). You don't know which local study or world study your placement school will focus on, or which pre-1066 strand of British history will be explored, but as with the previous NC for history, you do know that you will be teaching a significant amount of British history from 1066 onwards. Once your course of training starts, the emphasis changes, and rather than working on broad overview knowledge of British history, you need to focus primarily on the subject content knowledge you will need for the classes you are going to teach. Although there are several facets to subject knowledge, discussions amongst one group of history tutors concluded that in making judgements on student teachers' subject knowledge, the most important consideration was 'the degree to which student teachers had used their initiative, intelligence and energy to prepare effectively for the classes they had been assigned to teach'. (Minutes of UEA history tutors' meeting.)

Developing your subject knowledge

A decade or so ago there was perhaps a tendency for courses of initial teacher education to 'take as read' student teachers' subject knowledge, and to assume that as most student teachers had to at least some extent, a degree background in history, attention could be focused on other issues, such as pedagogy, theories of learning, and classroom management.

Since then, research evidence and inspection findings have suggested that there is a close relationship between teachers' subject knowledge and the quality of pupils' learning, and that without secure knowledge and understanding of the concepts and skills in their specialist subject, 'the quality of teaching and learning in the classroom suffers' (Baker *et al.*, 2000: 211).

Fordham makes the point that as well as having sound knowledge of the event or issue being studied, it is helpful to have an understanding of the historiography surrounding the topic:

> Take, for example, an enquiry question which can be found in classrooms across the UK: why was the British slave trade abolished in 1807? Those familiar with the debate will recognise the historiography: the primacy of 'saints' such as Wilberforce and Clarkson, as advanced by Coupland; the centrality of economics, as argued by Williams; the role played by slave rebellions, advanced by Hart; the role played by popular support for abolition in Britain, more recently argued by Drescher.... a history teacher clearly has to reflect carefully not just on the substance of what is studied, important as that is, but also on the way in which that question has already been approached within the discipline. (Fordham, 2012: 247)

As we will argue in Chapter 10, the internet and the availability of popular history magazines has made it much easier to *quickly* become familiar with the basic historiography pertaining to the topics you are required to teach.

Even single honours history graduates are unlikely to possess graduate level knowledge of every period and topic which is taught in secondary schools. Most of you will have some 'black holes' in terms of subject content knowledge. As soon as you have been offered a place on a course of initial teacher education, you should work on addressing gaps in your subject knowledge; once you are on teaching placement, you are unlikely to have time to read weighty tomes and biographies. This does not mean that there are no other useful strategies for acquiring subject knowledge. Popular history magazines, history education websites, podcasts and Twitter feeds, television history, newspaper articles on history – all of these sources can be helpful (see Chapter 10 for further development of this point). Diligence, initiative, resourcefulness and good organisational skills are important attributes which will, if deployed, make some student teachers much more effective than others in this area.

You should also keep a record of all the things that you have read and done which contribute to your developing subject knowledge. This needs to be well organised and easy to access, as it is a 'working document' which you should be able to refer back to throughout your course of initial training, and into your NQT year. It serves two purposes; as an audit or check on your developing history subject knowledge, and as a 'working document', which will be useful in the years ahead. You may have instructions and formats for auditing your subject knowledge development which are specific to the course you are undertaking, but if you are 'a free agent' in this respect, it can be helpful to simply keep a 'subject knowledge folder', which contains the things you have read, with articles, resources and handouts annotated and organised in a way which make sense to you, so that they can be accessed and deployed when necessary in your subsequent teaching or for Masters level work if you are pursuing a Masters level course.

Task 3.2 *How will you develop and audit your subject knowledge?*

If someone asked you what you had done on your course to develop your subject knowledge, what would you say?

Conduct a brief audit of your subject knowledge, reviewing it against the NC for History at Key Stage 3, and noting down any areas of weakness. Keep a record of the steps you make to develop your subject knowledge. This need not be reading and/or note taking, and might include familiarisation with history films, podcasts and television programmes. Try to be systematic about this monitoring process and keep a record in such a way as to be able to demonstrate to an external examiner or interview panel that you have been taking action to develop, enhance and update your subject knowledge. How can you do this in a way that is 'time effective' and not just a pointless administrative chore? How might you categorise and organise a subject knowledge folder? (Things to do with ICT, assessment, second order concepts, exam teaching, NC 'strands', year groups, substantive topics…?)

The requirement that pupils should gain knowledge and understanding of the substantive past (i.e. history as *a body of knowledge*) is explicitly stated in the current version of the NC for history:

> A high-quality history education will help pupils gain a coherent knowledge and understanding of Britain's past and that of the wider world…. The national curriculum for history aims to ensure that all pupils:
> * Know and understand the history of these islands as a coherent, chronological narrative, from the earliest times to the present day: how people's lives have shaped this nation and how Britain has influenced and been influenced by the wider world.
> * Know and understand significant aspects of the history of the wider world: the nature of ancient civilisations; the expansion and dissolution of empires; characteristic features of past non-European societies; achievements and follies of mankind.
> * Gain and deploy a historically grounded understanding of abstract terms such as 'empire', 'civilisation', 'parliament' and 'peasantry' (DfE, 2013: 1).

Understanding history as a discipline

If the study of history is to be of maximum benefit to pupils, it is important that there is a shared understanding of what 'history' is. If pupils are to make sense of the past it would be helpful if they understand why history is important and what are we dealing with when we study the past – what is the nature and status of the body of 'knowledge' which is the raw material of history lessons? What is the difference between 'history', and 'the past'? Although many undergraduate history courses now include elements of historiography, not all history graduates can confidently answer the question, 'What is a fact?', or the distinction between 'sources' and 'evidence'.

It is particularly important to be aware of the difference between what are sometimes termed 'substantive' and 'second order' concepts in history. Figure 3.2 provides a helpful explanation of these terms.

It is necessary to distinguish between *substantive* history on the one hand and *second-order* or *procedural* ideas about history on the other. Substantive history is the content of history, what history is 'about'. Concepts like *peasant*, *friar* and *president*, particulars like *the Battle of Hastings*, *the French Revolution*, and *the Civil Rights Movement*, and individuals like *Abraham Lincoln*, *Marie Curie* and *Mahatma Gandhi* are part of the substance of history. Concepts like historical *evidence*, *explanation*, *change* and *accounts* are ideas that provide our understanding of history as a discipline or form of knowledge. They are not what history is 'about', but they shape the way we go about doing history.

Figure 3.2 The difference between 'substantive' and 'second order' concepts in history (Lee and Ashby, 2000: 199)

If the history teacher is quite clear in her own mind about the nature of the discipline, there is more chance that the pupils will have a sound understanding of what they are working with in the history classroom. Although there are those who argue that there has been a tendency to undervalue the importance of pupils' acquiring knowledge of the past, it would seem reasonable to suggest that they should also become acquainted with some of the rules of procedure of the discipline of history.

HMI feedback from Initial Teacher Education (ITE) inspections again provides useful insights into what good subject knowledge entails. Although they attach particular importance to strong knowledge of the substantive past, they also stress the importance of student teachers possessing 'a clear understanding of the nature of the subject and its guiding principles... key concepts, key questions... key words' (Baker *et al.*, 2000: 212, 216). They argue that student teachers who have a clear understanding of 'the nature of history' will be more likely to be able to use the potential of the subject 'to promote pupils' spiritual, moral, social and cultural development' and the ability 'to relate the present to the past, for instance recognising the long-term effects of historical events such as the Reformation' (Baker *et al.*: 218-19).

Good subject knowledge is not just about having a sound grasp of the substantive past. It should include an understanding of the nature of history as a form of knowledge, with its rules, conventions and procedures, its organising concepts. It is also about inducting pupils into the language of historical discourse (see Chapters 6-8).

If we are going to teach children history, shouldn't they know something about what history is – what they are dealing with, as well as information about what happened in the past? Pupils need to develop an understanding that history is not 'what you are told about the past'; (information = what happened); history is a construct. It has been 'put together' by someone. As Lee and Ashby point out, if we are taking 'knowledge' seriously, shouldn't pupils understand the nature of historical knowledge, as something that has to be 'understood and grounded?' If pupils have some grasp of the nature of the relationship between facts, claims and accounts, 'as well as acquiring knowledge of the past, students develop more powerful understandings of the nature of the discipline, which in turn legitimate the claim that what they acquire is indeed knowledge' (Lee and Ashby, 2000: 200).

The statement that history is 'an account of what happened in the past' (Thatcher, 1995: 595) does not equip pupils to deal with the fact that there are *differing* accounts of the past. As Lee and Ashby point out:

> Many stories are told, and they may contradict, compete with or complement one another, but this means that students should be equipped to deal with such relationships, not that any old story will do... Students who understand sources as *information* are helpless when confronted by contradictory sources. (Lee and Ashby, 2000: 200)

Arnold reminds us that 'the Greek word which has become 'history' originally meant "to enquire", and more specifically, indicated a person who was able to choose wisely between conflicting accounts' (2000: 18). Postman and Weingartner have less elegantly described history as a 'crap-detecting' subject (quoted in MacBeath, 1998). It is precisely this facet of history as a discipline that can be helpful in persuading pupils of its utility and relevance.

It is therefore important that you understand and are able to explain to pupils what historians do, and why they do it; what 'facts' are, the difference between 'sources' and 'evidence', and why it is in the nature of accounts to differ. If you are not clear about these things, what chance have your pupils got of making sense of history?

Another helpful resource for developing a sound understanding of the nature, status and purposes of historical knowledge can be accessed in a short article by Richard Evans in the *Times Higher Education Supplement*. An extract from this article is provided below:

> History is, in the first place, the study of the past in order to find out the truth about it. Unlike novelists or film-makers, historians do not invent things that did not happen or conjure up characters that did not exist.... They deal with fact, not fiction. This distinction has been made by all historians ever since the first serious historical work to have come down to us from the ancient world, the History of the Peloponnesian War. Its author, the Greek writer Thucydides, rejected the romantic myths purveyed by the poets and checked all his evidence, as he told his readers, 'with as much thoroughness as possible'. But he went on to complain, as historians have done regularly ever since, that the truth was far from easy to discover: 'Different eyewitnesses give different accounts of the same events, speaking out of partiality for one side or the other or else from imperfect memories.' In the two and a half millennia or so since Thucydides wrote his great work, historians have elaborated a whole battery of sophisticated methods of checking the evidence and dealing with the gaps and partialities of their sources. But they can never attain perfect or total knowledge of the whole truth. All they can do is establish probabilities – sometimes overwhelming, sometimes less so, sometimes hardly at all – about parts of the past: those parts that can be accessed by means of the remains it has handed down in one form or another to posterity. History only ever involves a selection of what is knowable about the past because it has a second essential quality apart from the search for truth: it aims not just at reconstructing and representing the past but also at understanding and interpreting it.... The historian's job is to explain. (Evans, 2003)

The requirement that pupils should learn about history as a form of knowledge as well as a body of knowledge is stated explicitly in the current NC for history, which states that:

> Teaching should equip pupils to ask perceptive questions, think critically, weigh evidence, sift arguments, and develop perspective and judgement.... The National Curriculum for history aims to ensure that all pupils:
> - understand historical concepts such as continuity and change, cause and consequence, similarity, difference and significance, and use them to make connections, draw contrasts, analyse trends, frame historically-valid questions and create their own structured accounts, including written narratives and analyses;
> - understand how different types of historical sources are used rigorously to make historical claims and discern how and why contrasting arguments and interpretations of the past have been constructed. (DfE, 2013: 1)

It is important to get beyond simplistic polemics which characterise school history as a choice between knowledge and skills based approaches (see for instance Peal, 2013). As well as Lee and Ashby's point that if we are taking knowledge seriously, pupils ought to know something about the nature and status of historical knowledge (Lee and Ashby, 2000), Stephan Levesque lucidly points out the dangers and inaccuracies of the simplistic presentation of 'knowledge versus skills' in the popular media:

> It is important not to construe the distinction and transition from substantive to structural knowledge as the simplistic dichotomy of content versus skills, as too often happens in school history. It is impossible for students to understand or make use of procedural knowledge if they have no knowledge of the substance of the past. To claim, for example, that there has been remarkable *progress* in human rights over the last century makes no sense unless one knows some *content* (key dates, events, declarations, charters etc.) relating to the history of human rights. To understand the various claims made about the past, therefore, students need to be introduced to the disciplinary concepts and procedures that led to the crafting of these historical claims. (Levesque, 2008: 30)

Part of the 'knowledge versus skills' problem is the rather lazy and loose use of the word 'historical skills'. As Lee points out, skills are generally regarded as things that can be learned and improved by repeated practice, such as riding a bicycle or learning to write neatly. There is no guarantee that looking at and analysing thousands of historical sources will improve pupils' understanding of historical evidence. Progression in pupils' understanding of evidence might more accurately be understood as making particular cognitive moves towards a more sophisticated understanding of what evidence is and how it can be used. It is more about gains in understanding than the acquisition of a 'skill' (Lee, 2011: 64). Examples of such moves include addressing common misconceptions that many pupils have, such as the belief that primary sources are necessarily 'better' than secondary sources, the tendency of many pupils to see change entirely in terms of events rather than processes (Lee and Cercadillo, 2013), and uncertainty over the difference between causes and correlations.

Task 3.3 *Handling the 'So what?' question*

 Why do historians bother to 'do' history? Is it just a hobby, like stamp collecting or trainspotting? In addition to trying to establish what happened in the past, historians research into the past to see what insights historical perspectives might shed on the present and the future. Teachers of history must remember to do the same, if pupils are not to ask the 'So what?' question after studying a particular facet of the past.

One history student teacher wrote in the evaluation of a lesson (honestly but worryingly) 'I have no idea why I am teaching this.' If the grownups don't have a clue about why they are inflicting particular 'chunks' of the past on their pupils, what hope is there that the pupils will commit themselves enthusiastically to learning about it? Whether or not a pupil puts their hand up and asks why you are doing a topic, it can be helpful to think through the answer to this question before you start planning how you are going to approach the subject.

Spend a few minutes thinking about why pupils should have to learn about the following:

- castles (no-one's built one for hundreds of years);
- peasants (we don't have them any more);
- life in a medieval village;
- roads and canals in the seventeenth century;
- Hargreaves' Spinning Jenny; and
- The Agrarian Revolution.

(See Chapter 4 for some suggestions for approaching such topics. Some guidance is also given in Hunt, 2007.)

Part of becoming an effective history teacher entails developing a sound structural understanding of the discipline of history, and the nature of historical knowledge. The 'Golden Nugget' of this chapter (see Chapter 5), is that there is more to subject knowledge than just 'knowing your stuff' in terms of content knowledge, important though that is.

Pedagogic subject knowledge

One of the main challenges of initial teacher education is developing the art of transforming your subject knowledge into effective learning experiences for pupils. There is such a thing as 'pedagogy' – the science of teaching, and it is as important to develop expertise in this as to possess and develop your subject knowledge of the NC for History. In the words of Jacqui Dean:

> Pedagogical content knowledge includes knowledge both of how children learn and of a range of teaching strategies; in short, the teacher's craft knowledge of how to teach...

> History teaching thus involves craft knowledge which is underpinned by academic subject knowledge and shaped by the teacher's concept of the nature of the discipline. (Dean, 1995: 4)

Michael Fullan provides a useful reminder that 'even when people are sincerely motivated to learn from you, they have a devil of a time doing so. Transferability of ideas is a complex problem of the highest order' (1999: 63). Although it is important that you have a good grasp of the topic you are going to teach, this is not enough to guarantee effective teaching. One problem is that sometimes, the teacher's familiarity and confidence with the topic can lead them to overestimate the gap between their understanding of the topic and what pupils know and understand:

> Every teacher has got to the end of the lesson and realised that their students just don't get it.... When explaining ideas, you are most at risk of ambiguity when you are discussing a topic with which you are very familiar. This can lead to false assumptions about what the students already know and understand... familiarity with a subject can cause us to overestimate students' prior knowledge, leading to a lack of clarity in what we are asking them to do. (Gershon, 2014: 34)

Another potential problem is the misapprehension that the more the teacher knows, the better pupils will learn. It's just not a simple as this. The teacher needs to develop the skill of deciding which elements of their knowledge to use with pupils – which stories, quotes, examples, metaphors, comparisons, analogies – so that pupils develop a coherent grasp of the topic being studied. Shemilt (2009) and Dawson (2012) have argued that too much detail can clutter and hamper pupils' understanding of a topic. Dawson argues for providing pupils with a basic overall framework of the topic before 'filling in' the complexities and intricacies of causes, interpretations and significance of the topic being discussed (see Chapter 5 for further development of this point). So, it's partly about intelligence, understanding and good judgement in *selecting* which aspects of your (hopefully extensive) knowledge to deploy in your lessons. It is also about your skills of explanation; the extent to which you can convey often complex ideas cogently and clearly to pupils of different ages and abilities. A study of over 700 pupils which asked them to comment on what teacher characteristics were most helpful in enabling them to learn found that the two most influential attributes were 'knows their subject well', and 'explains things clearly' (see Figure 3.3)

Fordham makes the point that in addition to strong substantive knowledge of what is to be taught, and a grasp of the historiography surrounding the topic, teachers require 'an understanding of how pupils might be navigated through that complexity to some meaningful outcome' (Fordham, 2012: 247).

Knowing how to teach something in a way that all learners will understand is a complex and sophisticated skill. In a hugely influential article, Lee Shulman (1987) argued that effective teaching required teachers to know the subject content to be taught, what curriculum materials were available to teach the topic, how classrooms work, how pupils learn, what teaching approaches might work best with this content, as well as knowledge of school cultures and educational aims and values more generally. Shulman defined pedagogic

Teacher characteristic	% of pupils regarding this characteristic as 'very important' in having a positive influence on their attitude to learning
knows their subject really well	78.3%
explains things well	76.1%
makes it interesting	67.4%
is good at stopping other pupils from spoiling the lesson	65.2%
doesn't set too much written work	65.0%
talks to you 'normally'	63.0%
is friendly	63.0%
is enthusiastic about their subject	54.3%
has good ideas for lesson activities	54.0%
has a sense of humour	52.2%

Figure 3.3 10 most influential characteristics, judged by percentage of pupils rating the characteristic as 'very important' (online at www.uea.ac.uk/~m242/nasc/cross/cman/overallchar.htm, accessed 30 March 2014. Full paper describing the project, Zamorski, B. and Haydn, T., 2002)

subject knowledge in terms of 'the blending of content and pedagogy into an understanding of how particular topics, problems or issues are organised, represented and adapted to the diverse interests and abilities of learners and presented for instruction' (Shulman, 1986). A history teacher might therefore be very accomplished in teaching the Industrial Revolution, but struggle to teach the Glorious Revolution of 1688. The difference in effectiveness would depend not just on the strength of substantive subject knowledge of the two topics, but on their awareness of, and skill in deploying the best 'analogies, illustrations, examples, explanations and demonstrations as conduits for their subject knowledge to engage and enthuse pupils' (Husbands, 2011: 85).

Task 3.4 *The importance of checking for understanding*

It can be salutary to see to what extent pupils have fully retained and understood what you have taught them. Select a topic or lesson which you feel you taught reasonably well, and – a few weeks after teaching it – devise a test which explores how much knowledge and understanding of the topic the pupils have retained. Unless you are an exceptional and unusual teacher, you will find that some of the pupils will not have remembered or fully understood everything that you were trying to teach.

Historical consciousness

History education in schools varies in form and purpose in different parts of the world. There are still countries where school history and history textbooks are regarded as a vehicle for promoting loyalty to the state and national pride, and where less salubrious elements of the national past are excised (Epstein, 2009; Foster and Crawford, 2006; Macmillan, 2009). However, there are other differences in approach. Seixas (2013) makes the point that whereas in England, the United States and elsewhere, there has been an emphasis on the development of pupils' historical thinking (in terms of their understanding of the second order concepts referred to above), in other countries, including Germany, parts of continental Europe and Canada, more attention has been paid to the idea of young people's historical consciousness. If you are going to teach history, you should have some understanding of what the term 'historical consciousness' means. In rough terms, it might be understood as the ways in which people are aware of the past, the ways they interact and make use of the past, and can include their ideas about which ways of finding out about the past are most trustworthy. Influenced by the ideas of Rusen, the idea is that historical knowledge and understanding plays 'a role in the mental household of a person' (Rusen, 1993), and that there are differing levels of sophistication and 'usefulness' in terms of the ways in which people understand and use the past. (For a more developed explanation of this, see Instone, 2013; Lee, 2004; Rusen, 2006; The Pasts Collective, 2013). The *Usable historical pasts project* aimed to explore 'the extent to which students acquire a coherent framework of knowledge that links past, present and future and vitally offers a usable structure to help young people make sense of their place in the world' (Foster *et al.*, 2008; Howson, 2007). The ways in which young people make use of the past, and how their ideas about the past develop are clearly areas of interest to anyone who is a history teacher. The 'Canadians and their pasts'

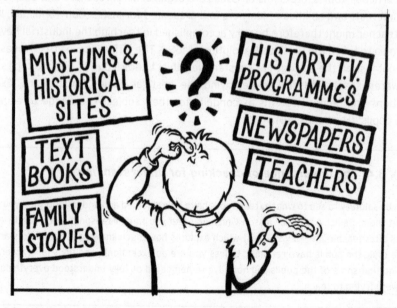

Figure 3.4 Developing pupils' ideas about the trustworthiness of information from different sources

project found that only one in a hundred adult Canadians did not engage with the past in any way (museums, family history, films, computer games, books, TV programmes etc), and that adults had different levels of sophistication in terms of which sources of information about the past they found most trustworthy. Your teaching can have a helpful influence on pupils' ideas about the reliability of different sources of information about the past (and the present), and developing pupils' ability to handle information intelligently is an important facet of a historical education for young people growing up in the twenty-first century (see the section on history and citizenship later in this chapter).

There is an important strand of 'progression' involved in understanding and developing pupils' ideas about the uses of the past, and the trustworthiness of information about the past. In the words of Peter Seixas:

> North American media have devoted considerable attention to the public's knowledge (or lack thereof) of discrete historical facts... The more significant measure of public historical literacy is one that captures not the number of facts they remember but rather the sophistication of their strategies for coming to know the past. (Seixas *et al.*, 2008: 11-12)

Pupils' ideas and feelings about history

Pupils' ideas about history

It is important not to *assume* that pupils understand why they are doing history, or particular aspects of it. There is a degree of paradox here – often at the 'micro' level, the learning objectives for the lesson are written up on the board in every lesson, but at the 'macro' level ('Why do we have to learn about the Stuarts?'), the understanding is not there and we have to be explicit about getting ideas about 'purposes' and 'benefits' across to pupils. It can also be helpful to keep in mind the idea of 'historical perspectives', the idea of the discipline of history providing one way of developing our understanding of the world we live in (see Aldrich, 1997). Everything has a history: food, jobs, transport, clothes, weapons, schools, television. Part of our job is convincing pupils that many of the things that have happened in the past have an effect on their lives when they leave school, and that it can be helpful for them to have an understanding of some of these changes and developments. It is a question of persuading them that in the words of William Faulkner (1953), 'the past is not dead, it is not even past'.

Several surveys of pupils' views about studying history in schools have revealed that substantial numbers of them feel that the subject is boring and useless. One of the reasons that some pupils do not do well in the subject is not that they lack ability, but that they are not wholeheartedly committed to learning and doing well in history. One of your responsibilities is to ensure that pupils feel that history is relevant, important and essential – it is one of the tests of your ability as a teacher. As Burston and Green noted in 1962, 'The problem for historians and the history teacher is how to demonstrate the relevance of history to the present in a sufficiently convincing manner to gain the interest of the pupils' (Burston and Green, 1962: 34). This is as true today as it was in 1962. You must look for opportunities to relate the past to the present and the future so that pupils can 'see the point' of learning about the past.

It can be helpful to know what pupils find difficult in history, what misconceptions and gaps they have in their understanding of the past, what sort of ideas they are 'operating with', and what sort of ideas are suggested for helping them to progress in history. This knowledge comes from reading about research in history education, accessing inspection evidence, and considering it against your own teaching experience.

Task 3.5 *What are pupils' ideas about why they do history in school?*

'Throughout the lesson, the teacher stressed to the pupils that the skills they were learning would be of use in the wider world when they left school.' (Extract from a student teacher's notes from observing an experienced teacher).

Recent surveys have revealed that many pupils do not have a well-developed understanding of why they are doing history in school, or the ways in which it might be helpful to them in their lives after school (see, for example, Adey and Biddulph, 2001; QCA, 2005).

Some responses from the 2005 QCA survey:
'I'm not being rude but it doesn't actually help you in your daily life.'
'I don't really know but some people really enjoy it.'
'I don't have a clue.'
'They don't tell us why.'
'So that you can know a bit more knowledge you don't use much.'
'To get a bit of ancient stuff into your brain.'
'So if you dig something up in the garden you know what it is.'
'I don't know, but it helps you on quiz shows and pub quizzes.'

 Go to www.uea.ac.uk/~m242/historypgce/qcafinalreport.pdf and click on the link to 'Pupil perceptions'. Read the summary of what pupils said when asked to explain why they thought the government made it compulsory for them to do history at school (pages 8-16). What implications does this research have for your practice as a history teacher? Pick out 2-3 lessons which you will be teaching and think how you incorporate some component which establishes or clarifies some of the ways in which the study of the past is useful to young people.

Pupils' feelings about history as a school subject

Perhaps surprisingly, not everyone thinks it is desirable to make lessons interesting for pupils, or develop pupils' critical literacy. Former Chief Inspector of Schools Chris Woodhead has argued that too much attention has been paid to what pupils think and feel: 'The aim should not be to develop 'critical thinking skills' and they should not be encouraged to express their opinions on the texts. Who cares what they think or feel?' (Woodhead, 2010: 9).

However, this is a minority view. Most commentators believe that it is generally helpful if pupils can be engaged in the process of learning. Not all pupils are driven scholars but many are 'biddable' to the idea of learning history, if the subject matter and learning objectives are presented in an accessible and intellectually intriguing way, and if they feel that they can gain something and achieve in the lesson (Banham, 2014).

It is important to remember that not all pupils share your love of the subject. The historian Norman Stone suggested that pupils should have the national culture 'rammed down their throats' (quoted in Crawford, 1995). Most experienced history teachers believe that this strategy is not effective, and that pupils learn best when they are interested in what they are learning, and feel that it has some relevance to their lives.

Figure 3.5 Not all pupils share your love of history

Survey and date	Useful	Not very useful
Schools Council Survey (1967)	29%	71%
Hargreaves Report (1984)	53%	47%
2005 QCA Survey	69.3%	30.7%

Figure 3.6 Pupils' views on the usefulness of school history

Survey and date	'Enjoyable'	'Not enjoyable'
Schools Council Survey (1967)	41%	59%
Hargreaves Report (1984)	61%	39%
2005 QCA Survey	69.8%	30.2%

Figure 3.7 Pupils' views on enjoyment of history

For further detail on these surveys, see Aldrich, 1987 and the Qualifications and Curriculum Authority (QCA) report, 'Pupil perceptions of history at Key Stage 3', online at www.uea. ac.uk/~m242/historypgce/qcafinalreport.pdf. The latter survey found that the teacher was one of the most influential factors determining whether pupils enjoyed the subject or not.

It has been claimed that the attempt to engage pupils in 'active learning' and 'fun activities' has been at the expense of academic rigour, and has led to meretricious activities which children might find enjoyable (for instance poster work) but which do little to enhance their understanding of the past. There is some truth in Lawlor's claim that there has sometimes been a degree of 'dumbing down' in education, where pupils are given low level and unchallenging work 'to pass the time', and 'keep them happy' rather than advance pupils' learning (Lawlor, 1989). (How many of you remember sometimes being given a piece of work to do, or a video extract to watch which you suspect was prescribed because it 'passed the time', until the end of the lesson?) While accepting that there might be times when this is true, as a general rule, there is more chance of real gains in learning where pupils are interested and motivated to learn.

This is not to suggest that history needs to be reduced to constant game playing, poster drawing and group work. 'Engagement in the process of learning history can be simply listening to the teacher's exposition, and thinking about the past. James Schick claims that in the United States, students often express a preference for lectures over other types of class:

> They want the teacher to tell them what's important, to select appropriate facts, to focus on the important issues. They want the teacher to provide all the answers... This low-stress arrangement puts as much burden as possible on the teacher and demands little intellectual growth by students. As teachers of history, we must not only revere truth, honour courage, and smash icons, we must require our students to do the same. We must not abet students' intellectual passivity.... In education, the vital interaction should take place in the student's mind. Without this the potential for learning diminishes significantly. No teaching has occurred if students do not understand. (Schick, 1995: 11–12)

It is not about making learning easy, it is about making it interesting and challenging. Coffey (2011: 201) warns of the dangers of setting work that is too easy for pupils:

> It is a common mistake of beginning teachers to set work that is too easy in the hope that it will please pupils and keep them occupied. In fact the opposite happens: pupils enjoy the level of challenge that allows them, with effort, to succeed.

In terms of the implications for your practice, a key challenge is to learn how to devise activities which are challenging, but not so far beyond the capabilities of your pupils that they simply give up and don't even try to engage with the work.

Another contested area is the extent to which history teachers should go to try and make the topic 'relevant' to pupils' lives. Michael Gove, Secretary of State for Education at the time of writing this chapter has argued that 'We should pull back from seeking to make content more relevant to the contemporary concerns and lives of young people' (Gove, 2010). However, the majority of history teachers believe that it can be helpful if pupils can see some connection between what they are learning and their own lives (Harris and Rea, 2006; School History Project, 2012). Coffey echoes this view:

> Pupils respond more positively when invited to draw on their own experience rather than with reference to an abstracted reality. This is true of all pupils but has been shown to be especially effective in increasing participation of disaffected low-achieving boys. (Coffey, 2011: 205)

Whatever your views about which aspects of the past are most important to teach to your pupils, pupil *attitudes to learning* can make a difference to the effectiveness of your teaching.

The history teacher's knowledge and understanding of subject pedagogy, and research and inspection findings can be a significant influence on their willingness to commit wholeheartedly to learning history. Successful history teaching depends in part on the ability of the teacher to present history in a way which makes the pupils want to find out about the past. We return to the point made by Burston and Green, 'The problem for historians and the history teacher, is how to demonstrate the relevance of history to the present in a sufficiently convincing manner to gain the interest of the pupils' (Burston and Green, 1962). Part of the challenge is to get pupils to 'care' about the past (Kitson, 2013). An exploration of whether Elizabeth the First should or should not have cut off the head of her sister, Mary Queen of Scots, will not be very animated if the pupils don't give a damn either way. It helps if you can get them to want to learn. In the words of Sue Hallam (1997), 'If you lose that, you lose just about everything.'

Understanding progression in history: what does it mean 'to get better at history'?

Another important aspect of subject knowledge is an understanding of what it means 'to get better' at history. It is now generally accepted that there is more to getting better in history than simply acquiring a greater depth and breadth of subject content knowledge, important though those things are. How can you help to move pupils forward in the subject if you are not clear about what it means 'to get better' at history? You therefore need to develop a clear grasp of ideas about progression in history. In terms of the implications for your practice, the main aim of this section of the chapter is to develop your awareness of the wide range of ways in which pupils can make progress in history. This can be helpful when you are planning lessons (see Chapter 4).

The inception of a National Curriculum for History brought about a much more clearly defined framework for progression in the subject than had existed hitherto, based on 45 statements of attainment, divided into three main strands or 'ladders' of progression:

- the development of historical knowledge and understanding;
- the development of pupils' ability to use historical sources; and
- the development of pupils' understanding of historical interpretations. (DES, 1991)

This assessment framework suggested that as well as getting better by knowing and understanding more about the substantive past, there were steps that pupils could take to get better at understanding how to use historical sources, and in their understanding of 'interpretations' of the past.

In 1993, Lomas suggested a list of 12 ways in which pupils might demonstrate progression in their learning. In addition to 'greater historical knowledge', these included greater skill in the selection of relevant information, a greater ability to make connections and comparisons across time, and to explain rather than simply describe. Greater independence of thought, the ability to balance differing viewpoints and increased awareness and acceptance of uncertainty were also to be encouraged.

The various revisions to the NC for history (see Chapter 2) increased the number of 'areas for attention' and by the time of the 2007 version of the NC, there were six 'key concepts' (chronology, diversity, change, cause, significance and interpretation) and three 'key processes' (evidence, enquiry and communication) to be considered (QCA, 2007).

During this period, a number of researchers explored pupils' ideas about pupils' understanding of history, in order to gain greater insight into children's thinking about these concepts, in areas such as accounts, cause, rational understanding, explanatory adequacy and objectivity, and 'big picture' understanding of the past (see, for example, Blow, 2013; Foster, Ashby and Lee, 2008; Lee and Ashby, 2000; Lee and Shemilt, 2004; Wineburg, 1997). Byrom (2003, 2013) also pointed to the complex interrelationship between elements of progression in pupils' learning and the problem of retention – the extent to which pupils were prone to regression and forgetfulness in their understanding of history, particularly in terms of pupils' ability to retain substantive historical knowledge and use it to build a coherent mental map of the past. Taylor's framework for historical literacy provides a reminder of the importance of developing pupils' understanding of the language of historical discourse (Taylor, 2012), and the Council of Europe (2001) also provides some interesting ideas about progression in history, including the development of pupils' understanding that the work of historians is usually subject to the scrutiny of other historians.

Counsell (2000) and Vermeulen (2000) make the point that there is often a need to address a particular aspect of historical thinking in order to move pupils forward, but warn against attempting to define progression primarily in discrete domains of second order concepts. This might be as unhelpful as the discredited 'levels' system. There also needs to be some consideration about the extent to which the pupils are developing 'a sense of history' (Fordham *et al.*, 2013), in a more holistic way. Wineburg provides a helpful explanation of what someone who 'knows history' might look like:

> Such a person knows how to determine and weigh an author's perspective when evaluating a piece of history.... Someone who claims to know history, as opposed to someone who possesses a great deal of historical information, has an understanding of the strengths and weaknesses of historical claims, the power and the fallibility of evidence, the nature of imaginative reconstruction from fragmented sources, and a sixth sense about when reconstruction ventures into fabrication. Such a person has 'a historical cast of mind' – she or he 'thinks' like a historian, asking questions about context, showing caution at the pronouncement of a unilateral causal statement, and seeking corroborating evidence.... To know how to construct a historical argument, to know how to evaluate and question sources, to know when analogies to other events are appropriate and when they are misleading is not a generic 'thinking skill', a 'process', or a disembodied system of 'metaknowledge'. It is content knowledge in its richest form. (Wineburg, 1997: 260)

These qualities are not just important for deploying in historical contexts, they are useful in helping young people to make sense of and evaluate information on the news, in the newspapers and on the internet. They are part of what makes school history useful.

There is evidence to suggest that pupils often do not have a clear grasp of what it means to get better at history, with many of them thinking that it is mainly about writing longer answers and 'knowing more stuff' (Haydn and Harris, 2009). Ian Dawson's *What is history? A starter unit for year 7*, is one of the few text books to address the question of what it means to get better at history (Dawson, 2003: 38–43). Not only do you have to acquire a sound grasp of progression issues in history, you need to be able to make these ideas explicit to your pupils.

 The complexity of what exactly constitutes 'progression' in history means that it is difficult to provide a comprehensive explanation within the confines of this book , but further detail and suggestions for further reading can be found at the UEA History PGCE website, http://terryhaydn.wordpress.com/pgce-history-at-uea.

Knowledge and understanding of the National Curriculum for history and examination specifications

Even if you are teaching in a school which is not obliged to teach the National Curriculum for history, it can be helpful to have some knowledge or understanding of it, in order to inform and guide your practice. If you are in a school which is obliged to teach the National Curriculum, it is essential that you have a precise grasp of 'what children should be taught...'. Similarly, if you are teaching examination groups, it is essential that you have a clear understanding of what the exam specification stipulates, the form of the examination and the assessment objectives which will be tested. This seems so obvious as to be hardly worth saying, but sometimes teachers have not 'thought ahead' in terms of covering the content for the exam, and leave themselves with insufficient time for revision, or have to rush through content having spent too long on aspects of the course which they enjoy teaching.

The Historical Association's Final Report of the *History Transition Project* can provide helpful information about the issues and problems surrounding pupils' transition from primary to secondary school in history: www.history.org.uk/resources/primary_resource_3616_127.html.

Knowledge and understanding of research and inspection findings in history

Subject-related educational research can play an important role in trainee teachers' learning since it provides a disciplined perspective from which trainees can derive new ideas and understandings related to their own developing practice as well as a critical basis from which to formulate, examine and justify their views through reference to a wider, collective pool of experience (Counsell *et al.*, 2000).

Counsell *et al.* make the point that educational research is not *automatically* useful, and some research 'may not seem applicable to the classroom, or it may seem very technical or full of jargon' (Barton, 2007: 1). However it does provide access to some ideas and evidence about teaching which are outside your own professional experience and sometimes, that of the colleagues with whom you are working.

As noted in Chapter 1, there is a degree of arrogance in thinking that you can work it all out for yourself, and that you don't need any knowledge, information or guidance from anyone else. The important thing is to keep in mind Stenhouse's precept that the purpose and value of educational research is to test it out in your own practice, to see whether it works or not, and how it might be adapted, improved, or discarded (Stenhouse, 1975).

- Succinct and up-to-date summaries of recent *scholarship* in history can be found in *BBC History Magazine* and *History Today* (both magazines provide an online index which helps to locate particular topics, www.historyextra.com/index-search, www.historytoday.com/archive).
- *Teaching History* provides access to summaries of recent research in history education. The 'Move me on' section provides guidance on relating particular teaching challenges in history teaching to relevant literature.
- Levstik, L. and Barton, K. (2008) *Researching history education: theory, method and context*, New York, Routledge.
- Davies, I. (ed.) *Debates in history teaching*, London, Routledge.
- Harris, R., Burn, K. and Woolley, M. (eds) *The Guided reader to teaching and learning history*, London, David Fulton.

Figure 3.8 Accessing research on history education

Another useful source of information which should inform your practice is the online material provided by Ofsted. Although Ofsted inspections are a source of stress and anxiety for teachers, it would not be accurate to say that Ofsted processes, outcomes and feedback, at an HMI level, are not transparent and available for scrutiny (this is not the same as saying that all judgements are accurate or that all inspection teams adhere to the criteria specified). Ofsted have gone to considerable time and trouble to provide feedback on the outcomes of their inspections, in terms of providing insight into problematic and weaker areas of practice, and examples of good practice in history teaching.

Task 3.6　*Developing your awareness of recent inspection findings, grading criteria and examples of good practice in school history*

- Access the Ofsted Report *History for all*, which provides a summary of recent Ofsted findings on history teaching in English schools: www.ofsted.gov.uk/resources/history-for-all. Read pages 5–8, 21–26 and 45–57, which focus on history in secondary schools and note the main findings in terms of 'areas of strength' and 'things that need to be worked on'. What are the implications for your own development as a teacher?
- Access and read the 'Professional development materials for history teachers' section of the website: www.ofsted.gov.uk/resources/subject-professional-development-materials-history.
- Access and read the secondary 'Case studies of good practice' which are on the website: www.ofsted.gov.uk/inspection-reports/our-expert-knowledge/history-0.
- Access and read the grade criteria which provide Ofsted descriptions of the quality of history teaching which they observe: www.ofsted.gov.uk/resources/generic-grade-descriptors-and-supplementary-subject-specific-guidance-for-inspectors-making-judgement.

Understanding how children learn

It is helpful to know something about how children learn. The QED documentary 'Simple Minds' (BBC2, 19 September 1994) demonstrated that in many cases, fewer pupils understood a topic after the teacher had taught it than before it was taught – teaching can actually reduce pupil understanding. If we decide that something is worth teaching, it is worth spending some time thinking about how to teach it effectively. There is a body of research evidence which gives us some ideas and suggestions about achieving this. It would be churlish to disregard this source of help. Pupils arrive at your lessons with strongly rooted ideas and preconceptions about many aspects of how the world (including the past) operates. It is important that you try to understand and take account of pupils' preconceptions and ways of thinking if you are to move them on to more sophisticated and powerful ways of understanding both the past and the present. Without taking their understandings into account in your teaching, you may well leave their misconceptions undisturbed (see Lee, 1994: 141-48 and Lee and Ashby, 2000: 199-222, for further development of this point).

There is also the problem of knowledge retention (Willingham, 2009; Shemilt, 2009): why does so much learning 'slip away' over time, and how can we reduce such slippage? Knowledge retention is important in history – 'the more capacity I have for holding and using detailed knowledge, the stronger is my ability as a historian' (Byrom, 2003: 13). Recap, reinforcement and revisiting of knowledge can help consolidate knowledge and understanding, as is being able to place knowledge within a bigger 'framework' (Shemilt, 2009). Much cited, Willingham argues that 'memory is the residue of thought' (Willingham, 2009: 54), and that if learners have been 'made to think', and process information in some way, they are more likely to remember it. Wiliam (2011) and Vermeulen (2000) also argue that pupils remember best what they have, to at least some extent, worked out for themselves.

Desforges (2002) argues that knowledge *application* is also a major problem, in the words of Wineburg, 'the chasm between knowing X and using X to think about Y' (Wineburg, 1997: 256). If you want to make sure that pupils really have understood a concept such as 'appeasement', whilst studying the Munich Crisis of 1938, it can be useful to see if they can identify and explain the use of appeasement in a different historical context.

All this is before we get to the problem of pupils not learning because they are not really bothered about doing well in history (see earlier section of this chapter).

In terms of the implications for your practice, keep in mind that just because you've taught it doesn't mean that they've learnt it.

Knowledge and understanding of the role that new technology can play in enhancing teaching and learning in history

This is partly about developing pupils' digital literacy. Taylor (2012: 1) identifies 'ICT understandings – using, understanding and evaluating ICT based historical resources', as a key component of historical literacy. However, it is also about the extent to which history teachers are able to use new technologies to enhance teaching and learning in their lessons.

Over the past 30 years, new technology has become an increasingly influential component of 'a historical education' (Haydn, 2012), particularly in terms of teacher and pupil use of a wide range of ICT applications. Ofsted report that 'its impact in accelerating gains in pupils' historical knowledge and understanding varied, particularly in the secondary schools visited' (Ofsted, 2011: 7). The report also provided four pages of guidance on the use of ICT to promote achievement (Ofsted, 2011: 50-54, www.ofsted.gov.uk/resources/history-for-all). Further guidance on this facet of history teaching is provided in Chapter 9 and on the website http://terryhaydn.wordpress.com/pgce-history-at-uea.

Knowledge and understanding of the Teachers' Standards

In England (at the time of writing this chapter), *The Teachers' Standards* (DfE, 2012) identify eight areas of teaching capability, and several requirements which relate to 'personal and professional conduct' which you must acquire if you are to be licensed to teach in England (unless you apply to teach in an academy, or free school, in which case, no teaching qualification is required). You need to keep in mind the full breadth of the Standards in the course of your initial teacher education. They might be considered as 'the things which you need to consider if you are to develop into a fully effective teacher'. It can be helpful for you to keep in mind the full breadth of the *Teachers' Standards* when you complete your evaluation of lessons. It is not unusual for student teacher evaluation of lessons to focus on a limited number of these facets of teaching (typically, and not unnaturally, 'How was my teaching?' 'Did the pupils learn what I was trying to teach?' 'How did the pupils behave?'). From time to time it can be helpful to keep the *Teachers' Standards* document to hand as you complete your lesson evaluations, and consider other strands of the Standards ('How did my subject knowledge influence the lesson?, 'How effectively am I assessing pupil progress?', 'How should I approach the *British Values* strand of the Standards?).

Task 3.7 *Developing your breadth of subject knowledge*

How would you respond if someone asked you...

- What history are pupils likely to have encountered before secondary school?
- What are 'key skills' – and what can history do to help pupils make progress in them?
- Can you think of anything you have read about teaching history which has had an influence on your thinking about how children learn in history?
- What do you understand by the term 'New history', and what are some of its advantages and disadvantages compared to the 'Old' history?

What would you say in response to these questions if you were asked them at an interview? By the end of your course of ITE, you should be able to give a cogent and well-informed answer to these questions.

Summary and key points

It is possible to have a First Class Honours degree in history, and yet not be an effective and accomplished teacher of the subject. *As well as* being a good academic historian, you need to have a clear grasp of the rationale for teaching history to young people (including an awareness that there are differing views on this).

You need to be able to relate your subject knowledge to the demands of the NC for history, and the criteria for GCSE and post-16 specifications.

It helps to know something about how children learn in history; what they find difficult, what mistakes they commonly make, and about some of the ideas which have emerged for helping them through these difficulties. You should therefore develop an awareness of relevant literature in these areas, by reading *Teaching History*, the professional journal for history teachers and student teachers, and other books, journal articles and Ofsted findings.

Above all, you must also keep in mind the full breadth of benefits which pupils can derive from the study of the past. History can make a profound difference to the sort of citizens who emerge from our schools. It can contribute to their ability to handle information critically and intelligently, to their spiritual and moral development, their self-esteem and ability to work well with others, their ability with language, numbers, and ICT, and other 'key skills' which are valued by employers, and which can also contribute to your pupils' chances of living happy, worthwhile and fulfilled lives. But it will not necessarily do all or any of these things. It depends how thoughtfully and skilfully the subject is taught. (Remember; some pupils have considered school history to be 'useless and boring'.)

As the opening quotations to this chapter indicate, it is the breadth and depth of your subject knowledge, together with your commitment, teaching expertise and skills of communication that will persuade pupils to value history as a school subject, and work hard to do well in history. Without a clear grasp of the purposes and benefits of school history, the best you can hope for from pupils is desultory compliance with things they neither care about nor understand. As well as the benefits for the pupils in your care, a clear sense of purpose enables you to feel confident that what you are doing is important and worthwhile, so that you enjoy your teaching, and find it rewarding.

Perhaps above all, you should remember that just because you've taught it, it doesn't mean that the pupils have learned it. Always keep in mind 'the messiness, the unpredictability and the elusiveness of learning' (Yandell, 2014: 153).

Remember that not all of your pupils are driven scholars

'They must want to learn. If you lose that, you lose just about everything.' (Hallam, 1996)

Figure 3.9 Remember that not all of your pupils are driven scholars

Suggestions for further reading

Department for Education (2013) *History programmes of study: Key Stage 3, National Curriculum in England*, London, DfE, online at www.gov.uk/government/uploads/system/uploads/attachment_data/file/239075/SECONDARY_national_curriculum_-_History.pdf, accessed 30 March 2014.

DES (1991) *Final Report of the National Curriculum History Working Group*, London: HMSO.

Evans, R. (2003) 'Our job is to explain', *Times Higher Education Supplement*, 13 June 2003, online at www.timeshighereducation.co.uk/features/our-job-is-to-explain/177421.article, accessed 30 March 2014. A succinct and eloquent explanation of what historians do and why they do it.

Husbands, C. (2011) What do history teachers need to know? A framework for understanding and developing practice, in I. Davies (ed.) *Debates in History Teaching*, London: Routledge: 84–95.

Husbands, C. (2012) Using assessment data to support pupil achievement, in V. Brooks, I. Abbott and P. Huddleston (eds) *Preparing to teach in secondary schools*, Maidenhead: Open University Press: 132–44. This is one of the best resources currently available which provides a succinct and clear explanation of what is quite a complex issue.

Lee, P. (2011) History education and historical literacy, in I. Davies (ed.) *Debates in History Teaching*, London: Routledge: 63–83.

Lee, P. and Ashby, R. (2000) Progression in historical understanding amongst students aged 7-14, in P. Sterns, P. Seixas and S. Wineburg (eds) *Knowing, Teaching and Learning History: National and international perspectives*, New York: New York University Press: 199–222. Pages 199–201 are particularly helpful for understanding the nature of history as a discipline, and the ways in which ideas about the purposes and benefits of school history have changed over the past 30 years.

Lee, P. and Shemilt, D. (2004) A scaffold not a cage: progression and progression models in history, *Teaching History*, No. 113: 13–23.

Seixas, P. (2013) Historical consciousness and historical thinking, paper presented at the international seminar on research in historical culture and historical education, Las Navas, Madrid, 4-6 December.

Teaching History (2000) 'Defining progression', No. 98. Issue focusing on progression.

References

Abulafia, D., Clark, J. and Tombs, R. (2012) History in the new curriculum: 3 proposals, London, Politeia, online at www.politeia.co.uk/sites/default/files/files/Final%20Appendix%20to%20Lessons%20from%20History.pdf, accessed 20 March 2014.

Adey, K. and Biddulph, M. (2001) The influence of pupil perceptions on subject choice at 14+ in geography and history, *Educational Studies*, Vol. 27, No. 4: 439–51.

Aldrich, R. (1987) Interesting and useful, *Teaching History*, No. 47: 11–14.

Aldrich, R. (1997) *The end of history and the beginning of education*, London: Institute of Education.

Baker, C., Cohn, T. and McLaughlin, M. (2000) Inspecting subject knowledge, in J. Arthur and R. Phillips (eds) *Issues in History Teaching*, London: Routledge: 211–19.

Banham, D. (2014) Seminar for History PGCE students at the University of East Anglia, 31 January.

Barton, K. (2007) *Applied research: educational research as a way of seeing*, presentation to the joint conference of the Dutch History Teachers' Association and the History Teacher Education Network, University of Amsterdam, 23 June.

Blow, F. (2011) Everything flows and nothing stays': how students make sense of the historical concepts of change, continuity and development, *Teaching History*, No. 145: 47–55.

Burston, W.H. and Green, C.W. (eds) (1962) *Handbook for History Teachers*, London: Methuen.

Byrom, J. (2003) Continuity and progression, in M. Riley and R. Harris (eds) *Past Forward: A vision for school history 2002-12*, London: Historical Association: 12–14.

Byrom, J. (2013) Alive ... and kicking? Personal reflections on the revised National Curriculum and what we might do with it, *Teaching History: curriculum supplement,* December: 6–15.

Coffey, S. (2011) 'Differentiation in theory and practice', in J. Dillon and M. Maguire (eds) *Becoming a teacher: issues in secondary education,* Maidenhead, Open University Press.

Council of Europe (2001) *Recommendations of the Committee of Ministers to member states on history teaching in twenty-first-century Europe,* Strasbourg, Council of Europe, online at https://wcd.coe.int/ViewDoc.jsp?id=234237, accessed 2 April 2014.

Counsell, C. (2000) Historical knowledge and historical skills: a distracting dichotomy, in J. Arthur and R. Phillips (eds) *Issues in History Teaching,* London: Routledge: 54–71.

Counsell, C., Evans, M. and McIntyre, D. (2000) The Usefulness of Educational Research for Trainee Teachers' Learning, *Oxford Review of Education, 26* (3–4): 467–82.

Crawford, K. (1995) A history of the right: the battle for control of the National Curriculum history 1989-1994, *British Journal of Educational Studies, 43* (4): 433–56.

Dawson, I. (2003) *What is history? A starter unit for year 7,* London: Hodder.

Dawson, I. (2012) *The Wars of the Roses,* London: Hodder.

Dean, J. (1995) *Teaching history at KS2,* Cambridge: Chris Kington.

DES (1985) *History in the Primary and Secondary Years,* London: HMSO.

DES (1991) *History in the National Curriculum (England),* London: HMSO.

Department for Education (2013) *History programmes of study: Key Stage 3, National Curriculum in England,* London, DfE, online at www.gov.uk/government/uploads/system/uploads/attachment_data/file/239075/SECONDARY_national_curriculum_-_History.pdf, accessed 30 March 2014.

Desforges, C. (2002) *On Learning and Teaching,* Cranfield: NCSL.

Epstein, T. (2009) *Interpreting National History: Race, Identity and Pedagogy in Classrooms and Communities,* London: Routledge.

Evans, R. (2003) 'Our job is to explain', *Times Higher Education Supplement,* 13 June 2003, online at www.timeshighereducation.co.uk/features/our-job-is-to-explain/177421.article, accessed 30 March 2014.

Faulkner, W. (1953) *Requiem for a Nun,* London: Chatto and Windus.

Fordham, M. (2012) Disciplinary History and the Situation of History Teachers, *Educational Sciences, 2:* 242–53, online at www.mdpi.com/2227-7102/2/4/242, accessed 30 March 2014.

Fordham, M., Burn, K., Foster, R. and Counsell, C. (2014) A sense of history, *Teaching History,* No. 154: 2.

Foster, S. and Crawford, K. (eds) (2006) *What shall we tell the children? International perspectives on school history textbooks,* Charlotte NC: Information Age Publishing.

Foster, S., Ashby, R. and Lee, P. (2008) *Usable Historical Pasts: A study of students' frameworks of the past: ESRC grant reference: RES-000-22-1676,* online at www.esrc.ac.uk/my-esrc/grants/RES-000-22-1676/outputs/Read/1d94b76c-8117-4356-ba95-d7b088a04b5a, accessed 2 April 2014.

Fullan, M. (1999) *Change Forces: the sequel,* London: Falmer: 63.

Gershon, M. (2014) Classroom practice – Five simple steps for raising achievement, *Times Educational Supplement,* 28 March: 34, online at www.tes.co.uk/article.aspx?storyCode=6420273, accessed 30 March 2014.

Gove, M. (2010) Online at www.matthewtaylorsblog.com/public-policy/michael-goves-response/, accessed 31 August 2012.

Harris, R. and Rea, A. (2006) Making history meaningful: helping pupils see why history matters, *Teaching History,* No. 125: 28–36, online at www.history.org.uk/resources/secondary_resource_566.html, accessed 4 April 2014.

Harris, R. and Haydn, T. (2006) Pupils' enjoyment of history – what lessons can teachers learn from their pupils?, *The Curriculum Journal, 17* (4), pp. 315–33.

Haydn, T. (ed.) (2012) *Using New Technologies to Enhance Teaching and Learning in History,* London: Routledge.

Haydn, T. and Harris, R. (2009) Children's ideas about what it means 'to get better' at History: a view from the United Kingdom, *International Journal of Historical Learning Teaching and Research*, 8 (2): 26-39, online at www.history.org.uk/resources/secondary_resource_2593_149.html, accessed 3 April 2014.

Howson, J. (2007) Is it the Tuarts and then the Studors or the other way round? The importance of developing a usable big picture of the past, *Teaching History*, No. 127: 40-47, online at www.history.org.uk/resources/secondary_resource_706_8.html, accessed 30 March 2014.

Hunt, M. (ed.) (2007) A Practical Guide to Teaching History in the Secondary School, London, Routledge.

Husbands, C. (2011) What do history teachers need to know? A framework for understanding and developing practice, in I. Davies (ed.) *Debates in History Teaching*, London: Routledge: 84-95.

Instone, M. (2013) Moving forwards while looking back: historical consciousness in sixth form students, *Teaching History*, No.152:52-60, online at www.history.org.uk/resources/secondary_resource_6882_12.html, accessed 30 March 2014.

Kitson, A. (2013) 'The Georgians', keynote address at the SHP November Conference, British Library, November.

Lawlor, S. (1989) Correct Core, in B. Moon, P. Murphy and J. Rayner (eds) *Policies for the Curriculum*, Open University Press.

Lee, P. (1994) 'Historical knowledge and the National Curriculum', in H. Bourdillon, (ed.) *Teaching History*, London: Routledge: 41-48.

Lee, P. (2004) Walking backwards into tomorrow: historical consciousness and understanding history, *International Journal of Historical Learning, Teaching and Research*, 4 (1): 69-114.

Lee, P. (2011) History education and historical literacy, in I. Davies (ed.) *Debates in History Teaching*, London: Routledge: 63-83.

Lee, P. and Ashby, R. (2000) Progression in historical understanding among students ages 7-14, in P. Stearns, P. Seixas and S. Wineburg (eds) *Knowing, Teaching and Learning History*, New York: New York University Press.

Lee, P. and Cercadillo, L. (2013), Historical accounts, significance and unknown ontologies, paper presented at the international seminar on research in historical culture and historical education, Las Navas, Madrid, 4-6 December.

Lee, P. and Shemilt, D. (2004) A scaffold not a cage: progression and progression models in history, *Teaching History*, No. 113: 13-23.

Levesque, S. (2008) *Thinking Historically: Educating students for the twenty first century*, Toronto: Toronto University Press.

MacBeath, J. (1998) *The Observer*, 22 February.

Macmillan, M. (2009) *The Uses and Abuses of History*, London: Profile Books.

National Curriculum Council (1991) History: non-statutory guidance, York: NCC.

Ofsted (1995) *History: a review of inspection findings 1993/4*, London: HMSO.

Ofsted (2011) *History For All*, London, Ofsted, online at www.ofsted.gov.uk/resources/history-for-all, accessed 2 April 2014.

Peal, R. (2013) *The Battle of Ideas: History Wars, Institute of Ideas debate*, online at http://goodbyemister hunter.wordpress.com/2014/03/02/the-battle-of-ideas-history-wars, accessed 28 March 2014.

QCA (2005) Pupil perceptions of history at Key Stage 3, London, QCA, online at www.uea.ac.uk/~m242/historypgce/qcafinalreport.pdf, accessed 4 April 2014.

QCA (2007) *History programmes of study for Key Stage 3 and attainment target*, London: QCA.

Rusen, J. (1993) 'The development of narrative competence in historical learning: an ontogenetical hypothesis concerning moral consciousness'; 'Experience, interpretation, orientation: three dimensions of historical learning'; 'Paradigm shift and theoretical reflection in Western German historical studies'. In P. Duvenage (ed.) Studies in Metahistory (Pretoria: Human Sciences Research Council), 63-84.

Rusen, J. (2006) Historical consciousness: narrative structure, moral function and ontogenic development, in P, Seixas (ed.) *Theorising Historical Consciousness*, Toronto: Toronto University Press: 70-78.

Schick (1995) 'On being interactive: rethinking the learning equation', *History Microcomputer Review*, 11 (1), 9-25.

School History Project (2012) SHP principles, online at www.schoolshistoryproject.org.uk/AboutSHP/principles.htm, accessed 20 March 2014.

Seixas, P., Ercikan, K. and Northrup, D. (2008) 'History and the past: towards a measure of "Everyman's epistemology"', paper presented at the AERA Conference, New York, 27 March.

Seixas, P. (2013) Historical consciousness and historical thinking, paper presented at the international seminar on research in historical culture and historical education, Las Navas, Madrid, 4-6 December.

Shemilt, D. (2009) 'Drinking in ocean and pissing a cupful: how adolescents make sense of history', in L. Symcox and A. Wilschut (eds) *National History Standards: The problem of the canon and the future of teaching history*, Charlotte NC: Information Age Publishing: 141-210.

Shulman, L. (1986) 'Those who understand: knowledge growth in teaching, *Educational Researcher*, 15 (2): 4-14, online at http://ccnt5.wcu.edu/WebFiles/PDFs/Shulman.pdf, accessed 30 March 2014.

Shulman, L. (1987) Knowledge and teaching: foundations of the new reform, *Harvard Educational Review*, 57 (1): 1-23.

Stenhouse, L. (1975) *An Introduction to Curriculum Research and Development*, Oxford: Heinemann.

Taylor, T. (2012) Teaching historical literacy: the National History Project, online at www.civicsandcitizenship.edu.au/cce/expert_views/teaching_historical_literacy_the_national_history,9323.htm, accessed 3 April 2014.

Thatcher, M. (1995) Margaret Thatcher: the Downing Street years, London: Harper.

The Pasts Collective (2013) *Canadians and their Pasts*, Toronto: University of Toronto Press.

Vermeulen, E. (2000) What is progress in history?, *Teaching History*, No. 98: 35-41.

Wiliam, D. (2011) *Embedded Formative Assessment*, Bloomington IN: Solution Tree Press.

Willingham, D. (2009) Why do students remember everything that's on television and forget everything I say?, in D. Willingham, *Why don't students like school?*, San Francisco: Jossey-Bass: 53-86.

Wineburg, S. (1997) Beyond 'breadth and depth': subject matter knowledge and assessment, *Theory into Practice*, 36 (4): 255-61.

Wineburg, S. (2000) *Historical Thinking and Other Unnatural Acts*, Philadelphia: Temple University Press.

Woodhead, C. (2010) 'Answer the question', *Sunday Times*, News Review, 25 October: 9.

Yandell, J. (2014) Classrooms as sites of delivery or meaning-making? Whose knowledge counts, *Forum*, 61 (1): 147-55.

Zamorski, B. and Haydn, T. (2002) Classroom Management and Disaffection, *Pedgagogy, Culture and Society*, 10 (2): 257-78.

4 Planning for learning

My problem Miss, is how the different bits fit together' (Quoted in Ward, 2007).

Figure 4.1 The history jigsaw

Introduction

Do you have a clear idea, or plan, of what you are trying to achieve, both within a lesson, and in the longer term, over a series of lessons? Why are you telling these children about something that happened hundreds of years ago, what good will it do them?

Given the pressures on you in your first weeks of teaching (will they behave, will I remember my script, have I enough to get through the lesson?), it is easy to lose sight of why we are teaching children about aspects of the past (exactly what *do* you want them to 'get' from learning about the Industrial Revolution?). Along with lack of clarity about the purposes of school history, one of the most common causes of indifferent or unsatisfactory teaching by student teachers is the absence of precise, clearly thought out and appropriate learning objectives for pupils. There is also the issue of progression in learning linked to previous lessons, and future lessons. There is an understandable tendency for student teachers to think of lessons one at a time, especially in the early stages of teaching experience. An important element of progression in your planning skills is the extent to which you can 'think long-term', refer back to previous lessons, and have a coherent plan for developing pupils' knowledge, skills and understanding in history. If you don't recap, reinforce, check, make connections, and link 'depth' studies with 'overviews' of history, there is a danger that pupils forget what they have learned, do not have a sound grasp of what happened in the past, and do not really understand what history is about.

If you can manage to maintain a clear sense of direction and purpose to your lesson planning, and an awareness of the breadth of factors involved in planning, this can have a positive influence on many of the other preoccupations which dwell in the minds of student teachers. Most pupils are more likely to behave and respond well if the lessons have been well planned and 'make sense' to the pupils.

If you explain (for instance), the causes of the outbreak of Civil War in 1642 in the same way that you acquired your knowledge of it at GCE A Level, or at university, you may as well explain it in a foreign language for all the sense it makes to many 12 year olds. Subject application – being able to teach effectively – is as important as subject knowledge. Being clear in your own mind about exactly what benefits the pupils will derive from the study of the topic is also important (NCC, 1991). It is also important to keep in mind that just because pupils are 'on task' and well behaved, it does not guarantee that valuable learning is taking place. You have to beware that you do not 'fill up their days with dull, repetitive tasks that make little or no claim on their intelligence' (Holt, 1982: 119). A clear grasp of the full range of learning objectives which might be relevant to school history can help you to minimise this danger.

Objectives

At the end of this chapter, you should be able to:

- identify how the purposes of school history might interact with the process of lesson planning;
- understand the relationship between short, medium and long-term planning;
- use the NC for History to structure learning;
- understand the range of learning objectives which can be relevant to the study of history in the secondary school;
- formulate precise and appropriate learning objectives; and
- use the idea of a 'planning loop', where teaching, assessment and evaluation inform your further planning and teaching.

What questions are worth asking?

Another point for consideration in terms of historical knowledge is to focus on the sorts of questions that historians ask. As Lee points out, 'even questions have their standards –

some are uninteresting, and some merely foolish' (Lee, 1994: 44). To some extent, the quality of your history teaching is a function of the quality of the questions you ask. One of the common early difficulties which student teachers encounter is in devising questions which go beyond recall and comprehension, and which focus on historical understanding. Even a topic as important as the Holocaust can be rendered sterile and meretricious if time and thought is not given to the quality of questions to be posed, and why it is useful and important to find out about the Holocaust.

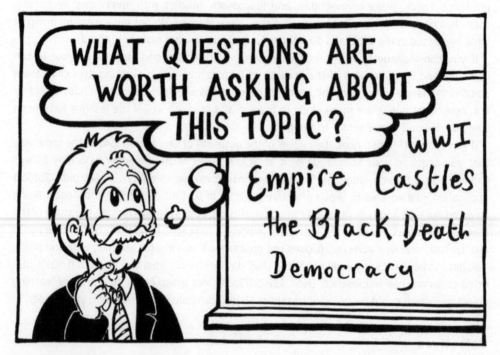

Figure 4.2 What questions are worth asking...?

Connecting learning objectives to the purposes of school history

As Chapter 2 demonstrated, there are very different views on the purposes of school history, and no universally accepted consensus on either why or how it should be taught. How are you to reconcile this divergence of opinion with the suggestion that what you attempt to achieve in your history lessons should bear in mind the purposes of school history? One helpful way forward is to make sure that you have a secure grasp of the NC for history: this is the current official 'warrant' for teaching history in schools. The NC documentation translates the accepted purposes of school history into 'what this means when you teach pupils in school', in a way that tries to ensure that you give pupils a broad and balanced 'diet' of history, which reflects *the full range* of ways in which being in your history classroom can be of benefit to your pupils. This means keeping in mind not just all the components of the NC for History, but agendas such as 'key skills', citizenship, inclusion, and all the other factors mentioned in Chapter 3.

There are two things of overarching importance which you should keep in mind when planning for learning:

- Although developing pupils' knowledge of the past is an essential part of school history, it is possible to teach it in such a way that it is also helpful to pupils in other ways. There is more to it than just getting them to know 'more stuff' about what happened.
- Although developing pupils' historical knowledge and understanding of the past should be central to planning for learning, more general educational objectives should also be considered if pupils are to derive maximum benefit from the study of history in your classroom.

Task 4.1 *Keeping in mind the full breadth of learning objectives in history*

There is a tendency for student teachers to concentrate mainly on the transmission of substantive content knowledge of topics in the early stages of their school experience. It is not unknown for tutors and mentors to look through a student teacher's teaching file at the end of a first school placement and find that there is little or no mention of words such as 'evidence', 'enquiry', 'significance', 'interpretation', 'chronology' or 'cause' – concepts that are central to progression in historical understanding.

When you are at a stage of your school experience where you have had at least several weeks of planning, teaching and evaluating lessons, look through your teaching experience file together with the NC for History at Key Stage 3. In addition to covering some of the seven areas of substantive historical content that 'pupils should be taught about', to what extent has your planning and teaching of lessons helped your pupils to make progress in the aspects of historical understanding which are specified in the NC for History? (DfE, 2013):

- their 'mental map' or 'big picture' of the past (chronologically secure knowledge and understanding of British, local and world history)?
- their ability to make connections, draw contrasts and analyse trends within periods and over long arcs of time?
- their ability to use historical terms and concepts in increasingly sophisticated ways?
- their ability to pursue historically valid enquiries including some they have framed themselves?
- their ability to create relevant, structured and evidentially supported accounts in response to these enquiries?
- their ability to understand how different types of historical sources are used rigorously to make historical claims?
- their ability to discern how and why contrasting arguments and interpretations of the past have been constructed?

Is it clear from your lesson evaluations that they are *history* lessons, with history specific comment, rather than largely general comment on task and class management? (For more detailed suggestions on how to approach your lesson evaluations, see the website, www.uea.ac.uk/~m242/historypgce/planning/evals.htm).

One of the difficulties which student teachers encounter in the early stages of school experience is formulating precise and appropriate learning objectives. Many students have found Martin Hunt's work *Thinking it through* (Hunt, 1997) useful in helping them through this problem. Extracts and examples from the paper, and other resources on objectives and evaluations can be found at http://terryhaydn.wordpress.com/pgce-history-at-uea/pgce-student-teacher/planning.

Hunt makes the point that student teachers need to 'think through' objectives into lesson activities and their evaluations – if your objectives are meaningful, it should be possible to make connections and 'track through' objectives through the various components of the lesson plan, from where you set out the learning objectives, through to the timings of activities and then in the evaluation of the lesson.

Figure 4.3 'Thinking it through'

There may be some lessons where the principal aim is to transmit to pupils information about what happened in the past, but if *every lesson* were to have this objective, and this objective alone, this would limit the benefits which might accrue from the study of the past (they are not all going to go on to take history at university) and is there not a danger that it may be difficult to elicit and sustain pupils' enthusiasm, interest and desire to learn if attention is limited to this objective?

So what other objectives might there be? What should student teachers keep in mind when planning schemes of work and individual lessons? Figure 4.4 attempts to make the point that there is more to think about than simply subject knowledge in putting together a history lesson. The generally accepted purposes of school history enumerated in the non statutory guidance (NCC, 1991), and by all five versions of the NC for history embrace both the development of knowledge and understanding of the past, and the development of pupils' understanding of the discipline of history – what history is, and its rules and conventions. This stems from the belief that some aspects of historical method might imbue pupils with 'transferable skills', which will be of use to them in life after school. Thus at the core of the teacher's aims are the twin pillars of knowledge and understanding of the past, and understanding of the nature of history – what history is, and what the rules and conventions of the discipline are. These are considered in detail in subsequent chapters.

Then there are more general educational objectives; you are not just teaching pupils history, you are attempting to develop oral skills, writing skills, listening skills; the ability to record and recall information and deploy it appropriately. All teachers should contribute to the development of children's language skills, and to their digital and information literacy (Haydn, 2012). Your planning also needs to consider 'inclusion' – the provision of accessible and challenging learning opportunities for all pupils (DfEE/QCA, 1999: 26-36). There are also the 'cross curricular' areas which obtrude into the study of history; there are times when the study of history sheds light on pupils' understanding of economic issues, or provides insight into moral and ethical issues, citizenship, and links into geography or philosophy. All school subjects have a responsibility to contribute to pupils' 'spiritual, moral, social and cultural development'. During history lessons, pupils might also develop some of the 'Key Skills' which the Dearing Report noted as being essential elements of education for all pupils – numeracy, problem solving, communication skills, ICT, team working and 'learning to learn' (Dearing, 1994). Remember, you can't do *all* this in every lesson, or even every study unit, but you should be aware of opportunities which might present themselves in these areas.

In planning lessons, there are also pragmatic considerations, which must take into account the nature of the pupils who are to be taught. One is the question of *differentiation* – how can the lesson be structured so as to maximise access to learning, and meaningful gains in learning, for all pupils in the teaching group. Dale Banham argues that 'the mindset problem' – pupils' attitude to learning in history, and their confidence that they will be able to get better at history – is perhaps the biggest problem that history teachers face: 'When pupils leave your lesson, do they feel more positive about their ability to do history than when they came in?' (Banham, 2014).

Another issue is *pupil progress* – giving thought to moving pupils forward in history, to higher levels of understanding, increased knowledge of the past, and more expert levels of accomplishment in skills of analysis, synthesis, selection and evaluation. Differentiation is about challenge as well as access, and there is an art to getting pupils to enjoy doing work that is at the limits of their capability. Clarke stresses the importance of getting this across to pupils:

> Discuss the importance of challenge and having a go at difficult tasks – we shouldn't be afraid to get things wrong, because that's how we learn. If work is easy, it means we are not learning – if it's hard, we need to keep trying, as that is how we learn. (Clarke, 2008: 25)

It is also important that there should be challenge for all pupils, not just for the most able. One way of building this into a lesson is to offer the pupils a 'difficulty challenge', which asks them to find out the meaning of a word or concept which they don't currently understand for the next lesson – all pupils can at least have a go at this. (More guidance on setting homework can be accessed on the website.)

Task 4.2 *Thinking about progression*

Read Christine Counsell's article in *Teaching History* No. 99, 'Didn't we do that in year 7? Planning for progress in historical understanding' (Counsell, 2000a). The article describes an activity based around a collection of sources about the Blitz. Counsell makes the point that how useful the activity is for developing pupils' evidential understanding depends on the questions we ask about the collection of sources. In Counsell's words, it's not just about coming up with 'nice little activities', it's about moving pupils forward in their learning.

There are also what might be termed 'tacit' considerations or objectives, and although even the most accomplished and experienced history teachers have to take account of them, they loom particularly large in the planning of student teachers. They include considerations such as classroom management – how do I settle the class down, how can I draw the lesson to a conclusion in an orderly and effective way, how can I reduce the chances of child X messing around and disrupting the learning of others?

Some of these 'tacit' objectives are a function of the comparative inexperience and limited repertoire of the student teacher. Because you do not as yet possess a vast archive of successful and proven teaching techniques and ideas on all aspects of the NC for History, there are times when pupil learning has to be balanced against classroom management and 'survival' strategies in your planning. Student teachers and NQTs have at times to devise 'coping strategies', in order to get through lessons as best they can. If student teachers are honest with themselves, there are times when some of the learning activities are designed more for classroom management purposes than to advancing learning in history. If you have 'the class from hell', on Friday afternoon, a video extract which the class might enjoy, followed by a worksheet which 'keeps their heads down', and 'keeps them occupied', might seem an enticing option, and make for a more controlled and effective lesson than a roleplay on the Battle of Hastings. Such strategies may well have diminishing returns in terms of their effectiveness. If you become over-reliant on 'anaesthetic', 'this will pass the time' strategies, pupils may well grasp that child minding is taking the place of learning, and their behaviour and respect for you as a teacher will deteriorate accordingly. One of the central challenges of your education is to progress as rapidly as possible towards consistently purposeful learning for pupils, as your expertise as a history teacher develops, whilst making appropriate use of 'coping strategies' where necessary. There may well be legitimate reasons for not always placing the development of historical knowledge, skills and understanding at the centre of your planning for the whole lesson or series of lessons. Some pupils may be reluctant scholars, who need to be lured into learning history, and will be 'biddable' to learning history if it is presented in an interesting and accessible manner. A common strategy is to try to ensure that lessons have a good 'starter' or 'initial stimulus material': some form of intriguing or entertaining prologue to the 'serious' history which will follow (Phillips, 2001). If your control of the class you are teaching is not secure, you may have to think carefully about what is attempted, and opt for 'settling activities', (such as setting written tasks, or taking notes from a video extract), which are more conducive to a quiet working atmosphere, rather than 'stirring' activities, (such as drama, 'hotseating' or roleplay), which are more suited to eliciting the enthusiasm and commitment of pupils to actively engaging in 'doing' history. (For a fuller explanation of stirring and settling activities, see MacLennan, 1987.) There are times when you may need to concentrate on developing a calm and purposeful working atmosphere in the classroom, and history learning objectives are influenced (and limited) by this imperative.

There is also sometimes a difficult tension between the long-term need to do interesting and stimulating work which wins the pupils over to the study of history, and the short-term agenda of staying within 'the comfort zone', and sticking to a tried and tested 'survival agenda' which is comfortably within your compass. Tempting though this may be at times, you must remember that by the end of your course, you want to have as full a repertoire of teaching experience and methods as possible. Progression in learning is just as important for student teachers as for pupils, and one of the reservations about teacher education is the tendency of some student teachers to 'plateau' in their learning (Baker *et al.*, 2000: 199).

In addition to there being many things to consider in planning for learning in history, there are also tensions between some of the factors involved. It is important that you think about these tensions, and discuss them with your tutor, if you are to make maximum progress in the course of your initial teacher education. 'Tacit' lesson objectives rarely feature in student teachers' lesson plans; it might be helpful to acknowledge them if you are to gain insight into the full range of factors influencing planning for learning. The way forward is not to pretend that they don't exist, but to think, talk and discuss how to get beyond tacit lesson objectives.

'I hate teaching this class and have major discipline problems with them. Forget the history, I just want to get to the end of the lesson without feeling shattered. I'll show an episode of 'Blackadder' and then give them a War and Peace scale worksheet with lots of drawing work and copying little stick men cartoons, that should do the trick.'

Figure 4.4 Tacit lesson objectives

Tempting though some aspects of these strategies might be, they do not offer a long-term way forward. Not only is such an outlook ethically indefensible – you shouldn't be teaching history if you don't believe in it – but it is likely that pupils will become aware that you are merely passing (or wasting) time rather than teaching anything of value. As one student teacher noted in her observation of such a lesson, 'A number of pupils expressed frustration at being given yet another drawing and colouring in exercise' (Extract from student teacher assignment, January 1997).

A popular series of history textbooks pre-National Curriculum, the *History Alive* series by Peter Moss, contained many pages of easy to copy cartoon diagrams (Moss, 1970). If used imaginatively, the books could be very useful; if they were used to get pupils to copy the diagrams and cartoons on a regular basis, they would do little to develop children's historical understanding. There may be a justification for using 'low value' activities which entice reluctant scholars into learning, but only if something educationally worthwhile is to follow. Your aim should be to build up an archive of worthwhile activities, information, questions and problems on an increasingly broad range of historical topics. You cannot construct a comprehensive archive in the first few weeks of teaching practice, and may at times have to resort to 'low value' activities as a coping strategy because of classroom management or other concerns, but these should be kept to a minimum, and reduced, as your competence and confidence develops.

Low and high value activities in the history classroom

Heafford's typology of tasks in modern language teaching illustrates the idea that some pupil activities might be of more value than others in planning for learning (Heafford, 1990: 88). Word searches, copying from the board and reading round the class are regarded as low value activities, dialogue in the target language, reading silently and 'doing written work of an error-avoiding nature' are cited as activities of high value.

Task 4.3 *Considering the value of classroom activities*

a)   Reading can be done in different ways in the classroom. If you want your pupils to read something, it can be done by either:
   - Pupils taking it in turn to read aloud.
   - You read the passage or extract to the whole class.
   - You ask the pupils to read the passage in silence.
   - The pupils read the passage to each other in pairs or small groups.

   What might be the advantages and disadvantages of these options, for the teacher, and for the pupils?

b)   Drawing on your experiences and observations in history lessons (both as a pupil and a student teacher), draw up a list of other activities which might occur in a history classroom, and consider what they lend themselves to in terms of usefulness (for the teacher) and value (for the pupils). If possible discuss your views with other student teachers. It might also be helpful to test out your views on the advantages and disadvantages of the various activities in your teaching, to see if 'theory' accords with practice.

Why do teachers not always use high value activities? In some instances, it may be due to limitations in teacher competence – no history teacher has a *comprehensive* archive of high value scripts, questions, problems and tasks for every historical topic, although good history teachers are constantly extending their repertoire of purposeful and valuable activities or explanations. A key point here is that some activities are valuable because they help to develop pupils' knowledge and understanding of the past, and others are useful for other reasons; for settling a boisterous class down, for instance, or devising an 'enabling' task, which introduces a difficult historical concept in an accessible or striking manner. Although it should be central to planning for learning, developing historical understanding is not the only factor which you have to consider when putting together a lesson or series of lessons (see Figure 4.5). It is important to remember that good teachers often use strategies which might be considered 'low value' very adroitly, and in a way that leads on to positive learning outcomes.

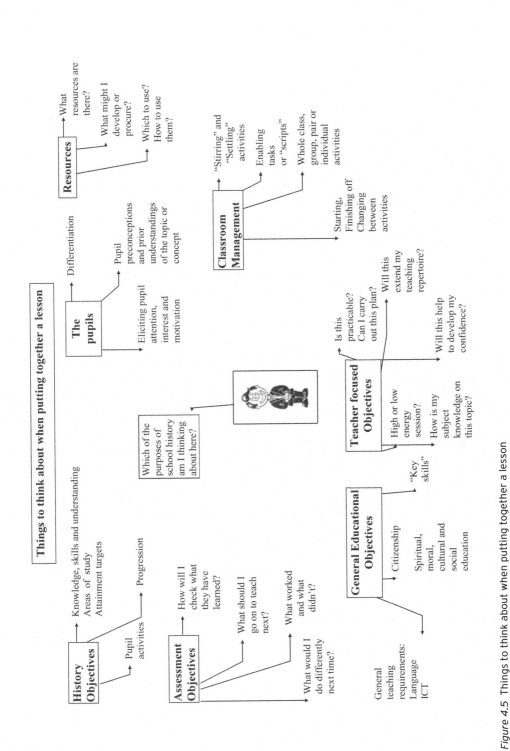

Things to think about when putting together a lesson

History Objectives
→ Knowledge, skills and understanding
Areas of study
Attainment targets
→ Progression
Pupil activities

The pupils
→ Differentiation
→ Pupil preconceptions and prior understandings of the topic or concept
Eliciting pupil attention, interest and motivation

Resources
→ What resources are there?
What might I develop or procure?
Which to use? How to use them?

Which of the purposes of school history am I thinking about here?

Assessment Objectives
→ How will I check what they have learned?
→ What should I go on to teach next?
→ What worked and what didn't?
What would I do differently next time?

General Educational Objectives
→ "Key skills"
→ Citizenship
Spiritual, moral, cultural and social education
→ General teaching requirements: Language ICT

Teacher focused Objectives
Is this practicable? Can I carry out this plan?
→ Will this extend my teaching repertoire?
→ Will this help to develop my confidence?
High or low energy session?
How is my subject knowledge on this topic?

Classroom Management
→ "Stirring" and "Settling" activities
→ Enabling tasks or "scripts"
Whole class, group, pair or individual activities
Starting, Finishing off Changing between activities

Figure 4.5 Things to think about when putting together a lesson

Tensions in planning for learning

In addition to the awareness that there are many factors involved in planning for learning, there is the complication that there is sometimes a tension between them. For instance, your needs as a student teacher attempting to broaden your teaching repertoire by experimenting with new teaching methods might conflict with the reality that you are faced with a teaching group over which your control is tenuous – you might need to 'play safe' and consolidate your control and confidence with this group rather than take risks and end up with a lesson which drifts out of control. If your relationship with the group is poor because they are sick to death of work sheets, drawing pictures, and other 'low value' containment activities, trying something different may be the way forward. You need to develop skills of judgement, in order to find the best way through these tensions. Hopefully, your 'percentages', and sureness of touch will improve with experience and reflection. There are many such continuums in planning for learning, and you need to deploy perceptiveness, professional integrity and determination to find the right point on them.

Another important tension in planning for learning is reconciling long- and short-term planning. Teachers sometimes think about what would constitute a good next lesson, given the resources available, the teacher's ideas and knowledge for that topic, and the nature of the pupils to be taught. But they also need to think about planning for learning in the longer term: over a topic, a study unit, a whole key stage. What do the pupils need for a comprehensive and coherent education in history? If you were to teach a class right through from the start of year 7 to the end of year 9, what benefits would they have derived from your teaching, in terms of knowledge, understanding, skills and experiences? If teachers do not give some thought to 'curriculum mapping', pupils might receive many high quality individual lessons, but have studied history in a way which has only bestowed a fraction of the potential benefits which might accrue from the study of the past. One of the reasons behind the formulation of the NC was the belief that pupils needed a broad and balanced diet of history teaching, rather than one which was driven by the particular talents, specialisms, idiosyncrasies (and limitations) of individual history teachers. The guidance provided in the NC for KS3 History is designed to help ensure that pupils receive a broad and balanced 'diet' of history (DfE, 2013). You must keep in mind all the 'components' of the NC for history in your medium and long term planning.

Your school department is responsible for constructing a programme to teach the NC for history in an effective way. Long-term departmental planning encompasses issues such as progression, differentiation, coherence, continuity, assessment, and the provision of a wide range of learning experiences. Short-term planning, including the planning of individual lessons, is still generally in the hands of individual class teachers, who decide on resources and teaching methods within the framework of school policies and the department's scheme of work. You have to work within these parameters and guidelines, whilst developing the range of your teaching approaches.

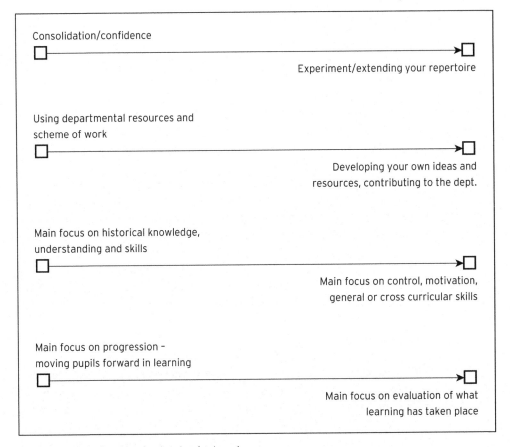

Figure 4.6 Some tensions in planning for learning

The list above is not a comprehensive one, but gives an indication of some of the processes involved in planning for learning.

As well as trying to ensure that you have a good 'starter' for the lesson, it is helpful if you can 'pull together' and reinforce the learning which you are hoping to achieve at some points in the lesson (plenaries do not necessarily come at the end of a lesson, and you may well have more than one plenary in a lesson).

Jamie Byrom provides some helpful guidance on starters and plenaries on the SHP website: www.schoolshistoryproject.org.uk/blog/author/jamie-byrom.

Figure 4.7 Starters and plenaries

Starting points for planning for learning

There is often a difference in the degree of latitude accorded to student teachers in terms of what and how they teach - some departments give you a fairly free hand in terms of *how* you deliver the topics you have been assigned - in others, you have to teach closely to the schemes of work which have been devised by the department.

Given that you are not a free agent in the classroom, and must adhere to school and departmental policies, and be guided by the framework of the NC for History, there are some factors which might be helpful to consider in putting together history lessons.

1 **Some aspects of the past might lend themselves to particular approaches.** When you first consider the historical topic, event or question you have been asked to teach, think about which purpose of school history it lends itself to. To many experienced teachers, issues such as the Norman Conquest, the Glorious Revolution, Hargreaves' Spinning Jenny and the Holocaust immediately suggest ways into the topic in terms of what questions to ask, and what teaching approaches might be most appropriate. All of these topics pose very important questions, but very different ones. This is not to say that there is one definitive, best way of translating the topic into classroom experience, but that the topic might lend itself to, or easily relate to, a particular second order concept or teaching approach. A history topic might even be considered as a piece of raw meat - you have to think what you are going to do with it to make best use of it.

2 **It is important to think about what questions or problems are posed by the topic.** What important and/or interesting questions does the topic pose? How can you 'problematise' the topic in a way which makes pupils think? When we present pupils with information about the past, the purpose is to get them to think about what questions one might usefully ask of that information, in a way which develops their historical understanding. It is not until questions are asked that the information can be thought of as 'evidence'. A helpful way forward for lesson planning can be to think what questions you pose for the pupils to work on and attempt to resolve, and for you to present and discuss some of the answers which have been suggested. In the long term, we want the pupils to be able to work out for themselves what are the intelligent and important questions to ask of the past. (See 'asking and answering historical questions', later in this chapter for further development of this issue.)

Task 4.4 *What questions are worth asking about these topics?*
Which second order concepts do you think might relate to
these topics?

The Norman Conquest	The 1832, 1867 and 1884 Reform Acts
Women in medieval society	The French Revolution
The Munich Crisis of 1938	The Gunpowder Plot
The Factory Reform Acts of the 1840s	The Glorious Revolution of 1688

3   **You should keep in mind and sometimes draw on, the pupils' ideas about why and how things have happened in the past.** It is important to take account of the understanding and ideas that pupils bring with them to the lesson. They may not know a great deal about the topic itself, but they will have their own ideas about how and why things happen, and if you are to help them to progress to more powerful and effective ideas about why and how things have come to be are as they are, you need to be sure that you are talking to pupils in a way that engages with their ideas rather than passes over their heads.

4   **A useful starting point from which to approach the topic can be the present rather than the past.** One of the commonly cited purposes of school history is 'to understand the present in the light of the past'. There are few topics in the NC which do not have in some way a relation to questions and problems which pertain to the present. Making links between the present and the past can be an effective tool for persuading pupils of the importance and relevance of history.

Making comparisons with the present also helps to clarify concepts and ideas about the past. Husbands makes the point that:

> learning about the concept of kingship frequently involves two sets of simultaneous learning: learning about power and its distribution in past societies, and learning about power and its distribution in modern society. The former cannot be given any real meaning until pupils have some more contemporary knowledge against which to calibrate their historical understandings. (Husbands, 1996: 34)

In some cases, this means trying to explain how the present is explained by the past – how the Bill of Rights was an important step towards our present mode of government, why there is conflict in some areas between Catholics and Protestants. In other cases, it may be a question of pointing out that many of the major problems and questions of human existence remain the same, but ways of resolving them are affected by changes which have taken place. How do rulers control their citizens, and how do dissidents oppose them? 'Work' is still an important part of the way societies are organised, but the way in which people work, how work is distributed and problems relating to work have changed over time. The place where we draw the line between what is the state's concern and what is private has changed over time; why and to what effect? In essence, a doctor does the same job now as 2,000 years ago, but the problems which confront doctors have changed. It can be helpful to 'work from the known to the unknown'; to start from the present, and work back to the past. Robbins (2004) provides some useful suggestions and strategies for linking the past to the present.

5   **Sometimes it can be helpful to approach the topic in an oblique or eclectic manner in order to draw pupils into learning**. You do not have to confine yourself to the historical narrative, and the 'straight' history which is in text and topic books. Sometimes points can be made very powerfully and effectively by the use of analogy, anecdote, cartoon, newspaper article or video extract, before concentrating on the more formal historical record. These are sometimes referred to as enabling or engaging strategies. Their purpose is to secure the interest and commitment to learning of the pupils, or to

put over an important idea or concept in an arresting or striking manner. The concept of appeasement might be understood more readily by pupils if it was explained that teachers and parents often use it as a strategy, instead of explaining its use in the Belgian Crisis of 1831–32 or at Munich in 1938. A common strategy for introducing ideas and language about causal reasoning is Arthur Chapman's article about Alphonse the camel (www.youtube.com/watch?v=zZwVM6NWCDM). Having used the story of Alphonse the camel, the teacher might then try to get pupils to go through the same processes of reasoning, and use of language, in relation to events leading to World War I, the Franco-Prussian War, or other crises which lend themselves to this form of analysis or comparison.

Lawlor (1989) has pointed out that teachers might go too far towards turning learning into low-challenge 'fun and games', which remove intellectual rigour from learning, and avoid the reality that sometimes worthwhile learning can require patience and determination. School history has at times been brought into disrepute by the use of drawing and copying work, wordsearches and low value 'pass the time' type activities. However, you face the reality that not all your pupils are driven by a burning desire to do well in history, and that one of the first steps in putting together a history lesson is to try to engage the attention and commitment of the pupils to the learning activities which are planned, and to ensure that they *understand* what you are talking about. If they are not listening, or if they do not understand, no learning can take place. Initiative, imagination and an awareness of your pupils' abilities and prior understandings are as important as your subject knowledge in planning for effective learning. All history teachers find that some topics offer more obvious opportunities for learning activities than others; many would feel that World War II is perhaps a more 'user friendly' topic than 'Roads in the 17th Century' or 'The wool trade in the 14th century', but by adopting an imaginative and eclectic approach to seemingly intractable topics, and thinking carefully about what questions to ask, experienced teachers can often render them just as intriguing and valuable to pupils. Some topics need to be 'opened out', and interpreted in a broader context. 'Roads in the 17th century' could be taught in a way which concentrates on transmitting to pupils knowledge of the improvements wrought by Telford and Macadam, or it could examine the question of transport in a broader sense, by considering in what ways transport problems have changed over time. 'Historical perspectives' can help to shed some light on transport problems today – same issue, different problems – why, and what are the implications of these differences for the future?

6   **Sometimes, the starting point for putting together a history lesson can be a resource rather than a lesson plan.** Although the traditional 'theory' of lesson construction tends to place the resources to be used after the 'ideas' which are to be addressed in the lesson, there are times when history teachers read a newspaper article, see a cartoon, watch something on the news, or a history programme on TV, or visit a museum, which gives them an idea for a successful lesson, or a component of one. They then have to think carefully about how to make best use of the resource, and how to incorporate it into their teaching. Part of planning for learning is being alert to possibilities, scavenging for good resources, and displaying initiative in building up an archive of materials and ideas which can be used to augment the department's reserves.

Task 4.5 *Initiative with resources*

Sometimes lessons can be to at least some extent, 'resources led', rather than 'ideas led'. Good teachers are continually on the look out for resources which might help to teach something more effectively.

For a period of about a week, make a conscious effort to scan newspapers, magazines, television schedules, and spend some time browsing the internet, to look for resources on topics you may encounter in your teaching. Cut out, bookmark, or record them. At the end of the week, compare your collection with fellow history student teachers. Hopefully, this will lead to the realisation of how many 'gems' there are which can help you in your planning if you keep your eyes open for things.

The following is an example of how the topic of the Industrial Revolution might be approached in terms of 'first thoughts' in planning for learning.

At the end of this topic, I would hope that the pupils would have a better understanding of questions such as:

- What do we mean by 'industrial revolution'?
- Why was Britain the first country to have one?
- In what ways did the Industrial Revolution change what Britain was like? (The difference between feudal/agrarian societies and industrial ones, how and where people lived and worked, changing role of land and commerce and industry on wealth and power in Britain.)
- What effect did the Industrial Revolution have on Britain's position in the world in relation to other countries? (What part did the Industrial Revolution play in making Britain a great power, what factors make countries 'great' and do those factors change over time?)
- What happened when other countries had industrial revolutions?
- How does all this affect us in Britain today?
- What are the connections between industrialisation and the environment and how have they changed over time?
- What are the important questions to ask about industrialisation today?
- When did the Industrial Revolution end? Did it end?

At the end of this topic, I hope pupils will have a better understanding of the following concepts and vocabulary:

resources	Colony	capital
feudal system	domestic industry	factory system
technology	Privatisation	manufactured goods
'the class system'	division of labour	alienation
supply and demand	Monopoly	profit
luddism	laisser-faire	protection
free market	'mixed economy'	nationalisation
regulation	Deregulation	balance of payments
labour	trade unionism	trade

While addressing these questions and ideas, in addition to developing the range and depth of the pupils' historical knowledge and understanding, I hope that pupils develop their understanding of the nature of history as a discipline (in particular that there are differing interpretations of these events), their ability to structure their enquiries into the past and work things out for themselves, and their ability to organise and communicate the results of their enquiries, both orally and in writing.

In order to derive these benefits from the study of the Industrial Revolution, pupils will engage in a variety of activities which will develop their historical knowledge and understanding, and also some more general educational skills (such as oracy, proficiency in information technology and writing skills). In the course of the unit they might work with artefacts, visit a site, do a group presentation to the class on an aspect of the industrial revolution, do an extended piece of writing, study written sources, read, listen to teacher exposition, do a data handling exercise and in groups, produce a newspaper front page on an aspect of the industrial revolution in order to demonstrate their understanding of some of the concepts or questions above.

Figure 4.8 Thinking about how to approach the treatment of the Industrial Revolution

Task 4.6 *Thinking how to make your teaching of a topic coherent and worthwhile*

Read Byrom and Riley's article about planning to teach the British Empire at Key Stage 3 (*Teaching History*, No. 112: 6-14). The article shows very powerfully what difficult choices history teachers have to make when planning for learning in particular topics. Think of another fairly substantial topic (World War One, The English Civil War, The Norman Conquest of Britain, The French Revolution...) and draw up an outline plan of how you would teach six to eight lessons on the topic. How would you divide it up, what would be the main focus within the topic, what would be the main learning outcomes you would hope for, how would you build in plans to assess the extent to which the learning outcomes will be achieved? You may find it helpful to consider the information in Figure 4.6.

Task 4.7 *'Opening topics up': approaching challenging aspects of the history curriculum*

Although in theory, outstanding history teachers should be able to render all aspects of the past intriguing and accessible to pupils, the reality is that some topics might offer more obvious opportunities, ideas and resources than others. As Byrom and Riley point out, some topics are 'important but boring' (Byrom and Riley, 2008: 6). The following suggestions may be your favourite bits of history, but some student teachers have mentioned them as topics that they feel they are comparatively intractable in terms of being able to transform them into interesting and enjoyable experiences for their pupils:

- Life in a medieval village.
- The Agrarian Revolution.
- The Chartists.
- The League of Nations
- The coming of the factories.

How might you 'open up' these topics so that the pupils might find the topics powerful, interesting and relevant?

Ask the history teachers you work with, and fellow student teachers, how they approach less propitious topics, and what engaging and enabling strategies and tasks they use to try and draw pupils into learning.

 Some suggestions on 'opening up' topics can be found in the web section on planning: http://terryhaydn.wordpress.com/pgce-history-at-uea/pgce-student-teacher/planning.

Task 4.8 *Working out what key enquiry questions might be used to explore particular historical topics*

One of the major changes on planning for learning in history over the past decade has been a tendency to move away from planning 'grids' and towards the use of 'enquiry questions' (see, for example, Riley, 1996). Care in getting your enquiry questions right in the first instance can make the detail of subsequent planning much easier. Remember that often you will have an overarching enquiry question, and some 'sub-questions' arising from the main enquiry question.

The questions posed by study of the Industrial Revolution, (and the concepts involved), might be very different from those which arise from a consideration of other historical events. In the form of a spider diagram, draw up a list of possible 'key questions' and concepts which might provide a basis for teaching a series of lessons on a) The Crusades; b) The Renaissance; c) The Reformation; d) The Enlightenment. These terms are sometimes known as 'colligations', where we 'bundle together' a number of events and changes and give them a particular name. It is worth thinking about what percentage of pupils leave school with a sound grasp of what these terms mean.

Examine some fairly recent history textbooks and explore how they often use enquiry questions to structure learning around particular topics and 'colligations'.

There are some things that all these topics have in common; in teaching all of them we are considering information about what happened in the past, we are developing children's knowledge and understanding of the past, and there are some recurrent themes or questions which pertain to the study of many historical topics, such as 'Why did this happen?', 'What effect did this have?', 'How do we know about this?', and 'How reliable is this information?'

However, different topics offer different *opportunities* to the history teacher, can suggest different 'key questions', and offer insights into very differing sorts of ideas and concepts. Study of the Industrial Revolution generally enriches the pupils' grasp of economic concepts and the cross-curricular theme of economic and industrial awareness. Study of the events of 1688 might prove an excellent opportunity to develop *political* concepts, and be the point at which to give an *overview* of how government has developed in this country, from 1066 to the present day, culminating in an examination of pupils' understanding of the present system of government, and the way in which the events of 1688 relate to this. The events of 1066 might not throw as much light as 1688, or 1867, on how Britain is governed today, and so instead of focusing on the purpose of 'explaining the present in the light of the past', the main focus might be developing pupils' understanding of evidence, the nature of history, how we know about the events of 1066, and what criteria we use to assign significance to events. Although there are several approaches to the Holocaust, (including evidence and the Holocaust) many history teachers use the topic to focus on moral and ethical questions.

Guidance on teaching sensitive and controversial issues in history can be found from the following sources:

Arthur J., Davies, I., Wrenn, A., Haydn, T. and Kerr, D. (2001) History, citizenship and diversity, in *Citizenship through secondary history*, London, RoutledgeFalmer: 101-113.
Harris, R., Burn, K. and Woolley, M. (2014) *The guided reader to teaching and learning history*, London, David Fulton, Chapter 6: 65-76.
Historical Association (2007) Teaching emotive and controversial history 3-19, London, H/A: online at: www.dfes.gov.uk/research/data/uploadfiles/RW100.pdf.

Figure 4.9 Teaching controversial issues in history

The importance of concepts in school history

Historical knowledge includes an understanding of certain ideas and concepts. These are more than glossaries of historical terms; they are aids to categorising, organising, analysing and applying historical information. They can only be understood when they are used in illustrating a variety of different historical circumstances. 'Revolution', for example, is a historical idea. But a simple definition does not help pupils to understand why the word is applied equally to events in France after 1789, in Russia in 1917, or to the history of industry in later eighteenth-century England, or whether it can equally usefully describe events in seventeenth-century England. Ideas such as 'left wing' or 'right wing' have their value, but only if pupils begin to appreciate their limitations and the oversimplifications they sometimes suggest. (HMI, 1985: 14)

Understanding concepts helps pupils make sense of the world they are living in, and in order to make sense of the past, pupils need to understand the ideas and concepts which emanate from the study of a historical topic as well as the factual details they are presented with, if they are to transform the learning experience into knowledge and understanding.

Part of a study of the Russian Revolution of 1905 is an understanding of the groups opposing the Czar. The aim of the exercise is to extend the pupils' understanding of the different ways in which the state can be opposed, as well as their grasp of the continuum between terrorism and peaceful protest which can be adopted by opposition groups, both in Russia in 1905, and at other points in history, including the present day. This could lead on to a consideration of which methods of opposition are 'justifiable', which methods were available to the protesters of 1905, whether what is justifiable varies according to the way in which the state exercises its power and control, and what are the advantages and disadvantages of the various forms of opposition.

1   Pupils are given an explanation of the events leading up to the 1905 revolution, including the actions and motives of factions opposing or criticising the Czar's regime.

2   Pupils are asked to brainstorm a list of ways in which citizens oppose governments today in different parts of the world, including Britain.

3   Pupils are given two quotes about opposition which are written on the board at either end, with a line drawn across the width of the board to represent a continuum between the two statements.

        Quote A: 'Nothing is ever done in this world until men are prepared to kill one another if it is not done.' (George Bernard Shaw)

        Quote B: 'No revolution is worth the effusion of a single drop of human blood.' (Daniel O'Connell)

3   Pupils are asked to place the methods of opposition which they have thought of in order, from those which accord with Shaw's view, to those which accord with O'Connell's, or given cards which outline methods of opposition and asked to place them in a continuum between the two positions.

Voting against govmt. in elections	Threats of poisoning of water/food supplies	Hunger strikes	Bomb/sniper attacks on govmt. security forces
Placing anti-govmt. advertisements in newspapers	Damage to public/ govmt property (slashing paintings, setting fire to post boxes)	Drawing up petitions and presenting them	Sit-down protests/ blocking public highways to govmt.
Peaceful protest marches	Hijacking of airplanes	Kidnapping and ransom threats	Assassination of govmt. agents
Random bomb attacks in cities	Graffiti/poster campaigns against govmt	Non-payment of taxes	Public suicides

4   Pupils are asked to categorise types of opposition (some classes or pupils within classes could be given categories, i.e. peaceful/nuisance/violence against self/damage-violence to property/violence against government agents/random violence.

5   Pupils are asked to position the groups opposing the Czar along the continuum between Shaw's position and O' Connell's, to state which methods of opposition were available to them in Czarist Russia in 1905, and why different opposition groups used different methods of opposition.

The idea of continuums of opposition can obviously be applied in other historical contexts, (for example, discontent in Britain after the Napoleonic Wars), and can encompass understanding of the concept of radicalism – including the fact that there can be conservative as well as progressive radicalism.

Figure 4.10 An example of the integration of concepts into learning about the past

---

Task 4.9 *Linking content to concepts*

Think of a topic which you expect to teach to a class, and a concept which might arise in the course of covering that topic. How can you structure the work in a way which develops pupils' understanding of the concept, as well as developing their knowledge of the historical content involved. (The concept might, for example, be appeasement, in the course of covering Hitler's foreign policy; imperialism, in the course of covering Britain in the nineteenth century; trade, in covering the Roman Empire, or propaganda, in covering Nazi Germany).

For further discussion of the use of concepts in history teaching, see Haenan and Schrijnemakers, 2000, 2003; Chapman, 2003; Howells 2002 and van Drie and Boxtel, 2003.

Planning to develop useful frameworks of the past for pupils

Not all commentators on school history are convinced of the utility and importance of concepts in the study of history. Several pamphlets from the Centre for Policy Studies argued that the centrality of a coherent historical narrative and sound grasp of the record of the past had been undervalued at the expense of themes, concepts and skills (see, for example, Deuchar, 1992; McGovern, 1994). More recently Ofsted (2011) and Abulafia *et al.* (2012) suggested that many pupils lack a general overview or 'mental map' of the past. As the pupil testimony at the start of the chapter suggested, one of the problems which many pupils have is how the different bits that they do in lessons fit together. For many pupils, history is just 'one damn thing after another'. This is why you should give some thought to long-term planning in history. What will pupils end up with at 14 or 16 in terms of a general understanding of the past?

Harris, R., Burn, K. and Woolley, M. (eds) (2013) *The guided reader to teaching and learning history*, London, David Fulton, Chapter 11: 128–41.

Howson, J. and Shemilt, D. (2011) Frameworks of knowledge: dilemmas and debates, in I. Davies (ed.) *Debates in history teaching*, London Routledge: 73–83.

Wineburg, S. (2001) 'Making historical sense in the new millennium', in *Historical thinking and other unnatural acts*, Philadelphia, Temple University Press: 232–55.

Figure 4.11 Further reading on frameworks of the past

The interplay of overview and depth studies

There is a tension between simply thinking about what would make a good lesson, and planning for a 'balanced diet' of school history which incorporates a broad range of learning objectives, and which links together to provide a coherent understanding of the broad sweep of the past. There is also the question of the time allocation for covering a study unit. You have to think about how a broad and balanced programme of learning in history can be delivered in the teaching time available (the exact amount of which will vary from school to school).

At times you are linking together work which has been done over the course of the year or key stage, in order to help pupils to see 'the long arc' of history, and aid progression in key areas of the subject, while at other times, you will be studying a particular event in considerable detail. Riley suggests that it is the skilful interplay between depth and overview that enables teachers to entice pupils into learning with details of the stories of real individuals and human-scale stories, and yet enables them to get a meaningful grasp of the 'bigger picture' of the past, arguing that 'pupils will only make sense of the past if we let them step back and take a panoramic view' (Riley, 1996). The new NC for history states explicitly that teachers should 'combine overview and depth studies to help pupils understand both the long arc of development and the complexity of specific aspects of the content', and that pupils should:

> gain historical perspective by placing their growing knowledge into different contexts, understanding the connections between local, regional, national and international history; between cultural, economic, military, political, religious and social history; and between short- and long-term timescales. (DfE, 2013: 2)

There is thus a much greater emphasis on coherence, and on providing pupils with 'a big picture' of the past in the most recent version of the NC for history.

In order to guard against the risk of thinking too much about 'What would make a good lesson?', at the expense of 'How can I ensure that pupils receive a broad and balanced diet of school history?', many departments use planning grids, so that it is easy to check whether and where breadth and balance is achieved. Figure 3.10 shows an example of a planning grid for a scheme of work for a series of several lessons on the Norman Conquest.

Although planning grids can be helpful in checking breadth of coverage, variety of focus, and range of teaching methods, Tim Lomas makes the point that 'the matrix approach can obscure much that is significant and critical in pupils' learning – the links, echoes and threads and 'the spontaneous responses of pupils' (Lomas, 2000: 3). Make sure that your lesson plans, evaluations and schemes of work do not become mechanistic, cosmetic and divorced from the reality of your pupils' experiences. HMI observe that although nearly all student teachers keep records to meet their professional obligations, some of them 'failed to reflect on why they kept the records, or whether keeping them in this or that particular form was either the most efficient means or helped them and their pupils achieve their ultimate teaching and learning objectives respectively' (Baker *et al.*, 2000: 200). In the words of Counsell, are you converting the curriculum 'into something that *means something* to the students'? (Counsell, 2000b: 2).

Key Questions	Concepts, vocabulary	Historical content	Resources	Pupil activities	Teaching objectives	Assessment opportunities
Why did the Normans invade England?	invasion, heredity, power, resources	The quarrel for the throne, England before the invasion	Briefing sheet on claims, Medieval Realms, pp. 15-19	Listen to story, groupwork preparing claims for court, presentations	Understanding of motives for invasion and nature of govmt pre-invasion	Oral presentations on claims to throne
What happened at the Battle of Hastings, how do we know, why did William win?	evidence, accounts and chronicles	The military campaigns of 1066	Video extract of battle, worksheet on death of Harold miniature of Bayeux Tapestery	Sequencing exercise, extended writing, "How and why Harold lost"	Understanding nature of hist. record-interpretations	Extended writing exercise on 1066 campaigns
How did William gain control of England with only a few thousand men?	power, authority, administration, deterrence	From Hastings to 1086; castles, The Domesday Book	Maps from Medieval Realms, pp. 21-2. "The Normans" software	Mapwork, sourcework exercise from Medieval Realms, p. 22, IT suite	Accounts and explanations, taxation, role of individual in history	Sourcework exercise on interpretations
Why were these events important, what difference did it make to life in England?	kingdom, feudal system, heirarchy	The changed social and political order	Visit to museum, Normans YouTube clip, Medieval Realms, pp. 24-6	Construct timeline, newspaper front pages and obituary for class display	Significance, notion of "turning points", factual grasp of main events and changes	Recap test on main events and key vocabulary

Figure 4.12 An example of a planning grid for a series of lessons on the Norman Conquest

Look at the specimen schemes of work which were commissioned by QCA and the DfEE for an earlier version of the NC for history at: http://webarchive. nationalarchives.gov.uk/20090608182316/http://standards.dfes.gov.uk/ schemes2/secondary_history/?view=get.

Although the schemes were formulated for an earlier version of the NC for history, they were drawn up by a number of experienced and accomplished history teachers and teacher educators, and should give you some ideas about how to put together a series of lessons on particular topics.

Figure 4.13 Developing your ideas about medium term planning

Asking and answering historical questions

One of the things which student teachers of history sometimes find difficult is how to ask questions of the past which go beyond recall and comprehension, and which develop pupils' understanding of history as a body of knowledge, and as a form of knowledge. If we are to develop the skills and understandings referred to in Chapters 1 and 2, we must attempt to get beyond questions which simply ask pupils to locate information and write it down, or reiterate what we have just told them.

One way of doing this is to think of the processes and areas for progression outlined in the NC for History at KS3 when constructing lessons. Second order concepts such as chronology, time, change cause, evidence, interpretation and motive can often be a way of leading pupils into the problems and difficulties which historians face, and which require discussion, debate and thought, rather than pupils consistently being asked to do no more than write down or repeat what they are told.

What are historians trying to do when they investigate the past? Why do they bother?

What happened? Events, time periods, time lines, story lines, chronology, accounts, sequencing.

Why did it happen? Explaining things, actions, events, developments, cause, motive, ideas, beliefs.

What changed? What stayed the same? Patterns in/of the past, looking for similarities and differences, charting change.

How did what happened and what changed affect things? Consequences and significance for people at the time, for us now.

How do we find out what we want to know? What problems are there in finding out and being sure? What claims can we make? Looking at sources, asking them questions, deciding whether they can be used as evidence for a particular question or what they can be used as evidence for.

Why might we get different answers to our questions? Purposes, interests, concerns for reconstructing the past, *why* was this produced? Problems of available evidence, issues of interpretation.

(Ros Ashby, An introduction to school history, Workshop, Institute of Education, University of London 11 February 1995)

Figure 4.14 Things we want to know about the past

Sources are not evidence until we start to ask questions of them. It is the asking of questions which renders the study of the past meaningful, and which can help to explain to pupils why historians bother to do what they do, and why it might be helpful to understand these processes. So having thought of the questions we wish to pose of the historical content we are teaching, the next stage is to look for sources, stories or ideas which problematise those questions, in a form which your pupils can engage with. Although the questions relating to second order concepts permeate the history curriculum, there are times when you are also addressing substantive concepts, and trying to develop pupils' understanding of ideas such as *government, democracy, collectivism, oligarchy* etc. Keeping in mind substantive and second order concepts can be a way of ensuring that you are asking historical questions, rather than comprehension ones. The following is a small selection of the type of historical questions you may find helpful suggested by Tim Lomas, in his Historical Association pamphlet, *Teaching and Assessing Historical Understanding* (Lomas, 1989).

Cause and consequence
- What was the importance of economic factors in causing the Russian civil war?
- What influence did Robespierre have on the outcome of the French Revolution?
- Why were the children evacuated from this town but not that town?
- Who would be most upset/pleased when the law said that children could not work in the mine anymore?
- What long-term factors may have led to the decision to send the Spanish Armada?

Time/Change
- What might a cotton worker have noticed different about conditions at work between 1750 and 1850?
- Look at the picture of the Victorian school. What has changed in most schools, since the time of that picture?
- Why did the renaissance happen at the time that it did?
- The events in this story about the murder of Thomas Beckett are jumbled up. Put them in the order which you think makes the most sense.
- Why did it take 20 years before Germany took revenge for the Treaty of Versailles?

Evidence

- What do you think this artefact would be used for?
- Look at the two sources about World War 2. Where do they not agree with each other?
- Which parts of this newspaper account are just the opinions of the person who wrote it?
- How reliable do you think the author is even though she was an eye witness?
- Why might the Bayeux Tapestery have been compiled?

Significance

- Why can 1485 be described as a 'turning point'?
- Did the legislation of 1918 solve all the problems of inequality which British women faced?
- Which of these do you think an ordinary villager in the Middle Ages would have felt was more important in her life?
- What might have happened if the Jacobites had not been defeated at Culloden?
- Put the following sixteenth-century events in what you consider as their order of importance giving reasons for your choice.

Similarity and Difference

- Compare the peace treaties after World War 1 and World War 2
- Why might France have felt differently about Germany in 1918, 1940 and 1980?
- Could the events which caused the French Revolution have produced a similar effect in Britain?
- What differences can you find in the way these two battles were fought?
- How typical was this of Richard the Lionheart's policies?

Figure 4.15 Examples of questions relating to second order concepts

The link between planning and evaluation of pupil learning

Another important aspect of planning for learning is to consider how you assess what pupils have learned, in order to think of what elements need to be gone over again or reinforced, what pupils might go on to learn next, and what might be done differently, the next time you teach the lesson. There should be a 'planning loop' of planning-teaching-assessing-evaluating-revised planning and teaching. It is important to keep in mind that effective learning requires you to think carefully about two questions. How much that you have taught has been learned? Once the pupils have learned something, what should you teach next? Holt makes the point that these two questions are not always asked:

> I assumed for a long time that my students knew when they did, or did not understand something. I was always urging them to tell me when they did, or did not, understand, so that with one of my 'clever explanations', I could clear up everything. But they would never tell me. I came to know by painful experience that not a child in a hundred knows whether or not he understands something, much less, if he does not, why not. The child who knows, we don't have to worry about, he will be an 'A' student. How do we find out when, and what, the others don't understand? (Holt, 1982: 276)

Holt goes on to attempt to provide possible ways of exploring the problem of understanding. A key element is that pupils are not simply regurgitating information in exactly the same form as it was given, but are asked to manipulate or analyse the information in some way to demonstrate that they have assimilated it into other, contingent areas of knowledge and understanding. In Counsell's phrase, they need to move from being 'knowledge tellers' to knowledge transformers' (Counsell, 1996).

Holt gives the following descriptors of situations where understanding has taken place:

It may help to have in our minds a picture of what we mean by understanding. I feel I understand things if I can do some, at least, of the following:

1   state it in my own words;
2   give examples of it;
3   recognise it in various guises and circumstances;
4   see connections between it and other facts or ideas;
5   make use of it in various ways;
6   foresee some of its consequences;
7   state its opposite or converse.

This list is only a beginning; but it may help us in the future to find out what our students really know as opposed to what they can give the appearance of knowing, their real learning as opposed to their apparent learning. (Holt, 1982: 177)

Figure 4.16 Assessing for understanding

The following table is an attempt to assess how well pupils have grasped the relations between the major powers of Europe in 1914. They are asked to give a mark out of 10 to each relationship, with 10 out of 10 representing the most solid and committed of alliances, and 0 out of 10 representing countries which were intensely hostile to each other. In addition to shedding light on their understanding of the two main camps (the Triple Alliance and the Triple Entente), it tests their understanding of the comparative strength of the different alliances and relationships.

Relations between the Great powers of Europe, June 1914

	Great Britain	France	Germany	Italy	Russia	Austria-Hungary
Great Britain						
France						
Germany						
Italy						
Russia						
Austria-Hungary						

Figure 4.17 Assessing for understanding; an example

Another example of a format for assessing whether pupils have understood relationships is provided in the National Curriculum Council's booklet, *Teaching History at Key Stage 3* (NCC, 1993).

The following 0 - 5 scale is about how much power different groups or people had in the country at a particular time.

0   -   1   -   2   -   3   -   4   -   5

No power   Some power   All power

Fill in this table and then stick it in your book.

In a group, put the number from the scale which you think applies to that person or group of people in that particular year on the table, e.g., if you think the King had all the power in 1649 put 5 under 1649 in the first line across. Discuss your group's findings with another group.

	1640	1649	1701
The King			
The House of Lords			
The House of Commons			
The Church of England			
The Army			
The Common People			

Figure 4.18 Worksheet designed to help pupils understand changes in the distribution of power, 1640–1701 (from NCC, 1993)

A further example of assessment for understanding can be found on the School History website, see the 'What did Hitler believe in?' homework exercise at: www.schoolhistory. co.uk/gcselinks/sourcework/masterrace.pdf.

In many lessons, you will have what Battersby calls a 'golden nugget', a key idea or fact that you hope all pupils have grasped, to take away from the lesson with them (Battersby, 1996). In a lesson on propaganda in Nazi Germany, an example of this might be that all pupils understand that propaganda is not something that only happened in Nazi Germany; its use is widespread and it still exists today, particularly in time of war. In addition to 'the golden nugget', it is also helpful to try to have at least one resource or component of each lesson which (hopefully) elicits the interest or engagement of the pupils.

As your assurance and competence develops, your lesson evaluations should increasingly focus on the central issue of pupil learning, rather than simply evaluating your own teaching performance. They should move from 'Was I OK?', to 'How was it for them?', by considering questions such as:

- How many of the pupils grasped the main points I was trying to make?
- Which aspects did they understand and which aspects do I need to return to?

- How can I try and put this across in another way for those who did not grasp the key points of the lesson?
- How can I reinforce and consolidate what they have learned?
- What points should I move on to for those pupils who have grasped the 'golden nugget' which was the key point of the lesson?
- In what ways might I teach this more effectively next time – what would I change, what would I retain?
- Were they listening to what I was saying or looking out of the window, bored stiff and inattentive?

Teaching is a creative activity. Don't be surprised if you find planning difficult and time consuming at first. As a teacher, you have to in effect 'put on' 15 to 20 'shows' a week. You are the director, the producer, the props manager, the casting manager. But you are not the star. At the centre of your planning is concern for the quality of pupils' learning, progress and performance. Most teachers get better at the 'technical' aspects of teaching. As intelligent graduates, it would be surprising if they did not improve with practice. But what marks out the teachers who go on to be inspirational and exceptional is the quality of thinking and preparation that goes into their lessons.

Summary and key points

- Planning goes on after the lesson has finished: reflect on how you might teach the lesson more effectively next time.
- Don't forget to make connections to pupils' prior learning, so that they develop a coherent overview of the past.
- Try to formulate precise and appropriate learning objectives for history in your lessons, and 'track them through' in the lesson activities and your evaluation of the lesson. This can make the written aspect of lesson planning seem purposeful and worthwhile, instead of seeming like pointless paperwork.
- Keep in mind the full breadth of the NC for History; it's not just about covering subject content.
- As well as moving pupils forward in history, you are also responsible for the development of their general educational skills, whether in terms of language, ICT capability or other 'key skills'. Make sure that your lesson planning incorporates these factors.
- You also need to consider your own learning needs, departmental policies and classroom management concerns. You have to balance these as adroitly as possible – this requires skills and qualities of tact, perseverance, insight and determination.
- Initiative and imagination are also important attributes in planning; sometimes it may be necessary to adopt an eclectic 'way in' to the topic.
- Give some thought to the interplay of high and low value activities to maximise pupil engagement and learning.

More information on planning, lesson objectives and evaluations and suggestions for further reading can be found at www.uea.ac.uk/~m242/historypgce/planning or at http://terryhaydn.wordpress.com/pgce-history-at-uea/pgce-student-teacher/planning/.

Suggestions for further reading

Byrom, J. and Riley, M. (2003) Professional wrestling in the history department: a case study in planning the teaching of the British Empire at key stage 3, *Teaching History*, No. 112: 6–14. A helpful insight into the complexities of planning a topic.

Fordham, M. (2012) Out came Caesar and in came the Conqueror, though I'm sure something happened in between: a case study in professional thinking, *Teaching History*, No. 147: 38–46. A helpful insight into how one might approach planning a topic which traces an aspect of history back beyond 1066.

Kitson, A., Husbands, C. and Steward, S. (2011) Teaching and learning history 11–18: understanding the past, Maidenhead: Open University Press. Chapter 9 focuses on long-term planning issues.

McFahn, R. (2013) Curriculum planning section of the History Resource Cupboard website, online at www.historyresourcecupboard.co.uk/content/?page_id=1812, accessed 14 April 2014. Richard McFahn's site has some interesting and useful ideas about medium- and long-term planning.

Ofsted (2013) History, case studies of good practice: Good practice resource – 'Putting the local community at the heart of the Key Stage 3 history curriculum: Copleston High School', online at www.ofsted.gov.uk/resources/good-practice-resource-putting-local-community-heart-of-key-stage-3-history-curriculum-copleston-hig. A good example of how to link local history into a broader scheme of work.

Riley, M. (2000) Into the Key Stage 3 history garden: choosing and planting your enquiry questions, *Teaching History*, No. 99: 8–13. This remains a very useful guide to using an 'enquiry-based' approach to planning.

Shemilt, D. (2009) 'Drinking in ocean and pissing a cupful: how adolescents make sense of history, in L. Symcox and A. Wilschut (eds) *National History Standards: The problem of the canon and the future of teaching history*, Charlotte NC: Information Age Publishing: 141–210. Pages 162–69 provide interesting examples of how one might trace an aspect of human development through from 60,000 B.C. to the present.

More detail on medium and long-term planning can be found on the website.

References

Abulafia, D., Clark, J. and Tombs, R. (2012) History in the new curriculum: 3 proposals, London, Politeia, online at www.politeia.co.uk/sites/default/files/files/Final%20Appendix%20to%20Lessons%20from%20History.pdf, accessed 20 March 2014.

Baker, C., Cohn, T. and McLaughlin, M. (2000) 'Current issues in the training of secondary history teachers: an HMI perspective', in J. Arthur and R. Phillips (eds) *Issues in History Teaching*, London: Routledge: 191–202.

Banham, D. (2014) Workshop for PGCE students, University of East Anglia, 31 January.

Battersby, J. (1996) 'Discipline and Control', Unpublished lecture, University of East Anglia, 4 November.

Byrom, J. and Riley, M. (2008) Professional wrestling in the history department: a case study in planning the teaching of the British Empire at Key Stage 3, *Teaching History*, No. 112: 6–14.

Chapman, A. (2003) Conceptual awareness through categorising: using ICT to get Year 13 reading, *Teaching History*, No. 111: 38-43.

Clarke, S. (2008) *Active learning Through Formative Assessment*, London: Hodder.

Counsell, C. (1996) 'Progression at Key stage 3: What does "getting better at history" mean?', *Address to Historical Association Conference*, York, 14 September.

Counsell, C. (2000a) 'Didn't we do that in year 7?' Planning for progress in evidential understanding, *Teaching History*, No. 99: 36-41.

Counsell, C. (2000b) Editorial *Teaching History*, No. 99, May, 2.

Dearing, R. (1994) *The National Curriculum and its Assessment*, London: SCAA.

DES (1985) *History in the Primary and Secondary Years*, London: Department for Education and Employment/Qualifications and Curriculum Authority.

DfE (2013) *History programmes of study: key stage 3: National Curriculum in England*, London, DfE, online at https://www.gov.uk/government/uploads/system/uploads/attachment_data/file/239075/SECONDARY_national_curriculum_-_History.pdf, accessed 20 July 2014.

DfEE/QCA (1999) *History: The National Curriculum for England*, London: DfEE/QCA.

Deuchar, S. (1992) *History on the Brink*, York: Campaign for Real Education.

DfEE (1998) *Teaching: High Status, High Standards Requirements for Courses of Initial Teacher Training*, London: Department for Education and Employment.

Haenen, J. and Schrijnmakers. H. (2000) Transforming Year 7's understanding of the concept of imperialism: a case study on the Roman Empire, *Teaching History*, No. 98: 22-9.

Haenen, J., Schrijnmakers. H. and Stufkens, J. (2003) Transforming Year 7's understanding of the concept of imperialism: a case study on the Roman Empire, *Teaching History*, No. 112: 28-34.

Hallam, S. (1996) Unpublished lecture on Differentiation, Institute of Education, University of London, January.

Haydn, T. (2012) ICT and citizenship education, in J. Arthur and H. Cremin (eds) *Debates in citizenship education*, London: Routledge: 169-80.

Heafford, D. (1990) 'Teachers teach but do learners learn?', in C. Wringe (ed.) *Language Learning Journal 1*, quoted in N. Pachler and C. Field (1997) *Learning to Teach Modern Foreign Languages in the Secondary School*, London: Routledge.

HMI (1985) *History in the primary and secondary years*, London: HMSO.

Holt, J. (1982) *How Children Fail*, New York: Delacorte/Seymour Lawrence.

Howells, G. (2002) Ranking and classifying: teaching political concepts to post-16 students, *Teaching History*, No. 106: 33-7.

Hunt, M. (1997) *Thinking it through*, Unpublished paper: Manchester Metropolitan University.

Husbands, C. (1996) *What is History Teaching*, Buckingham: Open University Press.

Lawlor, S. (1989) 'Correct core', in B. Moon, P. Murphy and J. Raynor (eds) *Policies for the Curriculum*, Milton Keynes: Open University Press.

Lawton, D. (1985) *Education, Culture and the Curriculum*, London: Hodder and Stoughton.

Lee, P. (1994) 'Historical knowledge and the National Curriculum', in H. Bourdillon (ed.) *Teaching History*, London: Routledge: 41-48.

Lomas, T. (1989) *Teaching and Assessing Historical Understanding*, London, Historical Association.

Lomas, T. (2000) Letters, *Teaching History*, No. 99, May 3.

MacLennan, S. (1987) 'Integrating lesson planning and classroom management', *ELT Journal*, 41 (3), 193-96.

McGovern, C. (1994) *The SCAA Review of National Curriculum History: A Minority Report*, York: Campaign for Real Education.

Moss, P. (1970) *History Alive 55 B.C.-1485*, London: Hart-Davis.

National Curriculum Council (NCC) (1991) *Non-Statutory Guidance for History*, York: NCC.

National Curriculum Council (NCC) (1993) *Teaching History at Key Stage 3*, York: NCC.

Ofsted (2011) *History For All*, London: Ofsted.

Phillips, R. (2001) Making history curious: using initial stimulus material to promote enquiry, thinking and literacy, *Teaching History*, No. 105: 19–25.

QCA (2005) *History 2004-5 Annual report on curriculum and assessment*, London: QCA.

Riley, M. (1996) 'Beyond a superficial scamper', *Times Educational Supplement*, Extra: History, 6 September.

Robbins, D. (2004) Learning about an 800 year old fight can't be all that bad can it? *Teaching History*, No. 117: 44–8.

Van Drie, J. and van Boxtel, C. (2003) Developing conceptual understanding through talk and mapping, *Teaching History*, No. 110: 27–31.

Ward, R. (2007) 'Creating a curriculum that will help all young people in Britain understand the world in which they live', paper presented at the *Why history matters* Conference, Institute of Historical Research, 13 February.

It helps if you can somehow get them interested. In the words of Hallam (1996) 'They must want to learn, if you lose that you lose everything.'

5 Teaching approaches and methods

What can you do in a history lesson?

Highly imaginative, fun activities are not an attempt to bypass the serious work of history, but rather, to provide access to it for those pupils who were previously fobbed off with low level colouring in, missing words exercises and model making. The problem is that some commentators confuse 'accessible' with 'easy'. History teachers only make things 'accessible' in order to help refractory learners into a truly challenging task that they would otherwise shun or fail in. (Counsell, 1999: 20)

Introduction

One of the many skills you need to develop as a history teacher is the ability to select teaching methods which are appropriate for the particular pupils you teach and for the achievement of the learning objectives for the lesson. The choice of method usually resides with the class teacher for, although the NC for History outlines in general terms areas of content which should be taught and the ways in which pupils' historical understanding should be developed over time (DfE, 2013), the methods by which the NC is delivered are left for the teacher to decide.

Most methods have their strengths and their weaknesses. Your skill as a teacher knows which approaches are most likely to maximise the learning achieved by the pupils. Different methods suit different circumstances, so you need to be competent in the use of a range of styles and methods, sometimes within the same lesson. *Over-reliance on one approach limits the learning potential of the pupils.* Ofsted reports have noted a narrow range of teaching styles as a weakness in school history (see, for example, Ofsted, 2005, 2011). Also, most lessons consist of several 'components' or phases, so you will often be using a range of teaching approaches within one lesson. It is unusual for a lesson to consist of just one activity, but this does not mean 'the more components the better', or that there is a standard number of components which should be fitted into the lesson. Although there are departmental handbooks and aging National Strategy materials which talk about 'the three part lesson', 'the four part lesson', or the necessity for all lessons to have a 'starter', 'main bit' and 'plenary', there seems to be a general acceptance amongst the history teaching community (as evidenced in *Teaching History*, and the most influential history websites), that there will be major variations in the number of different components or activities which a history lesson will have, and that is not generally a good idea to have a standard format for your lessons, which means that they unfold in pretty much the same way. You should beware of falling into a cosy 'rut' of falling into a standard pattern of activities for your lessons.

A range of factors may inhibit your choice of method, particularly in the early weeks of your school experience. There may be times when it is unwise to move away too abruptly from the methods the pupils have usually experienced. There may be classes where the choice of methods is influenced by issues of control and discipline, and the extent to which you feel in relaxed and assured control of the group. Above all, remember that there is no hard and fast rule which guarantees success: teaching is a context dependent activity. Sometimes adopting a different approach with reluctant learners is just what is needed – but it won't always work, you need to be pragmatic and adaptable.

Whatever style you choose to employ, how you make use of language is often the key to successful learning. This chapter will also address the ways in which use of language is one of the key issues in effective history teaching.

Objectives

At the end of this chapter you should be able to:

- examine the subject specific nature of some teaching methods and skills;
- discuss the strengths and limitations of various teaching approaches; and
- consider the linguistic demands and the potential difficulties which the learning of history makes on pupils.

Beware of simplistic generalisations about teaching methods

In thinking in terms of 'High' and 'Low' value activities (see Chapter 4) it is important to keep in mind that 'fitness for purpose' is equally important to effective planning and teaching. You must beware of the danger of thinking that 'active' learning (such as roleplay, groupwork, drama) is a priori better than 'chalk and talk'. There are times when talking to pupils to explain aspects of the past to them is the most efficient way of teaching the class. Sometimes student teachers quote the Chinese proverb, 'I am told, and I forget, I am shown, and I remember, I do, and I understand.' Less quoted, but equally valid is Lawton's reminder that it all depends who you are teaching and what you are trying to achieve:

> There are important distinctions to be made between memorisation without understanding, acquiring knowledge by traditional didactic methods but with a grasp of its significance, and learning experientially. Because learning experientially is excellent for some aspects of the curriculum however, it does not follow that all learning must be active and experiential. (Lawton, 1985: 84-5)

Recent years have seen the return of some 'pedagogical fundamentalism' of differing forms, in the sense that teaching approaches have been characterised as 'good' or 'bad' irrespective of the skill with which they are executed, or the context in which they are applied. We have taught with history teachers who were so accomplished at storytelling, and exposition and questioning, that pupils audibly sighed with disappointment when they stopped talking to set the class an activity. However, a 2005 survey of pupil perceptions of what teaching approaches were most helpful in enabling them to learn effectively found that teachers talking too much and for too long was one of their main things that put them off learning in history (QCA, 2005; Harris and Haydn, 2006). Instruction is not *per se* a good thing, it depends how well it is done. Group work is not *necessarily* 'in practice, children chatting to each other' (Gove, 2013), but neither does it necessarily deliver high quality discussion and 'dialogic learning': group work can be desultory, unfocused and a waste of teaching time. Effective history teachers can adopt both these teaching approaches and make them work well, indeed it could be argued that the more adroitly the teacher has 'led the learning' from the front of the class, and introduced a topic in a way which has elicited the interest and attention of the class, the better the subsequent group work will be, as the pupils will be engaged and positive about the task in hand. Christodoulou (2014) makes the point that teacher instruction does not necessarily mean that the class is passive. Being made to think, and absorbing knowledge, and integrating it into your current understandings of the way the world works are not passive experiences. However, if the teacher talks for too long, and does not explain things clearly, pupils can 'switch off', and if they are 'playing truant in mind', they are not learning. Although at times dismissive of the feelings and thoughts of pupils (see Chapter 3), former Chief Inspector of Schools Chris Woodhead argued that 'whole class teaching doesn't just mean standing at the front of the class, lecturing, boring pupils, it means engaging them, stimulating them, questioning them (Woodhead, 1996).

Teaching approaches: some guiding principles

It is helpful to be able to deploy a wide range of teaching approaches

It seems reasonable to suggest that because you may eventually be teaching the same group of pupils for a whole year or even over several years, you need to make a conscious effort to build up an 'archive' of teaching ideas and resources, some of which may be adaptable to differing topic areas.

As you grow more confident in the classroom, you begin to think more about the quality of learning you are providing and to evaluate the methods and the materials you are using. With that growth of confidence also comes the opportunity to try out new approaches and to take a few risks. Be prepared to experiment even though you may not have seen an approach before. Although your course provides you with experience in more than one school, you would be very fortunate if the amount of observation of experienced teachers you can manage covers the breadth of methods available to the history teacher (this is why *reading* about teaching history is so essential). If you are trying out a method for the first time and it does not work particularly well, try to work out why this was the case but do not dismiss it forever. Try it again perhaps with a different class and a different topic. Variety of method is often a key ingredient for a successful scheme of work. The ideas and principles which underpin the NC for History are themselves very varied in their demands and emphasis and you need to have a range of teaching styles and approaches if all these major 'domains' of history are to be successfully developed (see DfE, 2013). Ofsted have consistently pointed out that a limited and staple diet of textbook work and worksheets runs the danger of pupils becoming disaffected and disengaged from the subject (Ofsted, 2005, 2011).

There are times when learning in history can take place through teacher instruction; the teacher talks, the pupil listen. There are times when learning occurs through dialogue and interaction between pupils and the teacher, or through pupils talking to each other. And there are times when pupils can learn on their own, working in silence, reading something. It is the skill with which these forms of activity are set up and executed, and the judicious balance between them, which determines how much learning will take place.

You have got to learn to be effective teaching 'from the front of the class'

However accomplished you are at devising pupil activities, however assiduous you have been at hunting down 'impact' resources, there are times when you need to be able to 'lead the learning' from the front of the class. This is partly because you have got to tell the pupils what to do, you have to give them instructions, you are the 'director' of the lesson as well as its producer. It is also your job to introduce the topic to them, in a way that makes them want to find out more about it. There are times when the most time-effective way for them to learn something is for you to explain to them clearly. You have to 'pull the learning together' at the end of the lesson, and recap and reinforce what has been learned. Another important skill, and one which is difficult to acquire, is to handle what are sometimes termed 'QUAD' activities (question, answer and discussion) – and it can be quite challenging to foster vigorous, focused and high quality discussion and argument with some teaching groups. All these aspects of 'teaching from the front of the class' can be done well or badly. Every time you talk, it can be boring or interesting. It can ease the pressure on you as a teacher if you become accomplished in these areas as you are not constantly needing high quality impact resources and activities to provide all the learning for the lesson. You might use the video camera or roleplay only occasionally, but you will be using these teaching approaches to at least some extent in every lesson, so it is important to develop your skills in these areas, particularly in terms of your skills of exposition and questioning. In a survey of over 700 pupils which asked pupils to identify which teacher characteristics pupils felt had the most positive influence on their attitude to learning 'Explains things clearly' was the quality that most pupils thought was next to the most important characteristic for the teacher to possess (after 'knows their subject really well') (NASC, 2002). It is not uncommon for history student teachers to be given the task of preparing a two-minute talk on an aspect of history, to be given to their peers, towards the start of the course. It can be a salutary reminder of how difficult it can be to make 'teacher talk' a riveting experience for learners.

Figure 5.1 Have you got anything interesting or worthwhile to say about this topic?

You should try to teach in a way which motivates and engages pupils, and in way that makes them want to try their best and do well in history

This seems so obvious as to be hardly worth saying. Chris Woodhead is one of the few commentators to suggest that we should not be concerned with what pupils think or feel (see Chapter 3). However this issue is complicated by the existence of differing views on the lengths to which teachers should go to persuade pupils of the relevance of history to their lives, and who argue that the transmission of a 'canon' of historical knowledge should be the main concern of a historical education (see Chapter 2). This is not a party political issue. Former Conservative Secretary of State for Education Sir Keith Joseph posed the question of whether:

> We fail to make the connections which could be made between the content of syllabuses and pupils' own environment and experience. Is it not an important part of history teaching to bring home to pupils the implications of what they are learning for life in British society today? (Joseph, 1984: 12)

The specifications for the National Curriculum for History (DfE, 2013) and the proposals for GCSE and A level history (DfE, 2014) all state that one of the aims of the syllabus is that it should encourage further study of the subject. The test for the teacher is to be able to deploy teaching approaches which achieve this aim, without reducing the rigour and value of what is learned. As indicated in Chapter 3, this can be quite challenging with some topics, which can be important, but not easy to turn into a thrilling experience for learners (Byrom and Riley, 2003). This is one of the reasons that teaching is such an intellectually challenging activity.

Try to use teaching approaches that make pupils think

'Active learning' does not have to be about 'kinaesthetic' learning, or groupwork. Dylan Wiliam (2011) and Daniel Willingham (2011) both make the point that one of the key things in making learning effective is to try to use methods that force pupils to think, using activities which demand more than retention and comprehension of information. The idea is that pupils will remember best that which to at least some extent, they have worked out for themselves, they have in a sense 'gone ten rounds with the information'. Willingham argues that although factual information is an important component of what is necessary for learning to occur, it is best taught in 'a wider context of understanding' (Willingham, 2012: 34). In his book about effective teaching in history, *Why won't you just tell us the answer?*, Lesh also warns against 'spoon feeding' of pupils, where they are told things, and have to remember and regurgitate them for the assessment of their learning. This is in spite of the fact that many pupils like teachers who teach in this way (Lesh, 2011).

One strategy for making pupils think about the history they are learning is to require them to reduce information. Selecting information and being obliged to make decisions about what to keep and what to leave out forces some sort of decision on pupils. Figure 5.2 suggests some ways of structuring tasks which require pupil thinking.

- In no more than 6 PowerPoint slides...
- Summarise in 50 words...
- Which event was the most important cause of...
- Who had the most important impact on...
- Underline the five most important words or phrases in the article.
- Which ten historical figures should we learn about if we want to understand World War One?
- Which is the most important paragraph and why?
- Top ten British heroes/moral exemplars from history?
- Which was the most significant event of World War Two?

Figure 5.2 Asking pupils to select and discard information

Van Boxtel suggests that oral discussion and debate can help to develop and consolidate pupils' knowledge and understanding of the past; pupils were asked to choose which Dutch people should go in a museum to celebrate the development of democracy in the Netherlands, and Van Boxtel points to the existence of discussion terminals in some museums where students gather to talk about what they have seen in the museum in relation to particular questions about the present and the past. A prompt for this can be 'What did your group think about...?' (Van Boxtel, 2010).

Tasks should develop pupils' historical knowledge and understanding in some way

As noted in Chapter 4, history teachers sometimes use a judicious blend of 'low' and 'high' value activities in order to sustain the engagement of all learners in the class (while trying to go for as high a proportion of 'high value' activity as possible in the circumstances). It is difficult to defend low ability pupils doing history if they are mainly doing colouring in or copying work. 'Reading round the class', wordsearches, crosswords and comprehension type exercises are also less than ideal. Pupils should be asking and answering *historical* questions, pursuing historical enquiries, and doing work involving the second order concepts mentioned in earlier chapters. At the highest levels, activities will have these characteristics and will provide access and challenge for all pupils, with formative assessment and checks for understanding built into the lessons to guide pupils to higher levels of attainment and provide information which enables the teacher to refine and improve the activities for future use. Over a series of lessons, the teaching approaches should contribute to the development of pupils' understanding of history as a body of knowledge, and as a form of knowledge, and develop pupils' understanding of the relationship between 'stories and sources' (Hake and Haydn, 1995).

Your teaching approaches should help pupils to make progress in their ability to communicate their historical knowledge and understanding, both orally, and in writing

There is more to this than just helping them to write better essays, or deliver better oral presentations; it is about developing pupils' ability to select, organise and deploy their historical knowledge and understanding, their understanding of the relationship between evidence and enquiry, their use of historical vocabulary and their ability to construct and take part in historical arguments (Chapman, 2011). The desirability of developing pupils' grasp of history as both a body and form of knowledge is not a function of 'New' history. As early as 1927, Happold was extolling the virtues of getting pupils to construct cogent and valid explanations or accounts in response to a particular historical question or problem:

> The ability to collect, examine and correlate facts and to express the results in clear and vivid form... the ability to think and argue logically and to form an independent judgement supported by the evidence which is available, and at the same time, the realisation that every conclusion must be regarded as a working hypothesis to be modified or rejected in the light of fresh evidence. (Happold, 1927: 4)

This statement demonstrates the close interconnection between evidence, enquiry, and communication - described in the previous version of the NC for history as 'key processes' (QCA, 2007), and still important components of the present version of the NC for history (DfE, 2013).

Teaching approaches should provide opportunities for pupils to engage in historical enquiry, to make progress in their ability to pursue historical enquiries and to formulate their own questions about the past

The idea of historical enquiry encourages pupils to use sources not as discrete and often arid exercises, removed from their context, but as a means of conducting an investigation of a real historical issue or problem. In other words, 'sources' may be seen as an aspect of the 'resources' available to aid the development of historical knowledge and understanding.

The word enquiry, with its implication of searching, activity and problem-solving, has been usefully adapted to describe overarching questions which form the basis of a series of lessons. They can be helpful in enabling your pupils to see the 'big picture', and usually incorporate the use of evidence. Riley defined such an historical enquiry as:

> A planning device for knitting together a sequence of lessons, so that all the learning activities – teacher exposition, narrative, source-work, role-play, plenary – all move toward the resolution of an interesting historical problem by means of substantial motivating activity at the end. (Riley, 2006: 2)

Riley also suggests ten questions, which can be asked to inform planning:

1   Is this area of content significant?
2   How can we turn this area of content into a rigorous and motivating enquiry question?
3   Can we focus the enquiry on individual people?
4   How will pupils communicate their understanding through an engaging end product?
5   How will we hook them in at the start of the enquiry?
6   How will we sequence the learning for maximum motivation?
7   How can we help pupils to choose and use information?
8   How can we create learning activities which appeal to different intelligences?
9   How will we create 'mini-hooks' to engage learners with particular tasks?
10   How will we create rich resources rather than grubby gobbets? (Riley, 2006: 2)

Ian Dawson's *Thinking History* website provides helpful sections on the importance of historical enquiry: www.thinkinghistory.co.uk/EnquirySkill/EnquiryImportance.html, and how to develop pupils' enquiry skills: www.thinkinghistory.co.uk/EnquirySkill/EnquiryImportance.html.

The site also provides links to examples of 'worked' historical enquiries, for Key Stage 3, GCSE and A level pupils.

It is not just a question of pupils doing more enquiries as they progress through school, but of making progress in their ability to undertake historical enquiry in a rigorous, intelligent and intellectually autonomous manner. The idea of ascribing precise 'levels' to pupils in terms of their ability to undertake historical enquiries is a rather artificial and contrived affair. Progression in history does not usually work so neatly, but there are some 'moves' towards better understanding which are harder to make than others. The list below is roughly ordered in terms of 'things we would like our pupils to be able to do/understand', from 'lower level' or 'easier things to grasp', to more sophisticated understandings and abilities related to historical enquiry:

- pupils can find answers to questions from sources of information and make simple observations;
- pupils can start to make inferential judgements on sources/information;
- pupils can make intelligent decisions about selecting information from sources which are relevant to the enquiry questions;
- pupils can select and combine information from a range of sources in order to make judgements in response to the enquiry questions;
- pupils are able to critically evaluate sources of information relevant to the enquiry questions;
- pupils can devise their own historical questions and understand why they are good questions to ask;
- pupils are able to refine their enquiry and amend their views in the light of new information;
- pupils use appropriate language to phrase their conclusions and have a sense of how strongly a claim can be made;
- Drawing on their historical knowledge and understanding, pupils can use sources of information critically, carry out enquiries about historical topics and independently reach and sustain substantiated and balanced conclusions.

Two good examples of well-structured enquiry activities which provide a sound 'model' on which you might base your own enquiry activities can be found at www.keystagehistory. co.uk/free-samples/battalion-101.html, and at www.historyresourcecupboard.co.uk/content/ ?page_id=1907. Both feature the idea of feeding in more information as the enquiry progresses, to explore the ways in which explanations might change in the light of new information, and the extent to which conclusions might be more confidently held. Other examples of enquiry activities can be found on the website.

Task 5.1 *An enquiry into the issues of 'identity' and 'Britishness' in the context of the history classroom*

a) The issue of 'identity' has become politically high-profile in recent years, particularly in the context of 'Britishness', and what it means to be British in the twenty-first century. How would you approach a lesson on 'Britishness' in a lesson with Key Stage 3 pupils?
A list of readings and resources on the issue of school history and identity can be accessed at www.uea.ac.uk/~m242/historypgce/purposes/welcome.htm.

b) What other forms of identity do people have, and to what extent should school history address forms of identity other than 'national' ones? (It can be interesting to ask pupils to make a list of loyalties, affiliations and 'identities' and then ask them to put them in order of importance, although this idea often needs to be 'modelled' by the teacher so that pupils get a clear idea of the full breadth of 'identities' that people have).

Local history sources can provide the basis for many stimulating enquiries for pupils of all ages and abilities in the secondary school. They are particularly useful if your locality can provide examples, which help your pupils to understand national history. Fieldwork, site investigations and the use of local history libraries can give an extra dimension to the learning of history.

The following activity for Year 7 classes can help to develop their understanding of the use of sources for a series of enquiries. As with all valuable lessons involving enquiries, appropriate materials need to be accumulated. For this activity you need to acquire a set of census returns for, say, 1861 for the area in which you are teaching, then:

1   Divide the data into approximately equal amounts of data for six groups (a population of 800 people would result in two A4 pages of data per group).
2   Explain to the class that they are going to find out what occupations the people living in their area had in 1861.
3   Using the entry for a particular household, explain each of the columns and give the class some details of how the census returns were acquired.
4   Appoint two pupils whose task is to move round the groups collecting and collating the data.
5   Appoint another pupil who will then use to data to create a bar chart on the board.
6   The groups will then complete the following sheet and the collators complete their totals (suitably amended for your area and data).

GROUP...

We have found that in .... in 1861 there were:

1. _____ servants or house servants   _____
2. _____ labourers; farm labourers   _____
3. _____ laundresses; washerwomen   _____
4. _____ housewives; housekeepers   _____
5. _____ gardeners   _____
6. _____ cotton factory workers (winders, weavers, spinners, calico printers, dyers, agents)   _____
7. _____ farmers   _____
8. _____ craftsmen (blacksmiths, stone masons, wheelwrights, joiners, shoemakers, carpenters.   _____
9. _____ warehousemen   _____
10. _____ salespeople (beer house keepers, butchers, grocers, saleswomen, provision dealer, hosier)   _____
11. _____ jobs related to travel (railway porter, carter, grooms, coachmen, carriers, footmen, paviours)   _____
12. _____ craftswomen   _____
13. _____ professional jobs (teachers, police, nurses, clerks, cashiers)   _____
14. _____ merchants, manufacturers   _____

Figure 5.3 An enquiry activity based on local history

An important part of the investigation will be a discussion of the final bar chart and the questions that can emerge. Further enquiries using the same data could include an analysis of the age range of the population and an investigation into their places of birth.

 Linking the census data to the maps of the time can add interest to the enquiry, especially when the pupils can make a connection with past and present place names. The first edition of the 6″ series of Ordnance Survey maps are now accessible through the website of the Landmark Information Group. The website includes details of such an enquiry-based project on the Peasants' Revolt. www.old-maps.co.uk.

Teaching approaches should contribute to the development of progression in pupils' understanding and use of evidence

As you will find in subsequent chapters, evidence is central to historical method and understanding, and your teaching approaches should therefore keep in mind the need to include pupil understanding of 'evidence' as an element of their planning. Burn makes several useful points relating to how to approach the development of pupils' evidential understanding, arguing that textbooks often contain unhelpful activities in this area, and that the use of evidence should be related to real historical questions. As with other areas of historical understanding, there are particular 'moves' which pupils need to make (such as understanding that 'primary' sources are not necessarily more useful or reliable than 'secondary' sources, moving pupils from ideas about 'bias' to ideas about 'position', and Hexter's concept of 'the second record' in history):

> The effective use of evidence involves a range of different sorts of skills and abilities... Evidential understanding thus needs to be built gradually, with careful planning for progression... Our goal is to enable pupils to understand how accounts of the past are constructed... Constructing their own accounts can help them to understand this process. (Burn, 2006)

A comparatively neglected or understated facet of school history relating to evidence is that of 'veracity', in the sense of respect for evidence and intellectual integrity in the processing of information and formulation of judgements about the past (and the present). Many of the bad things that happen in the world are done by people who are very clever, who did well in history at school, and who often have history A level, or even a degree in history, and who are at one level 'good' at handling evidence. However, they are not good at handling evidence in the way that Sir Keith Joseph suggests is important: 'the teaching of history has to take place in a spirit which takes seriously the need to pursue truth on the basis of evidence.' He goes on to say that 'The aim of the history teacher is to help pupils form a picture of the past which is consistent with the facts, to bring the pupils to the point where they can make their own interpretations of historical evidence; (Joseph, 1984: 12).

As with other facets of school history, there are language related aspects to developing pupils' understanding of evidence (see Figure 5.4)

It seems possible/probable/plausible/likely...
This suggests/demonstrates/supports...
Valid/reliable/corroborate/contradict/gaps/doubt/tenable/tentative/sceptical
hypothesis/theory/revisionist/on the other hand/however
audience/purpose/context/position

Figure 5.4 Vocabulary related to pupils' understanding of evidence

For members of the Historical Association, a number of articles about developing pupils' understanding of evidence can be accessed at www.history.org.uk/resources/secondary_resource_2575_61.html.

Teaching approaches should contribute to pupil acquisition of a coherent mental map or 'big picture' of the past

One of the few things that almost all commentators on the history curriculum agree on is that many pupils are leaving school with only a very limited and fragmentary mental map of the past (see Chapter 3). This limits the use of history to provide some form of 'orientation' and understanding of how things got to how they are today. Your teaching approaches should make some provision for 'providing a general picture in terms of which the relations between things encountered earlier and later are made as clear as possible' (Bruner, 1960: 12). This means making connections across time, and revisiting earlier learning so that we do not put too much emphasis on 'the accumulation of unrelated facts' (Joseph, 1984: 11).

Your teaching approaches should contribute to the development of pupils' language and literacy skills

Concern over pupils' literacy skills can be traced back to at least as far as the Bullock Report, ('A Language for Life', 1975), which gave an impetus towards a greater concern for the use of language in the teaching of all subjects across the secondary curriculum.

It has long been established that history is well-placed to make a significant contribution to pupil literacy. Burston (1963) asserted that 'history, more than any other school subject, depends upon literacy in its pupils as a prerequisite to success and increased literacy is perhaps its most important by-product'. This is one of the things that makes history useful to young people.

As a student teacher, you will soon appreciate how much the ability (or lack of it) of your pupils to read, write and generally communicate their knowledge and understanding will influence the planning and execution of your lessons. History has much to offer in the development of language capability, and history teachers must be constantly alert to opportunities to enrich this aspect of pupils' learning.

The study of history also requires the use of a host of *abstract terms* and, although the subject cannot claim a monopoly of such terms, because subjects such as economics, policies, sociology and perhaps, theology are usually studied after the age of 16, it is often through their study of history that pupils have their first acquaintance with concepts such as 'revolution', 'democracy', 'colonialism' 'representation', 'taxation', 'inflation' and so on.

In addition to the vast array of names of people and events, pupils are faced with *subject specific labels,* often implying interpretations, such as 'The Glorious Revolution' and the 'Peterloo Massacre' and colligations such as 'The Renaissance' and 'The Reformation' that we probably have a reasonable grasp of, but which are probably quite mysterious to many of our pupils. Hence you need to be constantly aware of the problems presented by your language in your teaching of historical evidence and historical interpretations. Similarly the DfES publication, *Literacy in history* aims to demonstrate how focused literacy teaching can enhance historical understanding with due attention to the way the history teacher approaches speaking and listening, reading and writing (DfES, 2004).

All present real problems for pupils unless they are anticipated by the teacher and adequately explained. This means we have to give particular thought and attention to the needs of pupils with very limited or low levels of literacy (see Chapter 8). Pupils need to be encouraged to use such terms in a way that shows they do understand them and are not repeating other people's language without fully understanding it.

Although attention and concern tended to focus on pupils' abilities in 'extended writing' after the drastic reduction in the role of essay writing in external examinations in history after the introduction of the GCSE exam, more recently, attention has focused on the desirability of getting pupils to 'read history', and to move away from their reading being limited to dismembered gobbets of text and 'death by sources a-f'. Counsell makes the point that the moves away from extended texts have been profoundly unhelpful for history teachers (Counsell, 2008).

Strategies for the use of reading:

1   Seek to establish the role of reading in history by taking steps to build up the pupils' confidence, taking measures to ensure success. These could include making sure the pupils have sufficient background knowledge so that the reading makes sense; identifying beforehand the words and phrases that could stop the reader's progress, both subject-specific and non-technical language; and, where significant, the use in the text of structure words such as 'if', 'although', 'nevertheless'; giving them an overview of what the reading involves by summarising the arrangement of the paragraphs. Encourage the pupils to appreciate the value of re-reading. ('A quick reader is not necessarily a good one.') Make a point of praising pupils' reading and emphasise that a good effort at reading is comparable with a good effort at writing.

2   Make sure the pupils' can see the purpose of the activity (e.g. questions to be answered), diagrams or charts to be completed. Try to ensure that they are given not just comprehension questions but tasks which encourage reflection and opinions on what has been read. Hellier and Richards (2005) make the point that it is also useful to remind pupils what they are not reading for, as discarding information can be difficult for pupils regardless of ability.

3   Use active or 'guided' reading strategies. Reading can make an important contribution to your lessons if you have chosen and planned strategies appropriate to your lesson objectives. There are a wide range of activities for your choice, several well-documented in DfES (2004), *Literacy in history* and Hellier and Richards (2005). These include asking your pupils to:

- Highlight, underline, label, or annotate the text to meet a specific search; at times you could set the challenge to find information against a specified time.
- Transfer information from the text to a list, grid, chart, Venn diagram, etc, for example for categorising the causes of an event.
- Summarise the content in a sentence or present, say, the essence of a piece of source material as a speech bubble.
- Work in pairs on completion activities such as cloze exercises or putting paragraphs into their correct sequence.
- Work in groups on a collection of sources, in which individuals describe and summarise for each other.
- Read one section of the material at a time as you seek to scaffold their reading.
- In addition you might consider the merits of reading aloud. This could involve yourself modelling your approach to reading having notes the issues and questions that can arise in your preparation. Lewis and Wray (2000) advocate the value of inviting pupils to read aloud as a means of helping understanding as some pupils would welcome this use of an auditory approach to reading, including bi-lingual pupils.

4   Ensure the pupils have the necessary reference skills. Some pupils can become frustrated and disillusioned if they spend their time unprofitably, simply because they lack the appropriate reference skills – the ability to use the indexing system, dictionaries, encyclopaedias and contents pages. To this we can add internet materials, which again will require reading ability.

5   Chapman (2006) argues that pupils can cope with quite challenging documents if the teacher helps and guides them through in a skilful manner.

In your use of reading in the history classroom it is of benefit to your pupils, and your lessons if you emphasise the status of reading in learning history. Seek to create an environment for reading both in the classroom and beyond.

Loy (2008) offers suggestions for getting pupils to enjoy reading history, and a collection of 'good examples of historical prose' can be accessed at http://historyandict.wikifoundry.com.

A comparatively recent development in history education in England is the exploration of the work of academic historians in the history classroom. In a sense, this is at the opposite end of the continuum to the use of decontextualised sources in history teaching. A series of articles in *Teaching History* has described how departments have attempted to use the work of academic historians to develop pupils' historical knowledge and understanding (see Figure 5.5). This development addresses both the development of pupils' understanding of *what history is*, and the moves toward getting pupils to engage with longer pieces of reading than those which prevailed in the early years of National Curriculum textbooks and the GCSE exam.

Bellinger, L. (2008) Cultivating curiosity about complexity: what happens when year 12 start to read Orlando Figes' *The Whisperers*, *Teaching History*, No. 132: 5-15.
Burn, K. (2014) Making sense of the eighteenth century, *Teaching History*, No. 153: 18-27.
Foster, R. (2011) Passive receivers or constructive readers? Pupils' experiences of an encounter with academic history, *Teaching History*, No. 142: 4-13.
Hollis, C. (2014) Waking up to complexity: using Christopher Clark's The Sleepwalkers to challenge over-determined causal explanations, *Teaching History*, No. 154: 48-54.
Laffin, D. (2013) Marr: magpie or marsh harrier? The quest for the common characteristics of the genus 'historian' with 16- to 19-year-olds, *Teaching History*, No. 149: 18-25.
Richards, K. (2012) Avoiding a din at dinner or, teaching students to argue for themselves: Year 13 plan a historians' dinner party, *Teaching History*, No. 148: 18-27.

Figure 5.5 Using academic history in the history classroom

Another important resource which is often underused in terms of making use of academic history in the history classroom is the popular history magazine. Magazines such as *BBC History Magazine* and *History Today* can be very time-effective ways of helping to ensure that whatever your chosen teaching approach, your teaching is informed by strong subject knowledge and up-to-date scholarship. Much of the content of these magazines is based on newly published history books, and can help make the point to pupils that history changes, it is not monolithic. Articles can be used just to strengthen your subject knowledge and aid your exposition and questioning, or extracts from the articles can be incorporated into lesson activities. Both magazines provide online indexes so that you can locate articles which relate to the topics which you are required to teach (www.historyextra.com/index-search, www.historytoday.com/archive). *History Review* has recently put its exam advice guidance articles online, and these can be very helpful if you are involved in helping pupils to revise for their public examinations (www.historytoday.com/students). A combination of Neville Chamberlain's own explanation of his policy of appeasement (www.historyguide.org/europe/munich.html), and the *History Review* article on historiographical debates about

www.european-crossroads.de/

The EHISTO Project is a European collaboration to explore the use of popular history magazines in history teaching. Based around the concept of 'multi-perspectivity' in history, and the development of pupils' media and critical literacy skills, it provides popular magazine articles on the Outbreak of World War One, and Christopher Columbus, which have been translated into English from Spain, Sweden, Poland and Germany and enables national differences in the treatment of these topics to be examined (https://media.sodis.de/ehisto/en/index.html). https://media.sodis.de/ehisto/wwl/en/en/transnational_comparison.html.

Figure 5.6 The EHISTO Project

that policy (www.historytoday.com/frank-mcdonough/chamberlain-guilty-man-or-national-saviour) could make a big difference to how well you would be able to teach this topic to an examination level class. Even if you cannot afford the subscription fee for the journal, if your university has a history faculty, they will generally subscribe to these magazines.

Task 5.2 *Language problems in history teaching*

Acquire three or four history textbooks, which have been produced at different times in the last ten years. Select from each book a paragraph and try to identify those words and phrases which you think might prove to be problematic for the pupils for whom they are intended. If the opportunity arises, talk to pupils about their understanding of such extracts. Consider the difficulties, which might arise from the conciseness of the text, the style and the use of metaphorical language, the use of abstract concepts, of vague descriptive words, of words related to time and place and the use of quotations from sources.

Select one of the passages and try to re-write the content so that the potential problems have been eliminated. There will be some occasions when you have to re-write material to make it accessible to your pupils.

Teaching methods involving the differing use of language in history

Teacher talk: developing your skills of exposition

As a history teacher it is difficult to avoid the use of teacher talk as a significant element of your lessons. The reason for this is the fact that history is one of those subjects which involves a vast amount of content, so there can be a great deal to talk about. There is and always will be an important place for teacher talk whether it be questioning or exposition and the subject offers plenty of topics, which can be described in a stimulating way. The development of your skills both in exposition and in questioning is an essential feature of your competence as a history teacher. Such teaching figured highly in the traditional approach and there is little doubt it can be overdone. Yet, however accomplished you become at devising purposeful and worthwhile learning activities for pupils, you must at some point be able to use the skills of exposition and questioning to explain the past to pupils in an engaging and effective manner.

An important part of your role as a history teacher is to be able to sell the subject, to transmit your enthusiasm for the topic to the pupils. Reluctance to develop exposition skills can encourage the uninspiring use of the textbook or an overreliance on duplicated handouts. At times you can call on the assistance of a dvd extract to stimulate interest in the topic, but there are times when you are dependent on yourself, your knowledge and classroom personality. You need to have a good command of the topic and to have selected from it the significant points you want to stress and the kind of detail appropriate to the age and ability of your class. It is useful to have your notes at hand but try to remember as much as you can. If you appear to be tied to your notes, this serves only to reinforce your inexperience and limits your movement about the class. One of the ways of avoiding frequent reference to notes is to use visual aids, be it the board, the visualiser, PowerPoint, pictures or your own creations. These not only serve as an aid to your memory, they help the pupils follow your exposition and also focus their attention away from you. They can also help in reinforcing and recapping key points. Some teachers have found it useful to practice exposition skills at home, not exactly declaiming from the top of the stairs, but possibly using a digital voice recorder to help them reflect on their use of language, about any assumptions they may be making about the pupils' understanding and about how they use their voices. If you feel you have a problem with the way you use your voice, most courses have a specialist available to help you.

Task 5.3 *Developing your skills of exposition*

Make notes on the topic you wish to transmit to the class. Then identify those details, which will benefit from the use of visual aids and how you use the board or whiteboard. Underline those *key* points that you consider to be the ones that need emphasis and which are related most clearly to your lesson objectives.

Record about ten minutes of your exposition and on listening to the play-back, assess the extent to which you have used your voice to make the topic interesting, relevant and stimulating for your pupils.

In at least one of your lessons, make a conscious attempt to undertake a piece of teacher exposition which, *above all other considerations*, interests and engages pupils.

You should find that your worries about exposition skills recede as you teach more lessons. Whereas in the early stages of school experience, a ten-minute explanation can appear a daunting prospect, after a while the use of teacher talk can present a different challenge - that is, *how to avoid talking for too long* (with most classes 15 to 20 minutes is a maximum). Effective teacher talk is better measured by quality rather than by quantity.

You will find that there are times when there is a place for self-denial. You must learn to judge how long to talk for, and when to stop. That is, to be aware of what has been termed, 'discursive intrusiveness' - the belief that if the teacher 'bangs on about it' for long enough pupils will understand. At times there may be a negative correlation between the quantity of teacher talk and pupil understanding. Although you might be tempted to display your knowledge ('I know it, therefore I will tell them about it...'), such loquacity may not be in the best interests of your pupils. You need to develop a sense of when you may have 'lost' your audience, and need to move quickly on to something else.

 A dataset giving pupils' views about what they do and don't like about being in classrooms, and the factors which they think either help or hinder their learning is accessible at: www.uea.ac.uk/~m242/nasc/welcome.htm. Excessive teacher exposition and teachers 'not explaining things well' are two of the most commonly cited things that put pupils off learning.

'He's not my sort of teacher, he's like a Duracell battery, he just goes on and on.'
(Pupil describing his history teacher)

Your competence in talking to pupils should include an awareness of the disadvantages and advantages of this approach:

1   *The disadvantages.* This style of teaching does invite questions about the quality of learning that might be involved, particularly if overused or used with content for which this 'transmission mode' is not really appropriate. Criticisms of this mode are most valid when its use may be seen to reflect an attitude towards the learning of history, which places the teacher too exclusively in the role of the 'expert', the fount of all knowledge to be covered and the pupil in the role of the receiver, who sits like an empty receptacle waiting for 'knowledge' to be poured in. Teaching through teacher exposition raises fundamental questions about how pupils learn and specifically acquire language in a way they can understand and make use of it.

2   *The advantages.* Advocates of the value of teacher exposition usually emphasise its efficient use of time, a precious commodity for a subject often restricted to two or even one lesson per week. The material can be thought through ready for presentation, given a logical structure and pared down to the essentials so that due emphasis can be given to key points. Any subject-specific words can be explained as the talk proceeds. The material can be presented with a style and organisation suitable for meeting the needs of assessment, particularly external examination syllabuses. There is little doubt that, with an accomplished practitioner, there are times when this approach can be an effective learning experience, perhaps even the highlight of the lesson, and it is perhaps significant that Ofsted (2005) have commented critically

about the lack of input by the teacher. Part of that input should be the development of your narrative skills.

The narrative art of the history teacher

It has become evident that there has been a reappraisal of the role of exposition within the context of a curriculum that emphasises skills as well as knowledge and understanding. Story has long been used as a means of addressing wider complex, abstract ideas. *Great Tales from English History* is an attempt to revive this tradition (Lacey, 2006). Husbands welcomes this 'reshaped' narrative tradition as a means of stimulating ways of thinking about the past and about the ways the past was experienced (Husbands, 1996). He is mindful of the obligations of the teacher adopting a narrative approach, stressing the importance of factual accuracy, consistent with historical evidence, the need for authenticity to period and character and the need to ensure the pupils realise that this is not the only story. It is also important to think through how you engage the pupils in the course of the narrative. Given a dilemma, what could be done about it?

The success of the narrative approach often lies in the detail and the nature of the details. Wilkinson questions the capacity of the double-page spread of a typical textbook to be of real use in understanding a topic or the arguments being explored. He advocates a narrative skill that gives 'the opportunity to flesh out people, figures and events and to add some of the colour, sights and smells that children love but often miss out on' (Wilkinson, 2006: 17). To succeed with the narrative approach you need to acquire the sort of detail that makes a story. Such information you accumulate over time as you select to read more detailed books on topics you think likely to benefit from the narrative approach. Wilkinson (2006) and Goodwin (2006) offer the following advice for the successful use of narrative, the latter particularly with beginning teachers in mind.

Guidance for successful use of narrative

Wilkinson	Goodwin
1. Learn the plot and revise in the light of the response.	1. Move around the room to emphasise the movement of the story but stand absolutely still to emphasise key events.
2. Vary your voice – do not keep the same flat tone and do not be afraid to repeat things to emphasise them.	2. Lowering the classroom lights will help to focus the pupils' attention on you and any visual material you use to support your narrative. This will signify a different type of activity.
3. Entertain – act it up even more than usual.	3. Vary the volume of your voice for emphasis. Once you have the pupils' attention try lowering your voice so they strain just a little to hear you.
4. Plan. Consider carefully how you are going to follow up the story – what aspects you are going to focus on and build on in the follow-up.	4. Beginners may find there is reassurance in giving the pupils a written version for reference if you are losing the thread.

How good are your skills of exposition?

A) I'm fairly confident about this aspect of my teaching; when talking to my teaching groups, I think I can generally interest them and hold their attention, whatever the topic. Question, answer and discussion activities are usually lively and stimulating.

B) I'm OK; I feel relaxed and confident in talking to my teaching groups, and talk quite fluently and effectively to them most of the time. I think I explain things quite well. Sometimes they are interested in what I say, and they enjoy the bit of the lesson where I am talking to them. I can think on my feet fairly well and feel comfortable with QUAD activities with most groups.

C) Reasonable, but it's an aspect of my teaching that I will need to work on whilst on second placement. Sometimes I suspect that they do not find my exposition helpful or interesting, and I don't really enjoy this bit of the lesson. I find QUAD activities quite difficult and sometimes they don't really take off.

D) Definitely a weakness; I am aware that pupils are frequently bored and restless when I try to talk to them at any length, even on topics where my subject knowledge is quite good. I don't feel confident or relaxed when doing QUAD activities with them.

E) I'm so bad at this that I avoid doing it as much as possible, I talk for about ten seconds and then set them some written work or a group work task.

Use of questioning

A common classroom strategy is that of exposition interspersed with questioning. Questioning is an important skill for any teacher. It has been calculated that teachers spend about 30 per cent of their time asking questions. However, the rate and the nature of oral questioning vary from subject to subject. How you formulate questions and use them is a good indicator of what you think the pupils are gaining from your history lessons. Much has been written since the 1950s about the type of questions used in lessons, which demonstrates the link between objectives and questions. Bloom made an early contribution to the classification of types of questions and since then there have been many variants to his original attempt to place the questions in a hierarchical order, from the easiest to the most difficult (Bloom, 1956). A common list would be recall, comprehension, translation (e.g. transfer from one medium to another such as writing a description of a picture), analysis, comparison, interpretation, synthesis, hypothetical (invention), evaluation. Opinions vary about the order for it is important to stress that some comprehension questions can be very difficult as will be very clear from a glance at some historical sources and some interpretations can be relatively straightforward. The following taxonomy with particular reference to the use of evidence in history teaching can be helpful:

1   *Recall questions:* Give details of events, people, places mentioned in the source.
2   *Comprehension questions:* What does the evidence say? Do I understand it? Can I picture to myself the scene that it represents?
3   *Interpretation questions:* How does the evidence compare with my knowledge of the historical context? What was the writer's purpose in writing?
4   *Extrapolation questions:* Does it contradict other evidence? What new light does it shed?
5   *Invention questions:* If you had been there questions? 'What if' questions.
6   *Evaluation questions:* What is the value of the evidence? Is it trustworthy? What is your opinion about the course of action taken?

Such lists give you a useful basis for an analysis of the type of questions to use in your lessons. A familiar criticism of lessons is that too much emphasis is given to what are thought to be the undemanding questions; that is an overuse of what may be called the 'lower order' questions involving recall, comprehension and translation with only a limited use of the 'higher order' questions which encourage the pupils to think, such as interpretation and evaluation. Of course, the difficulty of a question depends on the context and materials being used, even so your aim is to encourage your pupils to think for themselves and to try and use the 'higher order' questions as much as the situation allows. It should be noted that there is also the skill of listening and responding to questions in a way which encourages pupils to volunteer answers.

Task 5.4 *Using 'thinking' questions*

1   Using the hierarchy of questions presented above, analyse a selection of worksheets and try to identify the types of questions that have been asked. What is the distribution of 'lower' and 'higher' order questions? If there are few 'higher' order questions, try to formulate some that might be added.
2   Use the same method with questions on two or three topics in a textbook.
3   When you are planning a question and answer session within your lesson, write out the principal questions you will be asking. McCully (1997) has shown how there are times when the whole lesson can be structured around a set of key questions. Think about the sequencing and how you might include some 'thinking' questions. After the lesson reflect on how you used such questions and on how the techniques you used might differ from the asking of recall questions.

Questioning should not all be one-way, that is the teacher questions, the pupil responds. *Pupils should be encouraged to ask questions both of the teacher and of each other.* Much can be learned about pupils' historical understanding or lack of understanding from the questions they ask. There is a connection here with your own subject knowledge, because you are more likely to wish to monopolise the questioning if you feel insecure about your knowledge of the topic. Ofsted (2005, 2011) noted how, in circumstances that indicated good practice, pupils raised their own questions, developed and tested hypotheses and undertook investigations. A methodology, in which the pupils undertake their own historical enquiries, gives you the opportunity to encourage them to ask questions about the topic and their sources of information they are using.

There are also interesting issues arising out of 'wait time': how long do you give pupils to think about an answer before providing it, or asking someone else or moving on? You can give pupils, individually or in pairs, some time to come up with an answer, in order to get them to think in a bit more depth.

Task 5.5 *Encouraging pupils' questioning*

1   When you have taught some lessons, look back on your lesson plans and consider whether there might have been some opportunities for the pupils to have done some questioning.
2   Try to list the range of situations that could generate pupils asking questions of yourself, of each other or for interrogating sources. Here is a list to get you started: asking questions of you as Oliver Cromwell; mock trial of Charles I; questioning group reports on a decision-making exercise; questioning the producer/author of a costume drama seen on video; researching family history; questioning a group presentation. Now try to add to these.
3   Think of, and experiment with, strategies for dealing with problems such as:
     (a)   the reluctance of some pupils to answer questions;
     (b)   how to deal with 'wrong' or inappropriate answers;
     (c)   overenthusiastic or attention-seeking pupils wanting to answer all the questions.

Pupil talk

There are occasions when you ask the pupils to be quiet and talking constitutes a breach of classroom rules. Nevertheless, there are other times when pupils need to be encouraged to talk as a means of advancing their learning. 'Speaking and listening' was an important part of the National Literacy Strategy. The learning of history offers many opportunities for the effective use of speaking and learning. Strategies to use a variety of activities involving pupils talking and listening need not be seen as an imposition. With experience you learn that well-prepared use of pupil talk can considerably advance your pupils' historical knowledge. In their report for 2004/05 HMI noted that history lessons showed too little emphasis given to discussion and group work, aware of how much the various uses of pupil talk can advance their learning in history.

How can the use of pupil talk advance pupils' learning in history?

1   It helps to combat the *diffidence* of some pupils, who either through shyness or a fear of being wrong prefer to remain silent. A reluctance to speak may also stem from the idea that learning a subject such as history requires the ability to speak in the formal standard English of the textbook, alien from most pupils' usual form of speaking. Luff (2001) makes the point that speaking and listening does not come naturally to many adolescents so that it is important to devise activities in which they are encouraged to

speak. Trying out their ideas in groups or even as a pair can be an enormous confidence booster, which might encourage such pupils to repeat them in a plenary session. Skill in 'drawing out' pupils so that they regularly contribute orally to the lessons can make pupils feel much more positive and involved in the subject.

2   Encouraging pupil talk can be particularly helpful in the development of pupils' *understanding of historical concepts.* The work of Lee *et al.* (1995) suggests that pupils can often develop more powerful ideas for understanding the past by talking to each other about problems of change, cause and explanation. Clark (2001) demonstrates how 'causal explanation' is about competing possibilities and pupils need to be comfortable with using the speculative language of possibility within their arguments. Hence the encouragement to use 'might have', could have', 'if' and 'probably'. Similarly, use can be made of 'oral frames' to help pupils speaking and listening. This can involve helping to structure pupils' discussion by involving useful phrases such as, for example, for explaining cause and effect, 'the result is', 'triggering', 'the effect of this was' or even 'precipitating'.

3   In contrast to writing, talk has the advantage of *speed. Literacy in History* (2004) notes how 'talk is quick, fluid and shared and can do some things better that writing, for example, exploratory work'. And Luff (2001) reminds us, speed appeals to young people. Pupil talk encourages the quick absorption of ideas and of opposing views. He sees value in speaking, which demands the ability to absorb and marshal ideas quickly, something which will be needed when writing under the pressure of time.

What kind of activities can be used to make constructive use of pupil talk?

- asking and answering questions;
- creating or identifying definitions of subject specific words;
- drawing out similarities and differences;
- defending and justifying a point of view;
- explaining a process;
- explaining or summarising the content of a source;
- creating mind or concept maps;
- participating in pair or group discussion;
- presentations - by individuals or groups, often illustrated;
- involvement in debates, controversies, sometimes with a competitive element;
- use of varieties of role play.

In planning to use activities involving pupil talk, it is important for you to consider how your choice maximises pupil involvement, not allowing certain pupils to dominate the talking but do their share of listening to others. It is also important to keep emphasising that activities involving pupil talk are not a 'light option'. Because they may also be enjoyable it does not make them any less valid as a serious learning activity. The point is often worth repeating in the plenary session, where pupils can often realise just what they have learned from the activity.

It is also important to keep in mind that there is a progression issue with the use of pupil talk. It can be helpful to move pupils on from being over reliant on reading from a prepared script, or from extensive written notes, and on towards 'thinking on their feet' as they move through the secondary school.

Use of group work

The value of the use of group work has over the years been a source of debate among teachers but it has now established an important place in the history teacher's repertoire of teaching methods. As with all methods, if group work is poorly or inappropriately organised, it provides little advancement in the pupils' learning. Much depends on your understanding of the potential problems and your ability to anticipate these. Such problems can include the following:

- the need to ensure pupils keep 'on task';
- the concern that some pupils in each group are not contributing;
- the likelihood that pupils are given too much control of the pace of the lesson;
- concentration on the obvious, eschewing the more thought-provoking issues;
- reluctance of any group member to give feedback in a plenary;
- can slow down the coverage of the content;
- at times, the classroom layout of desks or tables is not helpful to any whole class teaching which may precede or follow the group work.

Nevertheless, there are many situations when you find pupils can be more motivated in group activities than being a passive recipient of class teaching. Used well, group work is an excellent vehicle for all the positive values of pupil talk described above. The key, as so often, is in the planning.

Successful use of group activities in history may be positively influenced by the following strategies:

1 Ensure that the pupils have sufficient background knowledge to be able to complete the tasks they have been given. They are aware of this and it influences the enthusiasm with which they set about the activity. Furthermore the tasks should be sufficiently challenging to motivate and require collaboration. For example, try to turn the topic into a problem in a way that interests the pupils. A discussion on whether Queen Elizabeth I should order the execution of Mary, Queen of Scots, would not work well if the pupils are not bothered whether she dies or not.

2 Think about the way the groups are organised, by ability, friendship groups, mixed gender, choice of this depends on the tasks involved. The use of grouping by ability is not as frequently used as it might be in history lessons. You should explore the possibilities of this and the opportunities it can give you as a teacher to change your role from asking questions appropriate to the group, taking interim feedback or being a temporary group member. Goodwin (2006) recommends putting pupils in groups before entering the room or having place cards on the desks.

3 Think about how each group may have to allocate tasks or roles, e.g. recording discussion, completing pro formas, chairing to ensure all participate or presenter of group decisions.

4   Be precise in your thinking about the materials the groups need.

5   Give clear instructions. It is fundamental that the pupils have a clear idea of what they are to do and understand the value of what they are doing and how this contributes to their historical understanding. In particular, think carefully about the starting point of any group activity.

6   Employ strategies to maintain the pace of work. At times there are several stages to the activity so time-checks and interim targets can be employed. Many 'card sort' activities have successive stages. Perhaps most important is the need for group activities to have an end product, for example a decision or set of conclusions, a presentation or a display.

7   Finally, in your follow-up, there is value at times in discussing how the group work went, what has been learned so the pupils realise that pupil talk is real work with tangible results.

Although there are advantages in using the same group formation whenever you decide to use group work, such as the speed of the transition to the activity, there are times when it may be preferable to make use of different ways of organising group work. The methods cited below have the advantage of seeking to maximise pupil involvement by changing the audience, increasing listening skills and minimising the often tedious and repetitive reporting back stage. The *Literacy Across the Curriculum* material included the following strategies, which are all very adaptable for the teaching of history (DfEE, 2001).

Different ways of organising group work

Strategy	Example
Envoys Following group discussion, conclusions/decisions, one group member moves to join another group to explain and summarise these results and to find out what the new group thought.	This can be a useful format for encouraging discussion and decision making when dealing with contentious issues and ones, which require some understanding of attitudes at the time. Questions such as 'Did Louis XVI deserve to die?' and 'Was the Poor law Amendment Act of 1834 a good way to deal with poverty?'
Snowball This involves changing the group size. After the initial discussion and familiarisation with the content in pairs, the two become four and later an eight as they retell and develop ideas.	'Literacy in History' (2001) describes a snowball activity in which pairs are given a causation enquiry. The pupils are asked to divide a set of events/influences into two columns, share their answers with an enlarged group and add anything new. The feedback asks for two answers from each column.
Rainbow Another way of changing the audience is to give each pupil in a group a different colour and then later all those of the same colour join and retell the original's findings.	Given the need for the group to discuss from an informed position, some approaches may be best placed towards the end of a topic. For example when discussing the importance of a topic, 'Whose was the most important contribution to the Industrial Revolution? Or significance: Give a list of reasons why a topic is significant, which is most significant and why?

Jigsaw
This has the advantage of covering a range of material. The topic is divided and each group becomes an 'expert'. A spokesperson reports back in the plenary, when all the 'pieces of the topic are put together.

This approach can be useful when an enquiry involves the use of a range of sources some of which need time for reading. Groups can summarise their findings. The plenary must ensure pupils do not remain 'experts' in their own part of the jigsaw. Useful for the study of historical interpretations.

Role play

As you gain in confidence and seek to extend the range of methods you can employ, you will find that there are many topics, which are suitable for the use of role play. This is another learning activity, which can involve a wide range of pupils of different abilities and in some formats can be really beneficial to kinaesthetic learners, who enjoy learning when they are physically involved. Role play is often at its most useful when pupils have to deal with topics which are conceptually quite difficult such as the impact on a community of religious changes at the time of the Reformation. There has been a fear that role play can take up too much time as teachers struggle to cover the curriculum, but Banham and Dawson (2002) effectively show that this approach can save time because it helps pupils to understand more clearly through the visual representation and sheer physicality of the activity, the concepts involved and with that a substantial improvement in their writing. In another example of role play helping understanding, Duff (1998) presented some useful exemplar materials on helping a Year 10 class to understand the circumstances surrounding appeasement and the Munich Conference of 1938. Guscott (2006) shows how this approach can also be used for teaching historical skills and as a means of assessing pupils' historical understanding.

Remember that role-play does not have to be an 'all singing, all dancing' festival of active drama, with all pupils having to write and act their parts. It can sometimes involve a small number of pupils, who have been selected to perform for the rest of the class; it can be done without pupils having to move around the room; and it can be done by simply asking pupils to take part in decision-making exercises based on information sheets or film slides. Some student teachers are reluctant to use role-play because they envisage it will entail a full-scale dramatic production. Some of the most effective role-plays are quite modest in ambition. Ian Luff (2000, 2003) has proved several ideas for eminently practicable and useful role play activities, which do not require inordinate amounts of time and preparation.

For more detail on the use of roleplay, including some of Ian Luff's examples of roleplay and practical demonstration, and suggestions for further reading, go to: www.uea.ac.uk/~m242/historypgce/drama/welcome.htm

Writing

Of the range of activities, which take place in the learning of history, writing is one of the most important and, at the same time, the least popular among pupils (Adey and Biddulph,

2001; QCA, 2005). Yet, it is principally through pupils' writing that their knowledge and understanding is usually assessed. Writing has been an issue for concern and always presents a challenge to some pupils, but there is evidence of a positive response to the problems writing in history poses (Ofsted, 2002).

What are the problems which pupils face when given written tasks?

1   *Lack of audience and purpose.* Pupils are unlikely to produce the quality of written work of which they are capable if they are unclear about the purpose of the exercise and unsure about the intended audience. A vague, general invitation to write something about a topic is not likely to motivate the pupils, who may see it as a means of filling the remaining time left in the lesson and may well invite the usual delaying tactics. Instead the pupils need to have a clear idea of the purpose of the task and there is much to be gained by varying the audience and not just assuming this is always the teacher. Cottingham and Daborn (1999) found that teachers were able to note how writing improved when there was clarity of purpose and audience.

2   *Information.* A problem experienced by some beginning teachers is that they ask pupils to produce written work based on insufficient information. If they are asked to base their piece on a few sentences from a textbook then the pupils are unlikely to be motivated and are disappointed with the result. Basically insufficient time and thought has been given to the preparation for the task. By contrast, having too much information can also cause problems. Pupils seem overwhelmed by the detail, having to handle too much at the same time.

3   *Relevance.* Pupils have difficulties working out what information is relevant to the task. At worst some settle for selecting and copying those sentences, which they hope might meet the task. In this way weaker GCSE candidates will merely write out or paraphrase a sentence or two from a source in a hit or miss fashion. Counsell (1997) has noted pupils' difficulties distinguishing between the general and the particular; they have problems seeing the difference between the larger point and an example. Similarly, Cottingham and Daborn (1999) found that pupils have difficulty distinguishing significant conclusions and supporting evidence from the irrelevant and the superficial with the resulting tendency to write an unselective narrative. This is a problem that extends to A Level students, who often need to be taught how to make notes from an academic text with awareness of what they are looking for, otherwise their notes revealingly may be a random selection of facts.

4   *Language.* In addition to the considerable challenges of spelling and grammar written work in any subject presents to pupils, the specific tasks set in history have their own problems with language. Counsell (1997) has effectively identified the difficulties pupils have when they are asked to produce analytical and discursive writing. Pupils lack the skills and conventions required for such writing, for example, appropriate ways of beginning sentences and paragraphs and the use of modal verbs.

Strategies for improving the quality of your students' written work

1   *Preparation.* The problems which pupils can encounter with written work show the importance of preparation and clearly written work should not be perceived as the

'end-on' part of the learning process. Writing should not merely be an outcome but a valuable pedagogical tool for developing higher order thinking in history (Counsell, 1997). You will benefit from thinking about the ways different types of writing activities can be incorporated into your lesson planning. For doing this, it is useful to apply to history teaching the advice from *Literacy Across the Curriculum*:

● Establish both the purpose and the audience of the writing.
● Ensure the pupils have something to say and enough information for the task.
● Give the pupils opportunities to develop, shape and revise ideas.
● Encourage collaboration during planning and drafting.
● Make sure the pupils have access to reference material such as word banks, glossaries as well as historical resources.
● Build in opportunities for feedback both during and after writing. (DfEE, 2001)

2   *Presentation.* You will find your pupils will benefit from being made aware of your expectations of the final product of their writing. Be explicit about 'success criteria'. Cottingham and Daborn (1999) found that pupils responded positively to the exposure to and analysis of examples of extended writing as models for their own writing. At times there is a case for writing standard English, at others rough jottings will suffice. It could be that pupils use different ends of their exercise book for these different writing requirements. You need to *consider how the pupils' exercise book is to be used*. There may be a case, particularly with GCSE classes, for having two exercise books, each serving a different writing function and each intended for a different audience. Rough notes, jottings, draft versions, recording of ideas, summaries of group decisions in one book; more formal writing and recording of information in another. Do not always be concerned with tidiness as pupils work out their ideas. On some occasions work is set out on white boards or on separate paper especially if there is to be a display of pupil work.

3   *Clarity of Instructions.* A common weakness of student teachers is the limited quality of their instructions. To avoid having to stop the class when they have settled to their work to clarify directions and give further guidance, it is important that you have thought through exactly what instructions you need to give. You need to anticipate the pupils' requirements about layout, length of work, use of proper sentences, whether they write out the question, ensure they write in their own words and understand the basis upon which you will be marking the work.

4   *Process.* Behind these considerations of the mechanics of how written work is presented, lies a much more fundamental point about *how you encourage pupils to do themselves justice with their work*. It can be argued that in the past insufficient attention was given to the process by which pupils achieve the quality of work expected, especially extended writing. However, the last decade has experienced a considerable improvement in the way teachers have anticipated the problems outlined above and have adopted strategies by which they may be overcome. For this Counsell (1997) has provided valuable guidance. Her Historical Association booklet, *Analytical and Discursive Writing in National Curriculum History at Key Stage 3: A Practical Guide* is very much a positive document, which encourages you to discount the siren voices which deny pupils' capability. Her message is clearly that pupils can achieve a great deal in their writing if the problems are properly addressed. These are in many ways organisational. Hence the recommendation

to employ a whole range of sorting and classifying activities to help pupils deal with the information, encourage their historical thinking by various forms of classification, identify what is relevant, and structure their writing. The degree to which the 'scaffolding' of support for writing is provided can vary according to the extent to which the pupils are proficient in extended writing. With a Year 7 class, which is being introduced to the idea of essay work, this might entail writing a first sentence for each paragraph; where proficiency is variable within the same teaching group it might be achieved by providing suggestions for introductory and linking sentences on the classroom walls.

'Some sources suggest that...'

'However, others suggest...'

'Sources which have something in common are...'

'We cannot be sure about *x* because...'

'A source which sheds some light on this is...'

'Another important factor was...' (Counsell, 1997: 31)

Counsell also uses the idea of 'the zone of relevance', to help pupils to grasp that not all sources of information are relevant (and therefore 'evidence') for a particular question or enquiry. As an example, she suggests that the following statements are given to pupils whose task is to find out why the Great Fire of London got out of control and spread so quickly:

- town officials did not believe that it was going to spread and took no action at the start;
- houses in London were built very close together;
- most buildings were made of wood;
- someone started a fire in Pudding Lane;
- water supplies were unusually low in 1666;
- fire fighting equipment was not good enough to cope with a large fire;
- throughout London, heating and lighting were provided by fire.

They are asked to place in the 'zone of relevance' the statements containing information which helps to answer the question posed (Counsell, 1997: 42). The idea can also be used to develop the idea of 'topic relevance' and 'question' relevance', by incorporating statements which have neither topic nor question relevance.

Wray and Lewis (1994) were also concerned with helping pupils to structure their written work and advocated the use of writing frames, as long as they are flexible enough to allow able pupils to amend them. Bakalis (2003) gives a detailed account of how teaching pupils to structure a paragraph at the same time advances their historical understanding by considering the opening statement, its explanation, substantiation and conclusion. In this way pupils were encouraged to make their thought processes both logical and explicit and helped them towards greater understanding of history's key concepts.

Counsell (1997) again seeks to meet language problems with a range of strategies such as 'clever starters', a selection of starting phrases or words, sentence stems or paragraph openers, which can be on permanent display in the classroom. There can also be 'starters' for different types of historical questions such as causation. Other ways of helping pupils to start and to structure their writing include the use of mind minds and concept maps. Such activities bring together several of the language skills encouraged by the (now largely forgotten) National Strategy. Goodwin (2006) shows how through discussion the creation of a mind map of the First World War trenches became an effective plan for a piece of written work on that subject. Similarly, Van Drie and Van Boxtel (2003) showed how the value of pairs working with concept cards could be used not only to help pupils' understanding of the concepts, but also to create a structure for the outline of an essay. Counsell (1997, 2004) makes the important point that as pupils progress, 'scaffolding' such as writing frames needs to be removed. The long-term aim is to bring pupils to a point where they can write autonomously, without support.

The range of written work

You will find it helpful to keep in mind the range of written work that is possible in the learning of history. Curtis (1994) suggests an audit of how writing is used in history involving not only the types of written task undertaken by pupils but also how they are prepared for such tasks. There could be various ways of presenting such an audit. Here, six types of writing are identified and discussed.

Descriptive

You will find such writing is a prominent feature of Key Stage 3.

Types

These can include transferring into writing representations such as pictures, maps, diagrams and time-charts; describing historical sites; writing comparisons of photographs and sources.

Use and differentiation

Many pupils feel comfortable with descriptive writing, but the less able pupils may need something, which has already been written (e.g. completing a paragraph begun by the teacher or sequencing activities, which involve rewriting in the correct order statements linked to pictures). Gap-filling exercises are frequently used. These can offer useful support, but you should look for every opportunity to move the pupils on from such tasks and encourage them to use their own words. *Many pupils may also need to be encouraged to go beyond description.* A common experience is for pupils, when asked to compare two sources, to describe each in turn without commenting on the differences.

The nature of this writing particularly is determined by its function and the person for whom it is intended.

Types

Such writing could include rough jottings, notes for discussion, notes for group presentation or notes taken on a site visit. Alternatively the recording may be notes, which the pupil needs to use at a later date in preparation for an examination.

Use and differentiation

Note-making is an activity that plays a significant role in history teaching but Ofsted have noted as a weakness that drafting and note-making are often not well-developed. There may be a case for developing skills in note-making, but in such a way that the practice also serves to reinforce and extend the pupils' understanding. The emphasis therefore is not on 'note-taking' but on 'note-making' as the pupils use their own words and not those dictated by the teacher or copied verbatim from the board or the textbook. Your task is to help the pupils, in varying degrees according to their ability, to structure their notes. Following initial information, derived from teacher exposition, the viewing and discussion of a video, or the analysis of sources, the abler pupils in all years of the secondary school are quite capable of making their own notes given some structure in the form of sub-headings on the board, spellings of proper names and any statistics involved. The amount of information will be extended for the average pupils, whilst with the slower pupils note making follows greater reinforcement and requests to write a complete sentences extending what has been written on the board. The weakest may complete sentences the teacher has begun but still with some scope for their own words. If reference is to be made to information in books, *try to structure the work so that copying can be avoided*. Pupils are more likely to understand the content if they are required to express it in their own words.

Expressive

This is the 'personal' aspect of writing, where pupils are allowed to write with a more personal voice, in contrast to situations where the fear of making mistakes stifles opinion.

Types

Such writing can include the preparation for debate, comments on a dvd extract, on group decisions or participation in a role play.

Use and differentiation

Differentiation is often achieved by the extent to which evidence is used to support such opinion.

Imaginative

Another writing activity that is released from the more formal, impersonal kind of writing is that which is more creative and inventive.

Types

Such creative efforts can involve writing from the perspective of someone in the past, diaries, reports, eyewitness accounts, letters, plays, provided that the imaginative work is rooted in evidence to create a genuinely historical activity.

Use and differentiation

It is worthy of note that often through this type of writing a pupil can display a greater understanding of the historical context than other writing might suggest. Imaginative work can also cover the consideration of hypotheses, the 'what if' questions. Differentiation is usually by outcome and, again, the extent to which the work is rooted in historical evidence.

Analytical/evaluative

As made explicit in the task, which follows, the quality of this type of writing is greatly influenced by the methodology, which precedes it, as the problems inherent in this type of writing are tackled.

Types

Examples of such writing includes pupils being asked to group together and classify ideas and data and employ the relevant vocabulary to describe such grouping; the analysis of changes, causes and consequences or in the evaluation of sources and interpretations.

Use and differentiation

Much of Counsell's work (1997, 2004) is very relevant here with the intention to reduce gradually the support offered. For the able, beware of the restrictive nature of writing frames and also note the possibilities for the able to service their own analysis by creating their own categories, sorting cards and format of response.

Synthesis

This is arguably the most demanding of the written tasks you can set in the teaching of history, where pupils are required to reconstruct an event, create an extended explanation, answer a question at length or present an interpretation – all compositions based on a variety of evidence. Such a synthesis could take the form of a piece of narrative writing. Lang (2003) has described the writing of narrative as an underrated skill, which deserves to be restored as a valid intellectual exercise capable of rigorous assessment. The value of historical narrative is also considered in the Historical Association report, *History 14-19* (2005), with further emphasis on the construction of a narrative as a high order skill in need of rehabilitation.

Use and differentiation

For example, if pupils are to compile a comprehensive answer to questions such as 'What was it like living in (your home town) during the Second World War?' they need to be taken through a series of stages of research, recording, classifying and writing if they are to achieve a satisfactory synthesis.

Sources of good ideas for history lessons

The internet and the growth of social media has meant that history teachers do not have to come up with all their own ideas for lessons as was the case 20 years ago. It is however important to have a strong sense of initiative and resourcefulness in developing your repertoire of teaching approaches. Some student teachers tend to be reliant to a degree on 'what there is available in the department', others scavenge voraciously for resources and are constantly hunting for good ideas to use in their lessons.

It is not cheating, or plagiarism to look for ideas for your lessons from some of the many history internet websites which are available, but you must beware of thinking that such resources come 'shrink wrapped' and absolutely ready to use, without any research, adaptation and 'tweaking' to fit your purposes. Usually, you have to download the resources and instructions for their use well before you are due to teach the lesson, and spend time and care reading through the guidance, so that you are quite clear how to deploy the lesson you have acquired. It is very helpful that someone else has spent many hours putting together a 'learning package' on a particular topic, but occasionally, student teachers can get a bit lazy, and not do their 'homework' by rigorously preparing the package for teaching. Some useful 'repositories' of good ideas for history lessons are provided in Figure 5.6.

All these suggestions are based on feedback from student teachers who have recently 'been through the system'. In addition to the examples cited here, see the longer list of history websites in Chapter 9.

Ian Dawson's *Thinking History* website (www. thinkinghistory.co.uk). Particularly good for intelligent and well-focused active learning approaches and suggestions for the development of independent learning.

Amjad Ali's *Agility Toolkit,* http://cheneyagilitytoolkit.blogspot.co.uk. A very wide range of ideas to try out – not history specific.

Facing History and Ourselves, www.facinghistory.org/for-educators/educator-resources/teaching-strategies. Although dedicated mainly to Civil Rights and Holocaust Education, the 'Teaching approaches' section of the website contains a wide range of teaching approaches that could be adapted to work with other subject content.

Paul Ginnis's *Teachers' Toolkit* (book). Not history specific and first edition 2002, London Crown House, but recommended by large numbers of teachers.

National Archives website, www.nationalarchives.gov.uk/education. One of the world's leading history education websites, with a wide range of appropriate and well thought out activities relevant to most NC, GCSE and A level topics.

School History Project website, www.schoolshistoryproject.org.uk/index.php. SHP host one of the most popular and enduring CPD conferences for teachers and in recent years, the site has become much better for curating many of the keynote presentations and workshop featured at the conferences.

QCA schemes of work, http://webarchive.nationalarchives.gov.uk/20090608182316/http://standards.dfes.gov.uk/schemes2/secondary_history/?view=get. Although these resources were developed to support teachers working on the last version of the NC for history, the substantial element of continuity between the previous and current versions of the NC for history mean that much of the content is still relevant, and the schemes of work were devised by many of England's leading history teachers and history educators.

Schoolhistory (www.schoolhistory.co.uk). Another massive site, and the History Teachers' Forum is one of the main social media portals for history teachers, with over 100,000 posts at the time of writing this chapter.

Russel Tarr's Active History www.activehistory.co.uk, A subscription site with some free content. An astonishing range of ideas for history lessons, from a history teacher who was attacked by spokespersons for the DfE for his 'Mr Men' activities.

Figure 5.7 Some useful sources for lesson ideas

Summary and key points

You have been encouraged to consider what assumptions you may be making in how you choose to cover a topic, assumptions about the contribution to pupils' understanding when required to listen, read, talk and write. Such consideration helps you to anticipate potential difficulties in the approaches and the materials you choose to use and to employ strategies to help the pupils succeed. This often means helping pupils through such difficulties rather than helping them to get round them: in Counsell's phrase, not teaching by avoidance with a negative 'can't do' approach but seeking to help all pupils. The styles of teaching you adopt reflects your understanding of the processes by which the pupils learn.

The key points which this chapter has emphasised are that you avoid getting into too repetitious a style with a very limited range of approaches and are prepared to take some risks as your confidence grows. Look carefully at any reading material before you use it and try to anticipate any potential difficulties it may create. Remember it is your job to sell the subject, to demonstrate a genuine interest in the past and to ensure the pupils value the contribution of history to their education. Consider the value of using 'higher' order questions and also of creating situations for pupils to ask questions. Reading can be both underused and badly used – think carefully about how you can maximise the use of reading materials but be careful not to use the textbook as an easy option. This chapter has attempted to emphasise that pupils often only understand historical content if they are given the opportunities to express it in their own way. Hence the importance of activities which include the structured use of pupil talk and the opportunities to write in their own words. Finally you are encouraged to carry out an audit of the variety of writing activities you set over a period of time as a means of ensuring you employ the range covered by this chapter.

Suggestions for further reading

Barton, G. (2013) *Don't Call it Literacy: What every teacher needs to know about speaking, listening, reading and writing*, London: David Fulton. A really useful and concise guide for these areas, with sections on 'How to explain things more clearly', 'How to ask better questions', 'How to write discursively', and 'How to build a reading culture'.

Coffey, C. (2006) *Historical Discourse: The language of time, cause and evaluation*, London: Continuum.
Counsell, C. (2004) *History in Practice: History and Literacy in Y7: Building the lesson around the text*, London: Longman.
Gershon, M. (2013) *Secondary Starters and Plenaries in History*, London: Bloomsbury.
Ward, C. and Logie, S. (2009) *History Mysteries*, London: Chris Kingston.

For further resources on the issues covered in this chapter, and suggestions for further reading, go to www.uea.ac.uk/~m242/historypgce/.

References

Adey, K. and Biddulph, M. (2001) The Influence of Pupil Perceptions on Subject Choice at 14+ in Geography and History, *Educational Studies*, 27 (4): 439-50.
Bakalis, M. (2003) Direct teaching of paragraph cohesion, *Teaching History*, No. 110: 18-26.
Banham, D. (1998) Getting ready for the Grand Prix: learning how to build a substantiated argument in Year 7, *Teaching History*, No. 92: 6-15.
Banham, D. and Dawson, I. (2002) Thinking from the inside: je suis le roi, *Teaching History*, No. 108: 12-18.
Bloom, B.S. (1956) *Taxonomy of Educational Objectives: Cognitive Domain*, London: David McKay.
Bruner, J. (1960) *The Process of Education*, Cambridge Mass.: Harvard University Press.
Burn, K. (2006) *Professional Knowledge and Identity in a Contested Discipline: Challenges for student teachers and teacher educators*, paper presented at the EERA Conference, University of Geneva, 14 September.
Burston, W. (1963) *Principles of Teaching History*, London: Methuen.
Byrom, J. and Riley, M. (2003) Professional wrestling in the history department: a case study in planning the teaching of the British Empire at key stage 3, *Teaching History*, No. 112: 6-14.
Clark, V. (2001) Illuminating the shadow: making progress happen in causal thinking through speaking and listening, *Teaching History*, No. 105: 26-33.
Chapman, A. (2006) Asses, archers and assumptions: strategies for improving thinking skills in history in Years 9 to 13, *Teaching History*, No. 123: 6-13.
Chapman, A. (2011) *What does it mean to 'think historically and what do we know about how to develop children's historical thinking?*, online at www.ahdr.info/ckfinder/userfiles/files/October_workshop_Arthur_Chapman_write_-up.pdf, accessed 14 April 2014.
Christodoulou, D. (2014) *Seven Myths about Education*, London: Routledge.
Cottingham, M and Daborn, J. (1999) *What impacts can the development of Literacy Teaching have on the teaching and learning of history*. Conclusions at: www.tda.gov.uk/upload/resources/pdf/c/cottingham-daborn.pdf, accessed 10 October 2007.
Counsell, C. (1997) *Analytical and discursive writing in National Curriculum history at Key Stage 3, a practical guide*, London: Historical Association, online at www.history.org.uk/resources/resource_1948.html, accessed 12 August 2014.
Counsell, C. (1999) Teaching history, *History Today*, 49 (11): 18-21.
Counsell, C. (2004) *History and literacy in Year 7: building the lesson around the text*, London, Longman.
Counsell, C. (2008) 'Intriguing texts', *Times Educational Supplement*, 12 May.
Curtis, S. (1994) Communication in History, *Teaching History*, No.77, October: 25-30.
DES, (1975) *A Language for Life* (The Bullock Report), London: HMSO.
DfEE (2001) *Literacy Across the Curriculum*, London: DfEE.
DfES (2004) *Literacy in History*, London: DfES.

DfE (2013) History programmes of study: key stage 3 National Curriculum in England, London, DfE, online at www.gov.uk/government/uploads/system/uploads/attachment_data/file/239075/SECONDARY_national_curriculum_-_History.pdf, accessed 14 April 2014.

DfE (2014) *Proposed GCE AS and A Level Subject Content for History* and *History GCSE subject content*, London, DfE.

Duff, R. (1998) Appeasement Role Play: the alternative to Munich, *Teaching History*, No. 90, January, 17–19.

Edwards, A.D. and Furlong, V.J. (1978) *The Language of Teaching*, Oxford: Heinemann.

Garvey, B. and Krug, M. (1977) *Models of History Teaching in the Secondary School*, Oxford: Oxford University Press.

Goodwin, S. (2006) 'Learning Strategies and Approaches' in M. Hunt (ed) *A Practical Guide to Teaching History in the Secondary School*, London: RoutledgeFalmer: 27–36.

Gove, M. (2013) 'Michael Gove talks about the importance of teaching', speech, Department for Education, 5 September,

Guscott, S. (2006) 'Roleplay as active history', in M. Hunt (ed.) *A Practical Guide to Teaching History in the Secondary School*, London, Routledge: 53–62.

Hake, C. and Haydn, T. (1995) Stories or sources?, *Teaching History*, No. 78: 20–22.

Happold, F. (1927) *The Study of History in Schools, as a Training in the Art of Thought*, London: Bell.

Harris, R. and Haydn, R. (2006) Pupils' enjoyment of history – what lessons can teachers learn from their pupils?, *Curriculum Journal*, 17 (4): 315–33.

Hellier, D. and Richards, H, (2005) Do we have to read all this? Encouraging students to read for understanding, *Teaching History*, No. 118: 44–8.

Historical Association, (2005) *History 14-19. Report and recommendations to the Secretary of State*, London: Historical Association.

Husbands, C. (1996) *What is History Teaching?*, Buckingham: Open University Press.

Husbands, C, Kitson, A. and Pendry, A. (2003) *Understanding History Teaching*, Buckingham: Open University Press.

Joseph, K. (1984) Why teach history in school? *The Historian*, No. 2: 10–12.

Lacey, R. (2006) *Great tales from English History* (3 volumes), London: Little Brown.

Lang, S. (2003) Narrative – the underrated skill, *Teaching History*, No. 110: 8–13.

Lawton, D. (1985) *Education, Culture and the Curriculum*, London: Hodder and Stoughton.

Lee, P., Ashby, R. and Dickinson, A. (1995) 'Progression in children's ideas about history', in M. Hughes (ed.) *Progression in Learning*, BERA Dialogues II Cleveden: Multilingual Matters, 50–81.

Lesh, B. (2011) *Why won't you just tell us the answer? Teaching historical thinking in grades 7-12*, USA: Stenhouse Press.

Lewis, M and Wray, D. (2000) *Literacy in the Secondary School*, London: David Fulton.

Loy, M. (2008) Learning to read, reading to learn: strategies to move students from 'keen to learn' to 'keen to read', *Teaching History*, No. 132: 25–9.

Luff, I. (2000) I've been in Reichstag: rethinking role play, *Teaching History*, No. 100: 8–17.

Luff, I. (2001) Beyond I speak, you listen, boy! Exploring diversity of attitudes and experiences through speaking and listening, *Teaching History*, No. 105: 10–18.

Luff, I. (2003) Stretching the straightjacket of assessment: use of role play and practical demonstration to enrich pupils' experience of history at GCSE and beyond, *Teaching History*, No. 113: 26–35.

McCully, A, (1997) Key questions, planning and extended Writing, *Teaching History*, No. 89: 31–5.

NASC (Norwich Area Schools Consortium) (2002) *Classroom management*, online at www.uea.ac.uk/~m242/nasc/cross/cman/overallchar.htm, accessed 2 April 2014.

Ofsted (2002) *History in Secondary Schools*. Subject reports series 2001-2, HMI 813, London: Ofsted.

Ofsted (2005) *History in Secondary Schools*. Annual report for 2004/5, London: Ofsted.

Ofsted (2011) History for all, London, Ofsted, online at www.ofsted.gov.uk/resources/history-for-all, accessed 14 April 2014.

QCA (2005) Pupil perceptions of history at Key Stage 3, online at www.uea.ac.uk/~m242/historypgce/qcafinalreport.pdf, accessed 10 March 2014.

QCA (2007) *History: programmes of study: Key Stage 3*, London: QCA.

Riley, M. (2006) Quoted in Final report: Historical Association's key stage 2-3 history transition project, London, Historical Association, online at www.history.org.uk/resources/primary_resource_3616_127.html, accessed 3 April 2014.

Rudham, R. (2001) A noisy classroom is a thinking classroom, speaking and listening in Year 7 history, *Teaching History*, No. 105: 35-41.

Schools Council (1978) *Writing across the Curriculum Project, writing in geography, history and social studies*, London: Ward Lock.

Scott, A. (2006) Essay writing for everyone: an investigation into different methods used to teach Year 9 to write an essay, *Teaching History*, No. 123: 26-36.

Van Boxtel, C. (2010) *Something to Talk About: The potential of a dynamic approach to heritage*, address to the EUROCLIO Conference, Nijmegen, 26 March.

Van Drie, J. and Van Boxtel, C. (2003) Developing conceptual understanding through talk and mapping, *Teaching History*, No. 110: 27-31.

Wiliam, D. (2011) *Embedded formative assessment*, Bloomington IN: Solution Tree Press.

Wilkinson, A. (2006) Little Jack Horner and polite revolutionaries: putting the story back into history, *Teaching History*, No. 123: 16-20.

Willingham, D. (2009) Why don't students like school?, San Francisco: Jossey-Bass.

Willingham, D. (2012) Quoted in 'Education expert cautions Michael Gove over heavy reliance on exams', *The Guardian*, 28 December.

Wilson, M.D. (1985) *History for Pupils with Learning Difficulties*, London: Hodder and Stoughton.

Woodhead, C. (1996) Radio 4, 25 July.

Wray, D. and Lewis, M. (1994) 'Extending literacy in the junior school', in A. Littlefair (ed.) *Literacy for life*, London: UK Reading Assocation.

6 Developing historical understanding (1)

Time, cause, change, similarity and difference, empathy, significance

Introduction

One consequence of recent developments in the teaching and learning of history is an emphasis on the importance of concepts - substantive, as well as second-order concepts (see Chapter 2). This chapter considers how you might set about teaching some of these concepts. It is now generally accepted that the more sophisticated your pupils' understanding of these concepts, when related to historical content, the greater is the depth of their historical understanding.

Objectives

By the end of this chapter you should be able to:

- understand the contribution of the concepts of time, cause, change, similarity and difference and significance to pupils' historical understanding;
- recognise some common misconceptions which pupils may have when confronted with these concepts;
- identify some problems pupils may experience in understanding the characteristic features and diversity of particular periods and societies;
- devise a range of teaching strategies with which to develop your pupils' understanding of these concepts.

The importance of organising concepts in the teaching and learning of history

An awareness of the importance of organising concepts such as chronology helps to ensure that history is not reduced to dismembered and isolated gobbets of the past, which are not reconciled into a coherent framework or useable 'mental map' of the past by pupils. One of your responsibilities as a history teacher is to provide *an overview of the past* so that pupils emerge from school history with some sense of the stages which humans have gone through to get to where we are today. When covering particular events or topics, some attempt must be made to put them in their overall historical context if the pupils are to develop a meaningful sense of the past.

Concentration on such concepts helps the move away from an image of learning history as one represented by 'stories from the past' or of factual content which has, in the eyes of pupils, very little connection with the business of living at the beginning of the twenty-first century. Just as importantly:

> Focusing exclusively on the logic of history as an academic discipline, and distancing it from the variety of ways in which history is used in the wider society, may lead students to dismiss the subject as one that has little relevance to their own lives. (Barton, 2009: 265)

The understanding and use of key concepts in history helps to underline the significance of historical events and processes. Sansom (1987) argued that the application of these concepts, or 'tools of thought', helps to turn information into historical knowledge. It is also possible to assert that, even when a pupil's recall of specific detail diminishes, the understanding that comes from conclusions about the significance of an event or events is the enduring educational outcome.

Your pupils today live in a world of constant and rapid change and a historical perspective helps them to place such changes into a wider context and to begin to understand the complex and interrelated nature of the causes of change. At the same time there are aspects of life that do not change. Pupils today share a common humanity with people in the past and there is much to learn from the study of the response of different peoples, groups and individuals to situations that confront them. An emphasis on these concepts also presents a useful guide to the choice of topics within a syllabus, when the amount of time available means there has to be a discerning selection of the content you choose to teach. Finally, as we hope to demonstrate in the chapter, your pupils are more likely to succeed in developing this aspect of their historical understanding if they are actively engaged in their use of knowledge.

Teaching pupils about time

It would seem to be a reasonable proposition to suggest that part of the function of school history should be to give pupils some understanding of time and chronology. If pupils are to make sense of history, they need to have some idea about how we 'measure' and reference events in history in terms of when they occurred, and to build up a mental framework of the past. Although secondary pupils have studied history for at least six years, there may still be 'black holes' in their grasp of fundamental aspects of the concept of time.

It should be remembered that under the original NC for History, it was possible to get to Level 10 in all of the attainment targets for the subject, without knowing what century you were living in, or what A.D. and B.C. meant. Time was, at least to some extent, a neglected and forgotten element of the subject, and this was reflected in the textbooks which were published at the inception of the National Curriculum. A survey of over a thousand year 7 pupils found that many did not know which century they were living in, what A.D. meant, or what words such as 'reign', or 'chronology' meant (Haydn and Levy, 1995). When asked about the reasons for these deficiencies, some heads of history suggested that there was an assumption that 'all that had been covered at primary school', or that they had just taken such understanding for granted, or that as it was not part of the '45 boxes' of the original Attainment Targets, it had not been a focus for teaching and assessment. Whatever the reasons, it is important that you do not assume that all your pupils possess a clear grasp of the rudiments of time and chronology. Whereas time was a comparatively peripheral concern of the original NC for History, its status has been restored in the revised versions, and chronology is an integral part of the most recent version of the NC for History at Key Stage 3, introduced in September 2014, one of the aims stating that pupils should 'know and understand the history of these islands as a coherent, chronological narrative' (DfE, 2013: 1).

One advantage of the NC has been that all pupils have had some instruction in history at Key Stages 1 and 2, but as pupils are of differing abilities, and have come from different feeder schools, it would be surprising if they all arrived at secondary school with a similar depth or breadth of understanding about time. One of the tasks of the history teacher is to gain some insight into what knowledge and understandings pupils bring with them *before* you start to teach the topic or concept in question. Time may well have been approached in a very different manner in various primary schools; some have learned through family trees and timelines, others have started with ancient history and worked forward. Some already have a sound grasp of dating systems and some idea of a general 'framework' of the past, others may have passed through Key Stages 1 and 2 without having mastered even the lowest levels of attainment in this domain of history.

The complexities involved in developing pupils' understanding of time and chronology

Task 6.1 *A diagnostic exercise on children's understanding of Time*

The following weblink provides an example of a diagnostic test of children's understanding of some aspects of time, which might be given to year 7 pupils in order to elicit their grasp of some elements of the concept of time:

www.uea.ac.uk/~m242/historypgce/time/t1/time1.htm or http://terryhaydn.wordpress.com/pgce-history-at-uea/time-and-chronology

With the permission of your tutor and if the pupils have not already been subjected to such a test, give the test to a group of pupils and analyse their responses. The test should take pupils between 5 and 15 minutes to complete. The test attempts to address pupils' understanding of dating systems, their ability to understand and manipulate 'centuries', and their familiarity with some time-related vocabulary. If the pupils have already done a similar form of test, ask your tutor how the pupils performed, and what 'gaps' there were in their grasp of basic time concepts. When the pupils have completed the test, analyse their responses to examine where there are gaps in their understanding of time. What activities might you devise in order to rectify any deficiencies in their understanding of time?

Approaches to time and chronology

The activity in Task 6.1 addresses a particular strand of children's understanding of time; that of the 'mechanics' of time – dating systems and conventions, basic time vocabulary, how time 'works'. Although this is important, there are other aspects of time which children need to address. One of these is an understanding of chronology, and a developing sense of the order of events in history. Children should develop a mental framework of the past through the study of history. As the History Working Group's Final Report pointed out, 'A grasp of the sequence of events is fundamental to an understanding of the relationship between events, and such concepts as cause and change. Chronology, therefore, provides a mental framework or map which gives significance and coherence to the study of history' (DES, 1990). The tendency in recent years to study 'patches' or 'themes' in history, rather than a measured and even progression from 'The Romans towards the present day', has meant that not all pupils have a clear grasp of the overall unfolding of events in history, or of the 'duration' of different periods. The nature of the GCSE exam, with its emphasis on the critical examination of sources, means that it might be possible to gain full marks on a source-based question on World War II, without necessarily knowing who was on whose side, and who won. There are also some areas of history where is it essential to have a clear grasp of the precise *order* of events as a necessary, if not sufficient basis for providing a coherent explanation or analysis of a historical event, such as the outbreak of World War I, or the campaigns of 1066. Understanding of 'Deep Time' – the distant past stretching back to pre-history, the Stone Age and the formation of the earth might also be a facet of time which might be addressed in the course of school history. An understanding of what is meant by the term 'prehistory' can help to give pupils some insight into the nature of the discipline of history itself. Dawson (2012) points out that understanding 'duration' is also a facet of pupils' understanding of time. Giving pupils 'a sense of period' has also been mentioned as one of the desirable aims of teaching pupils about time (Dawson, 2009; Smith, 2014). There is therefore much more involved in developing pupils' understanding of time that simply teaching history in chronological order (Blow *et al.*, 2012). Barton points out that such an approach may be unhelpful:

> Research shows that children make sense of historical time by comparing people, events and periods to certain reference points.... A curriculum that proceeds in strict chronological order has the opposite effect: it limits the range of periods that pupils will become familiar with, thus limiting their temporal understanding. (Barton, 2009: 267)

It might be helpful to classify the teaching and learning of time into categories so that you have a clear sense of the various facets of time which need to be addressed in the development of pupils' understanding of the past. For convenience, we have labelled these, T1, to T6.

T1= The mechanics of time – dating systems and conventions, time vocabulary, how time works. In the same way that pupils need to understand the 24-hour clock, if they are studying history, they need to know 'the clock of history'.

T2= The framework of the past; building up a map of the past in terms of a developing sense of what bits of history fit in where. The chronology and sequence of strands of history, for example, the changing nature of monarchy in Britain over the centuries, the evolution of methods of transport, warfare, energy. Sometimes referred to as building up pupils' 'big picture' knowledge of the past.

T3= Building up an increasing range of historical topics or episodes where pupils have a sound grasp of the order in which events unfolded. This might include areas such as the changes in religious policy in England in the sixteenth and seventeenth centuries, the key events and turning points in World War II, or an understanding of the chronology of the French Revolution. If pupils have a confident grasp of the order of events *and* can explain why each event occurred, they are some way towards being able to construct an explanation of elements of the past.

T4= Developing pupils' understanding of 'Deep Time'. Giving pupils an understanding of the scale of the past, from the formation of the Earth, through prehistory to the development of writing and on to A.D. Part of this is helping pupils through misconceptions about when humans appeared on Earth, and when 'history' started.

T5= Developing pupils' understanding of 'duration' in the past, and understanding that there are 'overlaps' in history. For example, the Indus Valley civilisation and civilisation in Ancient Egypt did not come after one another, there was an overlap.

T6= Giving pupils 'a sense of period'; the idea that there were particular characteristics of certain periods of history.

It should be stressed that this list is far from comprehensive in terms of understanding time, but it might serve as a useful guide for what history teachers need to keep in mind when they are working to develop their pupils' grasp of time and chronology. If you are doing a Masters Degree in this field, Lorenz (in press) provides a useful guide to the complexities of this area.

Figure 6.1 Aspects of pupils' understanding of time and chronology

Teaching strategies

Your skills of exposition in providing narrative frameworks of the past are an important part of developing pupils' grasp of time and chronology, including an awareness that pupils do not possess the map of the past that some teachers take for granted. The use of timelines in the classroom, as well as in exercise books, can be helpful. The development of sequencing exercises, whether on cards, for group work, in exercise books, on the blackboard, or on a word processor can provide activities which require pupils to think through the precise order of events, using inference as well as knowledge, but there is a danger of sequencing for its own sake; that is, constructing arbitrary lists of historical events which have no necessary connection with each other. Dawson (2004) offers a range of well thought out 'overview' activities, and his website, *Thinking History* provides a number of eminently practicable 'active learning' approaches to the development of pupils' understanding of chronology (www.thinkinghistory.co.uk/Issues/IssueChronology.html).

The following are examples of exercises which might be given to pupils to develop their understanding of some of these facets of time and chronology.

T1 exercises

a) The following words are all used to note an amount or length of time. Organise them into the correct order, putting the shortest at the top, and the longest at the bottom.

shortest	year
	hour
	Decade
	second
	Millennium
	Century
	Minute
	Week
	Month
	Day
longest	

b) The following are all terms, which are used to describe periods of time in history. Place them in the table below, where you think they belong, and then put them in order, with the earliest at the top of each column, and the most recent at the bottom.

Renaissance   Stone Age   Tudor   Pre-Raphaelite   Bronze Age   Hanoverian

Ancient   Pre-Industrial   Plantagenet   Medieval   Modern   Reformation

Victorian   Gothic   Norman   Postmodern   Early Modern   Georgian   Dark Ages

Impressionist   Cubist   Space Age   Prehistory   Regency   Restoration   Windsor

(This is an example which might be appropriate for very able, or older pupils, but it would be fairly easy to draft simpler versions.) The most able pupils might be asked to identify their own categories.

Royal Family	General terms	Architecture	Named after historical events	Painting

For examples of T2/3/4 exercises, go to www.uea.ac.uk/~m242/historypgce/time/framework.htm

Task 6.2 *Devising an exercise on time*

1   With the permission of your tutor, try out an exercise on time, and evaluate its results.
2   Try to devise an exercise of your own, which might be used by pupils at Key Stage 3 or 4, which is focused on one of these aspects of pupils' understanding of time.
3   Try to devise a pupil activity which attempts to develop pupils' understanding of T4 ('Deep Time'), or ask pupils about their ideas about the distant past.

Putting time periods into chronological order

Chronology means putting things in the order in which they happened. Look at the images of these different time periods and try to put them into chronological order, that is to say, the order in which these time periods occurred, from the earliest periods, to the one closest to today.

Figure 6.2 An example of a 'T2' exercise

Are dates important? Differing views

A recent survey found that only 4 per cent of people knew that The Battle of Waterloo was fought in 1815. Is this a dreadful indictment of history teachers, or have history teachers better things to do than stuff children's heads with dates? How important is it that pupils should learn 'key' dates in British history? For the views of some pupils, history teachers and historians, see: www.uea.ac.uk/~m242/historypgce/time/dates/dateswelcome.htm.

Further information about children's understanding of time, research findings, and suggested activities can be found at: www.uea.ac.uk/~m242/historypgce/time or http://terryhaydn.wordpress.com/pgce-history-at-uea/time-and-chronology

Similarity and difference, within and across time periods

Under the previous Key Stage 3 specifications, 'cultural, ethnic and religious diversity' was identified as one of the six 'Key Concepts' in the NC for history (QCA, 2007). With the introduction of the new NC for history (DfE, 2013), there has been a tendency for history teachers to revert to earlier ideas of 'similarity and difference' (see, for example, McCrory, 2013).

The earlier requirement that pupils should be taught to describe and analyse the 'characteristic features' of periods and societies studied (DfEE/QCA, 1999) is no longer explicit, but this does not mean that helping pupils to understand characteristic features of periods and societies studied ceases to be a concern of history teachers. A real challenge for the history teacher is to prevent pupils lapsing into stereotypes and lazy generalisations about the past, and to get pupils to understand that periods and societies can have characteristic features, whilst still possessing diversity within those patterns and features (for example, urbanisation and the factory system were a feature of the Industrial Revolution, but this does not mean that everyone worked in factories and lived in cities after the invention of the Spinning Jenny and Compton's Mule).

What are the perceived educational outcomes of studying 'the range of ideas, beliefs and attitudes of people' of particular periods and societies? Why is it considered important that pupils analyse the 'social, cultural, religious and ethnic diversity' of particular societies? Is it possible that one of the objectives is the expectation that the analysis of societies, diverse in time and place, will produce in Britain a society which is more tolerant and understanding of people who hold beliefs and attitudes which are different to their own? Is it that through this study pupils are encouraged to re-examine their own system of values and beliefs? This is where the study of history makes a contribution to the pupil's growing personal awareness by having 'the richest storehouse of human experience and an unrivalled opportunity to reflect on other people's feelings and actions' (Wilson, 1985). The idea here is that school history should be more than just the pupils' cognitive development; it should also address the 'affective' domain of values and attitudes. Illingworth is firmly positioned among those teachers who emphasise history's contribution to the pupils' personal development (2000: 20). He wants pupils 'to feel outraged, inspired and moved by events in the past and to develop their own ideas of right and wrong from this experience'. So, for example, he has no difficulty extending the study of persecution in the past to present-day examples such as bullying in schools. History's role is seen as one of drawing out the moral issues that arise from the topics that are studied.

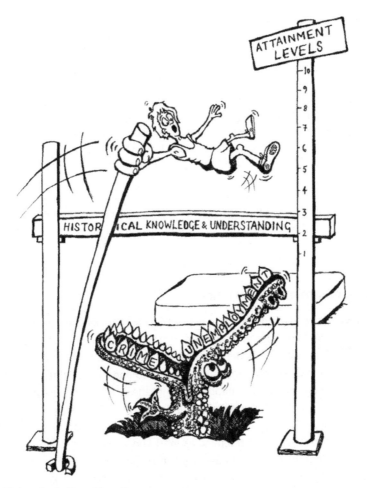

Figure 6.3 History for better citizens?

Some history teachers may prefer to stress that this concept should be seen more as an aspect of historical understanding. Thus, a second objective behind this concept is the necessity for the historian to try to explain why people thought and acted in the way they did in a particular situation. Such an emphasis sees the examination of past beliefs and attitudes as an aspect of historical causation and motivation. Hamilton and McConnell feel that to avoid empathy is 'to reduce history to a science' (Hamilton and McConnell, 2003: 19). At its core history is about what people have done and why they have done it and to ignore the importance of their mindset and the pressures of the influences upon them is to misunderstand the past. This emphasis would also contribute to the value of teaching about the social, cultural, religious and ethnic diversity in an explanation of events in the past.

Task 6.3 *School history and the affective domain*

1   Discuss with the history teachers and history student teachers with whom you work, their views on the idea of school history as a vehicle for developing particular values and attitudes in pupils, such as respect for cultural diversity and tolerance. What other values and attitudes (if any) should school history attempt to cultivate? How much should this be left to Personal, Social and Health Education (PHSE)?

2   Cunningham (2004) found in her research that teachers usually had difficulties with their approach because they were trying to negotiate complicated or irreconcilable goals. Discuss with your tutor and other history teachers how they seek to resolve these four dilemmas identified by Cunningham and discussed in this chapter:

    a)   How to harness imagination while keeping it tied to evidence.
    b)   Whether to frame empathy in personal or historical terms.
    c)   Whether to encourage identification and emotional connection with historical figures
    d)   Balancing empathy and moral judgement.

3   Discuss with colleagues and peers (and perhaps A Level pupils) what are the characteristic features of 'Britishness' in the early years of the twentieth century, as against the middle of the nineteenth century? This should give you an indication of the complexity and salience of such issues. What might be the pros and cons of discussing 'Britishness' with younger pupils?

Problems pupils might experience

The challenge you have of encouraging pupils to be able to understand past societies with a set of ideas, beliefs and attitudes very different from those commonly held today is one that has been a concern of history teachers for over 20 years. The experience of the GCSE has shown just how difficult that challenge has been with 15 and 16 year olds and so this is even more challenging when dealing with pupils at Key Stage 3. Many would agree with Lee and Ashby (1987) that 'entertaining the beliefs, goals and values of other people... is a difficult intellectual achievement'. It is hard, he continued, because 'it requires a high level of thinking to be able to hold such features in the mind as inert knowledge, but to be able to work with them in such a way that the pupil can understand and explain what people did in the past'. Let us try to analyse the problems and difficulties adolescents are likely to experience in trying to understand the characteristic features of societies remote in time and place from their own.

An important part of learning history is the ability to understand the ideas, beliefs and attitudes of different periods and societies. By understanding we mean not just the ability to recall and describe but to acknowledge that for those times and places, such ideas made good sense and did present a rational explanation of their actions. Yet this can create real problems for pupils in the secondary school. For them it is a major conceptual leap when the values and norms of behaviour might be so different from the world in which they live. For them, in the words of L.P. Hartley, 'the past is a foreign country, people did things differently there.' It requires significant adjustments to be made if they are to get to grips with the very unfamiliar ways of people living in the past. To achieve this, pupils need to discard a collection of notions that can detract from the quality of their understanding.

One such notion is the idea, common to many pupils in the secondary school, that people in the past were intellectually inferior to people today and that the further one goes back in time, the more inferior they get. This is not surprising as the evidence of material advances surround modern pupils and their understanding of the evolution of man would also encourage such thinking. Ashby and Lee (1987) have noted that the inability of the pupils to recognise that people in the past could not have known what the pupil of today knows and takes for granted and this can lead them to be contemptuous of past actions. Yet this dismissive attitude has to be surmounted if the pupil is to develop his or her historical understanding. You need to encourage your pupils to appreciate that what is 'strange' and 'different' is not necessarily 'stupid' or inferior. Although empathy 'got a bad name' in the years following the introduction of the original NC for history in 1991, partly because of the overuse of 'Imagine you are...' activities, it is now more widely acknowledged that pupils should understand 'the constraints under which the people of the past operated' (Gove, 2013).

Conversely, another notion that can often limit understanding of past societies and cultures, is one where the pupil makes too great an assumption that people in the past were the same as people today, a view that makes little concession to the changes that have occurred over time. Of course, we do have a common humanity with people of different times and places and the assumptions that pupils make are understandable for that reason. The danger is that such thinking is likely to encourage anachronistic representations of the past by the pupil attributing to people in the past, ideas and reactions, which could not have prevailed at the time. The short length of time that adolescents have lived and the limited situations they have encountered make it more difficult for them to project their experiences into past situations. Your task is to encourage pupils to understand why such ideas and attitudes were held and how these would influence peoples' actions.

To do this your pupils need to possess considerable background knowledge of the cultures and religions involved. Much of this knowledge involves abstract ideas, which are themselves difficult for most pupils to understand. The challenge to the teacher is first not to make assumptions about the pupils' prior knowledge but also to become skilled in expressing the generalisations in terms concrete enough for pupils to understand. For example, teaching the Reformation to Year 8 pupils can be a difficult task if pupils are to achieve a good understanding of the range of ideas and beliefs of the sixteenth and seventeenth centuries. Additionally, your pupils may find it difficult to communicate such ideas in a way that show that they clearly understand and are not merely repeating what they have heard or learned by rote. All these problems have profound implications for the strategies you choose when you come to teach this particular aspect of historical understanding.

Task 6.4 *Developing an understanding of pupils' ideas about past societies*

1   In your placement schools find out how the History Department seeks to meet the challenge of teaching about 'diversity'. Which topics are considered appropriate for the development of this concept?

2   With the permission of your tutor, discuss with a group of pupils the following questions:
 (a)   Do you think people in the past were less intelligent then people today?
 (b)   What different ideas would people in (the fourteenth century) have in comparison with people today?
 (c)   Why do you think ideas and attitudes were different?
 (d)   Do you think all people living in (the fourteenth century) held the same ideas?

Teaching approaches

As noted in Chapter 5 you are likely to be successful in developing your pupils' historical understanding if the pupils are more actively involved in their own learning. Whatever the unfamiliar ideas and attitudes are, they need to be able to apply them and re-work them in terms which are meaningful to them. This often means placing the use of such ideas in a specific context, which is not too vague for the pupil to handle. Pupils are more likely to understand ideas and beliefs which are new and strange to them if they are asked to employ them as if they were their own. They need to be presented with experiences and tasks which require them to express such ideas in their own words. Many pupils find this difficult and many make mistakes. Yet this is an important point for you to consider. By setting up situations and exercises that could lead to anachronistic statements you can assess more effectively the limitations of the pupils' understanding.

Many exercises designed to develop pupils' understanding of particular periods and societies have limited success because the pupils have been given insufficient background information with which to work. Too little background information encourages the far-fetched, fanciful and non-historical. Thus it is important that plenty of attention is given to setting a framework of background knowledge before any exercise is set. This can often involve the comprehension and analysis of evidence, for, as ever, many of these elements of knowledge, skills and understanding 'overlap'. This could be achieved by whole-class teaching and question and answer, or by pupils analysing sources in groups with the task of listing the ideas and attitudes that they think emerge from the sources. Having ensured the pupils have an adequate background knowledge, what else might you consider to achieve success?

The best efforts are often those which are set in a very precise time and place. Pupils find it easier to achieve some synthesis of the information available to them if it has such limitations placed upon it. Lack of precision and vague instructions often characterise the 'Imagine you were...' type of exercise. Such tasks tend to be overused and have at times opened this whole approach to ridicule. Bad examples of this method require pupils to place themselves in a situation, frequently gruesome, and describe their feelings. 'Imagine you are a soldier at the Battle of X' is one such example – some pupils have fought in several battles from Hastings to D-Day – and the descriptive writing which tends to emanate from such tasks is often more appropriate to the development of skills in English rather than the advancement of the pupils' historical knowledge and understanding. Such tasks only encouraged work of very limited value and, what is more, most pupils were aware of this.

Where such approaches were used, and overused, lack of detailed knowledge usually meant that pupils' responses were limited to statements which reflected common feelings, a transmission of everyday experiences and emotions into the past but lacking any real historical substance. As such the result was more creative writing than a vehicle to explore understanding of unfamiliar ideas, beliefs and attitudes. The task set needs to be well-structured and thoughtful. An example of such precision was an assignment, which sought to analyse the ideas and attitudes prevalent in a Lancashire textile town in 1866. Based on a real event, the pupils had studied the destruction by fire of two local mills, the consequences for the town in those days before the welfare state and also the contemporary attitudes of teachers and the clergy. For this they had used newspaper accounts, personal accounts and extracts from school log books. The exercise was a child's view of destruction incorporating the comments, which were made by significant adults about the disaster.

Task 6.5 *The role of historical empathy*

The word 'empathy' has given rise to a great deal of controversy.

1   To gain something of the flavour of that debate over time, read the following articles from *Teaching History*. They are 'Empathy and History' by Anne Low-Beer and 'Some Reflections on Empathy in History' by John Cairns. Both of these are in the April 1989. The third, 'Historical Empathy – R.I.P.?' by Peter Clements appeared in October 1996. A helpful 'thumbnail' summary of the empathy debate can be found in Empathy: In a nutshell', *Teaching History*, No. 100, August, 25. In 2004, *Empathy without illusions*, by Deborah Cunningham, in *Teaching History* No. 114, also contributed to the debate about empathy, and in 2011, Lee and Shemilt wrote 'The concept that dares not speak its name: should empathy come out of the closet?' (*Teaching History*, No. 143). Harris *et al.* (2013) also provide a useful overview.
2   After reading about empathy, discuss with your mentor the advantages and disadvantages of using historical empathy in the classroom.

Further consideration of 'empathy' in school history can be found at: www.uea.ac.uk/~m242/historypgce/empathy or at http://terryhaydn. wordpress.com/pgce-history-at-uea/empathy

---

It is usually helpful to consider the 'audience' of the task. This often works best if that 'audience' is also of the period, a contemporary audience, the recipient of a report or petition. Cunningham found that one of the difficulties teachers face is to decide whether to frame a task in personal or historical terms (Cunningham, 2004). She cites as an example the use of 'you' in setting a task. She decides that it is best used in a historical context such as 'You are (named contemporary person)', followed by details, rather than just 'you', meaning you, the pupil, placed in a historical situation, which can lead to much confusion.

Resolving dilemmas or decision-making can produce useful tasks. In such exercises pupils are required to describe a difficult choice of action which a person or group of people in the past may have had to make. In the United States, this is sometimes described as 'perspective taking', and can be used in teaching issues such as the decision to drop the atomic bombs in 1945 (Yeager and Doppen, 2001; VanSledright, 2014). The pupils have to examine those factors which might influence their choice and in so doing take account that such a decision involves the application of ideas and attitudes which were different from those prevalent today. For example, the pupil might be asked, as a novice in a monastery or nunnery, to decide whether to take the vows and stay or to leave, or to consider why people of varying social status and occupation might decide to fight in The Crusades (Byrom and Riley, 2013). What would be the pros and cons of such decisions for a person in medieval times? Such exercises are arguably better than the more familiar 'A day in the life of a monk'. Other examples of decision-making designed to develop understanding of diverse and unfamiliar attitudes could be whether, as a Member of Parliament, to vote against a Bill to abolish the Slave Trade in 1789.

It is important to emphasise that such exercises need to be 'rooted in evidence' and as such, while there is scope for the use of imagination, it must conform to what can be substantiated by the evidence available and not given a free rein. Lee has correctly emphasised that historical imagination 'must be tied to evidence in some way and so historical imagination cannot be creative in the same way as in literature, painting or music' (Lee, 1984: 86).

Historical imagination can be encouraged in many formats such as pages from a diary, which can cover successive days or significant days reflecting change and development. A well-used task is to invite pupils to write a letter in which a past ideas and attitudes are revealed. At times, two letters, where the recipient responds with different views although still consistent with those held at the time. Pupils can be asked to write newspaper accounts, eyewitness reports or petitions for or against some proposal, for example, a new canal or votes for women. In all cases whatever is written involves the use of the imagination but it must be grounded in historical knowledge, which can be substantiated by evidence. By using a medium such as a letter the pupils are being asked to transfer sometimes difficult abstract ideas into their own words and into more concrete situations that are meaningful to them.

More ambitious activities can include an attempt to utilise role-play as a means of developing understanding. This again can use a variety of formats and can also involve decision-making. Role-play can be used successfully to encourage the understanding of differing attitudes towards enclosures, of a parish's reactions to religious changes in the sixteenth century, to the ideas of a local Board of Health to the news of the arrival of cholera in the town in 1831. At a more advanced level, Hamilton and McConnell described their successful use of role play in helping Year 13 pupils to understand the concept of empire from the point of view of the colonial power by showing the pressures placed upon Bismarck, concluding with an activity where the pupils were Bismarck and had to make decisions bearing in mind the various problems and pressures he faced (Hamilton and McConnell, 2003).

Where appropriate, other evidence that can be successfully incorporated into imaginative work could be a historical site and the exercise makes use of a familiar landscape, for example a castle, monastery, street or canal. There may be times, perhaps with older pupils, although it has been done successfully by Year 7 pupils, where your pupils can be encouraged to reference the sources behind some of the statements. However, they also need to ensure their work does not follow the sources too closely and come close to paraphrasing.

Finally, although some teachers may still be reluctant to use historical fiction within the history classroom, Martin and Brooke have shown how this genre can be used effectively to encourage pupils themselves to create fictional pieces themselves in which they can develop their understanding of past attitudes and beliefs. They do emphasise as always that such activities must be solidly rooted in evidence studied beforehand. Provided the piece is not too ambitious, has not too many characters and is limited in time and space, then success can follow (Martin and Brooke, 2002). See Dave Martin's *Historical fiction in the classroom* website, for some examples of pupils' work (http://davemartin46.wordpress.com).

Much of the success of such tasks depends on the preparation you have done to enable you to set the work. You need to be very clear in your mind about the purpose of the task you are setting, to be able to articulate the precise objectives you have in mind. Careful thought here helps the way in which you formulate the task. When you have decided what you want the pupils to do, go back to the objectives and assess whether such a task enables the pupils to meet the targets you are setting. There are times when a poorly set exercise gives pupils little chance of indicating their understanding of past ideas, beliefs and attitudes. Having precise objectives means you also have to be clear about the assessment criteria you are going to employ when you come to mark the pupils' work. There is a good case here for letting the pupils know what these criteria are, so they can take account of them as they plan and complete their work.

Cause and consequence

Cause and consequence are arguably the most complex of the concepts that are under consideration in this chapter. They are difficult to teach because it is easy to make assumptions about the extent of your pupils' understanding of cause and consequence.

Traditionally causes were dealt with as a list of information. Any analysis that had been done was achieved by the teacher or the author of the textbook, rarely by the pupils. Pupils were presented with a list of causes and consequences of an event and committed these to memory to reproduce for assessment. There was very little attempt here to encourage pupils' thought about the nature of the concept involved and thus developing their historical understanding. The National Curriculum Council (NCC) noted that there have been critics of this traditional approach since the early days of this century. Some enlightened history teachers saw the important methodological implications of not relying on the teacher to do all the intellectual work but 'pupils themselves should be generalising, analysing, judging and explaining' (NCC, 1993). The challenge is in trying to get the balance right between providing structure and selected materials and allowing the pupils to have some ownership of an enquiry. This is not easy and usually involves adjustments and improvements as a topic is repeated. *Many teachers would now accept that the teaching of this concept needs to be the focus of a series of lessons rather than just one objective as part of a lesson.* Such a scheme would most likely cover different aspects of understanding causation. So, as ever, you need to be precise about what it is you want the pupils to understand about historical causation. Chambers includes the following:

- To know that there are reasons why an event happened.
- To highlight causes from a narrative account.
- To make links between causes.
- To organise causes into categories.
- To distinguish between the long-term (trends) and the short-term (triggers) causes of events.
- To order causes in a hierarchy of importance. (Chambers, 2006)

Common misconceptions about cause and consequence

1   *Pupils can look upon causes as being facts in themselves.* Shemilt (1980) noted in his evaluation of the 13-16 Schools Council project that many highly intelligent adolescents treated the word 'cause' as though it refers not to the connection between events but to the properties of one of the events. He also noted the prevalence of the opinion that causes are everything that happened before. For such pupils a cause is something of an agent, which has the ability to make something happen. Thompson (1984) suggested that *bad* 'traditional' teaching helped to reinforce this kind of misunderstanding by treating causes in exactly the same way as events in history.

2   *Monocausal explanations.* Shemilt also noted that many pupils are happy to settle for one cause for a particular event; they like the clear-cut conclusion without any complexities. To them any other causes are superfluous. Such simplicity of understanding is attractive but represents a very limited understanding of the concept. For example, if one asked pupils to account for the building of the turnpike road between Manchester and Rochdale in 1755 some pupils would feel that the fact that the existing roads were bad and in great need of repair to be sufficient for the answer; no additional explanation was necessary. Such a limited response fails to tackle the complexity of the question, where it would be necessary to know who were the people pressing for the setting up of a Trust and for what reasons; whether they had they the services of a well-known surveyor available at that time; where precisely would the road be built and did this bring advantages to some of the promoters; what trades or goods would be most likely to benefit and how had it been possible to defeat any local opposition. The challenge for teachers would be how to encourage pupils not to settle for the most obvious mono-causal explanation. This is not always that easy. Indeed, Lee (1999) has indicated that adolescent pupils may have difficulty with causal thinking because it is 'counter intuitive' to many of them who naturally think the last event is necessarily the most important.

3   Another possible disadvantage of listing causes in a traditional manner was that it took away any analysis which took account of the order in which the causes might have had their effect and the inter-play between events and causes. The Balkan Wars of 1912-13 were not as such a cause of the First World War but they contributed to the demands for self-determination and the heightened resistance of the multinational Empires towards this development. At times a distinction was drawn between long- and short-term causes

and similarly long- and short-term consequences but this was often a means of categorising information rather than a basis for discussion about the nature of the concept or indeed how distant a long-term cause had to be to qualify for this category.

4   We also have the problem of *causal determinism*. Scott (1990) indicates that this can occur when pupils liken the concept of causation in history to a scientific interpretation. This is encouraged when words such as 'catalyst' are used (it may be better to use words like 'triggers'). Confusion with *scientific causation* can lead to an almost mechanistic interpretation of causation. It is possible to see here the beginning of the attraction of adolescents towards the conclusion that some historical events were 'inevitable'. It is almost as if, given a certain combination of causes, an event was 'bound to happen'. The outcome is not only predictable, it is inevitable. This 'scientific' view of causation at least has the merit of logic and not least the importance of the interrelationship of causes. However, only the more sophisticated pupil is likely to be able to distinguish between the scientific and the historical mode of causal explanation and is able to understand the 'uniqueness' of a historical event, the sheer unpredictability of events involving both individuals and groups of people. Howells (1998) recommends the value of looking at an episode in some depth to consider chance factors and of relating conclusions of that episode to the wider question of inevitability. One of the challenges you face is to encourage pupils to be sceptical about claims that an event was inevitable.

5   This 'uniqueness', which is such an important feature of historical content, stems from the central fact that history is the study of human beings in the past and human beings are themselves unique and unpredictable. Consequently historians have to concern themselves with motivation, which is in itself an important aspect of the concept of causation. Pupils should be able to discriminate between understanding motive and cause and not see the two as synonymous.

6   Nevertheless, there may be something of a paradox here, which could be confusing to pupils. While emphasising the 'uniqueness' of events and their causes, the nature of the learning process often means there is a need to categorise and assimilate language, which describes categories and concepts. Consequently an important function of learning the concept of cause and consequence is to enable pupils to understand and use words such as 'social', 'political', 'economic', technological' and other adjectives we may wish to use to describe categories of causes, mindful of the fact such terms can be employed in the explanation of widely different events.

Task 6.6 *Identifying pupils' assumptions about cause and consequence*

When you have covered an appropriate topic, present the class with a list made up of causes and events. Ask the class, in pairs, to identify which are the causes and which the events and give reasons for their choice. Then consider:

1   The teaching points to make at the conclusion of this exercise.

2   With a class, or a group of pupils, discuss the following questions.
(a)   Do you think the (selected event just covered) was inevitable, i.e. was it bound to have happened?
(b)   How might you decide which cause was the most important?
(c)   What do you understand by the terms, short- and long-term causes?
(d)   Why might it be difficult to work out the consequences of an event?
3   In the light of this discussion, what points do you need to emphasise when teaching these concepts?

To remove many of the misunderstandings noted above, you should be prepared to invest time in the careful study of causal connections and give pupils the opportunity to work out their own ideas and thinking. To this end activities need to be meaningful and not just a question of labelling, processing and listing to meet assessment statements.

What to consider when planning a set of lessons focusing on historical causation?

- What experience the pupils have already had. Ask the teacher what has been covered and on which aspects of this concept there has been focus.
- When to introduce the concept? Various choices can be made, the choice often determined by the topic.
  1   *At the end.* A retrospective review of factors causing an event after the pupils have been informed of the preceding events. This has the advantage of a series of stories leaving the final outcome to reveal itself. A story with an interesting ending before any analysis begins.
  2   *At the beginning.* It has become increasingly attractive to begin with the final major event and then pose the question, 'Why did it happen?' Howells (1998) felt pupils find this approach attractive as 'big questions excite children'. Again, Clark (2001) believed causal skills need to be demonstrated within a 'problem-solving framework'. Coverage of the content then uses the overarching question as a constant reference point and as a means of adjusting hypotheses. Chambers (2006) used the execution of Charles I to begin a set of lessons on the causes of the English Civil War and describes the different activities to developing an understanding of why the king met his death.
- How prepared are the pupils?
  1   As ever, you need to ensure that the pupils have *sufficient knowledge of the content* of the topic in order to make sense of any causation exercises to set them. Categorisation exercises have little meaning if pupils cannot relate the activity to the content detail and may merely look for 'clues' in the words presented to them without having any real understanding. Without knowledge causation exercises can seem meaningless.
  2   Have they the *appropriate vocabulary* for their analysis? What are the range of words they need for different ways of categorising and explaining causes?

Chapman provides a useful way for you to consider this vocabulary. There would be words related to (a) 'content', for example, political, economic, religious etc; (b) 'time', for example, short-term, long-term etc.; (c) 'role', which could include words such as 'trigger', 'catalyst' and 'pre-conditions' and (d) 'weight', which encourages words that help describe the relative importance of causes. Chapman devised exercises, some unhistorical, to encourage his pupils to become familiar with the vocabulary of historical causation (Chapman, 2003). Woodcock (2005: 11) also provides useful suggestions for scaffolding the vocabulary of causation. Rogers (2011) has some very interesting and easily adaptable ideas about the use of causation maps or graphs.

Strategies for teaching the concepts of cause and consequence

Matching exercises

There are various ways such exercises can be approached. Often pupils are presented with two columns – one of events another of causes and the task is to match items from one column with another and then explain the reasons for the choice.

Group work using causation cards

Example (with a Year 9 class) After a detailed study of a topic on the coming of the railways, the pupils were placed in groups and each group received a set of cards on each of which was written a possible cause of the building of a specified (local) railway line. Each card was numbered to facilitate discussion.

1   Dissatisfaction with canal companies' freight charges.
2   Availability of a labour force prepared to move around the country.
3   Civic pride/rivalry.
4   Demands for the faster transport by many trades and industries.
5   Successful trials of steam locomotives.
6   Appointment of skilled engineer.
7   Leadership of local business people.
8   Use of wrought iron rails.
9   Defeat of opponents (canals, turnpikes, rival railway companies, land owners, coach firms) in Parliament.
10   Courage, foresight of bankers.
11   Spirit of the Age (Progress, eagerness to improve, enterprising climate).
12   Earlier experience of railroad traction using horses.
13   Discovery of steam power.
14   Existence of Iron Industry capable of meeting requests of engineers.
15   Availability of hard-working skilled engineers.
16   Dissatisfaction with the speed of land transport.
17   Knowledge and skill in Capital accumulation, share-holding, joint-stock capital.

Having received these cards the groups then were asked to perform a series of tasks, each followed by a class discussion. These tasks included the categorisation of the cause on the cards. With most groups it would be necessary to identify the categories and to explain these beforehand, but with some able groups it is a useful challenge to ask them to create their own categories. In the following feedback discussion the results of the groups are compared and from this activity it is possible to create a spray-diagram in which the categories of causes are grouped together. Later, a spray-diagram could assist the writing of a piece of extended writing on the reasons for the building of the specified railway.

A further activity was to ask the groups to identify from the cards those, which they considered to be short-term and long-term causes. An extension of this, in an attempt to deal with the issue of the ordering of the effect of the causes, could be to ask the pupils to try to place the causes along some imaginary or real timeline. Finally the pupils were asked to consider which causes were the most important and which the least important.

With able pupils, who have some familiarity with the use of causation cards, once a topic has been covered it may be possible for them to devise their own cards and for groups to compare the results. It is possible to use this approach with older pupils when the selection of particular causes as being the most important is seen to indicate something about the attitude towards causation of the historian. Questions such as which cards might a Marxist historian be likely to choose as the most important can be considered. In this there is a link with Chapter 7 on historical interpretations.

'Why then?' activities

It is important to keep asking this question, particularly in those circumstances when the long-term causes have been in place for so long. If the condition of the French peasants was worse in 1722 than it was in 1789, why did the revolution take place at the later date? Also, why not in 1722? This is useful to dissuade pupils from the attraction of the inevitability of events.

Research by Lee *et al.* provides not only interesting information on the development of pupils' ideas about causation and explanation, but excellent examples of 'pupil-friendly' tasks, which address some of the complexities outlined above, particularly with regard to the interrelationship of causes, and pupils' ability to discriminate between fact, reason and cause (Lee *et al.*, 1996).

Linking consequence and cause

In the development of such key concepts as cause and consequence over the past three decades, it is probably fair to say that consequence has been the poor relation and received far less attention. However, there have been recent attempts to take a more holistic approach by seeking to link consequence to cause as a means of achieving a better understanding of causation. Clark believes that 'the consequence of a chain of events generally need to be shown first' (Clark, 2001: 27). Chapman goes further and feels that work on causation should focus as much on consequence as it does on categorisation. He suggests this approach is particularly valuable when students are attempting to evaluate the relative importance of causes. By asking students to work out the effects of each cause he found that this not only encouraged useful debate but helped to sharpen historical understanding (Chapman, 2003).

See the 'trails' section of the Historical Association website which focuses on causation for a number of articles which give suggestions for activities to develop pupils' understanding of causation: (www.history.org.uk/resources/secondary_resource_2569_61.html).

Change and continuity

For many decades history teachers have been aware of the underlying importance of the concept of change and continuity but only in the last three decades have the reasons for its importance been articulated in pedagogic terms with attention to the way change in particular may be misunderstood by pupils and students. Again much of the research, which underpins this emphasis, comes from the Schools History Project (SHP). Attractive textbooks associated with this module were produced by Scott and organised in such a way that the concepts of change and continuity are given a clear and comprehensive emphasis (Scott, 1987). Textbooks, such as those covering the History of Medicine, offer plenty of ideas about utilising these concepts, which can be adapted to other content areas.

Common misconceptions about change and continuity

As in the case of the concepts of cause and consequence, you may find that it is possible that your expectations of your pupils' understanding of these concepts may be too high. You need to be aware of the possible misconceptions, which pupils may have if you are to succeed in developing their historical understanding.

Thompson (1984) concluded that 'change' is a historical concept that adolescents initially find difficult to entertain in any but everyday use. Pupils can understand change in relation to different times but their appreciation of the nature and scope of change varies very much from pupil to pupil. A feature of Shemilt's research (1980) was to note how many pupils saw change as an episodic not as a continuous process. One change (event) was not seen as in any way connected with changes (events) preceding it in time. This limited understanding tends to be reinforced by a syllabus, which is itself episodic, which moves from one topic to another with little apparent relationship to that which precedes or follows. There is a case to be made for a syllabus which has a chronological base so that the process of change can be better addressed.

Shemilt also noted the difficulty children may have with the idea of historical change seems to stem from their inability to imagine the daily life which give the events their meaning. History lessons can so often present pupils with a succession of events with little reference to the context in which they occur and as a result the pupils are not sure of what precisely it is that changes. Hence, the value of making such changes personal by the use of role play or writing from an individual perspective.

You may also find it rewarding to find out how pupils interpret the idea of 'progress' over time (see Chapter 7). It is quite common for young people to assume that the changes that occur over time may all be seen to be for the better. Consequently there is value in stopping to consider whether this was always the case. What were the consequences of the discovery of gunpowder? Did this represent progress? Such questions prompt a consideration of some of the wider issues that the study of history can generate, showing the subject is well placed in the Humanities.

A further misconception that often needs to be corrected is that through the pupils' tendency to compartmentalise their history, the episodic approach, they may assume that changes occur at once. Suddenly one changes from the domestic system to the factory system. Yet what can make the concept even more confusing for pupils is the fact that while some things change others do not. Change is not clear cut and to that degree requires a level of understanding which is quite sophisticated and not easily achieved by many pupils. Lee and Cercadillo talk of the 'eventification' of the past by many pupils, seeing change primarily in terms of things that happened suddenly which caused change, rather than slow, unfolding and non-observable change (Lee and Cercadillo, 2013). Google ngram (https:// books.google.com/ngrams), with its tools for exploring cultural change over time, can be a useful resource for addressing this misconception.

Strategies for the teaching of the concepts of change and continuity

1 Emphasising overviews

Arguably the most important of all the strategies used to teach change and continuity is the use of overviews. It is important to make sure the pupils are able to see how the content covered or to be covered presents an overview or framework from which a discussion of change and continuity may develop. Overviews help to give pupils a broader understanding of the past. The newly introduced NC for history includes the requirement that teachers should 'combine overview and depth studies to help pupils understand both the long arc of development and the complexity of specific aspects of the content' (DfE, 2013: 2).

Too often there has been a tendency to move from one block of content to another without sufficient emphasis on the overview, which helps to show the significance of the study. An episodic approach misses many opportunities to develop important features of historical understanding. As in the past overviews were simply used to link the chosen topics, in what was called the 'patch' method. However giving overviews a central role in a scheme emphasises the overall importance of the topics studied. Dawson argues for the advantages of providing a broad overview of a topic before going into more depth, so that the pupils have a better overall grasp of the topic they are exploring as they go into greater detail (Dawson, 2012).

Overviews can be used at different times during the teaching of a scheme. It may be useful to present an outline framework at the beginning of a topic or scheme to assist understanding and then return to the framework when the detail has been covered to ask questions related to the concept. Such a framework can also be used for reference while teaching a topic to aid the understanding of particularly complex content. For Banham (2000) the key is not to think of overview in isolation but to combine, blend and integrate it with topics dealt in depth. He shows how the study of the King John is enhanced by relating the content to a range of wider issues such as the nature of medieval kingship. Looking for the wider issues not only helps understanding but also contributes to covering the curriculum.

With some topics it may be preferable to study an overview at the completion of a topic. Here you can make good use of the knowledge the pupils have gained to encourage the consideration of a whole range of issues arising that help to develop their historical understanding, drawing out key issues and making connections with content covered earlier in the history curriculum or with their experience of life today.

A study of the Poor Law Amendment Act of 1834 raises the issue of how a country deals with poverty and pupils may be asked to recall how the poor were treated in the sixteenth century and then think about how they are treated today (see Chapter 7). The term 'zeroing' has been used to describe the rush to start a new topic just when the point has been reached when that content covered can be usefully developed to address pupils' conceptual understanding of important historical concepts and offer further challenges to the pupils. It is often important that you give thought to these 'matters arising' when completing the details of a study.

1   *Imaginative presentation of changes in the form of illustrated time-charts, time-lines, diagrams or graphs.* These may be drawn to highlight periods of slow or rapid change and again help to place the content under study in an overall context. There are times when it may be necessary to limit the precise accuracy of presentation in order to make general points in some imaginative diagrams.

    For example, a topic which benefits from a time-chart is the French Revolution, which may be said to be not one but a series of revolutions. To assist understanding it can be helpful to create a time-chart, which emphasises this succession of changes. Such a chart could also form the basis for a wall display. How much detail is included depends on the ability level of the class, but the idea of an overview is to ensure the changes are not obscured by too much factual 'clutter'. As the topic is covered in more detail, the chart is a useful reference point for pupils.

2   Graphs can also be an effective way of demonstrating change, or indeed, lack of change. Barnes (2002) and Foster (2008) show how effective use can be made of graphs to plot progress above time. Using information brought from three enquiries about progress in social conditions, in economic performance and in democracy and the franchise between 1750 and 1900, three lines were plotted and drawn in different colours. The resulting graph gave rise to them making valuable comparisons, connections and the relationship between different types of change.

3   *Comparative exercises.* For some time, 'similarity' and 'difference' have been identified as concepts in themselves. However, it is possible to use these terms more as an effective strategy for teaching the concepts of change and continuity. They are often used most productively at the beginning of a topic and make a relatively straightforward entry into the discussion of more demanding concepts such as causation. The use of 'similarity and difference' approaches nearly always involves pupils in making comparisons, which in turn can encourage varying degrees of analysis. Such comparisons often work well with pictures or other visual materials, but can also involve with effect cartographical and statistical material. You will find that most of the attractively produced textbooks of recent years make good use of comparisons and so material for their use is not too difficult to find. Even so, there is always scope for your individual

initiative in the acquisition of appropriate resources. Evidence from the local environment and from local history will usually add to the interest of lessons, as can skilfully chosen analogies from aspects of contemporary life closer to pupils' own interests and experiences. While most emphasis may be placed on the differences, it is also important to look for similarities.

There are a variety of ways in which comparative exercise can be used to further the pupils' understanding of the concepts of change and continuity (see Figures. 6.3 and 6.4). One is the *then-now technique*. This is most likely when pupils have some familiarity with the present-day example, especially involving the use of physical evidence. Contrasting a modern-day street with a photograph of the same street in Edwardian times encourages plenty of discussion about what has changed and what has remained the same. Booth *et al.* show how comparison of a Victorian and present-day kitchen can also bring out many facets of continuity and change (Booth *et al.*, 1987).

Town populations: comparison of the sixteenth century with recent times

As part of a lesson on towns in the sixteenth century, the following two lists were written on the board.

Sixteenth century	Recent times (1977)
1 London (200,000)	1 London (7,030,000)
2 Norwich (15,000)	2 Birmingham (1,050,100)
3 Bristol (12,000)	3 Leeds (734,000)
4 York (11,500)	4 Sheffield (547,000)
5 Exeter (9,000)	5 Liverpool (535,000)
6 Newcastle (9,000)	6 Manchester (491,000)
7 Chester (5,400)	7 Bradford (464,200)
8 Hull (5,000)	8 Bristol (409,000)
9 Coventry (4,000)	9 Coventry (340,000)
10 Manchester (3,500)	10 Nottingham (282,000)

After first identifying the changes featured in these lists, the pupils were asked to consider why such changes had occurred. How did we account for the disappearance of some towns and the appearance of others?

Figure 6.4 An example of a then-now exercise

This time pupils were given two maps, one showing the open fields, common lands and meadow and the nucleated village of pre-enclosure times and the other showing the effects on the landscape of the introduction of enclosures. The pupils were first invited to identify the similarities and differences between the two maps as a basis for a study of the changes, which had taken place and the reasons for those changes.

Figure 6.5 An example of a before-after exercise: the effects of enclosure

4   *Comparison of the implication of change for identified people living at the time or at contrasting times.* There is plenty of potential here for simulation exercises, role play and the use of 'radio' plays, for example, in approaching topics such as enclosures, the change from the domestic system to the factory system; religious changes of the sixteenth and seventeenth centuries.

5   *Encouraging speculation.* Teachers may gain useful insights into how pupils are assimilating the concept by asking them to consider what changes might be experienced by people living at a certain time, when they were 30 years older or by the time of their grandchildren.

> *Example.* Year 7 pupils have spent two or three lessons extracting information from the local census returns for 1861. From this information they have been able to construct bar charts showing the different occupations of the people living in 1861, the age and gender distribution and details of the inhabitants' place of birth. As an additional task, the pupils were set the following tasks:
> * Make a list of those jobs or occupations, which you think would *grow* in number in the next 30 years, that is, by 1891.
> * Make a list of those jobs or occupations, which you think would *decline* in number, that means, there would be less of them, by 1891.

Give reasons for your judgements.

The answers given would be quite informative of the pupils' understanding and also could be checked by a comparison with the 1891 census returns.

6   *Use of hypothetical questions.* Although there has in the past been some reluctance by history teachers to ask questions which invited speculation on what did not happen, it can be a useful way to emphasise the significance of a change or indeed lack of change. For example, consider what might have happened if Henry Tudor had been defeated at the Battle of Bosworth or what might have been the result had the Spanish Armada been successful in 1588?

7   *Sequencing activities* (such as those suggested earlier in this chapter on chronology, in which pupils have to reorganise events in the order in which they occurred). The best of these are where the selection of detail allows pupils to think through decisions using inference and their general understandings, rather than exercises which are purely reliant on memorisation. Such activities are a further example of how the concepts covered by this chapter interrelate as the concepts of change and continuity owe much to an understanding of chronology.

8   Following the completion of a topic, inviting discussion on what the pupils consider to be significant *turning points* in the events which have developed.

9   *Spot the anachronisms activities.* This can be both an amusing and yet revealing activity. Pupils are presented with a picture or a passage of writing which contains several errors of an anachronistic nature and are challenged to identify the deliberate mistakes. Alternatively they could be asked to identify which of two accounts is genuine and give reasons for their choice.

Significance

Although for decades many good history teachers have almost instinctively emphasised the significance of the topics they have taught, it can be argued that this particular element has not received the same attention as, for example, causation or historical interpretations. Lomas (1989) was able to indicate the possibilities of a greater emphasis on significance in his Historical Association pamphlet and those six pages remain a good starting point for your consideration of the concept. The NC for History mentions significance as one of the concepts which should be part of historical study, and significance can be a useful way into the question of why some topics, people and ideas are deemed worthy of being taught to young people, and others are not, and the factors influencing such decisions. The concept of significance raises important questions for history teachers.

1 How does the study of historical significance help pupils to value the importance and relevance of history?

The relatively recent emphasis on the use of overviews to counter the traditional episodic sequence of topics has helped pupils to understand how the topic they are studying fits into a bigger picture. Often this is achieved by placing content within a wider, overarching enquiry question. Emphasising historical significance is not the same as using overviews but it is not too great a leap for this to be done. Hammond (2001) was able to show how by placing the Holocaust within the bigger picture of persecution over time and the suffering of many groups of people in the Second World War, her pupils were able to identify the particular significance of the Nazi treatment of the Jews. Again, Phillips (2002) made the connection with overviews with the enquiry question, 'How important is the Industrial Revolution to our lives today?' He made the point that emphasising a topic's place within a wider perspective can often be a way of increasing pupils' interest in topics, which might have been deemed uninteresting by some teachers. He thought this was particularly the case with economic and social history topics. Similarly, Hunt showed that similar positive responses could be achieved in the study of the Agricultural Revolution by emphasising its significance within a wider context (Hunt, 2006). Often the value of local history can be underlined by drawing out its contribution to the understanding of national and indeed international developments.

As with other second order concepts, there is a vocabulary around change and continuity, and Foster (2013: 15) provides a helpful 'thesaurus' of words connected to the understanding of continuity and change. Foster also suggests the construction of a graphical 'roadmap' of historical change, for example, in helping to illustrate the processes involved in the changes brought about by the American Civil Rights movement (Foster, 2008).

Many topics require attempts to explain human conduct and motivation and the pupils' historical understanding is enhanced if an explanation can relate to the way people thought at the time. It is then a small step to make explicit the connections with other knowledge the pupils possess to be able to deepen their general understanding of what can motivate people in certain situations.

Consideration of themes such as how the country was governed, changes in trade and industry, public welfare and many others seem more coherent when pulled together.

Adolescents are particularly attracted by content that invites comment on the social and moral questions involved, as may be seen in the popularity of the unit on '*The Black Peoples of America*'. There are many topics where you can explore how the significance of specific events relates to a wider consideration of human conduct and motivation over a long time span, including links to the present. This raises fundamental questions which it is important for young people to consider. Harris and Rea (2006) have stressed the need to help pupils to understand how history is meaningful. They want history teachers to show how the past touches the pupils' own lives and how people in the past often had to deal with the same issues as people today. Such considerations in turn necessitate the use of generalisations and with them the need to understand and use a range of abstract concepts such as freedom, equality, inflation, slavery, taxation, class, depression and many more. Studying real people in real situations helps your pupils gain a better understanding of these terms. Part of the answer to this first question may lead to an accusation of 'presentism', the notion that for an event to be significant it must be related to the present, when that is by no means always the case. However, thinking through how the topics you teach do still touch the lives of today's citizens can only enhance your understanding and teaching of this concept.

2 What makes an event, person or issue significant?

The question, which is perhaps the most central to the teaching and learning of historical significance is: what makes an event historically significant? This may seem the most straightforward approach to the concept but, like so much about significance, it is quite complex. There have been various attempts to answer this question including an early one by Partington (1980) and also, by Phillips (2002) and Counsell (2004).

Partington

An event is historically significant if it has:

1 **Importance** - to people living in the past.
2 **Profundity** - because of the depth with which people's lives have been affected.
3 **Quantity** - because of the number of people who have been affected.
4 **Durability** - because of the length of time people's lives have been affected.
5 **Relevance** - because it makes a contribution to an increased understanding of present life.

Counsell' Five 'R's

An event is historically significant if it is:

1 **Remarkable** - was remarked on by people living at the time.
2 **Remembered** - was important at some stage in history with the collective memory of a group.
3 **Resonant** - is possible to connect with experience, beliefs, situations across time and space.
4 **Resulting** in change - had consequences for the future.
5 **Revealing** of some other aspect of the past.

Phillips (2002) suggests the mnemonic 'GREAT' to aid pupils' understanding of why World War One is often called 'The Great War' (Groundbreaking, Remembered by all, Events that were far reaching, Affected the future, Terrifying). Such attempts to help pupils remember things for examinations can also be used to get pupils to explore the limits of such scaffolding, and point to events and historical personalities who are significant but who do not conform to the criteria specified.

Task 6.7 *Evaluating historical significance*

It is a characteristic of this concept and debates about it that opinions differ about the validity and weight of these criteria, but they do help to stimulate your thinking.

1   To encourage thinking about how you might use these criteria in the classroom, take each of the ten criteria in turn and try to define then in words which you think most KS3 pupils would be able to understand.

2   Is it possible to rank these criteria in order of importance? Do all the criteria make a valid contribution? Can any be used on their own or do all the criteria of one or the other need to be fulfilled for an event to have historical significance? Would you add any others?

3   Study your department schemes for KS3 for the next term. Take each topic in turn and, using the criteria, consider how you would explain to your pupils the historical significance of the topic.

4   With a group of pupils, and the permission of your tutor, ask them to rank the following in order of their significance and to explain their decisions:

   ● An atomic bomb dropped on Hiroshima in 1945.
   ● A fire burns down a local factory in your town in 1893.
   ● A fire burns down much of London in 1666.
   ● Anne Boleyn executed in the reign of Henry VIII.
   ● The opening of the Manchester to Liverpool Railway 1830.
   ● The execution of Charles I 1649.
   ● The sinking of the Titanic 1912.

5   Select one major event from three of the Studies for KS3. Try to create a spray-diagram (some call them spider-charts) which shows the significance of the event. E.g. The Black Death, the Battle of Bosworth, the defeat of the Spanish Armada.

6   When observing a history lesson in your placement school, try to identify what you think is the significance of the topic being taught. How much is this being communicated to the pupils?

Osowiecki (2004, 2005) using Counsell's criteria and particularly that of remarkability, showed how effectively this could be applied to a study of the significance of Renaissance figures and through that of the Renaissance itself. On occasions you may be in a position to explain to your pupils why you chose to teach the topic they are studying in preference to other topics you might have taught. What gave your choice historical significance? Both Wrenn (2002), Counsell (2004) and Bradshaw (2006) stress the importance of encouraging pupils to offer their own ideas about why an event or person they have been studying is significant and so worthy of its place in the syllabus. It is likely that your able pupils will soon consider how the criteria might change depending on why you are studying a certain event or purpose. They may well feel the decision of a town to establish a local sanitary authority in 1870 is more significant for the local historian of that town than the Franco-Prussian war of the same year. So, can a local event meet the criteria listed in the table? Does, therefore, as Lee (1998) would affirm, the significance of an event only make sense within a particular account. Does significance for purpose make its contribution to what makes an event significant? What has been well established is that pupils should come to realise that the significance of an event or a person is not fixed in time, is not a 'given' as it might sometimes appear, is relative and is indeed a matter of debate.

3 Is there value in categorising types of historical significance?

In dealing with this concept it is useful to consider how the categorisation of various types of significance can help understanding. Both Partington and Counsell include in their criteria a reference to judgements about the significance of an event by contemporaries, events which may not be afforded the same significance today but which were at an earlier time. Such significance would come under the category of short term. By contrast, some events, which did not seem significant at the time, may be so regarded with the passage of time. Similarly, applying categories often used with causation, an event could be assessed from a choice of its political, economic, social, religious or military significance. And just as causation has 'triggers' and 'catalysts' so historical significance needs to use words such as 'symbolic' and 'cultural'. Cercadillo has also made an attempt at categorising types of significance. She identified six types: contemporary, causal, pattern – 'significance as part of a pattern of change or as a turning point', symbolic, revelatory – 'appealing to events or processes which reveal something about individuals or society' and present. She also showed how some of these types could be the basis for a progression model for the assessment of pupils' understanding of the concept (Cercadillo, 2006).

4 How can historical significance be used as a 'mega-concept'?

The complexity of the concept of historical significance may be partially explained by the notion that it is different from the other second-order concepts in that it is an over-arching 'meta-concept'. Counsell (2004) noted that, 'when pupils work on significance, they are really standing outside all the usual concepts and could be drawing on any of them'. Bradshaw (2006) suggests that 'in fact most of the second-order concepts are brought into play during a historical significance enquiry. Consider then its application to other second-order concepts. In many cases such application invites familiar decision-making activities, group work, 'elimination debates', and card-sorts. In the case of chronology and change, there is plenty of mileage for debate in selecting 'significant turning points'. For example, which of the series of acts to extend the franchise was the key turning point? Similarly, which of the education acts from 1833–1944 held the greatest historical significance and for what? When historical evidence is applied to the question of significance, it is territory that has been familiar to history teachers for decades. So many will have automatically stressed the significance of the Domesday Book, Sutton Hoo, the Rosetta Stone, the remains of WWI trenches and many more. And yet, there is also the issue of the selection of evidence that may be described as significant. When a historian reads a documentary source and sees certain parts as historically significant, what determines that choice?

Furthermore, the study of historical significance can enhance understanding of another key concept – interpretations. Hunt (2003) suggested that the application of significance can be a useful tool to challenge the promotion of particular perspectives when the question is asked, 'What is the significance of such an interpretation?' Wrenn picks up this point when he used Equiano's diary to help pupils to understand why others have judged a certain story significant and why this may not always be so. He concludes that work on 'interpretations' of history can both support work on significance and take it further (Wrenn, 2002).

In considering the significance of causes of events, once more the concept of significance demonstrates its potential for taking an explanation beyond its immediate context and making connections, that vital activity in studying significance, with other periods. What gives a cause a greater significance? Often the answer is in the way patterns and repetitions of such causes occur in different contexts, some disheartening such as religious and ethnic divisions and poverty, others more positive such as cooperation between individuals or nations.

Consequence is considered last because again, while, as with causes, one might consider the most significant consequence, it needs a more rigorous examination because there is real value in exploring the differences between consequences and significance. Hunt (2003) would claim that greater understanding of historical significance is more likely to be achieved if there is a clear distinction between the two. Thus, while the consequences of an event contribute towards its significance, it is the wider issues, often value-laden, that give it its significance, what Counsell (2004) describes as 'getting beyond consequences'. Also Bradshaw (2006) finds that 'for historical significance teaching to be meaningful it needs to be about more than just consequences, it needs to deal with the ethereal nature of judgements about historical significance and make them real'. For example, consider the Labour election victory of 1945. Listed among its consequences would be the establishment of the National Health Service, the nationalisation of steel, coal, transport and the railways and the continuation of rationing. However, it may be argued that the significance of installing a Labour government with a large majority was its contribution to the wider, enduring debate about the relative merits of nationalisation as opposed to privatisation, the role of the state and, with rationing, state-imposed equality restricting the free market. In this example, significance is seen to be concerned with enduring issues that arose from events and they are often more abstract than statements of consequences. In the Year 9 or 10 classroom, it is not impractical for you to try to draw out the historical significance in this way.

Task 6.8 *Matters for discussion*

Historical significance is a complex yet immensely rewarding concept. It does require much hard-thinking on how it is to be used and presents plenty of issues for discussion, many ongoing, continually revised and none resolved. Using the content of this section and your own knowledge and experience, consider the following:

1   When, how often, and with which topics would it be appropriate to employ consideration of historical significance with your pupils?

2　Must the historical significance of an individual, event or issue always be related to the present day for it to be meaningful and relevant to the pupils?

3　Can an event, which was a failure, have historical significance?

4　How can the study of historical significance contribute towards citizenship education?

5　How would you assess a pupils' ability to understand historical significance? What might serve as a progression model for the assessment of pupils' understanding of historical significance?

The principal objectives for learning the concept of 'significance'

As noted above, it is increasingly important that you should try to be proactive in asserting the relevance and significance of the topic you are teaching in the widest terms. Howells (1998) made a valid point when suggesting that 'this notion of significance' must inform the learning objectives at some period in the lesson sequence'. To this end you may find it helpful to consider the value of this set of objectives, developed and augmented from those of Lomas (1989), when you seek to meet the requirements of this concept.

The importance of significance in the teaching of history is that it enables the pupils to:

1　understand that history operates on the basis that some events and changes are more important than others;

2　establish criteria for assessing the significance of events, people or changes in the past;

3　understand that some events, which may have seemed significant at the time, were not, while the significance of other events is only recognised later, sometime many years later;

4　understand that different people have different ideas about which events, issues or changes are significant;

5　be able to understand *why* people may hold different ideas about what has been significant;

6　understand that the significance of an event or change is determined by the nature of the historical enquiry;

7　understand that relatively minor events can be highly significant, for example, they have 'symbolic' significance (see Chapter 7);

8　be able to distinguish between the consequences of an event and its significance;

9　understand that an event or change usually becomes significant because of its connection with other events.

Strategies for the teaching of historical significance

Strategies for emphasising significance can involve a range of approaches. Most frequently this occurs within your usual teaching routines, looking for opportunities to ask questions relating to the significance of events, people and changes either at the beginning or end of a lesson or topic. For example at the end of a topic or unit pupils could be asked to justify their selection of the six most important events covered.

Many successful strategies for teaching historical significance involve decision-making exercises. Hunt (2000) includes several examples of such activities. These included giving pupils a set of explanations why an event was significant and asking them to choose the best three, giving also the reasons for their choice. Alternatively, pupils could be given a set of cards explaining *why* the study of a topic is important and are then asked to decide which is the most important. There are opportunities for role-play in which rival inventors, political leaders, physicians, generals, reformers etc. assert the significance of their contribution. As a history teacher you should always try to keep abreast of current events and issues, and where appropriate, link these to the topics you are covering or have covered in your teaching. Try to look for opportunities to point out links, which will not always be obvious to your pupils, especially when they involve the wider issues such as attitudes and responses to poverty, crime, technological change, oppression and disease.

It can be helpful if you can get pupils *thinking* about what things in history have been most significant, and why. Richard Overy's suggestions for the 50 key moments in world history (https://sites.google.com/site/nccmnhistory/the-50-key-dates-of-world-history) offers an example for discussion, and can be adapted to explore other topics and periods.

Summary and key points

The teaching of the key concepts covered in this chapter provides you with the potential for some stimulating and successful lessons. That success is aided if you have a good understanding of the likely problems many pupils may experience in handling these key concepts. The challenge for you is to keep reinforcing the significance of the events you cover and the wider relevance of the concepts involved. In that way you help your pupils to realise that history is not just about the acquisition of knowledge but how you apply that knowledge.

Suggestions for further reading

Barton, K. (2009) The denial of desire: how to make history education meaningless, in L. Symcox and A. Wilschut (eds) National history standards: the problem of the canon and the future of teaching history, Charlotte NC, Information Age Publishing: 265-82.

Blow, F., Lee, P. and Shemilt, D. (2012) Time and chronology: conjoined twins or distant cousins?, *Teaching History*, No. 147: 26-34.

Counsell, C. (2011) What do we want students to do with historical change and continuity?, in I. Davies (ed.) *Debates in History Teaching*, London: Routledge: 109-23.

Dawson, I. (2012) Seeing the bigger picture – developing chronological understanding online at www.thinkinghistory.co.uk/Issues/downloads/SeeingTheBiggerPicture.pdf, accessed 14 April 2014.

Foster, R. (2013) The more things change, the more they stay the same: developing students' thinking about change and continuity, *Teaching History*, No. 151: 8-17.

Kershaw, I. (2004) Personality and power: the individual's role in the history of twentieth-century Europe, *The Historian*, Autumn: 7-19.

Levesque, S. (2008) *Thinking Historically: Educating students for the twenty-first century*, Toronto: University of Toronto Press.

Thinking History website, *Timelines and living graph activities*, online at www.thinkinghistory.co.uk/ActivityModel/ActModTimeline.html, accessed 14 April 2014.

Thinking History website, *Seeing the bigger picture: developing chronological understanding*, www.thinkinghistory.co.uk/Issues/SeeingTheBiggerPictureChronology.html, accessed 14 April 2014.

For further suggestions for further reading and more resources and information about the concepts discussed in this chapter, go to: www.uea.ac.uk/~m242/ historypgce/welcome.htm.

References

Ashby, R. and Lee, P.J. (1987) 'Children's Concepts of Empathy and Understanding in History', in C. Portal (ed.) *The History Curriculum for Teachers*, Lewes: Falmer Press: 62-88.

Barnes, S. (2002) Revealing the Big Picture: patterns, shapes and images at Key Stage 3, *Teaching History*, No. 107: 6-13.

Barton, K. (2009) The denial of desire: how to make history education meaningless, in L. Symcox and A. Wilschut (eds) National history standards: the problem of the canon and the future of teaching history, Charlotte NC: Information Age Publishing: 265-82.

Blow, F., Lee, P. and Shemilt, D. (2012) Time and chronology: conjoined twins or distant cousins?, *Teaching History*, No. 147: 26-34.

Booth, M., Culpin, C. and Macintosh, H. (1987) *Teaching GCSE History*, London: Hodder and Stoughton.

Banham, D. (2000) The return of King John: using depth to strengthen the overview in the teaching of political change, *Teaching History*, No. 99: 22-31.

Bradshaw, M. (2006) Creating controversy in the classroom; making progress with historical significance, *Teaching History*, No. 125: 18-25.

Byrom, J. and Riley, M. (2003) Professional wrestling in the history department: a case study in the planning and teaching of the British Empire at KS3, *Teaching History*, No. 112: 6-13.

Byrom, J. and Riley, M. (2013) *The Crusades*, London: Hodder.

Cairnes, J. (1989) Some Reflections on Empathy in History, *Teaching History*, No. 55: 13-18.

Cercadillo, L. (2006) 'Maybe they haven't decided yet what is right'. English and Spanish perspectives on teaching historical significance. *Teaching History*, No. 125: 6-9.

Chambers, C. (2007) Teaching causal reasoning, chapter 6 in M. Hunt (ed.) *A Practical Guide to Teaching History in the Secondary School*, London: Routledge: 49-58.

Chapman, A. (2003) Camels, diamonds and counterfactuals: a model for teaching causal reasoning, *Teaching History*, No. 112: 46-53.

Clark, V. (2001) Illuminating the shadow: making progress happen in causal thinking through speaking and listening, *Teaching History*, No. 105: 26-33.

Clements, P. (1996) Historical Empathy – R.I.P.?, *Teaching History*, No. 55: 11-16.

Counsell, C. (2004) Looking through a Josephine Butler-shaped window: focusing pupils' thinking on historical significance, *Teaching History*, No. 114: 30-33.

Cunningham, D.L. (2004) Empathy without illusions, *Teaching History*, No. 114: 24-9.

Dawson, I. (2009) What time does the tune start? From thinking about 'sense of period' to modelling history at Key Stage 3, *Teaching History*, No. 135: 50-57.

Dawson, I. (2012) *The Wars of the Roses*, London: Hodder.

DES (1985) *G.C.S.E.: The National Criteria*, London: HMSO.

DES (1990) *History in the National Curriculum, Final Report*, London: HMSO, para 3.18.

DfE (2013) *History programmes of study: key stage 3: National Curriculum in England*, London: DfE.

DfEE/QCA (1999) *The National Curriculum*, London: DfEE/QCA.

Foster, R. (2008) 'Speed cameras, dead ends, drivers and diversions': year 9 use a 'road map' to problematize change and continuity, *Teaching History*, No. 131: 4–9.

Foster, R. (2013) The more things change, the more they stay the same: developing students' thinking about change and continuity, *Teaching History*, No. 151: 8–17.

Gove, M. (2013) *Start the week*, BBC Radio 4, 30 December.

Hamilton, A. and McConnell, T. (2003) Using this map and all your knowledge, become Bismarck, *Teaching History*, No. 112: 15–19.

Hammond, K. (2001) From horror to history: teaching pupils to reflect on significance, *Teaching History*, No. 104: 15–23.

Harris, R., Burn, K. and Woolley, M. (eds) (2013) *The Guided Reader to Teaching and Learning History*, London: David Fulton, Chapter 13: 163–72.

Harris, R. and Rea, A. (2006) Making history meaningful: helping pupils to see why history matters, *Teaching History*, No. 125: 28–36.

Haydn, T. (1995) Teaching Children about Time, *Teaching History*, No. 81, October, 11–12.

Haydn, T. and Levy, R. (1995) *Partnership and School Improvement: Teaching children about time*, London: Institute of Education.

Howells, G. (1998) Being ambitious with the causes of World War 1: interrogating inevitability, *Teaching History*, No. 92: 16–19.

Howells, G. (2002) Ranking and classify: teaching political concepts to post-16 students, *Teaching History*, No. 106: 33–6.

Hunt, M. (2000) 'Teaching Historical Significance' in J. Arthur and R. Phillips (eds) *Issues in History Teaching*, London: Routledge: 39–53.

Hunt, M. (2003) 'Historical Significance', in *Past Forward: A Vision for School History 2002-2012'*, London: Historical Association: 33–6.

Hunt, M. (2006) 'Why Teach History', Chapter 2 in M. Hunt (ed.) *A Practical Guide to Teaching History in the Secondary School*, London: Routledge: 3–14.

Husbands C. and Pendry, A. (2000) 'Thinking and feeling: Pupils' preconceptions about the past and historical understanding', in J. Arthur and R. Phillips (eds) *Issues in History Teaching*, London: Routledge: 125–34.

Illingworth, S. (2000) Hearts, minds and souls: exploring values through history, *Teaching History*, No. 100: 20–24.

Kitson, A. (2001) Challenging stereotypes and avoiding the superficial, a suggested approach to teaching the Holocaust, *Teaching History*, No. 104: 41–8.

Lee, P. and Cercadillo, L. (2013), Historical accounts, significance and unknown ontologies, paper presented at the international seminar on research in historical culture and historical education, Las Navas, Madrid, 4–6 December.

Lee, P.J. and Ashby, R. 'Empathy, perspective and rational understanding in social studies', in O.L. Davis, S. Foster and E. Yeager (eds), *Historical Empathy and Perspective Taking in the Social Studies*, New York: Rowman and Littlefield.

Lee, P.J. (1984) 'Historical Imagination', in A.R. Dickinson, P.J. Lee and P.J. Rogers, *Learning History*, London: Heinemann: 85–116.

Lee P.J., Dickinson, A.R. and Ashby, R. (1996) Children Making Sense of History, *Education 3-13:* 13–19.

Lee, P.J. (1998) 'A lot of guesswork goes on'. Children's understanding of historical accounts, *Teaching History*, No. 92: 29–32.

Lee, P. (1999) 'A lot of guess work goes on': children's understanding of historical accounts, *Teaching History*, No. 92: 29–36.

Lee, P. and Ashby, R. (1987) Children's concepts of empathy and understanding in history, in C. Portal (ed.) *The history curriculum for teachers*, Lewes: Falmer: 62–88.

Levine, N. (1981) *Language, Teaching and Learning: 5. History*, London: Ward Lock Educational.

Lomas, T. (1989) *Teaching and Assessing Historical Understanding*, London, Historical Association.

Lorenz, C. (2013) Understanding historical time – some preliminary considerations, in M. Carretero, S. Berger and M. Grever (eds) *Handbook of Research in Historical Culture and History Education*, paper presented at the international seminar on research in historical culture and historical education, Las Navas, Madrid, 4–6 December.

Low-Beer, A. (1989) Empathy and History, *Teaching History*, No. 55: 8–12.

NCC (1993) *Teaching History at Key Stage 3*, York: NCC.

Martin D. and Brooke, B. (2002) Getting personal: making effective use of historical fiction in the history classroom, *Teaching History*, No. 108: 30–35.

McCrory, C. (2013) How many people does it take to make an Essex man? Year 9 face up to historical difference, *Teaching History*, No. 152: 8–19.

Osowiecki, M. (2004), Seeing, Learning and Doing the Renaissance, part 1, *Teaching History*, No. 117: 34–9.

Osowiecki, M. (2005) Seeing, Learning and Doing the Renaissance, part 2, *Teaching History*, No. 118: 17–25.

Partington, G. (1980) *The idea of an historical education*, Windsor, NFER.

Phillips, R. (2002) Historical significance – the forgotten 'Key Element'?, *Teaching History*, No. 106: 14–19.

QCA (2007) History, programme of study: Key Stage 3, London: QCA. Online at http://curriculum.qca. org.uk/subjects/history/, accessed 11 October 2007.

Riley, M. (1997) Big Stories and Big Pictures: making Outlines and Overviews interesting, *Teaching History*, No. 88.

Rogers, R. (2011) 'Isn't the trigger the thing that sets the rest of it on fire?' Causation maps: emphasising chronology in causation exercises, *Teaching History*, No. 142: 50–55

Sansom, C. (1987) 'Concepts, Skills and Content: A Development Approach to the History Syllabus', in C. Portal (ed.) *The History Curriculum for Teachers*, Lewes: Falmer Press.

Scott, J. (1987) *Medicine Through Time: a Study in Development*, Edinburgh: Holmes McDougall.

Scott, J. (1990) Understanding *Cause and Effect* (Teaching History Research Group). London: Longmans.

Shemilt, D. (1980) *History 13–16: Evaluation*, Edinburgh: Holmes McDougall.

Smith, D. (2014) Period, place and mental space: using historical scholarship to develop year 7 pupils' sense of period, *Teaching History*, No. 154: 8–17.

Thompson, D. (1984) 'Understanding the Past: Procedures and Content', in A.R. Dickinson, P.J. Lee and P.J. Rogers, *Learning History*, London: Heinemann: 168–86.

Wilson, M.D. (1985) *History for Pupils with Learning Difficulties*, London: Hodder and Stoughton.

Woodcock, J. (2005) Does the linguistic release the conceptual? Helping Year 10 to improve their casual reasoning, *Teaching History*, No. 119: 5–14.

VanSledright, B. (2014) *Assessing Historical Thinking and Understanding: Innovative designs for new standards*, London: Routledge.

Wrenn, A. (2002) 'Equiano – voice of silent slaves', *Teaching History*, No. 107: 13–19.

Yeager, E. and Doppen, F. (2001) Teaching and learning multiple perspectives on the use of the atomic bomb: historical empathy in the classroom, in O. L. Davis Jr, E. Yeager and S. Foster (eds) *Historical empathy and perspective taking in the social studies*, New York: Roman and Littlefield: 97–114.

7 Developing historical understanding (2)

Interpretation, accounts, substantive concepts

From Penelope Lively, *Moon Tiger* (1988: 14-15), where a dying historian recalls a history class on Mary Queen of Scots:

> I put up my hand. 'Please Miss, did the Catholics think Elizabeth right to cut off her head?' 'No Claudia, I don't expect they did.' 'Please, do Catholic people think so now?' Miss Lavenham took a breath. 'Well Claudia', she said kindly, 'I suppose some of them might not. People do sometimes disagree. But there is no need for you to worry about that. Just put down what is on the board.'

Introduction

In this chapter we will consider the teaching of three more facets or domains of historical understanding: interpretations of history, accounts and substantive concepts.

The revised version of Key Stage 3 to be introduced in September 2014 states that pupils should 'understand the methods of historical enquiry, including how evidence is used rigorously to make historical claims, and discern how and why contrasting arguments and interpretations of the past have been constructed', and that pupils should 'gain and deploy a historically grounded understanding of abstract terms such as "empire", "civilisation", "parliament" and "peasantry"' (DfE, 2013: 2).

Historical interpretations, while giving rise to some stimulating and enjoyable lessons, has also proved to be one of the most difficult elements of the history curriculum to implement. Successive Ofsted reports have identified interpretations as the weakest area and found schools reluctant to include the element as much as they should. An Ofsted Conference in 2004 focusing on the teaching of interpretations in history reported that 'there is little evidence that schools are giving sufficient time to understanding interpretations of history' (quoted in QCA, 2007b). While teachers often discuss contemporary viewpoints of past events, it is much less common for them to show pupils how different people today interpret the past: this is the area which has been seen by Ofsted as appearing to be the most problematic. There are also concerns about the difficulties of assessing pupils' understanding of interpretations. Student teachers often find this concept to be one of the most challenging aspects of their history teaching. For these reasons, we are devoting a substantial proportion of this chapter to the teaching of historical interpretations.

Objectives

By the end of this chapter you should be able to:

- explain what is meant by both historical interpretations and enquiry in the context of the secondary school curriculum;
- understand the challenges, issues and problems facing both teachers and pupils when studying historical interpretations;
- identify the wide range of interpretations and reconstructions which can provide material for the study of this element;
- deploy some of the strategies and approaches that can be used for the teaching of interpretations of history;
- understand how to approach the development of pupils' understanding of substantive concepts;
- understand some of the issues involved in developing pupils' understanding of the construction of historical accounts, and the status and nature of historical knowledge.

The challenge of teaching historical interpretations

The challenges with which you are faced may be briefly summarised. It is important that you make a clear distinction in your planning between 'sources' and 'interpretations'. Particularly in the early days of the NC there was much confusion of the two with the result that interpretations were approached with the already established 'source skills' approach such as reliability and bias. A clear understanding of the distinction helps you in your choice of appropriate learning objectives and selection of material. Other challenges stem from a variety of pupil misconceptions and stumbling blocks, which inhibit their understanding. You may well discover that some pupils find the idea of differing views of a topic or an individual to be a waste of time and they just want to know what is right, so this presents you with the challenge of explaining why they are studying historical interpretations. It is not always easy to convince pupils that there is not just one 'true' answer. While many pupils can identify *how* interpretations may differ, they struggle to explain *why* this should be the case. They particularly might struggle to explain why different people thought differently even when having available the same information. Other misconceptions you may need to challenge are pupils' conviction of the supremacy of 'eye-witness' accounts in contrast to those of people who were not living at the time; the pupils' preference for written interpretations and a distrust of other representations and indeed a general inclination to dismiss what may be termed 'opinion' with a preference for 'facts'. Finally, there is the thorny issue mentioned by Ofsted, that of assessing pupils' progress in understanding historical interpretations. This itself presents several problems. Firstly, there is considerable scepticism about both the validity and the appropriateness of the levels statements for interpretations, a concern that the progression implied does not relate to how pupils' understanding actually develops and thus making its application difficult for teachers; secondly, there is the problem that when the statements are linked to mark schemes they encourage formulaic responses, which mask the assessment of real understanding.

It can be argued that for many years teachers have encouraged their pupils to be aware that the way the subject-matter of history is presented is replete with interpretations. The very terms, in which some people and events are described, encourages some discussion of the reasons why such words are used. Why was 'The Glorious Revolution of 1688' so called? Who called the period between 1629 and 1640 'the Eleven Years Tyranny'? Who decided that Alfred was Great, Elizabeth I was Good, and her sister Bloody? It is also reasonable to ask how much the use of words such as 'revolution', 'progress' and 'civilisation' involve interpretations. Consider the use of the word 'reform'. Today pupils might well consider how the word 'reform' can be uncritically used in news bulletins implying 'a change for the better', even though it is a matter of opinion whether that is the case.

In her critique of the Interim Report of the NC History Working Group, Lawlor argued that the authors failed to consider that children might be confused by being given different versions and might be better off to master the facts (Lawlor, 1989). However, most history teachers working in England believe that learning about historical interpretations is an important aspect of studying history. Although some pupils might be confused, it is a lesser evil compared to the danger that pupils leave school not understanding *'what history is'*.

The study of interpretations is a further example of how *the processes by which history is communicated* may be used as a basis for developing your pupils' historical understanding. Encouraging pupils to be aware of the way historical events, people and situations may be differently interpreted, reduces the opportunities for the imposition of 'one version' history with all its potential dangers. An understanding of why such different interpretations occur might make a valuable contribution to the health of a democratic society. At the same time the range of historical interpretations can give you the basis for producing some interesting lessons, using materials which might not have been considered appropriate below A level teaching in the era before the NC for history.

Task 7.1 *Identifying the use of historical interpretations*

1   During your school experience discuss with your subject tutor how the department you are working in approach the issue of interpretations. Note which topics have been chosen as being suitable for the development of pupils' understanding of interpretations. Why are some topics perhaps more suitable for an interpretations approach than others? Find out what range of approaches are planned and discuss how these may differ according to the ability of the pupils.
2   Collect a variety of textbooks, which have been written for the KS3 Study Units and investigate the materials and task designed for the study of historical interpretations. Note any particularly useful examples for future reference.

Interpretations of history: issues and concerns

How can we define historical interpretations?

It is helpful to be clear in your own mind about what is meant by historical interpretations when used in the context of the secondary school. You need to be clear about how this aspect of the teaching and learning of history is distinguished from that range of skills associated with the use of sources. Sometimes the distinction has been made that interpretations are only linked to secondary sources. Yet the distinction between primary and secondary sources can sometimes be blurred and often depends on the purpose for which the source is used, rather than when the source was produced. It is perhaps better to think of an interpretation, as Sue Bennett has suggested, as 'a conscious interpretation of the past, which *normally draws together different sources of information*' (Bennett, 1995). In other words, as with the other second order concepts, interpretations is a *second-stage* activity that usually follows the study of the content and the completion of activities to develop an understanding of that content. Further clarification on this question was provided by SCAA (1996):

> Questions on representations and interpretations are likely to concentrate on the process by which the interpretation was created, its purpose, audience and validity. On the other hand, questions relating to source evaluation are likely to concentrate on comprehension, inference, utility and reliability.

Harrison made the point that 'the use of the word interpretations' 'is distinct from the generic term "to interpret", as in "interpreting sources of evidence"' (Harrison, 2004). Furthermore, 'conscious interpretations' will be found in a greater variety of representations than those normally covered by the 'use of sources' (for example, historical stories and novels, museum displays as well as pupils' own interpretations). Such variety increases the potential for adding interest and value to history lessons.

Potential confusion also lies between 'interpretations' and the use of the 'characteristic features of past societies' covered in the previous chapter. The concern of interpretations is *not* the knowledge of ideas and attitudes in the past, which may be very different from those prevalent today. It may, however, be necessary to explore how the ideas and attitudes of the past are related to different interpretations. Indeed, Tony McAleavy (1993: 15) made the point when he wrote, 'an interpretation of history is a conscious reflection on the past and *not* the ideas and attitudes of participants in past events'.

So, to summarise our definition, interpretations of history can be presented in many forms; they represent a deliberate and thoughtful attempt to reconstruct and explain events in the past; to be of any worth they must be rooted in genuine evidence and normally that means they are drawn from several different sources of information.

Debates on what constitutes an historical interpretation

As the study of historical interpretations has evolved since 1990 and teachers have sought ways of making the concepts involved accessible to secondary school pupils, several debates have emerged over what constitutes an historical interpretation. In one debate there is some tension between the conviction that pupils need to study 'real secondary sources', representations of historians' views and pupils being asked to create their own interpretations.

Mastin and Wallace (2006: 6) hold the view that 'the work of assessing interpretations must involve real interpretations', in other words, 'real' secondary sources. A pupil simply constructing their own opinion of say, the Empire, is not what is understood by this key concept. Similarly, a discussion paper for the Ofsted Conference (2004) noted that it had been argued that one of the common errors made by teachers in their planning of work on interpretations was that it is about pupils doing some interpreting on their own. Several found the activity 'Cromwell – hero or villain?', where pupils used sources rather than interpretations to form their answers, was not a study of interpretations. Mastin and Wallace do accept that pupils creating their own interpretations could be used as a way into understanding the concept and this highlights one of the challenges for you. What strategies can be employed to introduce pupils to this concept? Encouraging pupils to create their own interpretations is one strategy that is widely used. In doing this teachers are trying to get the pupils to understand the *process* by which interpretations are made by going through something akin to that process themselves. Such an approach could involve giving half the class one set of sources and the other half an alternative and contrasting set with a resultant variety of activities to explore and ask questions about the process. QCA (2007b) have stated 'that it is important that teachers help pupils to understand how individuals construct an interpretation and the constraints which influence their decision making and so they advocate the use of pupils making their own interpretations of the past. It is a means to an end and Pam Harper's (1993) conclusion from some time ago is still valid today when she wrote:

> activities where a class is divided into two and role play the story of the Boudiccan revolt from the point of view of the Iceni or the Romans will not in themselves enable pupils to work towards an understanding of interpretations of history. Only if the pupils spend time analysing their interpretations of events and compare them with the available evidence will such work be related to historical interpretations.

Another debate concerns what would be acceptable as interpretations. Within this there is a discussion about the validity of photographs in contrast to paintings – is the former 'a conscious interpretation of the past?' Then there is the question of the timescale. Does an interpretation have to be some time after an event for it to meet definitions of historical interpretations? Can an eyewitness account be an interpretation? Task 7.2 invites you to consider and discuss what you think constitutes a historical interpretation.

Task 7.2 *What constitutes a historical interpretation?*

Give a copy of the following list to your tutor or Head of Department and ask them to tick those items, which are thought to be historical interpretations and note the reasons for not ticking any items. Do the same yourself and compare notes.

Domesday Book

War memorials

Pepys' description of the Great Fire

Film 'Culloden'

Museum display re 'Trafalgar'

Firth's 'Railway' painting

Photograph of Wellington's statue	Dickens' 'Oliver Twist'
A castle	A newspaper cartoon
TV programme 'Blackadder'	Opinion of two fictional characters with opposing
History text-book	views e.g. Royalist /Puritan upon past events.

Issues of teaching historical interpretations

Apart from the challenges noted in the introduction to the chapter, the emergence of historical interpretations as an aspect of learning history in all years of the secondary school raises a series of issues for the teacher. You find that your lessons are more successful if you are able to anticipate the difficulties your pupils might encounter. Consider the following:

Knowledge

If the study of historical interpretations is to be a valuable learning experience, pupils and students must have a reasonably detailed knowledge of the topic which is the subject matter of the interpretations. They need a factual basis to enable them to understand the interpretation in the context of events and a basis for making worthwhile comparisons. As greater demands are made of the students, for example, to assess and evaluate interpretations, these could be of very limited value if the student is insufficiently informed on the subject matter.

However, how that content is initially presented or 'discovered' by the student could influence later work on interpretations. It may be a case of what information to give and what not to give. So, should you have some exercises involving historical interpretations to follow, then how the groundwork of necessary information is presented needs careful consideration. Basically, the question is, what do the pupils or students need to know and understand in order to complete work on interpretations with success?

Accessibility

Perhaps the most far-reaching and possibly frustrating problem for teachers seeking to teach historical interpretations is that of accessibility. The principal barrier to understanding is that of language; complex sentence structure and unfamiliar words have for many years presented a problem for teachers and examiners alike, as indicated in Chapter 4. To this may now be added the adult language of historians as they present their interpretations of people and situations in the past. At times such interpretations rest on nuances and shades of opinion too subtle for some pupils. While the variety and range of interpretations can add to the interest and stimulation of the study, the language of poetry or folk songs can also present problems of accessibility. Cartoons and satirical drawings may again be too subtle for some pupils. In all cases the challenge to you as a teacher is to try to make such interpretations and representations accessible to the pupils and without distorting the meaning or in the case of assessment removing too much of the skill or understanding one is trying to assess. The problem of accessibility therefore is linked to that of differentiation. Yet at the same time as being aware of the problems of accessibility, it is quite possible that your abler pupils could be capable of exploring more complex interpretations, especially if studied in a structured manner. Lengthier texts can increase the potential for analysing the process involved with the use of evidence as well as enabling pupils to match an interpretation with their own knowledge. Chapman (2006), Sinclair (2006) and Woolley (2003) have described such use of challenging interpretations.

Progression

As in other facets of historical understanding, it is difficult to argue that there is a clear and robust 'ladder' of progression which can be translated into levels; some pupils may grasp more complex ideas about interpretation, but not understand easier ones. However, a 'loose' framework for thinking about progression in this area might look something like this:

1   Understanding that different interpretations of historical events and personalities exist.
2   Being able to suggest why interpretations may differ.
3   Understanding that some interpretations are more valid or authoritative than others, and the criteria for making such judgements.
4   Being able to make a balanced and well-justified evaluation of the comparative authority of different interpretations.

Most pupils find it easier to explain *how* interpretations differ rather than *why*. Whereas many feel comfortable in describing the differences between the interpretations by analysing the data presented to them in a variety of media, they then struggle to explain those differences, particularly when they have to draw upon information not immediately before them. Many might settle for the obvious, for example, 'because they were written by different people living at different times', which while correct is not the depth of insight one might be looking for.

Even so, there are times when you may feel that the progression described does not conform to your experience in setting and assessing your pupils' work. Be prepared to find individual pupils responding differently when using different types of interpretations and different contexts. It is not necessarily regression but shows the complexity of the task. It is likely that any assessment would need to take account of a range of exercises, where assessment is enquiry and context specific. There have been criticisms of the level descriptions because they fail to give sufficient emphasis to the process by which interpretations are compiled and the suggestion is that if due attention is given to process in a succession of activities then determining pupil progress becomes much easier. Lee and Shemilt also identify the progression of pupils' thinking as pupils try to explain why historical accounts differ and seek to encourage pupils to go well beyond the kind of simple answers mentioned above (Lee and Shemilt, 2004). Lee advanced a set of levels often with a range of understanding within the level. They were:

- Stories are the same and only differ in the way they are told.
- Stories differ because of the availability of knowledge yet within this the responses range from 'not being there' to 'interpretation of evidence'.
- Different accounts differ about the past because the past is complex.
- Focus on the role of the author with a range of from biased views to selection of evidence as a legitimate personal move.
- Accounts are not complete so it is in the nature of historical accounts to differ. (Lee, 1998)

Some of these statements are quite insightful and sophisticated and demonstrate a burgeoning development of historical understanding. Lee and Shemilt indicated further developments of their research when setting the goal of pupils understanding that two historical accounts of an event can *legitimately* differ and be consistent with acceptable use of the evidence available. This approach is sophisticated but Lee and Shemilt believe this is possible with the younger pupils and can lead to pupils having positive thoughts about history and appreciate the value of different perspectives. To approach this goal the pupil needs to progress through several 'break through' points such as:

1   Abandoning the idea that only contemporaries could write a true account (a common misconception noted at the beginning of the chapter) and even worse, if contemporary accounts do not exist, all other histories are fabrications.
2   An appreciation that there can never be the *perfect* representation of an event but there can be an infinite number of possible descriptions of it.
3   An acceptance that accounts may differ legitimately without merely being matters of opinion. (Lee and Shemilt, 2004)

Another facet of progression in understanding interpretations is for pupils to develop the understanding that history is not just made by famous individuals. Hobhouse (2005) argues that modern history has been shaped less by the actions of humans than by the forces of population growth, food supply and disease. It is not just pupils who are prone to thinking that history is mainly about famous and important people, and wars, acts of parliament and significant deeds. Peter Mandler points out that in the draft version of the NC for history made public in February 2013:

> there was 'nothing about "Britain transformed" by the rise of the mass media (from radio and cinema to television and the internet), or by secularization, or by women's entry into the labour market, or by youth sub-cultures, or by consumerism, or by globalization, or by the ebb and flow of equality and inequality, or by family limitation, or by Americanization, or by social mobility, or by environmental change or ideas of history and heritage. (Mandler, 2013: 18)

Task 7.3 *Considering pupils' progression in understanding historical interpretations*

1 Using the information provided in this chapter about common misconceptions, which pupils may have of historical interpretations and the statements about progression from Lee and Shemilt's research, devise a list of questions, which you could employ at appropriate times when you are teaching a topic which targets this concept.

2 Ask your subject tutor or Head of Department if you could interview two groups of pupils of differing abilities, who have recently studied a topic, which targeted historical interpretations. Using some of your list and using the historical topic they have studied, consider how you will initiate a discussion with the groups. Although aware of the limitations of this activity, see if you can tease out their problems with this concept. Compare how the two different groups responded.

Background of the interpretations

Linked to the difficulties with progression, implying a progression of understanding, is that of knowledge of the background of the interpreters. That background information might be correctly but superficially expressed as 'He was a royalist' or 'She was a French protestant' or, with older pupils, 'He was a Marxist historian', but such information would need to have a fuller explanation, which requires further layers of knowledge. Should it be necessary to determine that an interpretation of a much earlier event reflected the spirit of the times of the person responsible for the interpretation, then that requires knowledge not only of the event being interpreted but also of the times of the interpreter. Card has called this process 'seeing double' – one historical period's visualisation of another. Using the example of painting, she shows how the artist – even one who has done a great deal of research – usually projects back into the subject, the values, ethics, manners and sometimes the costumes of the artists' own period (Card, 2004). The result is the double vision of studying two periods of history. However, sometimes when the background of the interpreter is reduced to a brief attribution, as for assessment, then there can arise the dangers of stereotyping as if say all Victorians held the same views.

Conveying genuine understanding

When presented with such issues as accessibility, progression and author background, one approach chosen, particularly if external examinations are involved, is for teachers to present user-friendly packages of interpretations for the examination candidate to recall and reproduce within the examination room. Then, what is being assessed is an awareness of the differing interpretations and the ability to recall accurately. What is less likely is that the candidates have had the opportunity to work through the processes involved in understanding interpretations. McAleavy (2003) doubts very much whether the use of 'gobbet questions' with minimal background is likely to encourage critical thinking but is more likely to produce a set of stereotypical responses (McAleavy, 2003). In Howells' view 'the one line source description and date encourages simplistic comments on creating an interpretation and this greatly diminishes the historian's art (Howells, 2005). For perhaps what is worse, many candidates will see this for what it is to the detriment of a positive attitude towards the subject. There is a danger here that assessment practices at GCSE could have a detrimental influence on the teaching of historical interpretations with younger pupils. The challenge for you as a teacher is how to create situations, which can *genuinely assess an understanding of historical interpretations*, an application of principles and knowledge rather than diligent recall and formulaic responses. There is the danger of lessons being reduced to 'coaching rather than teaching' (Abulafia, 2012).

Confusion of certainty and uncertainty

A problem inherent in the study of historical interpretations is that, while for some it encourages valuable insights into the nature of events, people and issues in the past, for others there is a danger that such a study could promote a rather negative attitude towards history as a subject. For the latter they need to be assured that they are learning something that is accurate and 'correct', knowledge that they can now 'possess' to put alongside their knowledge of other subjects. To them, if history is too frequently presented as a mass of uncertainty, represented by different viewpoints, they may become disenchanted with the subject. You need to constantly emphasise that what is accepted forms the framework of our historical knowledge and assure your pupils that a great deal of what they learn falls into this category. At the same time as stressing that what really adds interest to the subject are the questions such uncontested knowledge raises. We accept that the Normans won the Battle of Hastings in 1066, what may be open to interpretation is how much that event affected England and Wales in the years that followed. Perhaps for this reason, in your schemes of work for Key Stage 3 you need to limit the concentration on interpretations according to the ability of the class or pupils within a class. Pupils and students need to be able to understand the educational outcomes that arise from such study and be able to recognise their relevance for the world in which they are growing up. For all these risks, the successful use of informed scepticism and the ability to make discerning and considered judgements about alternatives is extremely helpful to pupils in life after school. And even in school Lee and Shemilt were able to show that there was a positive appreciation of historical interpretations when pupils came to understand that historians could hold legitimate differing interpretations of the same evidence (Lee and Shemilt, 2004). Perhaps, the key message here is to be always seeking to emphasise the positive.

Sensitivity

The final issue for your consideration is that of the need to be sensitive to the way differing interpretations could affect your pupils not just in mixed racial schools but in all schools. Many departments teach the Crusades and are very conscious of the need for sensitivity and balance in their selection of material, particularly the need to ensure the inclusion of positive images for all pupils. Be aware of the potential dangers. A recent study, *The British Media and Muslim Representation* (2007) complained that popular films have helped to demonise Muslims as violent, dangerous and threatening, thus reinforcing prejudices. Significantly, the report argued that it was not the fact that they were negative images but that they were the only images. Therein lies your guide – it is not a question of making topics 'no-go' areas for differing interpretations but rather ensuing balance and positive images. The same point may be applied to the treatment of the slave trade and its abolition. Wrenn, in an article about Equiano, noted that 'societies, people, religious cultures and states often create role models or people of iconic value to reinforce their identities. The same is true of black identities' (Wrenn, 2002: 15). He goes on to reassert one of the aims of learning interpretations, relevant to a consideration of sensitive content, by noting that 'interpretations of history is one rigorous, analytical tool, which we can use to help pupils to resist and question racist attitudes'. Grosvenor (1999) has noted how often the black experience has either been excluded or seen in problematic terms and suggests that one aspect of the study of interpretations would be 'to teach pupils how such interpretations and representations have arisen'. Sensitivity is not limited to different races and cultures but can also be a factor with pupils from different social backgrounds. Thus there is a case for the sensitive handling of interpretations of poverty and its causes. Finally McCully and Pilgrim (2004) have shown how by the use of two fictional characters to present opposing views of major events in Irish history the characters reflected their own allegiances. In this way the teachers were seeking to explore the relationship between particular contemporary perspectives and the way the past is interpreted and in so doing offered the pupils a way forward in understanding the forces that divide society. Using fictional characters made it less personal.

Task 7.4 *Sensitivity and interpretations*

A useful long-term pursuit for you to contemplate is to collect old history textbooks. This is not always that easy as many departments have problems of space and old books soon disappear. Even so there are plenty still around and they can provide some useful material for your lessons, especially on historical interpretations.

1   With a series of textbooks written over time (you could be lucky and find some over 100 years old), examine how they approach a set of topics which you think would or should be treated differently today.
2   Examine a set of modern history textbooks to note with what sensitivity and with what images presented, they cover topics and groups such as the Crusades, the Slave Trade, Poverty, the British Empire, China, the portrayal of different nationalities.

Approaches to developing pupils' understanding of historical interpretations

1 Planning development

The teaching of historical interpretations is more likely to be successful if there has been a sufficient investment of time in the preparatory activities *before* the interpretations can be considered. The following diagram gives some indication of the stages through which the teaching of interpretations can move.

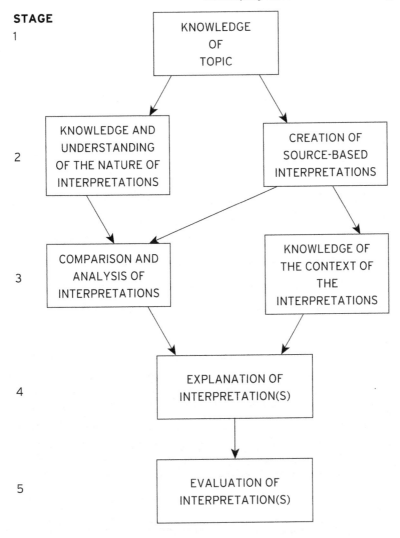

STAGE

1   KNOWLEDGE OF TOPIC

2   KNOWLEDGE AND UNDERSTANDING OF THE NATURE OF INTERPRETATIONS

    CREATION OF SOURCE-BASED INTERPRETATIONS

3   COMPARISON AND ANALYSIS OF INTERPRETATIONS

    KNOWLEDGE OF THE CONTEXT OF THE INTERPRETATIONS

4   EXPLANATION OF INTERPRETATION(S)

5   EVALUATION OF INTERPRETATION(S)

This diagram summarises some of the points made in the chapter to this point. Stages 1 and 2 represent the preparatory stages for the study of interpretations. The knowledge of the topic and the identification of the interpretation are vital preliminaries for the successful completion of the higher levels of analysis, explanation and evaluation. The key question is: do the pupils have sufficient information from which to be able to draw meaningful conclusions and to make valid comments on the interpretations they are studying? Without sufficient knowledge the pupils will become frustrated and lose motivation. It has been suggested that only when the activities described as stage 3 and above are reached is the real study of interpretations underway. Only if pupils spend time analysing their interpretations of the events and compare them with the available evidence can such work be related to the assessment of pupils' understanding of interpretations. Further knowledge about the authors of the interpretations and the context in which they were working would be needed if the pupils are to be able to tackle successfully stage 4 – an explanation of interpretations.

2 Explaining the purpose

There are times when studying the different interpretations might seem to some pupils a rather arcane and dry exercise, irritating in its uncertainties and lacking the interest of the original story. To counter this possible reaction, it is both advisable and educationally useful for pupils to be able to *appreciate the value of such exercises.* Your pupils always need to be encouraged to see the relevance of the aspects of the historical study they pursue to the world in which they are growing up. An important element of this is to *compare the varying interpretations of past events to current ones* and be able to show how sometimes what may be presented as an unequivocal truth is really an interpretation. Some current issues may be too complex for Key Stage 3 pupils. Even so they can probably understand why and how people who once wrote of Nelson Mandela as a terrorist are now prepared to accept him as a great leader.

3 The range and diversity of historical interpretations

An important feature of this element is the need for pupils to appreciate the breadth and variety of interpretations. Because they may regard history as a school subject with content that has to be learned, it is easy for them to fail to appreciate just how widely used history can be and that much of its use involves somebody's interpretation. They will soon appreciate the point when you refer to well-known cinematic interpretations such as 'Robin Hood' or 'Ben Hur'. References to interpretations, which are familiar to the pupils, form a useful starting point for the development of their understanding. This can be extended to include historical stories and novels, drama, cartoons, museum displays, guides and displays at historical sites, popular views about the past as well as your pupils' own interpretations. Valuable as it is for pupils to know the range of interpretations, Lee and Shemilt (2004) correctly warn against such knowledge being the height of your ambitions for your pupils. Many teachers have found them capable of much more.

Task 7.5 *Encouraging pupils to understand the range and diversity of historical interpretations*

The death of Thomas a Becket: see the Becket materials at: www.uea.ac.uk/~m242/historypgce/interp/welcome.htm.

Study the resources and suggested activities on the death of Becket. In most history departments the topic of Becket is covered in Year 7. Consequently any suggestions for activities involving interpretations must only consider those appropriate for such young pupils. The example and the activities set out on the website therefore have as their main objective the task of familiarising the pupils with the range and sometimes the unusual nature of interpretations.

---

4 Asking questions about interpretations

An important part of the teaching of historical interpretations is the development of pupils' skills in asking questions about an interpretation. It is possible to create a sequence of questions, which provides a useful basis for such questioning. The table shows two sets of questions which pupils could be encouraged to employ to a range of interpretations and a range of topics. The first list is taken, with some adaptations, from Pam Harper (1993) and the second a more recent one used by Counsell, Riley and Byrom (2004) at an OFSTED Conference. Compare the two and use them to design your own set, possibly for display on the classroom wall.

1993

- Who produced it? What was his or her starting point?
- What do we know about the person who produced it?
- Why was it produced?
- Where was it produced?
- What sources were used and how valid were they?
- Who was the intended audience?
- What was the purpose of the interpretation?
  - to amuse or entertain?
  - to sell the past or an image of it?
  - to inform?
  - to create myths?
  - to search for truth?
  - to justify or explain the present?
  - to influence current and future policies and discussions?
- Are some interpretations more believable than others?

2004

- What is it ?
- What is it saying?
  - What does it say/show explicitly?
  - What does it say implicitly?
- How and why was it constructed?
  - What was the purpose and the audience
    - i   to persuade?
    - ii   to entertain?
    - iii to inform?
    - iv to communicate?
    - v   to commemorate?
- What is the relationship between the interpretation and the available evidence?
- Which parts are factual, points of view or imagined?
- How has the interpretation been affected by the context in which it was created?
  - i   Ideology?
  - ii   Values?
  - iii Nationality?
  - iv Personality?
  - v   Expectations?

In spite of the passage of time the lists have much in common. However, with the greater experience now available the more recent list shows a clearer focus on purpose, process and perspective. However, take care in your use of questioning, selecting those which are appropriate for the materials you are using and the ability of your pupils. You need to ensure they have access to the information needed to answer the questions.

5 Identifying and explaining differences

You find that there is a logical sequence as you take your pupils to a point where they are in a position to begin to explain differences in interpretations. Your first task is to ensure your pupils understand the content of the interpretation. This might require some editing of the original statement or prompting to note the significant details of, for example, a picture or a poem. Then the pupils can be set the task of comparing the differences and the similarities. Once these have been identified the real task of explanation can begin. At this point your pupils can begin to apply the questions set out below. What is important is that your planning takes into account what the pupils will need, while *allowing pupils some scope for initiative and insight.*

Task 7.6 *Setting an exercise to identify and explain differences of interpretation*

Presented below are two extracts, which show two very different interpretations of Thomas Becket. On the left-hand side of each extract are the actual words of the author, on the right is an attempt to make the content more accessible.

Using these extracts work out a sequence of activities for your pupils to enable them to begin to offer explanations of these differing interpretations and to make some attempt at evaluating them. You may find these further extracts from John Harvey of use:

> Again and again kings with a truly regal achievement to their credit are found to have... their memory besmirched by historians.

> Becket got what he asked for, but Henry, as generous and as just as he was free from petty spite, was left burdened with murder and sacrilege for the remaining twenty years of his life.

Interpretation 1: From John Harvey, The Plantagenets', 1959, p. 45.

Nothing could be more misleading than the notion of a saintly man of God ill-treated by a tyrannical potentate. It was said that Henry was never known to choose an unworthy friend, but Becket's worthiness is a matter of opinion. Extraordinary mixture of well-to-do-man-about-town, witty and extravagant, and self-willed, self-torturing, and it must be said, self-advertising churchman, Thomas Becket won for himself an outstanding place in history by his genius for manoeuvring other parties into the wrong.

The idea that Becket was a saintly man of God, who was harshly treated by a cruel King is far from the truth. People said Henry always chose good friends, but whether Becket was a good friend is a matter of opinion. Becket was an unusual mixture of well-off man-about-town. He was witty but wasteful. He was a stubborn, self-torturing and, it must be said, a churchman who was keen to show off. Thomas Becket won for himself an outstanding place in history because he was a genius at making other people appear to be in the wrong.

Interpretation 2: John Morris, S.J., 'The Life and Martyrdom of Saint Thomas Becket, Archbishop of Canterbury', 1859, p. 91. Morris was a Jesuit, that is a member of the Catholic Society of Jesus, begun by Ignatius Loyola.

The personal hostility which King Henry was now beginning to entertain against St. Thomas, soon found rent in an attack upon the liberties of the clergy. This was a part of the King's policy of self-aggrandisement in which he had been restrained by the Saint, whilst he exercised influence over him.

The personal hostility, which King Henry was now beginning to show against Saint Thomas, was soon seen in an attack upon the rights of the clergy. This was a part of the King's policy of increasing his own importance. Before that, in the days when the Saint was able to influence the King, Thomas had been a restraining influence.

6 Explaining why historical interpretations might change

In order to meet the requirements of this area of knowledge, skills and understanding, pupils need to be able to explain 'how and why some historical events, people, situations and changes have been interpreted differently'. Part of that explanation involves an understanding of how circumstances might change which can influence an interpretation. To summarise these changing circumstances it is possible to create a spray-diagram. Here is an example showing some factors, no doubt there are others. Able pupils could be asked to try to design a diagram before being given a final version. Having drawn the diagram, most abilities might be asked to write a sentence or two explaining each point. Most would find it useful to have some examples of each point also.

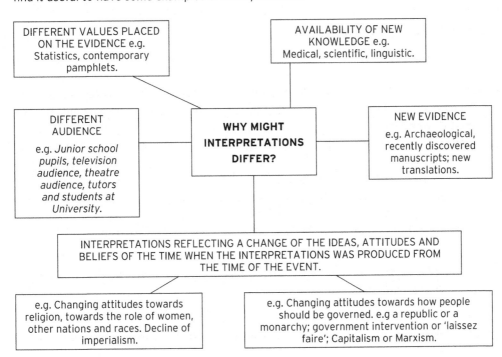

7 Evaluating historical interpretations

Some teachers are sceptical about whether the evaluation of historical interpretations is an appropriate activity for most secondary school pupils, believing it would be expecting too much of them to be asked to sit in judgement of what could be the result of long-term academic study by a reputable historian. Pupils are aware of their limitations and would see such an activity as contrived and artificial. However, there are situations when the evaluation of interpretations can offer rewarding insights for pupils studying this key concept. Such activity usually involves asking your pupils to apply their knowledge of a topic to certain types of interpretations and representations to see if they are consistent with their knowledge and understanding. Many rise to the challenge of offering their opinion as individuals or as a group. A further advance would be, after studying a range of sources, to evaluate an interpretation for its consistency with the understanding they have gained from their study of the evidence.

   To this end the following list of objectives deriving from the 2004 Ofsted Conference on interpretations should be helpful. Pupils should:

- know how to identify the internal evidence from the interpretation they are considering;
- be able to make inferences from the comparison of different interpretations;
- understand how the interpretation is affected by the context in which it was created;
- make judgements on the effectiveness of a history written as propaganda;
- understand the role of history where the context is unhistorical;
- make an informed judgement about the interpretation, which, depending on the type of question, might include objectivity, completeness, accuracy or the extent of these things. (Ofsted, 2004)

Examples of strategies

Although there are many challenges, debates and unresolved issues associated with the teaching of historical interpretations, the teaching of this concept can provide you with some of your most imaginative and stimulating lessons. In planning to teach this key concept, you may find that it is more likely to succeed if placed within a wider overarching enquiry. This means that your pupils will be better informed both to understand the interpretations presented to them and make informed comments about them. One-off interpretation lessons are more likely to have the same deadening effect as context-free source skill exercises. Furthermore, placing interpretations within an enquiry will also make it easier for pupils to understand the process by which an interpretation has been constructed and as noted, already understanding the process is a great step to a more sophisticated understanding of the concept. Also, studying interpretations makes it easier for pupils to answer those questions listed above.

The use of a variety of children's books, old-fashioned history textbooks and popular historical story books

For pupils who have had little experience in considering historical interpretations, the use of history books intended for a younger audience than themselves, can provide a useful introduction. The NCC (1993) described the use by Year 7 pupils of a view of William the Conqueror based on a Ladybird book by L. Du Garde Peach, published in 1956. Pupils were asked to compare that interpretation with their own knowledge and try to explain the limitations of the Ladybird view. Similarly, a Year 8 class could be presented with the following extract from *The Story of Queen Elizabeth*, Ladybird, 1958, by the same author:

> Queen Elizabeth reigned over England for forty-five years. When she came to the throne England was poor. When she died, England was rich, prosperous, united and happy. Her reign saw the beginnings of what came to be the British Empire. The fighting sailors of her reign and the great victory over the Spanish Armada, made England one of the greatest countries of Europe. Much of this was due to the character of Elizabeth herself. She never despaired and she never gave in.

Again, pupils could consider whether all these statements are confirmed by their knowledge and discuss why the author has chosen to present such an interpretation. This encourages a useful discussion of the relationship of an interpretation to its intended audience. With able pupils it could also be the starting point for an enquiry into 'How accurate is The Elizabethan Legend?'.

The study of historical interpretations can also generate a *revived use for some old textbooks*. Quotations from some such books, written in the late nineteenth century or early twentieth century can tell as much about the times in which they were written as the topic they were writing about. This particularly applies to comments about the British colonies and other countries, where the books often had an imperialist and condescending tone. Others sought to use the study of the past as a vehicle for moral lessons for the pupils; as such they encourage the consideration of the author's purpose in writing a historical textbook.

Drawings, paintings

Another relatively straightforward approach to the study of historical interpretations is through drawings and artistic reconstructions. Returning to the Ladybird books, these are attractively illustrated and yet it may be useful for pupils to think about such pictures as interpretations. How much do the pictures showing the social background of the times present a sanitised, attractive representation of what was often dirty and unhygienic. How much is the artist influenced by the nature of the audience? Similarly, artistic reconstructions in textbooks can be the subject of such questions.

An alternative approach to interpretations through drawing is *to encourage the pupils to draw their ideas about a topic*. This can offer useful clues about the pupils' understanding of that topic. Wilson (1985) has shown how successful this can be with pupils of generally low ability. Apart from using drawings as a welcome alternative to the symbolic meaning of language, encouraging pupils' drawing helps them to realise that what they produce is the product of their own imagination – 'history not necessarily as it was, but as they think it is'. The comparison of each other's interpretative drawings and the ensuing explanation of the differences enables the pupils to be operating at stage 3 of the diagram. Furthermore, as Wilson also points out, this subtle distinction between fact and interpretation is less clear when children are presented with visual material, which is the product of the imagination of others, including the illustrations of modern textbooks.

Much can be gained from the pupils' own interpretation of pictures. For example, a photograph of a painting by A.F. Tait of the Stockport Viaduct (1842), soon after its completion, was passed round a Year 9 class studying the nineteenth-century industrial town. Individually, they were asked to write down one or more adjectives that came to mind when they analysed the photograph. In the following feedback, a variety of contrasting interpretations emerged. Most saw a smoky, grimy factory town beneath this massive viaduct, while others produced words such as 'romantic', and 'magnificent'. These differences generated a useful discussion about the painter's purpose, about how people in 1842 might have felt about the new viaduct and its railway, and why so many pupils had emphasised the dirty aspect of the town. The discussion then moved on to consider further comparisons reflecting different viewpoints.

Use of historical fiction

In more recent years teachers have overcome some reluctance to make use of historical fiction in their history lessons. It has become generally accepted that such literature can be a useful aid to pupil interest and understanding. *By following the experience of individual characters placed in past situations, it is easier for many pupils to begin to comprehend situations very different from their own experience.* Any concern about the lack of authenticity of such a medium has been dispelled to a degree by the good fortune of having had in the past half century some excellent writers of historical fiction for young people. Such writers spent many hours of solid research on the background of their novel. The very nature of such fiction means that it represents an author's interpretation of an event or past environment. So, while extracts from such literature with the wealth of detail that is often included, are an excellent aid to understanding in themselves, they can also be used to develop further pupils' understanding of historical interpretations. Consider the following description of exploited child labour in the factories of the early industrialisation. The passage is taken from a novel, excellent for this purpose *The Devil's Mill* by Walter Unsworth.

> If Jeremy was overawed by the machinery and the noise, he did not fail to notice his fellow apprentices. What he saw was not encouraging: thin, ragged children with pinched faces, some only seven or eight years old and so tiny that they had to stand on stools to reach their machines. The boys wore only shirt and trousers, though the mill was damp and cold, the girls plain, pinafore dresses. All were barefoot, with unkempt hair, and incredibly dirty.
>
> Though these things in themselves were bad enough it was the faces of the children which alarmed Jeremy. Pale, sickly, their faces had set into a look of utter hopelessness. He felt a cold chill of apprehension to think that these were his companions of the future and he wondered whether he too would become like them.

Such a passage could precipitate the use of some of the questions about interpretations listed above. It would be particularly useful for pupils to consider not only the purpose of the author and the intended audience *but also the extent to which they think it represents an accurate picture of such factories.* Furthermore, such a passage could be used either to introduce the topic of child labour in factories to be followed by the use of contemporary sources to examine whether the passage was supported by such evidence. Alternatively, the use of the extract could, as in the procedure indicated by the diagram near the beginning of this section, follow the study of child labour and so enable the pupils to move from analysis through to evaluation. An alternative and effective way of using historical fiction is to encourage pupils to write their own. Martin and Brooke (2002) have shown that given structured guidance and using their own search for supportive evidence, pupils can find such an activity both stimulating and effective in developing their historical understanding.

Use of groups

Successful lessons may be based on *giving different sets of evidence to different groups* within the classroom. In their discussions the groups are asked to produce a set of conclusions based upon the information available to them. When their responses are fielded and recorded, one of the points that emerges from the ensuing discussion is the conclusion that interpretations will differ because they draw upon different evidence. A lesson using such an approach was given to a Year 8 class studying the Moghul Empire. The groups were asked to answer the question, 'Who won the battle of Panipat?' Two different duplicated and contrasting sheets were in use, some pupils had Sheet A, others Sheet B. Sheet A was fictitious. The different views were later recorded in a chart on the board. The teacher then analysed the results and asked the pupils a series of questions about the conflicting interpretations. Destroying the fictitious sheet before them, the teacher then asked the pupils to consider the significance for historians of having only one side of evidence on which to base their interpretation of events. *Again it is worth re-emphasising the importance of the follow-up work in re-informing the significance of issues that had emerged from the discussion.* Sometimes student teachers do not allow sufficient time for this important follow-up to the activity, assuming that the group activity itself will be sufficient for the objectives of the lesson to have been met.

In one of many card sort possibilities for teaching historical interpretations, Howells (2005) showed how, following lessons on the English Civil War, different distribution of cards describing long-term causes/blockers (actions which would stop the war/short-term causes), would reveal different interpretations of the war and lead on to a valuable debate about determinist/Marxist or chance/accidental factors. QCA (2007b) also advocate several card-sorting exercises to explore the question of the relationship between underpinning evidence and different interpretations of the past. One method begins with an explanation of the topic by the teacher. The pupils are then given a number of evidence cards and asked to sort them in a way that shows particular pieces of evidence can be used to support particular interpretations. For example, different views of the fairness of the Treaty of Versailles.

Group work may also be one way of studying how different periods have interpreted an event or an historical figure. For example, in compiling obituaries supposedly written at different times, thereby helping to develop Card's 'double vision' of interpretations. More elaborately, as part of a larger enquiry, groups might be used for understanding changing attitudes towards the British Empire. Mastin and Wallace (2006) described how different sources from (i) around 1897; (ii) 1960-70; and (iii) contemporary times can be used to show how different periods of history produced differing interpretations of the Empire.

This last example raises a further debate about the extent to which your pupils study of historical interpretations should concentrate on the process or whether some aspects of historiography present a legitimate approach to the study of the concept. McAleavy (2000) found teachers to be reluctant to use historiography but argued that it presents scope for introducing real historical debate at KS3, believing that academic histories are neglected and can be accessible to pupils of this age.

Use of video, film, internet

Among the most stimulating aids to the understanding of historical interpretations is the use that can be made of videos and films. These vary greatly in their nature.

The use of film material does raise legitimate questions about the use or neglect of historical evidence, the purpose of the interpretation and, again, how the nature of the intended audience can affect the interpretation. A familiar anecdote on this theme may be retold of how the film director, Eisenstein, in his reconstruction of the Bolshevik Revolution of 1917, did more damage to the Winter Palace when shooting the film than was ever achieved during the actual revolution. Clips from that film have been used in documentaries and news programmes for many years, since the film was made in 1922, to the extent that Eisenstein's reconstruction is often assumed to be the actual event. Pupils will be familiar with various historical 'epics', such as *Gladiator* and costume dramas frequently repeated on television. Such reconstructions could be useful starting points for the study of a topic. Useful discussion can focus on the degree of artistic licence involved to add drama to the reconstruction.

The rapid development of the internet has brought a range of opportunities and challenges to the teacher of historical interpretations. ICT has a chapter of its own and the wider issues and strategies are explored there. Even so, as a student you will already be familiar with some of its uses but it is well worth exploring it again through the eyes of the student teacher.

Task 7.7 *Using the internet for teaching historical interpretations*

1   Discuss with your department how they make use of the internet in their planning and teaching. Have they any rules or guidelines about how and *how not* to make use of this resource?

2   **Either** select a topic you are likely to be teaching in a few weeks time. Surf the web to find out what materials are available related to that topic. These might include: useful short summaries of content which extends the content of the textbook; various and differing visual images; controversial views/propaganda; academic debates; material on teacher-orientated websites.

Or collect material for studying historical interpretations of Richard I ('Richard Lionheart'). How could you make accessible the interpretations of: John Gillingham, Amin Maalouf, Réné Grousset, Bishop William Stubbs, Nigel Saul, Richard of Devizes and pictorial representations from the sixteenth to the nineteenth century?

Use of pupil made podcasts

Pupils working in small groups are provided with materials which will lead them to different interpretations of historical personalities and events. They use Audacity or Audioboo (see Chapter 9) to make short 'radio type' broadcasts about their interpretation.

The *real* work on interpretations will occur when the pupils are given an opportunity to compare the results and to try and account for the differences.

Use of role play

Another increasingly popular but valuable approach used in history teaching is that of role play. Its main purpose is usually to help the pupils to comprehend complex issues in format that they can understand by making situations more personal and immediate. Such an approach can also be used to help the understanding of historical interpretations.

The use of familiar media formats can also be used to good effect. A Year 9 class was asked, in groups, to prepare a radio programme on the Peterloo Massacre. Different pupils within the groups were to be interviewed presenting different interpretations of the event. Each interpretation was based on a collection of primary sources made available to the pupils. The discussion which followed the group work then sought in sequence to: (1) identify; (2) explain; and finally (3) evaluate the differences that emerged.

Use of articles from popular history magazines

As noted in Chapter 5, articles from popular history magazines can be a useful resource. Older and more able pupils should be able to cope with the reading demands of such articles, and articles can be 'filleted' for use with younger pupils, with the teacher leading pupils through the article with careful scaffolding where required. As noted in Chapter 5, such articles also have the benefit of moving pupils forward in their ability to cope with longer texts than are available in conventional textbooks. Many articles focus on issues revolving around controversies of interpretation, and some provide a historiographical overview of changes over time. A few examples are given below:

John Morill (2000) 'Oliver Cromwell, war criminal?', *BBC History Magazine*, May: 22–6.
Gary Sheffield and John Bourne (2005) 'Dropping the donkey epithet', *BBC History Magazine*, March 2005: 12–16.
Dennis Judd (2008) 'Empire: good or bad?', *BBC History Magazine*, January: 24–30.
Saul David and William Dalrymple (2007) Indian mutiny, *BBC History Magazine*, 15–21.
C.J. Bearman (2007) Confronting the suffragette mythology, *BBC History Magazine*, 14–18.
Jeffrey Green (2000) Before the Windrush: the forgotten blacks of British history, *History Today*, October: 29–38.
Chris Wrigley (2014) 'Smoking in the First World War', *History Today*, Vol. 64, No. 4.
Thomas DuBois (2013) 'Asia and the Old World Order', *History Today*, Vol. 63, No. 3.
Graham Seel (2012) 'Good King John', *History Today*, Vol. 62, No. 2.
Jonathan Steinburg (2011) 'How Did Bismarck Do It?', *History Today*, Vol. 61, No. 2.

In helpful advice on the formulation of appropriate questions to ask when teaching interpretations issues, Michael Riley offered the following suggestions:

- 'Why are people so angry about...?'
- 'Why can't historians agree about...?'
- 'Why has ... been interpreted so differently?'
- 'Why have people changed their minds about...?'
- Why have such different stories been told about...?'
- 'Why do Hollywood films about... leave out...?'
- 'What does ... tell us about American society in the late twentieth century?' (Riley, 2007)

Accounts

Closely linked to 'interpretations' of the past, accounts is the word suggested by Lee and Cercadillo (2013) to embrace the wide range of different forms of historical narratives, 'stories' and explanations which pupils might encounter, from 'big picture' studies, to depth studies, biographies, films, and statistical explanations of the past. A key issue here is the development of pupils' understanding of how historical accounts are constructed, and why they differ. The CHATA Project (see Lee and Ashby, 2000) found that when asked to try and explain how there could be different stories or explanations about the same bit of history, and how one could find out which ones were the most reliable, pupils varied widely in the sophistication of their responses. When asked why two stories giving different dates on the matter of when the Roman Empire ended, some pupils regarded the task as impossible as no one from those days was alive, others talked of bias or historians finding different evidence, but there were pupils who seemed to have some understanding that it was in the nature of accounts to differ, depending on what questions were posed of the evidence, and what criteria were used to make judgements. One year 8 pupil responded:

> People have different beliefs as to when the empire ended. Even after defeat, some would say the Roman Empire continued to survive but was not as great, as rich and big as before. There was a period of time when it could have been deemed to have ended but this is somewhere in between the two dates. [You would need to] assess when the empire stopped having an effect on the rest of the world. Beforehand, it almost ruled the world now you could decide when it had decreased in size and riches, and therefore when it ended. When the Eastern half stopped being like the old Roman Empire. (Lee and Ashby, 2000: 207-8)

Lee and Ashby suggested that there was a 'teacher effect' on pupils' degree of understanding of historical accounts, and why they might differ, and this clearly has implications for your teaching. Also, 'the ability to choose wisely from conflicting accounts' (Arnold, 2000: 18) is a useful life-skill to possess. The historian John Tosh has pointed out that 'The diversity and unevenness of the history which is publicly available raises the profound issue of academic authority' (Tosh, 2008: 136). History teachers need to devote time to educating students in the differences between 'good and bad history'. As Richard Aldrich (1997: 5) has pointed out:

If history is regularly used in the promotion of contemporary causes, it is incumbent on the professional historian of education to ensure that such usage is as accurate as possible, both in its representation of the past an in the connections established between the past, present and future.... Most historians do find more evidence about the past than they imagine or invent, and the quality of that evidence, coupled with the quality of the necessary selection, ordering and presentation of it, is one important distinction between good history and bad.

This is particularly important given the sophistication with which information is routinely distorted in the modern media, particularly in tabloid newspapers. Students therefore need to be able to discern between serious and rigorous or 'respectable' history, history which is primarily for entertainment (programmes such as 'Blackadder'), and history which attempts to distort the past for political purposes. This is an essential component of a historical education relevant to life in the twenty-first century. It can therefore be helpful to show pupils some 'bad history' and to develop their understanding of what makes it good or bad. There is no shortage of 'bad history' out there to make this point. A particularly important point is to get pupils beyond the idea that there is one completely and definitively accurate version of the past, and to understand that one of the skills or understandings which school history tries to impart is that there is a need to have an appropriate 'knowledge warrant' for the stories or accounts; that is to say, an awareness of how confident we can be in their accuracy and authority. The TED talk by Chimamanda Adichie, is a helpful resource for reminding pupils of 'The danger of a single story' (www.ted.com/talks/chimamanda_adichie_the_danger_of_a_single_story).

Marc Morris's article '1066: the limits of our knowledge', is another example of a popular magazine article which can help to make this point. He reminds us that there are some rulers, such as Harold Harefoot (1035–40), about whom we know absolutely nothing. Others that we know very little about, but where some modern historians deploy guesswork and amateur psychology to 'fill the gaps' and construct readable but dubious stories of their reigns, describing them as the 'why not make it up' brigade'. He goes on to praise William of Malmesbury:

> One of the greatest of all medieval historians... wrote his account of the Conquest period barely 50 years after 1066 itself, yet occasionally found enormous difficulty piecing together what had actually happened. 'I should like to warn the reader', he wrote, before describing the contentious events of 1051, 'that here I perceive the course of my narrative to be somewhat in doubt, because the truth of the facts is in suspense and uncertain'. (Morris, 2013: 15)

If you are working with A level pupils, Richard Evans' article, 'Postmodernism and history' is also very helpful in making this particular point about accounts, www.butterfliesandwheels.org/2002/postmodernism-and-history.

Just as important is to get pupils to understand why some bits of the historical record are sometimes elided from stories about the past, with the need to provide a 'heroes and villains' version of the past (Cannadine, 2013). The writer Alan Daniels criticises the film, *The motorcycle diaries*, which presents a romantic and sympathetic portrayal of the young Che Guevara, arguing that 'It is as if someone were to make a film about Adolf Hitler by portraying him as a vegetarian who loved animals and was against unemployment. This would be true, but… rather beside the point' (quoted in Usborne, 2006).

Even harder for pupils to understand, but a very important step to make, is that it may be possible to construct very different stories about the same events in the past, which both have an element of truth or 'validity'. The following quotation from the Irish Republican Gerry Adams makes this point:

> I am an Irish republican. British government involvement in Irish affairs and the partition of my country is, in my view, the core of the problem; but I recognise that others, for example unionists, have a different view and their own sense of truth. There will be those in the British system who also have a different analysis. There are many differing perspectives on the causes of the conflict, what happened and who was responsible; all have their own truth. There is no single voice for victims: some want truth; some want judicial processes. We need to respect all these narratives. (Adams, 2013: 50)

Russel Tarr very helpfully provides links to a wide range of sources about differing explanations for the outbreak of World War One, and other questions arising out of Britain's entry to the war, including, should Britain have stayed out, and should history teachers use the television programme *Blackadder* in their teaching of the war. The resources can be accessed at www.magzinr.com/user/russeltarr/ib_ww1_causes.

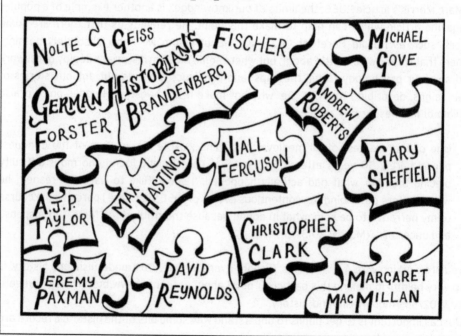

Figure 7.1 Exploring the outbreak of World War One

The richness of internet available resources for this topic makes it well suited to the use of tablet computers in the classroom if this resource is available to you. Pupils or small groups of pupils can be 'allocated' a historian, and asked to produce a brief synopsis of that historian's contribution to the debate about the outbreak of World War One. Some examples of 'historian cards' based around this activity can be found in Claire Hollis's article in *Teaching History* No. 154 (Hollis, 2014: 51).

The exercise can help to make the point that the search for a definitive 'truth' about the outbreak of World War One (i.e. 'It was Germany's fault', or 'It was mainly Germany's fault, with Serbia, Russia, and Great Britain having about 10% responsibility each', or 'It was not Germany's fault, the Triple Entente caused the war by not allowing for Germany to expand as England and France had done in earlier decades') is likely to be an elusive one, given the nature of history. In the words of Fowles (2014), 'The historian must master multiple meta analyses and the ultimate goal is not truth but understanding.'

The EHISTO exercise asking students to make comparisons between articles about the outbreak of World War One written by the German historian Stig Forster, and the English historian Christopher Clark can be useful in making the point that accounts differ because the historian is asking different questions. Forster's article focuses on the issue of responsibility for the outbreak of war, Clark's focuses to a large degree on the similarities between 1914 and 2014. (https://media.sodis.de/ehisto/wwl/en/en/transnational_comparison.html)

Figure 7.2 An example of accounts differing because historians are asking different questions about the event in question

History and numbers

Over the course of a key stage, pupils should learn that accounts and explanations of the past are not always 'written'. Sometimes historians use numbers to explain the past. Ian Phillips makes the point that lessons on slavery often confine their use of sources to text extracts and images depicting the horrors of slavery, and argues that this can limit understanding of slavery. Statistics on the profits made in just one voyage, the volume of trade in slavery, and the cost of slaves at auction provide another way of looking at, and explaining slavery:

> The cost of a slave in the eighteenth century was the equivalent of seven to ten years' income of a working man. Translated into twenty-first century terms, we are looking at an equivalent price of £75,000 to £100,000, or the price of a modern 3 bedroom semi in the North West. (Phillips, 2002: 39)

This throws a different slant on conditions on the slave ships transporting the slaves over to the United States. The question is perhaps not 'Why were conditions so bad?' on the voyage, but 'Why were they not worse?'

The first few minutes of Hans Rosling's TED talk on 'The joy of stats' (www.gapminder.org/videos/the-joy-of-stats) can provide interesting insights into the explanatory power of numbers, as can the use of history databases (see Chapter 9). A basic dataset on civilian and military casualties in World War Two can be accessed on the website (www.uea.ac.uk/~m242/historypgce/ict/welcome.htm). If you are doing a Masters Degree as part of your course (or are working with very able A level pupils), you may find it interesting to explore the world of correlation co-efficients and statistical significance (see the website). It can also be useful for pupils to understand the difference between causes and correlations (again, see the website). Graphs on climate change, easily available by internet search, can also be a way of demonstrating to pupils that history sometimes uses numbers to make sense of the past, and in this case, to also make the point that history is about linking the past to the present and the future.

This is another activity which lends itself to the use of tablet computers, which can be used to 'sub-contract' the task of finding out about the concept of progress by listening to the series of BBC Radio 4 podcasts on 'A history of Britain in numbers' (available at www.bbc.co.uk/podcasts/series/hbn).

Enquiry, Part 1: Terry Jones made a TV programme called 'So this is progress', which claimed that in many ways life was better in 'the olden days', even as far back as the Middle Ages (no commuting, less stress, better community cohesion etc.). To what extent can statistics shed light on this claim?

Using the podcasts from the recent BBC series, 'A history of Britain in numbers', examine this claim with respect to your assigned podcast, and write a summary response (some bullet points or 10-15 lines of text) to present your response. You will need to pick out what you feel are the most helpful or striking bits of evidence from the podcast.

An optional extension to the activity (which is probably only appropriate to use with older and more able pupils), is to follow it up by reading extracts which question the idea of an inexorable 'progress narrative' in history. See suggestions below:

Enquiry, Part 2: The podcasts suggest that in many ways, the human race has 'made progress' over the past few thousand years (technology, life expectancy, medicine etc.). Does this mean that 'things will continue to get better' (i.e. is there such a thing as a 'progress narrative in history')? Read the extracts by Ferguson, Wright and Rees (handouts).

Extract from Wright, R. (2010) *A short history of progress*, London, Cannongate: 2-14. (Available on Google Books)

Extract from Aldrich, R. (2008) Education for survival: an historical perspective, *History of Education*, Vol. 39, No. 1: 1-14 (see website).

Niall Ferguson's review of Fukuyama's book *The Great Disruption* (Observer, 20 June 1999).

(If you find it difficult to access these resources, you should be able to find some substitutes through a simple Google search.)

Figure 7.3 Using numbers (and texts) to look at the idea of 'Progress'

Developing pupils' understanding of substantive historical concepts

There has been so much attention paid to the development of pupils' understanding of second order concepts that it is possible that substantive historical knowledge and concepts have been comparatively neglected (Byrom, 2013).

Concepts are generalisations about data that are related. They are a form of 'shorthand' that enable us to group things together in an understandable way, and in a way that would make sense to others who shared an understanding of that concept. So, although 'revolutions' can take many different forms, to describe something as 'a revolution' conveys a degree of meaning, in this case in the form of an understanding that something represented a significant or radical change in a situation. There are degrees of understanding of a historical concept:

- can vaguely recognise an example of a concept;
- can think of other examples that fall within the definition of the concept;
- can think of examples in other contexts (for example, that you can have 'appeasement' in classrooms and families, not just national and political affairs);
- can offer a reasonably accurate definition of the concept;
- can justify why something falls outside the definition of a concept (for example, understand that Buckingham Palace, although it has some 'castle like' features, such as high walls, does not really count as a castle as it does not fulfil the generally accepted 'primarily defensive' function of a castle.
- can understand the elastic and uncertain boundaries of a concept, and that there may be differences of interpretation about them.

(There is a helpful article by Haenen and Shrijnemakers on substantive concepts in *Teaching History*, No. 98, 2000, with a table explaining five 'elements' of a concept on page 26.)

Ian Dawson (2010: 1) asks three important questions about knowledge in the Key Stage 3 NC for history:

1   How does knowledge fit into the overall plan of KS3 History?
2   What kind of historical knowledge constitutes a desirable to-be-aimed-for 'takeaway' when children complete KS3 History?
3   What do we want students to know and understand about individual events and people and, perhaps, individual themes within KS3 History?

The next section of the chapter focuses on some topics which are often taught at Key Stage 3, in the light of Dawson's question about what knowledge and understandings we want pupils to 'take away' with them after the teaching of the topic has been completed. This is done in order to give some ideas about the sort of thinking which might go into teaching these and other topics, in a worthwhile and meaningful way.

One of the arguments advanced is that pupils need to end up with a sound grasp of the event or topic in question (The Norman Conquest, The Black Death, The Glorious Revolution of 1688, the 1867 Reform Act, The Indian Mutiny etc.), but they also need to understand the event in the context of the 'bigger picture', the part it plays in a longer story. These 'thematic stories' (Dawson, 2010) can provide some coherence to the study of the past, so that pupils do not end up with the bits and pieces of a jigsaw puzzle that they are unable to put together. This 'opening up' of the topic can help pupils to make connections over time, and to the present, and help them to understand how life for human beings has changed over the centuries in different ways. In the words of Dawson, 'Yes, the Civil War may be new in terms of events, but remember, this is part of a bigger story, that of monarchy and parliament, and it's helping us to explain why we still have a monarch when most other countries do not' (Dawson, 2010: 2).

'Opening it up'

In 2007, Ofsted reported that pupils were 'generally unable to reflect on themes and issues or relate a longer narrative or story of the history of Britain, Europe or anywhere else over an extended period of time' (Ofsted, 2007: para. 21). This points to the need to link events from particular strands of history together, so that pupils can develop the coherent 'big picture' or mental map of the past that the NC for history advocates (DfE, 2013). Often we are teaching about events that are part of a longer or bigger story. Some examples:

The Indian Mutiny of 1857

We might be teaching pupils about the Indian Mutiny of 1857, and it is important that pupils should have a sound knowledge and understanding of the events involved in the mutiny, its causes and consequences. But it is also important *at some points* to link to the bigger story of the relationship between Britain and India, and important that pupils should understand that the balance of power between Britain and India was not always as it was in the nineteenth century, and that Britain was not the only country to have an empire.

Byrom and Riley show how difficult it can be to teach 'Empire' in a balanced and coherent way. We can't teach everything about the British Empire in the time available, so hard choices have to be made:

- **Chronology** – does our selected content give a fair sense of the rise, peak and fall of the empire?
- **Geography** – does our selected content give a fair sense of the spread of the empire?
- **Coherence** – does our selected content help us to give pupils a framework or a story where all the parts hold together?
- **Depth** – have we given sufficient opportunities for pupils to develop a strong sense of historical situations and processes?
- **Reality** – Have we chosen studies that have a strong sense of real people making real decisions in real places with real consequences?
- **Complexity** – does our selected content help them to see that history is a 'messy' business?
- **Impact** – does our selected content help to explain later events and developments in history?
- **'Icons'** – does our selected content help them to know about commonly accepted landmarks in history?

- **Interpretations** – does our selected content allow them to understand how and why the empire (including its 'icons') is interpreted differently by historians?
- **Variety** – Does our selected content allow us to study different 'types' of history, e.g. political, social, cultural, aesthetic, economic …?
- **Diversity** – Does our selected content reflect the experiences of rulers and ruled, men, women and children?
- **Morality** – does our selected content allow pupils to reflect appropriately on moral, social and cultural issues in their historical context?
- **Utility** – does our selected content help pupils to understand their world and their place in the world?
- **Motivation** – does our selected content help us to make the learners WANT to learn?
- **Progression** – does our selected content help us to move forward pupils' historical knowledge, skills and understanding, building on earlier experiences and preparing for later ones?

Figure 7.4 Some possible criteria for selecting content in a study of the British Empire (Byrom and Riley, 2008: 8)

But it is not *just* a matter of what content we select. There is also Dawson's point about what knowledge 'takeaway' we want pupils to have from a study of the British Empire, and in terms of their understanding of the concept of 'Empire'.

After encountering 'empire' at various points in their study of history at school, one would hope that pupils would emerge with some general understandings of the concept of empire at the end of their school career. These might include, for example:

- Pupils should understand what an empire is. Howe suggests that 'A kind of basic, consensus definition would be that an empire is a large political body which rules over territories outside its original borders' (Howe, 2002: 14). However, it could also be argued that empires can take different forms, and that these forms have changed over time (see below).
- They should also understand that there have always been empires – it's not just the Romans and the British who have had empires, and in the nineteenth century, the British Empire was not 'the only show in town'.
- It is instructive for pupils to know that empires are generally susceptible to 'rise and decline'. John B. Sparks 'Histomap' is an excellent resource for helping to make this point: (www.slate.com/blogs/the_vault/2013/08/12/the_1931_histomap_the_entire_history_of_the_world_distilled_into_a_single.html).
- Empires vary considerably in the way they operate. In the words of Porter: There were 'an extraordinary variety of relationships between the colonies and the mother country... which ranged from absolute despotisms and racist tyrannies, through colonies ruled paternalistically, in intention at any rate, and territories simply 'protected' by the British, to colonies whose (white) people were for more 'free' than stay at home Britons and whose non-white subjects were so little touched by the system that they could barely have been aware that they were colonies at all... To bundle these together under the rubric of 'empire' seems perverse. Equating the experience of a colonial Nigerian with a New South Waleseian... makes no sense at all (Porter, 2012: 2).

- Empires are not always 'wonderful' or 'evil'. History is more complex than that. (However, a study of the history of empires suggests that often/usually, people don't like to be ruled over by 'outsiders'.) Cannadine (2013) and Tosh (2008), point to the importance of history education helping young people to resist the oversimplification and distortion of history for political purposes.

- Different forms of empire have evolved over time. Modern times have seen the emergence of cultural forms of imperialism – with 'colonies' resenting and resisting the use and influence of 'soft power' (Mcdonalds, Coca Cola, Western music, etc.), and economic control exercised by the World Bank, Food Aid, the International Monetary Fund, and the European Central Bank.

- Historians disagree about the British Empire, and empires more generally. For older pupils, it can be helpful for teachers to provide pupils with a distillation of the arguments of, for example the generally pro-empire Niall Ferguson (2003), and the much more critical views of Richard Gott (2011), or other materials that help to illustrate the challenge and intellectual complexity of 'getting at the truth' about the British Empire, the pros and cons, rights and wrongs of Empire, and other 'big' historical issues and questions. (As with other topics, if you have not got time to read the books by Ferguson and Gott, a search of the online archives of *BBC History Magazine*, and *History Today* will lead you to magazine articles which summarise the arguments made in their books in a few thousand words.)

- Understanding empire is partly about understanding the nature and role that power plays in the creation and dissolution of empires, and that struggles over 'empire' often contribute to the outbreak of wars (see Haydn, 2014 for further development of this point). The first chapter of Howard Zinn's *A people's history of the United States, 1492 to the present day*, about 'Columbus, the Indians and human progress' is a very powerful piece of prose to make the point that the motives of colonisers were not entirely philanthropic and evangelical. The chapter is available online on Google books. The first chapter of Stephen Howe's *Empire: a very short introduction* (2002) contains a first chapter ('I read the news today'), which powerfully conveys what an important concept 'empire' is in everyday life.

The EHISTO Website also has a useful section on Empire: https://media.sodis.de/ehisto/en/index.html

The Poor Law Amendment Act of 1834

We would want pupils to understand why the act was introduced, what its provisions were, and what its effects were. A common enquiry question is whether the workhouses were 'Bastilles for the poor', or 'Pauper palaces' (see the magazine article by Fowler, 2007 for a helpful introduction to this debate). Using the history websites mentioned in Chapter 9 (The National Archives website is particularly helpful for this enquiry), it is not difficult to build up a 'learning package' of images and written sources to problematise this question, and look into the questions of why the poor were treated so harshly in the nineteenth century, and whether there were any changes in attitudes to the poor as the century progressed.

However, there is also a broader question of how societies have handled the problem of people who cannot (or are reluctant to?) provide for themselves. This debate goes back to (at least) Tudor times, and stretches forward to the present, as an important debate in public policy, in the UK and elsewhere. Pages 40 to 59 of Jeremy Seabrook's book *Pauperland: poverty and the poor in Britain* (Seabrook, 2013) provide a succinct outline of the ways in which attitudes and policies about how to deal with poor people have changed over the centuries, and Mudie *et al.* (2008) and the 2013 *Polychronicon* article in *Teaching History* (No. 152: 30-31), 'Changing interpretations of the workhouse?' also provide guidance on how to approach this topic. The issue of poverty can also be traced forward to the present, and using a combination of YouTube and searches of newspaper archives, it is not difficult to build up a 'learning package' focusing on contemporary controversies about poverty (for instance, footage and articles about the Channel 4 documentary 'Benefits Street').

You should try to get strong 'pieces' which represent a range of views on this issue, and this can persuade pupils that the study of history is relevant to the lives they will lead outside school, and after they have left school.

The 1867 Reform Act

Again, pupils should learn about why the act was introduced, what its provisions were and what its effects were. But alongside other important developments in Britain's system of parliamentary democracy, discussion should at some points be opened out so that pupils can see 'the bigger picture' of these developments including 'The history of democracy part 2': what happened after people got the vote? There is a case for playing 'Devil's advocate' with democracy as a concept as a way of developing pupils' understanding of democracy, including the idea that democracy is not perfect, and that the history of Britain has been marked by 'An executive zealously keeping their power and the people fighting to take it away from them' (Gove, 2013). Did women live happily ever after, once they had gained the right to vote? Did universal suffrage bring about a more equal society and social justice? Is there government 'of the people, by the people and *for* the people' as President Lincoln advocated? What about Pamela Hemsley's statement that 'Only the little people pay tax'? We need to trace the history of democracy up to the present day if young people are to leave school with a sound grasp of what liberal democracy is, and this includes their understanding of 'democratic deficits'. Extracts from the Adam Curtis series *The century of the self* (available on YouTube) can help pupils to understand the idea of 'the manufacture of consent', and the ways in which those in power have been obliged to manipulate the masses in order to maintain their control after 'the masses' were given the vote. Ian Dawson's unit on 'Power and Democracy' contains a range of ideas and activities for developing pupils' understanding of the ways in which power and democracy has changed from 1066 to the present: (www.thinkinghistory.co.uk/Issues/downloads/ThinkingAcrossTime.pdf) or www.thinkinghistory.co.uk/Issues/IssueKS3Power.html.

As with other facets of history, there is vocabulary related to an understanding of democracy, to remind pupils that there is more to a democracy than people having the vote. It can be useful to remind pupils that people in Nazi Germany and Stalin's Russia had the vote.

Liberal	Conservative	Authoritarian	Libertarian
Radical	Left-wing	Right wing	Fascist
Communist	Oligarchy	Plutocracy	Meritocracy
Dissident	Activist	Outsider group	Zenophobic
Chauvinist	Gerrymandering	Military-industrial complex	Oligopoly
Neo-con	Manufacture of consent	Separation of powers	Rule of law
Populism	Realpolitik	Corporate state	Globalisation
Hegemony	Lobbying	Executive	Legislature
Independent judiciary	Patronage	Freedom of assembly	Opposition
Freedom of information	Freedom of the press	Free speech	Suffrage
Republic	Constitutional monarchy	Sovereignty	Mandate
Manifesto	Demagogue	Polemic	Playing the race card
Referendum	Propaganda	Astroturfing	'Dog whistles'

Figure 7.5 The vocabulary of democracy

Propaganda in Nazi Germany

As well as providing pupils with knowledge and understanding of the role which propaganda played in Nazi Germany, pupils should at some points in their historical education develop an understanding of the concept of propaganda more generally. As Thomson points out:

> Amongst the most remarkable and least studied aspects of world history are the many examples of how easily led human beings can be.... From the awesome ceremonials round Stonehenge or the Temple of Karnak right through to the Romans, the Crusades, Napoleon, Hitler, Kennedy or Yestsin, the ability to deploy propaganda has been one of the major determinants of historical direction. (Thomson, 1999: preface)

Questions one might ask about propaganda:

- What does it mean?
- What is the origin of the word?
- Was it only used in Nazi Germany?
- What are the reasons for it?
- Is it used today?
- What forms does it take?
- How does it' work? What makes propaganda effective or ineffective?
- Is it necessarily a bad thing? Can you have 'good propaganda'?
- What is the relationship between propaganda and the truth?
- What effects have changes in media and technology had on propaganda
- What has propaganda got to do with the teaching of history in schools?

This brings us back to Norman Longworth's quote about the purposes of school history:

> It does require some little imagination to realise what the consequences will be of not educating our children to sort out the differences between essential and non-essential information, raw fact, prejudice, half-truth and untruth, so that they know when they are being manipulated, by whom, and for what purpose. (Longworth, 1981: 19)

The Act of Union 1707

An Ofsted Dissemination Conference held in Birmingham on 16 October 2013 pointed out that both in the previous and new NC for history, 'Pupils should learn about the changing relationship between England and the rest of the UK.' The Act of Union between England and Scotland is obviously only one of many steps in the changing relationships between England, Ireland, Scotland and Wales, but it does raise the point about 'what questions are worth asking?' about this topic. It is important not to make assumptions about pupils' knowledge in this area. Not all pupils will understand the difference between England, Britain and Great Britain (there are a number of short YouTube clips which provide clarification on this point), or understand the very complicated ways in which relations between England and Ireland have changed over time, indeed, McCall (2005) has suggested that 'Anyone who is not confused about Irish history is not well informed'. But given the high profile attached recently to 'Britishness' and 'Identity' issues, there are a range of other questions in this field which might be posed.

Why are we called 'Great Britain? What makes countries 'great'? Why are we less great than we used to be? To what extent are we 'a United Kingdom'? What is 'Britishness'? Are there such things as 'British values'? Do you think of yourself as English or British (or other things)? How important is national identity? How important an issue is it in terms of 'the challenges of our times'? What is social cohesion? What factors might have influenced changes in social cohesion since 1945? What part might school history play in social cohesion?

The sinking of the Titanic

Although it was a dramatic event, why has the sinking of this ship evinced so much attention? There have been many other ships which have sunk, often with more loss of life. How many people know of the sinking of the Wilhelm Gustloff, which resulted in the death of around 10,000 people, including many children? (www.wilhelmgustloff.com).

The journal *Irish Pages* (Vol. 7, No. 2, 'Memory') provides a rich source of materials which help to explain the resonance and symbolic significance of the event (the issue can be obtained from the journal's website, www.irishpages.org, for approximately £12). The contributions of Glenn Patterson in particular provide an excellent example of the interplay of depth and overview in thinking about the past. Two of his six meditations focus on the fate of two individuals on the ship, and one considers the sinking from a broader historical perspective. The sinking of the Titanic also provides some moral exemplars, and why shouldn't school history sometimes be about moral exemplars? It also provides stories of panic and cowardice. It might be interesting to ask how many of your pupils have heard of Jack Phillips, one of the radio operators on the ship.

In the journal, Michael McCaughan provides a two-page summary of what happened to the ship, ('A terrible silence'); a useful introduction to the story, and a good example of an 'impact' resource.

The BBC new magazine provides a useful summary of the role in the tragedy played by the two wireless officers (*Titanic: The final messages from a stricken ship*: www.bbc.co.uk/news/magazine-17631595).

After pieces telling the story of Jack Phillips, the radio operator, and one of the members of the band that played as the Titanic went down (see the website for these pieces), Patterson's fifth piece; part of the 'Requiem for the lost souls of the Titanic' at St Anne's cathedral Belfast, on 14 of April 2012, points out what those who died 'missed out on' because of the sinking. It offers one way of getting us to think about what happened in the twentieth century, and what history consists of:

> Because of what we hit we missed the trenches, the Crash, the hungry thirties, the Blitz, the camps, the bomb. We missed Chaplin, Keaton, *The Birth of a Nation*, we missed Jolson, Garland, *Gone with the Wind*. We missed TV. We missed Dixieland and swing, be-bop, hard bop, we missed Elvis, Little Richard, a wop-bop-a-loo-bop, pompadours and mop tops, and wondering what the world was coming to. We missed birthdays, wedding days, anniversaries and christenings and communions, we missed the other fates we might have met, the deaths we might have died, the influenzas, the cancers, the embolisms, the cirrhoses, the suicides, the simply slipping into sleep. We passed by instead into myth, launched a library full of books, enough film to cross the Atlantic Ocean three times over, more conspiracy theories than Kennedy, ninety-seven million web-pages, a tourist industry, a requiem or two.
>
> We will live longer than anyone of you. (Patterson, 2012: 93)

Other pieces in the journal include contributions by Michael Longley on the nature of remembrance, and articles by Patricia Craig, Keith Haines and John Wilson Foster about the aftermath of the tragedy.

Like the Space Shuttle Challenger disaster in 1986, and the crash of a Concorde aeroplane in 2000, the Titanic disaster was an example of an event in history which had a significance beyond the numbers of casualties involved. As G.K. Chesterton wrote in the aftermath of the sinking of the Titanic, 'Our whole civilisation is indeed very like the Titanic; alike in its power and its impotence, its security and its insecurity' (*Illustrate London News*, 1912).

In 2005, Martin Rees, the Astronomer Royal, and one of Britain's most eminent scientists, warned that in his estimate, humankind had an only 50/50 chance of surviving the twenty-first century (quoted in McKie, 2005). Similar warnings about 'the challenges of our time' have been issued by Ronald Wright in his book *A short history of progress*. This does raise the question of what are 'the challenges of our times', and whether the current NC for history relates to them.

---

1   As well as getting across to pupils a sound grasp of the substantive history of the topic being taught, try to get them to think about what issues/questions/problems the topic sheds light on, in respect of the insight it may provide into 'the challenges of our times'.
2   Give some thought to 'What questions are worth asking?' about the topic.
3   Try to collect some 'impact' resources around the problem/issue/question (resources which encourage pupils to *think* about the past and its connections to the present, and which might lead them to change their preconceptions and current thinking, and to get them to *actively engage* with the enquiry question).
4   Encourage them to 'problematise' the issue through an enquiry question/s, using the idea of historical perspectives, in a way that encourages pupils to ask their own questions about the topic.
5   Get pupils to think about the connections between the past, the present and the future, and spend at least some time 'opening' up the topic, putting the content in the context of change over time, making connections across time and to the present.

Figure 7.6 'Opening it up'

Among the criteria suggested by the Council of Europe for the teaching of history in a way which contributes to the development of a critical understanding of history are that pupils develop an understanding that:

- the past can be approached and represented from different perspectives;
- historical events and personalities can be interpreted in different ways;
- it is in the nature of accounts of the past to differ for a range of reasons;
- ideas and views about the past are time-bound and subject to change;
- sometimes there are people and organisations who seek to use representations of the past for their own present day purposes;
- events in the past were often the result of complex rather than simple causes;
- claims about the past need to be based on the scrupulous use of available evidence, and the use of established disciplinary procedures for evaluating that evidence;
- our knowledge and understanding of the past is often limited; claims about the past may have differing degrees of certainty or validity;
- the work of historians is usually subject to the critical scrutiny of other historians (www.coe.int/t/dg4/education/historyteaching/default_en.asp).

Summary and key points

The teaching of interpretations of history gives you the opportunity to plan and deliver lessons, which can be imaginative, interesting and of great educational value. We have seen that it is important that the pupils have a clear understanding of how the study of historical interpretations differs from source skills and also to know why we consider them to be important. This can be quite a challenge to the new teacher, who needs to be aware of the possible learning difficulties pupils might experience. The chapter has stressed that problems can arise through insufficiency of content, the pupils' limited comprehension, their need to have the confidence to move from describing to explanation and, where appropriate on to evaluation, and at the same time your pupils do not feel there is nothing in history about which we can be certain. Your pupils need to understand why it is important for them to study historical interpretations. Success is more likely if you try to utilise a range of types of interpretations, some of which the pupils might be surprised to find that they can form part of their history lessons. This in turn encourages you to employ a range of media and of teaching styles.

The chapter concludes by emphasising the point that the development of source skills is likely to be more successful if they are seen by the pupils to have a purpose. Such skills are to be seen as the means by which they can carry out historical enquiries rather than as exercises in source skills, divorced from their context and without any evident utility.

Further reading

Colley, L. (2014) *Acts of union and disunion: what has held the UK together and what is dividing it*, London: Profile. Provides a useful insight into changing relationships between England, Ireland, Scotland and Wales.

Dawson, I. (2010) Some thoughts on Knowledge in Key Stage 3, online at www.thinkinghistory.co.uk/Issues/downloads/IssueKnowledge.pdf, accessed 20 April 2014.

Evans, R. (2002) *Postmodernism and history*, online at 'www.butterfliesandwheels.org/2002/postmodernism-and-history. A lucid introduction to what can be a very abstruse concept.

Evans, R. (2003) 'Our job is to explain', *Times Higher Education Supplement*, 13 June, online at www.timeshighereducation.co.uk/features/our-job-is-to-explain/177421.article. Another helpful explanation of the status of historical knowledge.

Haenen, J. and Shrijnemakers, H. (2000) Suffrage, feudal, democracy, treaty... history's buildingblocks: learning to teach historical concepts, *Teaching History*, No. 98: 22-9.

Haenen, J., Schrijnemakers, H. and Stufkens, J. (2003) Transforming Year 7's understanding of the concept of Imperialism: a case study on the Roman Empire, *Teaching History*, No. 116: 28-34.

Haydn, T. (2014) How and what should we teach about the British Empire in English schools?, in *Annual Yearbook of the International Society of History Didactics*, Shwalbach, Wochenschau Verlag: 23-40.

Howells, G. (2002) Ranking and classifying: teaching political concepts to post-16 students, *Teaching History*, No. 106: 33-6.

For further resources and suggestions for further reading in these areas, go to: www.uea.ac.uk/~m242/historypgce/interp/welcome.htm.

References

Abulafia, D. (2012) Politeia Seminar, London, 5 March.

Adams, G. (2013) 'When the law aids killers', *The Guardian*, 22 November 2013: 50.

Aldrich, R. (1997) *The end of history and the beginning of education*, Inaugural Professorial Address, London: Institute of Education.

Arnold, J. (2000) *History: A very short introduction*, Oxford: Oxford University Press.

Bennett, S. (1995) *The Teaching and Assessment of Interpretations and Representations in History: A Discussion Paper*, London: SCAA.

Bowen, P. (1995) Secondary History Teaching and the OFSTED Inspections, *Teaching History*, No. 80: 12-16.

British Library (1994) *Medieval Realms*, CD-ROM, London: British Library.

British Library (1998) *The Making of the UK*, CD-ROM, London: British Library.

British Library, (2000) *Britain 1750-1900*, CD-ROM, London: British Library.

Byrom, J. and Riley, M. (2008) Professional wrestling in the history department: a case study in planning the teaching of the British Empire at Key Stage 3, *Teaching History*, No. 112: 6-14.

Byrom, J. (2013) Alive … and kicking? Some personal reflections on the revised National Curriculum (2014) and what we might do with it, *Teaching History*, Curriculum Supplement, September: 6-14.

Cannadine, D. (2013) *The undivided past: history beyond our differences*, London: Allen Lane.

Card, J. (2004) Seeing double. How one period visualises another, *Teaching History*, No. 117: 6-11.

Chambers, C. (2006) Teaching causal reasoning, Chapter 6 in M. Hunt (ed.) *A Practical Guide to Teaching History in the Secondary School*, London: RoutledgeFalmer: 49-59.

Chapman, A. (2006) What does it mean to 'Think Historically' and what do we know about how to develop children's historical thinking, online at http://www.ahdr.info/ckfinder/userfiles/files/October_workshop_Arthur_Chapman_write_-up.pdf, accessed 9 August 2014.

Counsell, C, Riley, M. and Byrom J. (2004) Presentation to Ofsted Conference on Historical Interpretations.

Dawson, I. (2010) *Some thoughts on Knowledge in Key Stage 3*, online at www.thinkinghistory.co.uk/Issues/downloads/IssueKnowledge.pdf, accessed 20 April 2014.

Dearing, R. (1994) *The National Curriculum and its Assessment*, London: SCAA.

DfE (1995) *History in the National Curriculum*, London: HMSO.

DfE (2013) History programmes of study: key stage 3: National Curriculum in England, London: DfE.

DES (1990) *History in the National Curriculum*, London: HMSO.

Ferguson, N. (2003) *How Britain Made the Modern World*, New York: Penguin.

Fowler, S. (2000) 'Pauper Bastille or Pauper Palace' Modern History Review, Vol. 11, February.

Fowles, S. (2014) The Complex Origins of the First World War, blogpost on the *History Today* Website, online at www.historytoday.com/blog/2014/01/complex-origins-first-world-war, accessed 20 April 2014.

Gott, R. (2011) *Britain's Empire: Resistance, repression and revolt*, New York: Verso.

Gove, M. (2013) 'Start the week', *Radio 4*, 30 December.

Grosvenor, I. (1999) History and the perils of multiculturalism, *Teaching History*, No. 97: 37-40.

Haenen, J. and Shrijnemakers, H. (2000) Suffrage, feudal, democracy, treaty… history's building blocks: learning to teach historical concepts, *Teaching History*, No. 98: 22-9.

Harper, P. (1993) Using the Attainment Targets in Key Stage 2: AT2, Interpretations of History, *Teaching History*, No. 72: 11-13.

Harrison, S. (2004) Address to Ofsted Conference on Historical Interpretations, June-July 2004.

Haydn, T. (2014) How and what should we teach about the British Empire in English Schools, *Yearbook, International Society for History Didactics*, Vol. 35 23-40.

Hollis, C. (2014) Waking up to complexity: using Christopher Clark's The Sleepwalkers to challenge over-determined causal explanations, *Teaching History*, No. 154: 48-55.

Hobhouse, H. (2005) *Forces of Change: An Unorthodox View of History*, London: Counterpoint.

Howe, S. (2002) *Empire: a very short introduction*, Oxford: Oxford University Press.

Howells, G. (2005) Interpretations and history teaching. Why Ronald Hutton's Debates in Stuart History' matters, *Teaching History*, No. 121: 29-35.

Lawlor, S. (1989) *Critique of the Interim Report of the National Curriculum Working Group*, London.

Lee, P. (1998) A lot of guesswork goes on: children's understanding of historical accounts, *Teaching History*, No. 92: 29-32.

Lee, P. and Ashby, R. (2000) Progression in historical understanding among students ages 7-14, in P. Stearns, P. Seixas and S. Wineburg (eds) *Knowing, Teaching and Learning History*, New York: New York University Press.

Lee, P. and Cercadillo, L. (in press) Organising the past: historical accounts, significance and unknown ontologies, in M. Carretero, M., S. Berger, and M. Grever, (eds) *International Handbook of Research in Historical Culture and Education*, Oxford: OUP.

Lee, P. and Shemilt, D. (2004) I just wish we could go back in the past and find out what really happened; progression in understanding about historical accounts, *Teaching History*, No. 117: 25-31.

Lively, P. (1988) *Moon Tiger*, London: Penguin.

Longworth, N. (1981) We're moving into the information society – what shall we teach the children?, *Computer Education*, June: 17-19.

Mandler, P. (2013) *History, National Life and the New Curriculum*, Keynote address at the SHP Conference, Leeds, July, online at www.schoolshistoryproject.org.uk/ResourceBase/downloads/MandlerKeynote2013.pdf, accessed 14 April 2014.

McAleavy, T. (1993) Using the Attainment Targets at KS3: AT2, Interpretations of History, *Teaching History*, No. 72: 14-17.

McAleavy, T. (2000) 'Teaching about interpretations', Chapter 6 in J. Arthur, and R. Phillips (eds) *Issues in History Teaching*, London: Routledge: 72-82.

McAleavy, T. (2003) 'Interpretations of history', in M. Riley and R. Harris (eds) *Past Forward*, London: Historical Association: 42-44.

Martin, D. and Brooke, B. (2002) Getting personal and making effective use of historical fiction in the history classroom, *Teaching History*, No. 108: 30-35.

Mastin, S. and Wallace, P. (2006) Why don't the Chinese play cricket? Rethinking progression in historical interpretations through the British Empire, *Teaching History*, No. 122: 6-14.

McCall, D. (2005) QCA history panel meeting, London.

McCully, A. and Pilgrim, N. (2004) They took Ireland away from us and we've got to fight to get it back, *Teaching History*, No. 114: 17-21.

McKie, R. (2005) 'Ace of Space', *The Observer*, 17 April.

Morris, M. (2013) '1066: the limits of our knowledge', *The Historian*, Spring: 12-15.

Mudie, C., Roe, A. and Dougall, C. (2008) Was the workhouse really so bad?, *Teaching History*, No. 130: 46-9.

NCC (1993) *Teaching History at Key Stage 3*, York: NCC, 50-58.

Ofsted (1993) *History: Key Stages 1, 2 and 3: The Implementation of the Curricular Requirements of the Education Reform Act*, London: HMSO.

Ofsted (1995) *History: A Review of Inspection Findings, 1993-94*, London: HMSO.

Ofsted (2004) *Report of Conference on Historical Interpretations*, June–July 2004.

Ofsted (2007) *History in the balance: history in English schools 2003-7*, London: Ofsted.

Patterson, G. (2012) Requiem for the Titanic: Literary meditations, in *Irish Pages*, Volume 7, No. 2: 90-94.

Pendry, A., Atha, J., Carden, S., Courtenay, L., Keegh, C. and Ruston, K. (1997) Pupil preconceptions in history, *Teaching History*, No. 86: 18-20.

Phillips, I. (2002) History and maths or history with maths: does it add up?, *Teaching History*, No. 107: 35-40.

Porter, B. (2012) Cutting the empire down to size, *History Today, 62* (10): 2-7.

QCA (2007a) History, programme of study: Key Stage 3, London, QCA, online at http://curriculum.qca. org.uk/subjects/history, accessed 11 October 2007.

QCA, (2007b) Innovating with History website, *How to Teach about interpretations at key Stages 1 to 3*, online at www.qca.org.uk/history/innovating, accessed 19 August 2014.

Riley, M. (2006a) Quoted in 'Final Report: Historical Association's Key Stage 2-3 History Transition Project, London, Historical Association, online at: www.historytransition.org.uk, accessed 11 October 2007.

Riley, M, (2006b) Historical Enquiries and Interpretations, conference presentation, online at http:// czv.e2bn.net/e2bn/leas/c99/schools/czv/web/riley.htm, accessed 11 October 2007.

Riley, M. (2007) *Advice about teaching historical interpretations*, Historical Association Newsletter, November.

SCAA (1996) *Exemplification of Standards in History, Key Stage 3*, London: SCAA.

SCAA (1997) *The Assessment of Interpretations and Representations and Use of Sources in GCSE History Examinations*, London: School Curriculum and Assessment Authority.

Scott, B. (1994) A Post-Dearing Look at History: Interpretations of History, *Teaching History*, No. 75, April, 20-6.

Seabrook, J. (2013) *Pauperland: poverty and the poor in Britain*, London: Hurst and Co.

Sinclair, Y. (2006) Teaching Historical Interpretations, Chapter 7 in M. Hunt. *A Practical Guide to Teaching History in the Secondary School*, London: Routledge.

Teaching History (2000) No.99, contains several articles, which are invaluable in giving guidance on the structuring of worthwhile and stimulating enquiry activities.

Tosh, J. (2008) *Why History Matters*, Basingstoke: Palgrave Macmillan.

Thomson, O. (1999) *Easily led*, London: Sutton Press.

Towill, E. (1997) The Constructive Use of Role play at Key Stage 3, *Teaching History*, No. 86: 8-13.

Usborne, D. (2006) Who was Che Guevara, and does he deserve his iconic status?, *The Independent*, 6 June: 29.

Wilson, M.D. (1985) *History for Pupils with Learning Difficulties*, London: Hodder and Stoughton.

Woolley, M. (2003) Really weird and freaky: using a Thomas Hardy short story as a source of evidence in the Year 8 classroom, *Teaching History*, No. 111: 6-11.

Wrenn, A. (1999) Substantial sculptures or sad little plaques? Making interpretations matter to Year 9, *Teaching History*, No. 97, November, 21-28.

Wrenn, A. (2002) Equiano-voice of silent slaves, *Teaching History*, No. 107: 13-19.

8 Ensuring inclusion in the history classroom

'Personal best' (The aim of athletics coaches – to coax out the best possible performance from the abilities which the athletes possess).

Introduction

Issues of equality of opportunity and educational inclusion are very high profile and important in current policy debates on education. Ensuring inclusion means responding to the needs of each individual pupil. This means respecting all kinds of diversity within the classroom, as well as making the curriculum accessible to all learners. It is the teacher's role to enable each pupil to feel part of the learning process, and to make sure that all learners make progress. Dale Banham (2014) makes the point that if you are to get all pupils to commit wholeheartedly to learning in their history lessons, every pupil must feel that they can get something out of the lesson, and there is an art to getting across to pupils that they can all make progress in history, whether they are able pupils, or struggling to do well in the subject.

The Statutory Inclusion Statement of the previous National Curriculum (QCA, 2007) and the new National Curriculum (DfE, 2013) state that the curriculum should provide relevant and challenging learning to all children, following two principles:

- setting suitable learning challenges;
- responding to pupils' needs and overcoming potential barriers for individuals and groups of pupils.

The importance of being able to address issues and equlity and diversity are also emphasised in the *Teachers' Standards* (DfE, 2012). These require teachers to 'have a clear understanding of the needs of all pupils, including those with special educational needs; those of high ability; those with English as an additional language; those with disabilities; and be able to use and evaluate distinctive teaching approaches to engage and support them'.

Objectives

At the end of this chapter you should be able to:

- understand the range of learning needs you are likely to encounter in school, including Special Educational Needs, and the needs of pupils who are learning English as an Additional Language, of the very able, and of pupils who are disabled;
- identify factors which are preventing pupils from performing to the best of their ability in the subject;
- understand how your teaching can be culturally relevant to your pupils;
- understand the educational context in which teaching and learning take place with regard to pupils with learning needs; and
- know about a variety of teaching and learning strategies to help pupils with different learning needs.

Valuing every pupil

Teachers need to respect all pupils as individuals and as learners. The previous government's 'Every Child Matters' initiative (DfES, 2004) distinguished five strands in a child's wellbeing. These are to be healthy, to stay safe, to enjoy and achieve, to make a positive contribution, and to achieve economic well-being. While trying to ensure that all our pupils make the best possible progress in history, we must not lose sight of affective dimensions of learning, such as motivation to do well and try hard, self-esteem, and perseverance, which have an influence on their progress in history. Effective teachers try to encourage a positive contribution from their pupils by creating a collaborative classroom ethos. An attempt to 'meet and greet' individuals as they enter your classroom, together with a positive word or an exhortation to improve as they leave shows that you are aware of their presence, and value their contributions (Taylor, 2012). Of course, like many other things in teaching, this can be done well or badly. If it is not done adroitly, it can come across as facile and patronising, or like 'Have a nice day', and 'Are you enjoying your meal?', something that is a 'technique' rather than a sincere concern.

Ian Grosvenor's chapter (2000) also gives further guidance on creating a positive classroom ethos. Effective classroom management is integral to this positive ethos. For example, a teacher who uses positive language, reminding pupils to stay on task or asking whether they need help, can be more effective than one who repeatedly challenges lapses of concentration.

Providing incentives for each individual to engage with learning is also essential to an inclusive classroom. The ideas in Chapter 11 on gathering instant feedback from pupils may also be helpful to involve all pupils in class activities as an alternative to the standard question and answer sessions. This chapter also suggests various approaches, including self and peer assessment, to encourage pupils to move on in their learning. Be aware of the possible anxieties of your pupils. For example, in a classroom where certain individuals, possibly boys, dominate talk, there is a risk of others feeling excluded. In this case the role of the teacher will extend to reaching the quieter pupils, through assessment for learning techniques, or group talk rather than class talk. You should also be aware of needs of pupils in Year 7, with the transition from primary school. The reorientation and more formal relationships required with subject teachers may be particularly testing for pupils with a disability or other additional needs (see www.historytransition.org.uk for history specific guidance on this issue). You may also discover certain religious or cultural sensitivities, so you need to exercise tact and sensitivity.

Task 8.1 Valuing the individual

Discuss with your tutor how teachers can encourage a sense of belonging from individual pupils. Observe a lesson, and list all the ways in which you see this happen. Can you identify any pupils with additional needs – either from the pupils' or the teacher's behaviour?

As you observe try to note down how many individual pupils interact with the teacher, and whether the interactions appear positive or negative. Can you learn anything about how a positive classroom environment is created and maintained?

A history curriculum for all

It is important that pupils perceive our teaching to be relevant to their own lives. For young people growing up in a multi-cultural society, as part of an increasingly globalised world, it is imperative to learn about world history, including a range of historical narratives, from a variety of perspectives. Diversity was previously enshrined as a second order concept in the National Curriculum Programme of Study (QCA, 2007) as well a component of substantive knowledge in history. The new programme of study for history (DfE, 2013) has lost the previous requirement to teach about diversity as a concept, although the inclusion of 'similarity and difference' provides a rough equivalent (see Byrom, 2013: 9) for further development of this point). While there is no longer a requirement to teach about movement and settlement as prescribed content, the 'purpose of study' statement does expound that 'History helps pupils to understand the complexity of people's lives, the process of change, the diversity of societies and relationships between different groups, as well as their own identity'. Mention of countries outside Britain appears to focus mainly on their role within the British empire, but there is a requirement for 'at least one study of a significant society or issue in world history and its interconnections with other world developments'. Mughal Indian and China's Qing dynasty are cited as examples. Furthermore, there is flexibility within this curriculum to decide what weighting is given to each topic, and even to teach about topics that are not mentioned. Pearson (2012) maintains, 'Whatever we are presented with in the next version of our subject we have a role in the translation of a National Curriculum into a curriculum for our own classes.' Grosvenor (2000: 149) stated, 'History is always about selection'. The way that you approach topics, and the selections and choices you make, can make a big difference to the extent to which history is relevant to the lives and situations of your pupils. Bracey, Gove-Humpries and Jackson (Davies, 2011) explain the place of diversity in the curriculum, whilst Bradshaw (2009) provides exemplification of how diversity can be embedded in the school curriculum, with progression ensured.

Positive curriculum choices at Key Stage 3 may involve learning about the various cultures within the British Empire, the transatlantic slave trade, groups of immigrants into Britain from the eighteenth to twentieth centuries, the Holocaust and other genocides, the role of the Empire in the two world wars. Britain's relations with the Commonwealth and wider world in the twentieth century could be explored through the lens of local communities and economy, examining where people have come from or emigrated to, or where trading partners are found. Often pupils enjoy this kind of study provided the teacher has the skills and enthusiasm to bring it alive for them. There are certain opportunities to teach non-European histories at GCSE and A level. An inclusive curriculum will also include study of women in the past (see Pearson, 2012). Ian Woodfield (Cole, 2009 – *Equality in the Secondary School*, Chapter 9, London, 2009) argues that the study of history inevitably leads students to consider questions of social justice and equality. His chapter lists websites and questions to explore around issues of gender, social class, sexuality, age and disability as well as ethnicity. At times the history teacher will engage with sensitive topics. A willingness to do so openly helps pupils to understand links between past and present, as well as exploring identities and diverse perspectives. The Historical Association's (2007) TEACH report explores some of the issues with examples of good practice.

Where the choice of topics is limited, try to adopt an inclusive approach. A few general principles follow.

Principle	Examples
Use resources that include people from all backgrounds (culture, gender, class)	Posters, pictures, books. See teaching materials available from 'Hidden History Express' (2006) for example.
Look into 'hidden histories'	<ul><li>Count references to women and to men, in the index of a textbook.</li><li>Discuss number of pages given to a topic such as the transatlantic slave trade.</li><li>Consider why certain groups do not feature in history textbooks, which could lead to research into their histories.</li></ul>
Show that Britain has been a diverse society for many centuries	<ul><li>QCA Respect for All web pages (2001b) give details of how one school broadened a study of the Norman Conquest into an investigation of the bigger question 'Who are the British?' Lyndon's article (2006) explains how black history can be woven into the curriculum rather than just visited at particular points.</li><li>Grosvenor (2000) gave examples of black people, whose role could be investigated as part of a traditional study of the English Reformation, radicals in the nineteenth century or the suffragettes.</li></ul>

Principle	Examples
Avoid presenting a picture of a particular cultural group solely as victims. Present positive role models and successes of different cultures.	• The successful slave revolution on the island of Saint-Domingue in the 1790s could be a case study. • Case studies of resistance to the Holocaust could be Rabbi Leo Baeck, who resisted Nazi authority by peaceful methods in Therersienstadt, or the armed uprising in the Warsaw ghetto in April 1943. The story of Abba Kovner, who advocated armed uprising in the Vilna Ghetto, is recounted in the DFEE Holocaust Memorial Day Education Pack (2000). • The struggle of enslaved Africans can be compared with the struggle of British workers in the nineteenth century, then with the struggle of British women for their rights, and the struggle of peoples in the British Empire to achieve independence in the twentieth century.
Show that victims of atrocities did not always belong to the same race.	• Some French Prisoners of war were transported to America through the transatlantic slave trade. • Sinti and Roma, as well as Jewish people, were murdered by the Nazis.
Show positive achievements within larger conflicts.	• Case studies of Christians who helped Jews during the Holocaust, for example Swedish diplomat Raoul Wallenburg or Albert Bedane in the Channel Islands, or Danish fishermen who ferried almost all of Denmark's Jewish population to safety in Sweden in 1943.
Keep in mind LGBT agendas	• Link to Ofsted 'Good Practice in reducing homophobic bullying: www.ofsted.gov.uk/resources/good-practice-resource-whole-school-approach-tackling-homophobic-bullying-and-ingrained-attitudes-st • The Historical Association has a range of resources to support LGBT Month in History: • www.history.org.uk/resources/student_news_2039.html • Guardian article on how one London school used history to address homophobic bullying: www.theguardian.com/education/2010/oct/26/lgbt-history-homophobia-schools

Figure 8.1 Some general principles of inclusion

Including pupils with Special Educational Needs: What the legislation says

Approximately one in five children, that is 1.62 million (DfE, 2012), have some form of SEN which will require additional provision in school. In 2012 boys in secondary schools were three times as likely to have a statement as girls, whilst pupils with SEN were much more likely to be eligible for free school meals than those without SEN. The Code of Practice for Special

Educational Needs, published in 1994, and revised in 2001, is designed to ensure that their needs are provided for. The Code confirms the key principle, present in policy since the Warnock Report of 1978, that, in nearly every case, pupils with special educational needs would be educated in the mainstream classroom. It states that children have special educational needs if they 'have a significantly greater difficulty in learning than the majority of children of the same age' or if they 'have a disability which prevents or hinders them from making use of educational facilities of a kind generally provided for children of the same age in schools'.

The Code of Practice requires all subject teachers to identify pupils with SEN in their classes. The Revised Code of Practice, 2001, specifies three stages of provision, once a pupils is identified as not learning effectively through the usual methods of differentiation. These are:

- School Action, whereby the pupil needs additional support, which can be provided within the school. This may involve extra tuition or in-class support, different learning materials or special equipment.
- School Action Plus, whereby some additional support is provided by specialist agencies external to the school.
- A Statement. This describes the pupil's needs and a plan of action for intervention.

10.8 per cent of pupils in English secondary schools were on School Action in 2011/12 (DfE, 2012), 6.0 per cent were on School Action Plus, and 2.8 per cent had a statement. The Code of Practice is currently being revised as part of a review of children's services. Statements, and existing categories of SEN, outlined above, will be replaced by joint education, health and care (EHC) plans with the aim of bringing about a more co-ordinated approach, for both education and medical care, from birth to the age of 25. Children should undergo fewer assessments of their needs. This will come into practice from September 2014. Parents will have more say in identifying needs. They will help to design a support plan for their child and will be given a budget to fund the costs. The current category of behaviourial, emotional and social difficulties will be redefined in the belief that it is overused. Some practioners are concerned that fewer children will be entitled to support and funding outside of the standard school provision, and also that families in areas of social deprivation will be further disadvantaged because they will have less power to campaign for their children than those who are highly educated and articulate. It is likely that current practice in schools of recording needs and strategies within an Individual Education Plan (IEP) will continue. It is the responsibility of the Special Educational Needs co-ordinator (SENCO) to write and review the IEP in collaboration with colleagues.

However, the changes highlight the need for classroom teachers to take responsibility for the learning of all children. The expertise of the subject teacher is essential in designing the best pedagogical approach for each individual.

The National Curriculum and Special Educational Needs: recognising barriers to learning

The statutory inclusion statement of the National Curriculum requires staff to modify the programmes of study to give all pupils relevant and appropriately challenging work at each key stage.

Firstly it is important to consider which pupils are struggling with tasks you set and why. History contains many abstract terms and concepts which, if not introduced at the right level, will cause ambiguity and confusion in the minds of some pupils. The linguistic demands of the subject are high and you need to be constantly aware of both the language you use in communicating with pupils, and of the demand placed on pupils' literacy skills and experience (see Chapter 4). Lomas (2005) identified some of the common difficulties experienced by learners of history. Teachers who are concerned about inclusion will attempt to address these difficulties as far as possible.

Pupils who have SEN may experience particular barriers. The history department and the SENCO at your placement school can be consulted about which of your pupils are identified as having SEN and what are their specific learning needs. Data such as reading ages, CATs and SATs scores will be helpful (see www.uea.ac.uk/~m242/historypgce/assess/welcome.htm for more detail). The main types of SEN are specific learning difficulties (such as dyslexia), non-verbal difficulties (such as dyspraxia), moderate or severe learning difficulties, physical, sensory and medical difficulties, speech and language impairments, social, emotional and behavioural difficulties, and autistic spectrum disorder.

There is a highly informative chapter on different types of SEN in Luff and Harris (2004), which gives details of the main characteristics for each type of need, and how the subject teacher can help to meet it. There is also a useful section on what you need to understand about SEN in Phillips (2008).

Task 8.2 *Recognising SEN*

During your school experience find out what the school and department policy is concerning the identification of pupils with SEN, including gifted pupils. Does the school have a whole-school approach to SEN with a written statement of policy? How does the history department interpret the school's SEN policy in terms of individual education plans and departmental strategies.

From the list of learning difficulties recognised by the Code observe one history class and try and identify any learning difficulties that the pupils have. In particular look at:

- ability;
- motivation and interests;
- maturity;
- preferred learning styles;
- behaviour;
- reading and writing skills;
- listening skills;
- communication skills; and
- memory.

Disability

The National Curriculum and the Equality Act of 2010 oblige schools to take reasonable steps to ensure that pupils who are disabled are not placed at a substantial disadvantage in their education. The Equality Act of 2010, which replaced all previous anti-discrimination laws, defines nine protected characteristics. It is illegal to treat people unfairly because they belong to one of the protected groups. Disability is one of the characteristics. Many pupils who have disabilities will learn alongside their peers. The National Curriculum (DfE, 2013) states that 'Many disabled pupils have little need for additional resources beyond the aids which they use as part of their daily life'. The Equality Act obliges schools and local authorities to supply auxiliary aids and services for disabled pupils, where these are not being supplied through SEN statements. In practice, medical and emotional needs, speech and language impairments or additional SEN, often necessitate further intervention. This might involve practical measures such as ensuring there is space for a wheelchair user to turn in the classroom, printing your resources in larger type, allowing longer to complete work, or reducing the amount of homework required. A sensitive and aware teacher can make a difference to the classroom climate, and therefore the extent to which disabled pupils are socially and logistically integrated. Inclusive classroom practice is particularly important for teenagers who are disabled. They will often want to be treated the same as other pupils without additional fuss.

Some approaches to teaching history to pupils with Special Educational Needs

A flexible, but carefully structured, approach to teaching and learning will help ensure that all of your pupils make progress. It is important not to teach to the lowest common denominator, simplifying everything or to simply supply a range of tasks that pupils with SEN can complete with relative ease. It is critical to consider the difficulties and capabilities of each individual pupil. HMI have made the point that this goes beyond the 'all, most, some' approach to differentiation (Maddison, 2014): you need to get to know your pupils really well, in order to provide precise and useful help to overcome barriers to learning. Your role is akin to an athletics coach, whose job is to try to ensure that all their athletes achieve their 'personal best'. You should be expecting and assessing progress in historical understanding from every pupil. Even in a mixed ability class, it is not productive to provide different learning experiences and differentiated materials *all of the time*. A useful start is to consider ways of stimulating your pupils and capturing their attention, by using a variety of approaches which will appeal to pupils of all abilities.

1 Planning and teacher input

The teacher concerned about inclusion holds high expectations of pupils with SEN, as of any other pupils. He or she seeks to recognise the difficulties faced by individuals in learning history, and to help them improve their conceptual understanding and literacy skills in order to access the learning more easily. Learning objectives are considered carefully, with appropriate cognitive challenge provided for all pupils. Planning will incorporate a range of strategies to bring alive the subject matter, as well as differentation. The new programme of study for history (DfE, 2013) contains a wide range of examples of content. Attempting to teach all of these will be unmanageable for pupils with SEN, and as they are non-statutory, teachers have a responsibility to be selective. In practice, much of the content is likely to be taught as an overview. As a class teacher, you will be responsible for ensuring that pupils of all abilities have opportunity to gather sufficient depth of understanding to develop a sense of period, allowing more time if necessary.

Rob Phillips emphasises the need to create a 'supportive environment in the history classroom'. This includes the need to allow 'time and space' (Phillips, 2002). Phillips wrote about the need to 'make time, take time' for pupils with SEN (Phillips, 2008). He argued that there may be a need to work more slowly through the curriculum, although this could be problematic with a mixed ability class. Teaching in a mixed ability setting may be challenging, but can be very positive if pupils support and challenge each other. Be careful to identify pupils who are struggling with work as quickly as possible. In a mixed ability setting, they can learn coping strategies such as copying from peers or copying out text. A slow writing speed may disadvantage pupils and appear to be a sign of lack of concentration, but could actually be a learning difficulty.

Consider how to build in opportunities for success for everyone early in the lesson sequence. A lesson which appeals to all pupils could focus on some kind of initial stimulus to 'hook' pupils into the lesson, and secure the motivation needed to pursue some difficult thinking, reading or writing. Use of historical narrative is often popular (see Chapter 4). The Foundation Subjects Strand of the Key Stage 3 National Strategy (2002) refers to the importance of starters. Useful to settle a class, the power of initial stimulus to engage the class in learning should not be underestimated. Use of pictures, artefacts, card sorts, puzzles to solve, DVD clips etc. could be interesting. Phillips' article (2001) contained helpful ideas on use of initial stimulus material. Harris (2005) argued that a suitable stimulus can help pupils to care about what happened in the past, and therefore engage them in learning from the start. He showed the pitfalls of over-simplification of complex topics for less able pupils, whereby they can be deprived of the knowledge necessary to make sense of the issues. If the work is made engaging and accessible, with obstacles such as reading and writing carefully placed, it can make a real difference to the extent to which pupils with learning difficulties *commit themselves* to learning in history.

As a trainee, you may be surprised at how often pupils require repeated reinforcement of what you have said. Teacher talk in class must be pitched at the appropriate level for the pupils to understand. Use open questions to permit some response from the pupils which you can build upon. Do not assume that closed questions are always easier, as they may require factual recall, which is difficult for some pupils.

Your planning should take into account difficulties in personal organisation linked with Special Educational Needs such as dyslexia. This should be considered as you plan their homework in particular. It is good practice to ensure that all homework is given to pupils in written form, and check that those who have SEN have recorded and understood the task. If they are slow workers, you may suggest that they stop work after a certain period of time. It is worth exploring what support is available to help with homework within the school.

2 Reading

Pupils with SEN will sometimes have a lower level of language development than that of their peers, and as suggested in Chapter 5, difficulties in reading can be one of the biggest obstacles in learning history. Many practical suggestions for strategies to aid reading are given in Chapter 5. Remember that your supporting explanation of written materials, and individual help given to pupils can help to make more difficult written materials accessible, as can shared reading of the text. Now that textbooks are used less in the classroom, there is a temptation to avoid reading at length. This is regrettable if pupils lose a sense of stories from the past and are rarely exposed to more complex historical language. You can help them to access such resources by guiding them through pieces of reading. Consider support given to pupils before, during and after reading. For example you might identify new vocabulary before reading, use highlighting or acting out during the reading and summarising the views of the characters in speech bubbles afterwards.

Task 8.3 *Guiding pupils through challenging pieces of reading*

Pick a newspaper article about history (see Chapter 10), collect some images from the internet to help you to 'illustrate' the article, with background use of PowerPoint, highlight some key sections of the text, and use the article in one of your lessons, interspersing asking pupils to read some passages, with your explanation of other sections.

---

3 Writing

Consider when writing is necessary, and how to support your pupils with developing their skills. Remember that it is not always necessary to complete written tasks in order to fulfil learning objectives. The figure below gives ideas to help pupils with SEN. Further ideas on improving pupils' writing in general are found in Chapter 5.

- Use appropriate tasks to aid understanding before writing – sorting, sequencing, exploratory talk.
- Repeat explanation of the task both orally and in writing.
- Question individuals to check that they have understood what is required.
- Think carefully about exactly what it is you are asking pupils to do. The use of imaginative writing, for example, requires first that the pupils be able to describe and record.
- Model the type of writing required, e.g. provide a first sentence or introductory paragraph.
- Beware of the difficulty in an apparently easy task such as copying from a board. Using a sheet on the desk is easier.
- If pupils are slow in starting the written task, check that the obstacle does not lie in reading text or instructions. If it does, try to give individual support, or to pair them with a classmate who can help.
- Reassure pupils as they work that they are doing the right thing.

Figure 8.2 Some advice on setting written tasks

Some suggestions follow about the mechanics of adapting written tasks for pupils with SEN:

- Use a high ratio of picture to print.
- Make instructions short and simple, possibly in the form of bullet points.
- Sources can be put into text boxes to make them more easy to find for reference.
- The language of any text may have to be adapted, or difficult words explained in brackets. Text can be broken up with diagrams and illustrations.
- Avoid fonts sizes below 14. Use a font in which the letters resemble handwritten letters, e.g. comic sans.
- Some specific learning difficulties or disabilities mean that pupils need text at font size 20 plus with double spacing between lines. Printing worksheets on pale coloured paper may also be helpful.
- Questions should refer to text on the same page, avoiding the need to turn pages to find an answer. It is better to print a two-page worksheet on one sheet of A3 than on two pages of A4.
- Give hints as to where to find answers.

Tasks can be broken up by:

- producing gap fills, with or without the missing words provided, or with first letters provided;
- deciding if a given statement is true or false;
- sequencing events;
- choosing the correct ending to a sentence from several;
- matching heads and tails of sentences; and
- cutting and pasting instead of writing out long answers.

Encourage some space for pupils to write down their own ideas, however briefly.

For ideas about checking the readability of a text, go to www.uea.ac.uk/~m242/historypgce/inclusiondiversity/welcome.htm

4 Differentiation

Differentiation means making the curriculum accessible and matching work to individual pupils' ability. All classrooms contain pupils of different abilities, even when they are theoretically setted or banded. When you are placed in a new school, you need to find out the policy on setting. If groups are setted, how many sets are there, and on what basis has their composition been decided? If sets apply across two or more subjects, for reasons of timetabling, problems may arise in placing individuals. Some schools prefer solely mixed ability teaching on the grounds of numbers, behaviour, self-esteem or encouraging peer support.

There are a number of ways of achieving differentiation. Some of these are explained in Chapter 10. Stephen (2006) gives an overview of the strengths and weaknesses of various methods. The starting point is an awareness of what and when to differentiate. Careful use of visual resources, and active learning activities, such as those outlined below, should reduce the need for differentiation of resources and tasks. Wendy Cunnah (2000) outlines the challenge to teachers to examine ther learning environment and the actual process of learning as a whole, affirming that successful differentiation includes a full range of approaches. Less obvious methods, such as the level of support offered to each pupil, or the use of different groupings to allow pupils to suport each other can be highly effective.

When written tasks are important to the learning objectives, some differentiation of the task will usually be required. An alternative to giving out different tasks could be to give pupils the choice of a 'help sheet' if they are struggling with a task. This may include glossaries, matching, sequencing, memory prompts, multi-choice answers, a cloze passage, tick boxes etc. It is good practice to allow space for pupils to compose some sentences of their own. Help sheets are also useful for homework. The advantages of using supplementary materials, rather than different materials, are that these can be given out with the minimum of fuss. Pupils with SEN can work from the same materials as their classmates, and may see progress at the point where they no longer need the help sheet. Remember, however, that most pupils will have been taught in mixed ability, and sometimes mixed age, classes at primary school, so that they will be quite used to different class members working on different tasks, at any given time.

Another popular method is stepped worksheets, where all pupils given the same materials but the tasks show an incline of difficulty with the simplest first. This can be clarified on the sheet, with tasks labelled as foundation, middle, higher. More able pupils do not have to waste time completing the simplest tasks. The advantage of this approach is that it is simple to manage, and it helps avoid any stigma attached to a separate resource given to less able pupils. However they may become disheartened that they never finish the sheet, or may be tempted to attempt tasks that are too difficult.

This was used as a help sheet where the standard task was to write a diary extract for a slave.

My Capture, 28th June 1777

1. Number the sentences in the order in which these events happened. The first one has been done for you.

We saw the white slave traders give cloth to the African chief who brought the slaves.	
They made us walk to the coast with our legs chained to each other's.	
They came at night and took me from my home.	1
They whipped us if we walked too slowly.	
They captured lots of people from my village.	
They crammed us into a rowing boat to take us to the slave ship.	

2. Now complete this sentence.
   My experience was .... because ....
   ....

Now consider the following:
1. What skills are being tested?
2. What input might be needed to give this pupil the knowledge to complete this task?
3. Where has challenge been left in the differentiated task?
4. Where might this pupil still experience difficulty with this task, and what kind of support would you offer?
5. If this task proved too easy, how could you add extra challenge?

Figure 8.3 An example of a task designed for pupils with SEN

Task 8.4 *Thinking about differentiation*

As preparation for this activity you should read Phillips, R (2002, pages 90-94) on recognising individual needs, creating a supportive learning environment, differentation, and language. You should then observe a particular pupil throughout a lesson or shadow them through a whole day of lessons. Make notes and comment on their performance in a range of activities in each of the classes.

From your notes try to identify:

- the extent to which pupils were on or off task;
- how interested they were in each lesson;
- how many contributions they made in the lesson;
- the quality of their written work;
- the extent to which they appeared to understand the purpose of the tasks they were engaged in;
- how they responded when they encountered difficulties with tasks assigned to them;
- to what extent pupils were able to work things out for themselves.

What do your notes tell you about differentiation? Try and meet with the school's SENCO to discuss the SEN policy in the school.

Task 8.5 *Building up a repertoire of approaches to teaching pupils with SEN*

During your school experience, if possible, observe a number of lessons of mixed-ability classes and observe with strategies the classroom teacher uses in working with pupils who have the following learning difficulties: poor organisational skills, lack of confidence, low level language skills, isolation from other pupils, poor writing skills, lack of interest, short concentration span, physical impairments, limited general knowledge, reluctance to contribute orally.

Discuss with your tutor the approaches which can be used to help pupils through their learning difficulties.

Read John Hull's article in *Teaching History* entitled 'Practical points on Teaching History to less able secondary pupils' (October 1980). Although from 'another age' of history teaching, as with other classic texts, it has useful things to think about. You will see that he lists a number of examples of how to exercise historical skills which include:

- analysis;
- vocabulary acquisition;
- synthesis;
- inference;
- comprehension;
- memorisation;
- sequencing.

Choose one of these skills and design a lesson plan and worksheet for a year 8 class which incorporates one of these skills as its aim.

5 The use of visual resouces

Many pupils learn well when they can visualise the concepts they are learning about, or when they are enabled to present their ideas in a visual format. Pictorial resources are critical in an inclusive classroom. See Stephen (2006) for ideas on how to use a picture as a starter. Luff and Harris (2004: 61) also included some practical ideas for use with visual learners. Sugarman-Banaszak (2008) gives various ideas about how to use images to help pupils step into the past and tease out learning, similarly, maps can be used as pictorial sources. Pupils could be given a number of maps of the local area at different dates, and could be asked to highlight the differences, before finding out how and why the area changed. Haward's (2005) *Seeing History: visual learning strategies and resources* is another valuable resource, as is Card's (2008) *History pictures: using visual sources to build better history lessons*.

Devising board games can be a very popular activity. Some examples could be a snakes and ladders game depicting the ups and downs of medieval town life, or those facing a factory worker during the industrial revolution. The board could include pictures or symbols from the time in question, to encourage use of knowledge and creative skills. Drawing on high levels of understanding and cognitive challenge, a board game can be motivating for very able pupils, including those who may have Special Learning Difficulties (SpLD). On the other hand, the task can be simplified by providing pupils with content to incorporate.

Many learners will benefit from the use of living graphs, charts, timelines, diagrams, mind or concept minds to display information rather than lengthy, written notes. A graph could be used, for example, to show changing attitudes in World War One where date is plotted against morale (from positive to negative). Pupils add labels to show why attitudes changed, instead of writing in paragraphs. The transfer of information from the written form to a visual format is quite a high level skill, which will need to be modelled by the teacher, or by able pupils in the class. Farmer and Knight (1995) suggest a variety of activities for working on diagrams, including completions of a diagram such as a pyramid showing the feudal system, whereby the task can be made easier by giving some of the answers or giving a list of points from which to choose, or correcting mistakes. They also suggest the drawing of strip cartoons to emphasise the key features of a story. To save time, these could be sequenced rather then drawn out. Cartoon strips can also be used to represent a specific point of view within a story. Visual representations can be made using ICT, with a range of apps, such as Comic Life, available for use on i-pads for example.

The process and benefits of concept mapping are explained in an article by van Drie and van Boxtel (2003). Mind maps can be effectively designed by pupils with SEN, as explained by Buzan (1993), who came up with the concept. A mind map is a complex tool to summarise information and categorise into big points and little points. Mind maps are simple to organise, and lend themselves well to differentiation by outcome, since they can display any amount of information and understanding of links between ideas. Some explanation of the process of classification will be beneficial to pupils before the technique is learned. They could recall familiar examples of classification, such as different aisles in a supermarket, then discuss why it is useful to classify information about history.

6 Use of active techniques

Many pupils with SEN prefer to learn by more practical methods. Card sorts are one example. Bear in mind that when a card sort is complete, the findings may not have to be written up. Cutting and pasting could be a time-saving alternative. A variation of card sorts is a pairs game, which involves pairing cards from a selection, explaining why they go together. Other approaches could be placing labels on a diagram or picture, making a model, putting together the pieces of a jigsaw, or human timelines, where individual pupils have large cards showing events and have to physically put themselves into the correct order. See Ian Dawson's *Thinking History* website for a wide range of examples of active approaches: (www.thinkinghistory.org.uk). Dawson's article (2008) explains how a large section of history can be learned actively as an overview. Luff and Harris (1994) refer to 'human continuums', which might involve 'best to worst' in the case of monarchs, or arranging ideas on a political spectrum. They further suggest that pupils organise themselves in a line of social order. This can similarly be done with sentences showing diverse views about a topic, whereby pupils have to group themselves according to the type of view. Another possible starter activity is 'Find the source', whereby pupils have to find sources which have been placed around the classroom in order to complete a chart containing a clue about each source. This encourages close study of sources, as well as immediate participation in the lesson. It can be a hook into complex analysis to be developed later in the lesson.

7 Oral and aural activities

Some pupils with SEN will respond better to auditory stimuli than to written or visual ones. Approaches may include story-telling, role play or drama. Group work is often a useful tool to encourage maximum participation and learning for pupils with SEN. Exploratory talk is crucial for pupils in development of their understanding and confidence.

Alternatively, pupils can present their ideas orally. These could be recorded using an ICT programme such as *Audacity* (http://audacity.sourceforge.net/) for assessment purposes. A further idea is the talking essay, a class effort whereby different groups take on different paragraphs of the essay, using 'talking frames' to guide them. They could be given prompts such as 'Our change was significant because...' Such group talk can also be fostered by giving groups a different extract from a story, or alternatively a picture, and asking them to sequence them as a class. This involves high levels of communication, especially when done to a strict time limit.

8 Working with a teaching assistant

A teaching assistant may be deployed to help pupils to learn. Pupils with SEN will not automatically make progress because he or she is present. It is the teacher's responsibility to plan for the progress of each child. The teachers' standards (DfE, 2012) outline the duty of teachers to 'deploy support staff effectively'. The DCSF-commissioned Blatchford Report found that whilst the support of teaching assisstants in the classroom was very helpful in keeping pupils on task, it did not always lead to improved progress for the child (DCSF, 2008). Both adults need to discuss the child's needs, and the teaching assistant should understand the historical learning objectives. Despite additional support, the pupil(s) may need differentiated learning objectives and resources. The assistant may help with assessment of the pupil's understanding. Close one-to-one support is not always required, and might harm a child's confidence or independence. It may be more effective for the teaching assistant to work with a group of pupils, or to circulate and work with different individuals.

Meeting the needs of pupils who speak English as an additional language

Teaching pupils who speak English as an Additional Language (EAL) is a growing challenge in secondary schools across the country. The Department for Education survey of January 2012 showed that one in six primary school pupils in England – 577,555 – did not have English as their first language. In secondary schools the figure stood at 417,765, just over one in eight (quoted from the NALDIC website). The barriers to learning for pupils with EAL may not derive solely from language issues. Pupils with EAL may also have SEN or may be gifted learners. Learning in two or more languages in an increasingly globalised world is an advantage. 'People who are learning successfully in two languages often do better than those learning successfully in one' (Warwick, 2009).

Some approaches to teaching pupils with EAL

1 Identifying need

The school should hold data on pupils' national and linguistic background. It may be harder to find out about the pupil's family circumstances, previous schooling and level of ability. Where possible, talk to the pupils or parents.

The situation that you encounter in different schools will vary. Each LA has an Ethnic Minority Achievement Service (EMA). EMA will allocate staff to schools where there is the greatest need. These specialist staff may run withdrawal groups for beginners in English, as well as supporting lessons. Where provision is streched, history lessons may not be prioritised for support and you may find pupils with very little English arriving in your classroom at any point. EMA staff, if present at the school, will be able to offer advice, and may assist in preparing resources. You may teach pupils at various stages of English language acquisition, and from a variety of different language backgrounds. Bililgual learners who have always lived in Britain, or have been through a British primary school, should be competent in the use of oral English, and often in written English. However, many who have a strong command of 'playground English' will struggle with the language of learning. The role of the history teacher in an inclusive classroom is to promote learning of history with a focus on the language necessary to understand the content and complete the tasks.

Some pupils, including asylum seekers, may be affected by traumatic experiences. Your priority here may be to make them feel welcome. A special effort to greet them, learn their name, use a 'buddy system', find a task for them to do, or involve them in any way, may enhance their motivation, as their language skills improve.

There are now some textbooks designed specifically for EAL pupils (see, for instance Ocana and Campos, 2010), and Babelfish (www.babelfish.com) and Google Translate - http://translate.google.com (for all their imperfections) can also go some way to providing some language support for EAL pupils.

2 The learning environment

Your overall approach is critical. Drawing pupils into your lesson can be achieved by the ideas outlined above under visual literacy, and careful thought about the use of classroom display and supplementary materials for EAL learners (see Stephen, 2006 and Parr, 1996 for further developent of these points).

Pupils who are in the very early stages of English language acquistion will find it hard to follow much of a history lesson. It is especially difficult in classes where there are only one or two learners with EAL, and it will be some time before they have the confidence to speak in class. Where pupils find themselves in a class with others who share their first language, it is easier to integrate, but arguably harder to make the shift to use of English for communication. The challenge for the teacher is to ease the process by giving as many cues as possible. These could involve gestures to reinforce what is being said, and use of pictures to help illustrate key points, for example in a PowerPoint presentation. For pupils whose first language employs a different script, there is a greater need than usual for clear writing on the board and in books. Try to watch these pupils to see how much they appear to understand. Give regular words of encouragement.

For beginners in English, it is worthwhile to develop separate work, such as labelling pictures, colouring certain parts of a diagram in a specified colour, matching words and meanings, writing out dates in order, completing sentences based on a short text or even copying in order to engage pupils in some way in your topic.

3 Interpreters and support teachers

Various types of support may be available in the classroom, including:

- support from an EMA-funded specialist teacher;
- support from an EMA-funded classroom assistant in the lesson;
- support from a pupil interpreter; and
- support from teacher/adviser with planning and resources outside the lesson.

The Ofsted report *Managing support for the attainment of pupils from minority ethnic groups* (DfES, 2001) stresses the need when planning jointly with EMA staff, to ensure that the focus is on the content of the lesson, with appropriate cognitive challenge, but with a parallel focus on the language necessary to complete the task. Useful guidance on the role of a support teacher can also be found in Malaya's chapter (1996). Hounslow Language Support services offer an excellent history specific booklet on supporting EAL pupils in history (Bousfield Wells, 2006). There are also lots of practical ideas for learning activities in Washbourne (2011).

4 Use of first language in the classroom

Encouraging use of the first language values the individual and his or her culture. Furthermore, pupils who can transfer their understanding from the spoken to the written word, or from one language to another, show understanding rather than rote learning. Some teachers are wary that use of first language may lead to exclusion of others or to disputes about what is being said. It also limits the teacher's control. Such concerns can only be allayed by setting specific boundaries. Many teachers prefer the use of English unless there is an express suggestion otherwise and for a clearly defined purpose.

Exploratory dialogue in the pupils' first language can take place within a group, and should then be fed back to the class through a pupil interpreter. It is most effective given the presence of another adult in the room. According to the paper 'Access and Engagement in History' (DfES, 2002), pupils should be encouraged to use their first language in lessons when:

- the cognitive challenge is likely to be high;
- they are still developing proficiency in English; and
- oral rehearsal will help reflection, for example, before responding to a text, artefact or historical source.

It may not, however, be appropriate for pupils to use their first language when:

- they need to practise the target language to improve fluency;
- they need oral rehearsal in the target language so that they are prepared for writing tasks; and
- they need to take risks in their spoken English in order to build confidence.

Bilingual dictionaries can help with transfer of language, although difficulties arise where there is more than one meaning or context for a given word. Dictionaries are best used with guidance. Various online translation services are now available, sometimes free of charge. These may be quite useful for translating particular words, but less so for translating longer passages. If there are interpreters working at the school, it is helpful to ask them to write out key words in both languages. Older pupils could also help with this. The lists could then be stuck on classroom walls or pasted into books. Pupils with EAL could be given lists of key words, with their meanings, for each topic, and then asked to write out the word in their first language. The learning of words could be set as homework.

5 Supporting oral work

Oral work is central to an inclusive classroom. Some suggestions as to its successful practice follow:

- In a question and answer session, inform your pupils with EAL in advance of the question to be posed to them, to allow them to rehearse an answer.
- Wait more than 15 seconds for a pupil with EAL to answer your question.
- Clarify the purpose of listening tasks and talk. Use listening or talking frames.
- Organise groups so that pupils with EAL hear a positive English language model.
- Use written prompt cards such as 'The evidence tells us that'... or 'The most likely explanation is...' to start sentences.
- Provide key words and meanings in advance.
- Consider using oral presentations as a form of assessment.

6 Supporting reading and writing

Many of the same techniques which apply to pupils with SEN can be applied. These may involve directed activities related to texts – see Eyre (1997: 79) for a summary of the DARTs approach), modelling reading and writing, paragraph headings for text or writing, structured questions and writing frames. Depending on your learning objectives, it will be possible at times to reduce the amount of written work required using methods outlined earlier in the chapter.

   The DfES publication, *Access and Engagement in History* (2002) points out specific confusions for pupils with EAL over the following:

- cultural references – for example, references to common aspects of life in Britain;
- the use of written sources from periods in the past where the use of English is different from the way the language is used today;
- reference in text, where meaning is carried across sentences and paragraphs through reference (to previously stated nouns) using pronouns (*it, they, he, she*);
- imagery – metaphors, similes, idiomatic phrases;
- use of the passive voice;
- contextual definitions of words that can have different meanings from those encountered elsewhere, such as *depression*; and
- subject-specific vocabulary.

The report also states that 'Pupils learning EAL may show patterns of error when writing in English in their history lessons which are related to their experience of the structures of their first language'. It suggests diagnostic marking to ascertain the most commonly made errors. These can indicate writing targets for individuals or groups of pupils.

Task 8.6 *Planning a lesson for pupils with EAL*

Plan a lesson using a short video extract. Watch the extract and note down any words that will need to be explained in advance. Devise a listening frame to encourage active listening. Then devise a group task exploring the new learning. This may involve picking out and weighing up different causes or interpretations of events, or explaining the achievements of an individual. Then write down some questions to be used as a plenary. Which questions would you direct to pupils with EAL?

Meeting the needs of academically able pupils in the history classroom

All schools are required to keep a register, by subject, of pupils who are gifted and talented (see DCSF, 2008). This is usually around 5-10 per cent of the school cohort, regardless of attainment against national standards. Learners are identified by ability, rather than attainment, even if some are underachievers. Talented learners are those who have abilities in practical subjects, whilst gifted learners are those with abilities in academic subjects, including history. Schools are required to evaluate their provision for these learners, and to monitor their progress. Whilst the school should adopt an overall approach to working with these pupils, it is the responsibility of the classroom teacher to ensure that suitable learning challenges are set and learning needs are met. Able pupils can quickly lose motivation and become distracted or disruptive if they are not challenged in their learning. From 2002, gifted and talented young people were supported by the National Academy for Gifted and Talented Youth (NAGTY). In 2007 this was replaced by the Young Gifted and Talented Learners Academy (YGT). This academy was disbanded in 2010 with cuts in funding specifically ring-fenced for gifted and talented pupils. There is still a requirement to provide for their needs. According to the DfE website, the term 'academically more able' pupils replaced 'gifted and talented youth' in spring 2012.

Your first task, as a trainee, is to identify your very able pupils. Generic guidance on gifted learners can be found in the DCSF (2008) guidance. The conclusions of the NAGTY History Think Tank (2005) identifed 21 characteristics of high achievement in history. These included an appreciation of the intrinsic value of historical learning and an enjoyment of the process, an unwillingness to be easily satisfied, a hunger for knowledge of the past, an ability to read historical materials actively and critically, as well as more sophisticated analytical powers. QCA (2008) also identified characteristics of gifted learners in history. Smith (2010) provides useful discussion of the merits of various criteria. However, Laffin (2013) warns of the dangers of over-generalisation about these categories, and making mistaken assumptions in assigning such labels and 'fixed categories' to pupils. It is important to keep an open mind and above all, to provide challenge and the opportunity to do 'difficult work' for all pupils.

As you begin teaching your own classes the class teacher should be able to offer information on gifted pupils. Some will rapidly identify themselves in discussion, whilst others prefer to keep their abilities well hidden. Early assessment of written work is helpful, but you may be surpirised to find that some articulate pupils with excellent powers of reasoning do not express themselves so fluently in writing. Schools may still identify such pupils as academically able. Barriers to writing, which may be connected with cultural background, can be alleviated by some techniques described elsewhere in this chapter.

Task 8.7 *Identifying able pupils in the history classroom*

With the permission of your mentor, when you have become reasonably familiar with one of your teaching groups, make a conscious attempt to identify any pupils who you feel may be particularly able in history, by examining their work and talking to them. What is it about their work and their oral responses which indicates exceptional ability? Look out for pupils who may appear very able because of motivation and workrate, but may fall behind their gifted peers when it comes to work requiring critical thinking. Consider the following characteristics, and see if your observations reveal any others:

- powers of concentration;
- critical judgement and evaluation of evidence;
- ability to argue logically;
- attention to detail;
- easy concept formation;
- originality and imagination; and
- fluency and sophistication of extended writing.

Your approach to teaching these pupils needs to begin with your own attitudes. In addition to expert subject knowledge, you will need to bring a willingness to listen to the exceptional learner and to learn with him or her. You will seek to encourage their intellectual curiosity, study skills and to be aware of needs for acceptance by peers which may mean that the learner does not want to be seen to be doing additional or different work, and does not want to meet you outside lesson time for extra coaching.

Strategies to meet these needs may involve extension or enrichment work as long as this is not restricted to extra work bolted on to standard classroom activities. Enrichment is defined by George (1997) as 'a function of the teacher's flexibility, sensitivity and individual needs, a sense of timing and a mastery of subject area'. As you begin to develop awareness of individual pupils' understanding, you may give the class a choice of activities, encouraging your very able pupils to select more demanding tasks. Activities may include posing their own questions, taking issue with the ideas of others, and use of more demanding source material, including primary sources. Many history teachers keep an 'archive' of newspaper and journal articles on historical topics which can be given as extension work or homework (see Chapter 10). Any reading of historical matter can help to extend vocabulary, and sense of period or place, as well as enhancing direct subject knowledge. Try to provide access to enhanced opportunities beyond the classroom, for example through online discussion with experts from local museums, universities or societies. Meetings with older, very able pupils or ex-pupils, might also be arranged, with learning outcomes to be a summary of a new historical topic in the form of an email proposal for a book or television programme. School visits can be a fantastic learning experience, particularly for those whose families cannot provide such opportunities. You could also direct pupils to visit key local places which are easily accessible, and set a challenge such as devising a trail for tourists or making notes on what steps need to be taken in order to do this. This might link with learning from other subjects such as geography or technology. Gifted pupils might also have heightened awareness and interest in links between the past and present. Encourage them to investigate media comparisons between current world affairs or leaders and historical wars or leaders.

Some exceptionally able pupils will respond directly to a challenge, whereas others might need quiet encouragement. The aim should be to intrigue all pupils so they are made to think hard about aspects of the past, whether this is through teacher exposition and questioning, whole class activities, pupil talk, or research and independent enquiry. This might be achieved through group talk activities like problem solving, mysteries (see Fisher, 2002), odd one out games, puzzles, counterfactual reasoning, ('what if' questions), decision making based on knowledge of the period and characters in question, answering questions in role. Eyre (1997: 55-84) provides 20 ways to create positive challenge in the classroom. Writing activities do not need to involve extended prose, but may comprise composing comments on a situation from the point of view of various different characters, and so on. Command words in questions can be varied to cater for different levels of challenge. Language such as 'investigate, justify, devise a hypothesis, discuss alternative reasons for...' can lead to exploratory learning, and a confirmation that there is rarely a single correct answer to historical questions. Differentiated learning objectives could also be shared with the class. The NAGTY report (2005) is worth consulting for detail on developing pupils' thinking about sources and interpretations of history. The historical concept of significance can be very complex, and decisions involving selection and application of appropriate significance criteria.

Groupings within a mixed ability classroom need to be considered carefully. Whilst the teacher may be tempted to place a more able pupil in each group, to stimulate the others, gifted pupils may benefit from working together at least some of the time. Sharing ideas, challenging each other's thoughts, and reading each other's written work are a learning process, as is peer marking.

Exceptionally able pupils might respond well to being asked to set their own enquiry question, and find their own sources to answer it, possibly in small groups. This could become a homework project as an alternative to the standard homework tasks. Ideally a few pointers would be given at the start, as well as occasional feedback on the process. Ongoing review and refinement of the methods used will also help the very able to engage with the process of study. Some pupils would welcome the opportunity to report their findings to the rest of the class, or to devise a short starter activity based on new learning. Others, who are less self-assured, might prefer a written dialogue with the teacher, through a learning journal or other written method.

Some of these questions may be appropriate for the whole class, with different levels of response expected.

- How was it that William the Conqueror's army of no more than 20,000 men managed to conquer a country with a population of over 1 million?
- In what ways and to what extent was life in England different in 1485 from 1065?
- William the Conqueror, Richard II and Henry VIII all had to put down revolts against their government. Which of them faced greater difficulties in crushing the revolts and why? Would it be easier or harder to put down revolts today? Give reasons for your answer.
- Why did William the Conqueror succeed where Philip II (1588), Napoleon (1805) and Hitler (1940) failed?
- Why did people stop building castles? Discuss alternative reasons.
- Devise a hypothesis about how the treatment of poor or elderly people had changed in Britain over the years. Then test your hypothesis by investigating how these people were treated in a) Elizabethan Times; b) in the years before and after 1834; c) in 1908-14; d) after 1945? Then evaluate and refine your hypothesis.

Figure 8.4 Questions for able pupils

Summary and key points

We have seen that ultimately, the inclusive classroom rests upon the teacher's efforts to make the curriculum accessible to all pupils. History is taught in such a way that all pupils want to learn. This is achieved partly by the provision of appropriate materials, partly by the careful planning of teaching methods and delivery of your lessons. It is an ongoing professional process, which needs to be adapted to individual learners. Support is available in schools from departmental colleagues, the SENCO, and possibly EMA staff. Where pupils are engaged in learning, the experience is more rewarding for the teacher. Finally, inclusion is not *just* a technical issue; the personality, warmth, skills of interaction, and care and concern of the teacher also contribute to pupils' sense of being valued in the classroom.

For further information and resources about aspects of inclusion in the history classroom, including a section on 'Taking equal opportunities seriously', go to www.uea.ac.uk/~m242/historypgce/inclusiondiversity/welcome.htm.

Further reading

Ajegbo, K. (2007) *Curriculum Review: diversity and citizenship*, available online at: http://publications. teachernet.gov.uk/eOrderingDownload/DFES_Diversity_&_Citizenship.pdf. The executive summary of this document is an important read in terms of developing an overall grasp of some of the challenges which schools face in this area.

Boulsfield Wells, D. (2006) *Bilingual Learners and Secondary History*, Hounslow, Hounslow Language Support Services, Martindale Road, Hounslow TW4 7HE, 020 8583 4166. One of the most wide ranging specialist publications for EAL approaches in history.

DfES (2002) *Key Stage 3 National Strategy: Access and Engagement in History - teaching pupils for whom English is an Additional Language* - Ref: DFES 0656/2002, London, DFES. A useful official source.

DfE (2010) *Children with Special Educational Needs 2012: an analysis,* online at www.education.gov.uk/researchandstatistics/statistics/allstatistics/a00214996/children-with-sen-analysis-2012, accessed 18 January 2014.

Grosvenor, I. (2000) History for the Nation: multiculturalism and the teaching of history, in J. Arthur, and R. Phillips (eds) (2000) *Issues in History Teaching,* London: Routledge: 148-58.

References

Banham, D. (2014) Seminar for PGCE students at the University of East Anglia, 31 January.

Boulsfield Wells, D. (2006) *Bilingual Learners and Secondary History,* Hounslow Language Support Services, Hounslow.

Bradshaw, M. (2006) Creating controversy in the classroom: making progress with historical significance, *Teaching History,* No. 125: 18-25.

Bradshaw, M. (2009) Drilling down: how one history department is working towards progression in pupils' thinking about diversity across Years 7, 8 and 9, *Teaching History,* No. 135: 4-12.

Buzan, T. with Buzan, B. (1993) *The Mind Map Book,* London: BBC Books.

Byers, R. and Rose, R. (1996) *Planning the Curriculum for Pupils with SEN: A Practical Guide,* London: David Fulton.

Byrom, J. (2013) 'Alive and kicking? Some personal reflections on the revised National Curriculum (2014) and what we might do with it, *Teaching History, Curriculum Supplement:* 6-14.

Card, J. (2008) *History Pictures: Using visual sources to build better history lessons,* London: Hodder.

Cole, M. (ed.) (2009) Equality in the secondary school, London, Continuum.

Cunnah, W. *History teaching, literacy and special educational needs,* in J. Arthur and R. Phillips (eds) (2000) *Issues in History Teaching,* London: Routledge: 113-24.

Davies, I. (ed.) (2011) *Debates in history teaching,* London: Routledge.

Dawson, I. (2008) Planning and teaching the story of power and democracy at Key Stage 3, *Teaching History,* 130: 14-21.

Department for Children, Schools and Families (DCSF) (2008) *The Blatchford report: DCSF-RR148,* London: DCSF. A summary of the report can be accessed at www.ioe.ac.uk/DISS_Research_Summary.pdf, accessed 24 April 2013.

DCSF (2008) *Identifying gifted and talented learners - getting started,* online at www.education.gov.uk/publications/eOrderingDownload/Getting%20StartedWR.pdf, accessed 18 February 2014.

DfE (1994) *The Code of Practice and the Identification and Assessment of Special Educational Needs,* London: HMSO.

DfE (2012) *Teachers' Standards, May 2012* found online at www.education.gov.uk/publications/eOrderingDownload/teachers%20standards.pdf, accessed 19 August 2014.

DfE (2013) *The National Curriculum in England Framework for key stages 1-4, September 2013* found online at www.gov.uk/government/collections/national-curriculum, accessed 19 August 2014.

DfEE(2000) *Holocaust Memorial Day Education Pack* P47/42392/1100/54 ref HMEP, London: DfEE.

DfEE/QCA (1999) *History: The National Curriculum for England,* London: DfEE/QCA.

DfES (2001) *Managing support for the attainment of schools from minority ethnic groups,* London: DfE/Ofsted.

DfES (2004) *Training Materials for the Foundation Subjects* ref: DFES 0350/2004, London: DfES.

Diversity and Inclusion Team (2006) *Hidden History Express,* Manchester.

Eyre, D. (1997) *Able Children in Ordinary Schools,* London: David Fulton Publishers Ltd.

Farmer, A. and Knight, P. (1995) *Active History in Key Stages 3 and 4,* London: David Fulton.

Fisher, P. with Wilkinson, I. and Leat, D. (2002) *Thinking through History,* Cambridge: Chris Kington.

Frederickson, N. and Cline, T. (2002) *Special Educational Needs, Inclusion and Diversity*, Buckingham: Oxford University Press.

Frow, M. (1997) *Roots of the Future: Ethnic Diversity in the Making of Britain*, London: Commission for Racial Equality.

George, D. (1997) *The Challenge of the Able Child*, London: David Fulton Publishers Ltd.

Gilborn, G. (2000) *Educational Inequality: Mapping Race, Class and Gender. A Synthesis of Research*, London: Ofsted.

Grosvenor, I. (2000) *History for the Nation: multiculturalism and the teaching of history*, in J. Arthur and R. Phillips (eds) (2000) *Issues in History Teaching*, London: Routledge: 148–58.

Hallam, S. (1996) 'Differentiation': unpublished lecture, Institute of Education, University of London, 17 January.

Harris, R. (2005) Does differentation have to mean different? *Teaching History*, No. 118: 5–13.

Hart, S. (ed) (1996) *Differentiation and the Secondary Curriulum: Debates and dilemmas*, London: Routledge.

Haward, T. (2005) *Seeing History: Visual learning strategies and resources for Key Stage 3*, Stafford: Network Educational Press.

Historical Association (2007) *Teaching Emotive and Controversial History, 3-19*, London: Historical Association.

HM Government (2003) *Every Child Matters*, London: HMSO.

Husbands, C., Kitson, A. and Pendry, A (2003) *Understanding History Teaching*, Maidenhead: Open University Press.

Imperial War Museum packs – *The Empire Needs Men, Together*, London: Imperial War Museum.

Laffin, D. (2013) 'Supporting and stretching your A level pupils', Historical Association Conference, York, 10 May.

Lomas, T. (2005) *New ideas in develping pupils' learning in Key Stage 3 and 4 history*, address to SHP Conference, Leeds.

Luff, I. and Harris, R. (2004) *Meeting SEN in the Curriculum: History*, London: David Fulton.

Lyndon, D. (2006) Integrating black British history into the curriculum, *Teaching History*, No. 122: 37–42. (See also Lyndon's website: www.blackhistory4schools.com)

Maddison, M. (2014) 'Securing improvement in secondary schools through highly effective history', Presentation for the Norfolk and Suffolk Secondary History Network, Norwich, 31 January.

Malaya, J. (1996) 'The case of bilingual learners', in S. Hart (ed.) *Differentiation and the Secondary Curriculum: Debates and dilemmas*, London: Routledge.

Montgomery, D. (ed.) (2009) *Able, Gifted and Talented Underachievers*, Chichester: John Wiley & Sons Ltd.

NAGTY History Think Tank (2005) *Supporting high achievement in History: conlusions of the NAGTY History Think Tank*, online at http://repository.edgehill.ac.uk/3028, accessed 19 August 2014.

Ocana, J. and Campos, M. (2010) *History for EAL/ESL/E2L pupils*, Oxford: OUP.

Parr, N. (1996) 'I belong here – they speak my kind of language' in S. Hart (ed.) *Differentiation and the secondary curriulum: debates and dilemmas*, London: Routledge.

Pearson, J. (2012) Where are we? The place of women in history curricula, *Teaching History*, No. 147: 47–52.

Phillips, R. (2001) Making History Curious: Using Initial Stimulus Material to promote Enquiry, Thinking and Literacy, *Teaching History*, No. 105: 19–25.

Phillips, R. (2002) *Reflective teaching of history 11-18*, London: Hodder & Stoughton.

Phillips, I. (2008) *Teaching history - developing as a secondary practitioner*, London: Sage.

QCA (2001a) *Planning, teaching and assessing the curricuum for pupils with learning difficulties: history*, available online at http://webarchive.nationalarchives.gov.uk/20080520223745/qca.org.uk/qca_11583.aspx, accessed 14 February 2014.

QCA (2001b) *Respect for All*, available online at: http://webarchive.nationalarchives.gov.uk/20081105160428/qca.org.uk/qca_6753.aspx, accessed 14 February 2014.

QCA (2007) *History Programme of Study for Key Stage 3 and Attainment Target*, London: HMSO.

QCA (2008) *Guidance on identifying and teaching gifted pupils in history* – found online at http://webarchive.nationalarchives.gov.uk/20080107211607/http://qca.org.uk/qca_2233.aspx, accessed 19 August 2014

Ofsted (2004) *Special Educational Needs and Disability: Towards Inclusive Schools*, 2004, ref HMI 2206, London: Ofsted.

Senior, J. and Whybra, J. (2005) *Enrichment Activities for Gifted Children*, Salisbury: Optimus.

Smith, N. (2010) *History Teacher's Handbook*, London: Continuum.

Stephen, A. (2006) *Ensuring inclusion in the classroom* in M. Hunt (ed.) *A Practical Guide to Teaching History in the Secondary School*, London: Routledge Falmer: 70-80.

Sugarman-Banaszak, C. (2008) Stepping into the past: using images to travel through time, *Teaching History*, No. 130: 24-29.

Sweerts, E. and Grice, J. (2002) Hitting the right note: how useful is the music of African-Americans to historians?, *Teaching History*, No. 108: 36-41.

Taylor, C. (2012) *Getting the simple things right: Charlie Taylor's behaviour checklists*, London: DfE, online at www.gov.uk/government/uploads/system/uploads/attachment_data/file/283997/charlie_taylor_checklist.pdf, accessed 4 March 2014.

Teaching History (2006) *Teaching the Most Able*, No. 124.

Teare, B. (2006) *Problem-Solving and Thinking Skills: Resources for Able and Talented Children*, London: Network Continuum Education.

Unwin, R. (1981) *The Visual Dimension in the Study and teaching of history*, Historical Association pamphlet number 49, London.

Van Drie, J. and van Boxtel, C. (2003) Developing conceptual understanding through talk and mapping, *Teaching History*, No. 110: 27-31.

Warnock, M. (1978) *The Warnock Report: Special Educational Needs*, London: HMSO.

Warwick, I. (2009) *Improving the Quality of Identification, Provision and Support for Gifted and Talented Learners from Under-Represented Communities through Partnership Working* in D. Montgomery (ed.) (2009) *Able, Gifted and Talented Underachievers*, Chichester: John Wiley & Sons Ltd.

Washbourne, A. (2011) *EAL Pocketbook*, Arlesford: Teachers' Pocketbooks.

9 The use of new technology in the history classroom

History cannot be taught without images; it is grotesquely and pathetically weakened if it fails to do so. (Simon Schama, Prince of Wales Trust Conference, Norwich, 2 July 2003)

A key question: to what extent are you able to make full use of the potential of new technology for improving teaching and learning in history?

Figure 9.1 Wired up?

Introduction

What do the *Teachers' Standards* (DfE, 2012) have to say about the use of ICT in subject teaching? Interestingly, nothing – this is in marked contrast to earlier competence specifications for entry into the teaching profession. This does not mean that new technology is of no interest or relevance to student teachers of history. Whereas a decade ago, there were many history teachers who were profoundly sceptical about the use of ICT in the history classroom, and some who argued that it was possible to be a perfectly effective history teacher without using ICT (see, for instance, Dickinson, 1998, Easdown, 2000), there are now few history teachers who believe that you can eschew the use of new technology without in some ways limiting the learning opportunities of your pupils (Haydn, 2012). Given that history is now seen by some as being about 'learning to manage complex subjects and manipulate data' (Rollason, 1998), it would be surprising if ICT was not capable of contributing to teaching and learning in history. If you are well informed, up to date and accomplished in this area it can make it much easier to teach history in a way that is varied, powerful and interesting for pupils. If you are a history teacher, new technology is your friend and ally.

All history teachers are somewhere on the continuum below. Very few of them are at either extreme of the continuum. Your overarching objective in this area of competence should be to be as far as possible towards the right hand end of the continuum as possible by the start of your NQT year.

Figure 9.2 Developing competence

Objectives

By the end of this chapter you should be able to:

- appreciate the importance of ICT competence for your professional development;
- identify the range and breadth of new technology applications which might be relevant to the history classroom;
- understand the various aspects of developing competence in ICT, particularly the difference between personal proficiency and classroom experience;
- understand that with many aspects of new technology, there is a continuum in terms of the degree of relaxed assurance and effectiveness with which you are able to use new technology to enhance the quality of teaching and learning in the classroom; and
- use new technologies to improve the quality of your lessons.

Some things to keep in mind

The use of ICT in history teaching poses difficult questions for history teachers and student teachers. Although politicians of all parties have waxed lyrical about the transformative potential of ICT, and have tended to see it as an unproblematic educational miracle, many official reports and surveys have presented a more ambivalent picture about the use of ICT in the history classroom (see Haydn, 2012 for more detail on this). Ofsted has pointed out that some history departments make much more effective use of ICT than others, in terms of improving the quality of the resources and learning opportunities open to pupils (Ofsted, 2011). Sometimes the technology can get in the way of the learning or be ineffective – it doesn't *necessarily* make your lessons better. Also, there are difficult choices to make in terms of what facets of ICT to explore in your teaching; there are now dozens of avenues to explore in terms of finding out about, and using new technology in your teaching, which ones should you prioritise? You have to think what to do with all this stuff, how to make intelligent use of it. You will have read about (and perhaps already been involved in) a world of Web 2.0, blogs, wikis, podcasts and so on. But how are you going to adapt them to improve your lessons? There are a lot of very boring podcasts out there whose best use might be as punishments for pupils who misbehave, and the number of 'dead' blogs, rotting and abandoned in cyberspace was estimated at 200 million as long ago as 2007 ('Why are so many people blogging off?', *Guardian*, 27 March 2007). Presentation software like PowerPoint does not have the same effect on learners as it did when it was first used. Is there anyone reading this who has not at one point or another been severely bored by a PowerPoint presentation (or heard the phrase 'death by PowerPoint')? There is no necessary correlation between the sophistication of the technology, and the degree to which it improves teaching and learning. Often very simple 'low-tech' applications can be very effective and powerful. The bottom line is the extent to which you are able to *apply* new technology to improve pupils' learning. It is not primarily a question of the extent to which you are technologically 'gifted' when you start the course, it is about how good a learner you are. It is an area where some student teachers make much more progress than others, and you need to be proactive, display initiative, and put aside some dedicated time to this agenda rather than just 'waiting for the answer lady to come round'.

Using ICT to 'build learning packages'

One of the most far-reaching consequences of the information revolution is the exponential increase in the speed and breadth of information dissemination. If there are good ideas about history teaching, it is now much easier to tell history teachers about them. Ben Walsh (2003) makes the point that one of the biggest advantages of ICT is the facility it offers to quickly and easily build up, store and organise a range of resources that will give them a rich archive of high quality materials on whatever topics they are teaching. It is also much easier to share 'collections' with fellow history teachers. Sites such as *Evernote* (www.evernote. com), *Dropbox* (www.dropbox.com) and *Skydrive* (www.skydrive.com) make it easy to store, organise and share digital resources. Although many people use sites such as *Delicious* (www.delicious.com), *YouTube* (www.youtube.com) and *Slideshare* (www.slidshare.com), to bookmark and collect resources, not all of them take advantage of the facility to offer access other people's collections.

The 'communications' strand of ICT can drastically reduce the amount of time which teachers have to spend collecting resources and ideas for their lessons. Many history teachers spend considerable amounts of time building up collections of resources on particular topics or what the Hampshire History Centre terms 'De luxe' lessons (www3. hants.gov.uk/education/hias/curriculum-resources/curriculum-resources-centres/history-centre.htm). Simon Harrison has spent hours of his time putting together a very useful package of resources on *Battalion 101*, which is available free at www.keystagehistory.co.uk/free-samples/battalion-101.html; Russel Tarr has a useful collection of links at www.delicious.com/russeltarr, and Russel Tarr and Dan Moorhouse have interesting collections on

YouTube (www.youtube.com/user/russeltarr, www.youtube.com/user/dmoorhouse1973). It can also be helpful to 'sub-contract' building up 'collections' between groups of learners.

There are many websites which are useful sources of information for student history teachers. You need to be familiar with these, if you are to keep abreast of recent developments in both history, and ICT. A list of some internet sites which history student teachers have found helpful is provided in Figure 9.4. In addition to the major internet sites for teaching history, there are also a number of online forums for history teachers to share their questions, interests and resources. Some student teachers use such forms to develop their capability in ICT; some sites focus on technology issues, others on providing ideas for pupil activities or the development of subject content knowledge. One further thing you should keep in mind is that web resources and sites are often transient; sometimes URLs change, content is pruned or sites become defunct, sometimes you find that they have moved elsewhere, other times, the resource has disappeared from cyber space altogether. It is worth refining your searching techniques (see, for example the 'advanced search' facility in Google), but if you find 'gems' on the internet, it is helpful to make your own 'capture' of them before they disappear. At the time of writing, the website keepvid (www.keepvid.com) was one option for doing this, but these things are subject to change, and you may find you have to 'google' or 'YouTube' to find an up-to-date way of doing this.

Making the most of history websites: building collections of 'impact' resources

The major history websites for history teachers in the UK offer an overwhelming number of resources. Just exploring one of the major sites would take months. It is not about building up the biggest collection of resources, it is about trying to 'cherry pick' the best, most powerful resources for the teaching points you wish to make. It is about discerning and focused use of history websites – and effective ways of sharing the 'gems' which have been unearthed. It can be salutary to check what proportion of the resources you have amassed that you are actually making use of in your teaching, rather than just cluttering up your hard drive or memory stick.

What is an 'impact' resource?

One of the 'variables' with my student teachers, in terms of being or becoming 'good at ICT', is the degree of resourcefulness which they devote to using ICT to get hold of what I call 'impact' resources.

By 'impact resource', we mean something that makes a particular teaching point in a vivid and powerful way; something that stays in learners' minds long after the lesson has gone (what Heath and Heath, 2008 term 'stickiness'). It is often something that disturbs learners' previous understandings, or which 'problematises' the issue or concept in a way that makes learners think further about it. It also encourages 'dialogic' learning, whereby learners are sufficiently interested by the resource that they are willing to clarify and modify their understanding through discussion with others. It intrigues learners to the extent that they are prepared to play an active part in constructing meaning themselves. It becomes part of learners' 'historical consciousness': what Rusen (1993: 87) refers to as 'playing a role in the mental household of the subject'. Impact resources can take various forms. They can be images, graphs, moving image clips, 'mysteries', pieces of prose, maps, newspaper articles, metaphors and ideas for pupil activities. A few examples are provided below; more can be accessed at http://historyandict.wikifoundry.com.

An extract from the BBC documentary *QED: Armageddon* (www.youtube.com/watch?v=7AYMS1poOL8) can convey an understanding of the gap between a large conventional bomb (www.liveleak.com/view?i=08f_1215297182) and an atomic blast which would be difficult to convey as vividly however good the teacher's skills of exposition. The moving image clip of the 'Blue Eyes, brown eyes' experiment, from '5 steps to tyranny' (www.youtube.com/watch?v=68GzOJQ8NMw) is much more powerful than just telling pupils about the experiment.

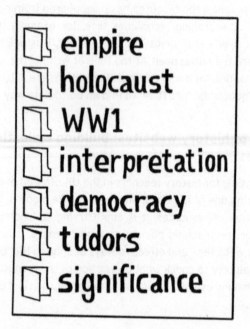

empire
holocaust
WW1
interpretation
democracy
tudors
significance

Figure 9.3 Building up image collections

Image libraries give easy access to many of the iconic images of the past century: the boy standing in front of the tank, the little girl burning from napalm, Tommie Smith's black power salute, Kohl and Mitterand holding hands at a memorial ceremony, the executed Vietcong soldier, the child and the vulture... All these images are ways into powerful and important stories about history (which can also be accessed on the internet). It is not about how many images you collect on a particular topic or concept, it's about getting hold of a small number of images which enable you to make a particular teaching point in a vivid and powerful way.

Most newspapers now archive their articles on the internet and at the time of writing this chapter, most of them are still 'free access'. Newspapers are an excellent source of high quality writing about history, and can often provide useful and homeworks or 'pre-reading' for teaching sessions.

(Some of these are 'free'; some are subscription sites with some free content)

Active History	www.activehistory.co.uk
BBC History	www.bbc.co.uk/history
Facing History and Ourselves	www.facinghistory.org
Historical Association	www.history.org.uk
History Resource Cupboard	www.historyresourcecupboard.co.uk
History Stuff	www.historystuff.co.uk
JohnDClare	www.johndclare.net
Keystage History	www.keystagehistory.co.uk/index.html
National Archives	www.nationalarchives.gov.uk/education
School History Project	www.schoolshistoryproject.org.uk/index.php
Spartacus Schoolnet	www.spartacus.schoolnet.co.uk
School History	www.schoolhistory.co.uk
Teachit	www.teachit.co.uk/history
Thinking History	www.thinkinghistory.co.uk
Timelines TV	www.timelines.tv
The e-help website	If you are particularly interested in the use
EHISTO	of new technology in history teaching,
	these two websites, based on European
	Projects might be of interest: www.e-help.eu.
	www.european-crossroads.de

Figure 9.4 A list of websites which students said they have found useful

Although you should be alert to the potential of communications technology for augmenting your resources, you should also keep in mind that access to information is the first step in learning, not the final one. You need to think through what you are going to do with the information, how you use it to improve your teaching, and pupils' learning in history. It is very easy to accumulate a bigger and bigger list of 'favourites', which you don't actually deploy in your teaching. Some time must be devoted to thinking what to do with all the information, and finding a balance between acquiring it, and deploying it. Becoming 'good at ICT' as a history teacher is not a genetic matter; like most aspects of teaching, it is a matter of intelligence and application.

What does it mean 'to be good at ICT' in history teaching?

Initial teacher education courses attempt to lay solid foundations to build on, they do not generally produce experts. It is important to be realistic about what can be achieved in initial teacher education, where you have many other areas of competence to develop. (If you are really struggling with class management issues, should you really be trying to learn 'Flash' software?). It is also important to stress that objectives should not be limited to the development of *personal* proficiency in ICT. Objectives might helpfully be divided into four discrete areas. You have to consider all four areas if you are to be in a position to use ICT effectively in your NQT year.

1   **Personal competence.** You should try to develop a reasonable 'base' of personal proficiency in the use of ICT. It may not be possible to develop assured and expert levels of competence in a comprehensive range of applications, but to think about what might constitute a foundation which would give you access to a wide range of eminently usable and realistic opportunities for using ICT in the history classroom in your NQT year.

2   **Awareness of what there is to think about in terms of history and ICT.** You should be aware of the breadth of ICT applications and ideas which can be used in the history classroom, even if you do not have time to fully explore the potential of all applications. It is important to keep abreast of new developments and ideas by reading the regular sections on ICT in *Teaching History*, the *TES*, and other relevant journals and websites.

3   **Levels of competence.** You must bear in mind that in all facets of competence in ICT, there is a continuum between ignorance and inadequacy on the one hand, and expert levels of proficiency and knowledge on the other. Ideas for progression in competence in some of the domains of ICT are suggested later in the chapter. The important thing is not to see competence as a line at which your development stops once you have achieved basic levels. A clear grasp of levels of expertise to aspire to, and a commitment to getting there are important attributes, even if you do not attain expert levels in the course of your education. Often progression is in terms of being able to get to a degree of confidence with the ICT application where the teacher can get *the pupils* using ICT applications constructively and creatively to 'do history', rather than just using ICT themselves.

4   **Classroom use of ICT.** Perhaps the most important – and challenging element – is to develop a depth of classroom experience in the use of ICT. No matter how sophisticated your personal levels of expertise in ICT, it is only when you can successfully incorporate that expertise into your classroom teaching that ICT can enhance the learning experiences of pupils. It is only by trying things out in a classroom with real, live pupils that you (eventually) develop a relaxed assurance in the classroom use of ICT. This is in some ways the most problematic of the four areas. History departments vary in the extent to which they have access to state of the art ICT facilities and departmental expertise in ICT, so you need to adopt a flexible and proactive approach, *and use your own initiative* to make progress in the use of ICT in the history classroom. It is partly (and perhaps largely) a question of application and attitude over the course of your training rather than your level of expertise in ICT when you start the course.

Easdown notes the negative preconceptions of some history student teachers in the early stages of their course, including one student who remarked that 'Computers are becoming increasingly important in education, and I'm afraid it's going to get worse' (Easdown, 1997). The process of developing classroom assurance in the use of ICT is in some ways akin to learning to ride a bike or learning to change gear in a car – effortless and enjoyable once proficiency has been acquired, but nerve-racking and requiring a degree of will and determination to persevere in the first stages. What is important here is that a climate of learning is created in which you are not afraid to experiment, to take chances, and even to 'fail' in some lessons, as long as this is not done with cavalier disregard of the needs of the pupils in your care (although reckless 'overdosing' on ICT by student teachers is a comparatively rare phenomenon). Short-term agendas of 'That was a reasonable lesson', need to be balanced against longer term consideration of developing a complete range of pedagogical skills and methods, so that you do not arrive at your NQT post having employed cautious and 'survival-oriented' teaching techniques, before going on to inflict a staple diet of worksheets and word searches for the rest of your teaching career. Because of this, it is better to attempt the incorporation of ICT elements into lessons, and risk the possibility of everything not working out perfectly on the first occasion, than not to use ICT at all. Given the variables in facilities, expertise and attitudes to ICT in different schools, departments and university tutors, the extent to which you progress towards expert levels of competence in the use of new technology in the classroom depends to at least some extent on the extent to which you are prepared to try things out and experiment, and use your initiative and make time for developing ICT skills over the course of the year.

You are pretty good 'technically'; you are relaxed and reasonably adept at working out how to use new applications and fix 'glitches'/minor or straightforward technical problems.

You are knowledgeable and up to date in your awareness of the range of ICT applications and programs which can be used to enhance teaching and learning in history.

You are accomplished in your use of the interactive whiteboard and PowerPoint: your use of these applications usually engages and motivates pupils.

You are well organised and efficient in terms of using ICT to save time in planning and assessment and to organise your personal 'archive' of resources effectively, clear emails etc.

You are good at using ICT to build up really good 'collections' of powerful impact resources on a wide range of topics. You are familiar with and make use of many of the 'gems' that are available on good history websites.

If you have got access to the internet and a data projector in your teaching sessions, you take full advantage of the wealth of resources on the net to improve the impact of your lessons.

You are able to deploy these resources to construct well-designed and intellectually rigorous pupil tasks using ICT – you can think of good ideas for deploying digital resources and structuring good activities for pupils using ICT resources and applications.

You are an 'early adaptor', quick to pick up on new developments and applications in ICT and work out ideas for doing something useful with them in the history classroom.

You make good use of ICT (websites, discussion groups, Blogs, Twitter etc.) to develop your use of ICT in history by being a proactive and diligent part of the 'community of practice' of history teachers in the field of ICT.

When you use ICT in your teaching, it usually works well.

Your use of ICT improves the quality of your lessons.

Your pupils use ICT to learn history outside taught sessions.

Your pupils are good at 'expressing themselves digitally'.

Figure 9.5 What does it mean 'to be good at ICT' as a history teacher?

Task 9.1 *Exploring how history departments use ICT*

Talk to the teachers you are working with in school, and to your peers on the course. What are their experiences and views on the potential of ICT for improving teaching and learning in history, and what avenues for exploration and development do they recommend?

Development of practical effectiveness in the use of ICT

If you are to arrive at your NQT post as a technologically enabled history teacher, you have to get to grips with a wide range of new technology applications. Part (but only part) of this agenda is your own range and depth of expertise in being able to use new technology. The following exercises were designed to get student teachers to think about what there is to think about in terms of the ontology of new technology – exactly what do you have to think about in terms of becoming technologically 'enabled' in ICT in the history classroom?

Task 9.2 *Which applications are most important to a history teacher?*
Prioritising your exploration of ICT agendas

New technology applications offer different advantages and opportunities according to the nature of the subject discipline. For instance, history teachers tend to make more use of the television and DVD recordings than maths teachers. Data logging is invaluable to science teachers, but of no interest or relevance to history teachers.

Look at the following list of new technology applications, and think about whether they are 1) essential; 2) fairly important; 3) of peripheral interest; or 4) irrelevant to the secondary history teacher. Also, what are the time implications of exploring the potential of these applications; are some going to be easier and quicker to get to grips with than others; what should your priorities be in exploring and developing your proficiency in ICT?

- wikis;
- video camera;
- mind mapping software;
- tablet computers;
- history websites;
- image manipulation;
- use of virtual learning environments;
- interactive whiteboards;
- history databases;
- presentation software (e.g. PowerPoint);
- history teacher forums;
- podcasts;
- blogs;
- web authoring;
- digital camera;
- webquests; and
- visualiser.

Task 9.3 *What is your ICT quotient? Thinking about what it means 'to be good' at ICT in history teaching*

1. **Computers-range of hardware platforms**
   I don't know how to use any computer hardware system. **0**
   I can only confidently use one computer hardware system. **4**
   I am confident using PC and Mac systems. **6**

2. **Computers-level of technical capability**
   None. **0**
   Very basic - can just about get round the system but sometimes get stuck. **3**

Quite confident; I feel I am reasonably capable in terms of knowing how to do most of the usual things. (file management, integrating and transferring bits and pieces from different applications. **7**

I feel I am pretty good technically and can do most things – I'm pretty quick and confident at technical stuff. **10**

All the above but also can usually reconfigure systems and fix problems without having to send for the mendy-person when something won't work. **20**

3. **Digital Camera**
    I am aware of what they are. **1**
    I can use one. **3**
    I can use a digital camera to transfer pictures into other applications. **5**
    I have occasionally used them in my teaching and preparation of lessons, on field trips etc. **8**
    I've had pupils using them in ways that have worked reasonably well. **10**
    I've used them quite a bit, in several ways with really positive outcomes. **12**

4. **Image editing packages**
    I know what they do. **1**
    I can make some sort of picture using them. **3**
    I am confident in using most features of imaging packages. **6**
    I can use them and am aware of how they can be used in teaching. **8**
    I regularly make use of them in my preparation of resources and teaching. **10**
    They have definitely improved my teaching repertoire and capabilities. **12**
    I've got a really good collection of images which really enrich my teaching. **15**
    The above plus I have got pupils to do interesting and worthwhile things using and manipulating images. **20**

5. **Word processing**
    I can't word process. **0**
    I can do basic word processing. (moving and adjusting text, saving and printing etc.). **3**
    I am confident and accomplished in word processing and can do most things. **5**
    I can use some of the advanced features of word processors. **7**
    I can 'find my way' around most word processing packages. **9**
    I am aware of the ways in which the word processor can be used by history teachers to help to develop pupils' historical understanding. **12**
    I've done some stuff with pupils using word processing activities that have worked really well. **15**

6. **Data-handling**
    I don't know what data-handling is. **0**
    I know what it is but I don't know how to do it. **2**
    I know how to use a data handling package or commercially produced datafile. **5**
    I know how to construct my own datafile using a data-handling package. **7**
    I know what sort of questions to ask of history datafiles. **9**
    I feel confident that I could teach/demonstrate how to construct a datafile to a group of students. **10**

I could do all this using a variety of data-handling packages. **12**

I can do all this and am confident that I could teach pupils how to use a data-handling package. **15**

I've had some really good lessons getting the pupils to do interesting and historically 'valid' things with datafiles. **20**

7.   **Spreadsheets**

I'm not sure what they are and what you can do with them. **0**

I know what they are but don't know how to use a s/s application. **2**

I know the difference between a database and a spreadsheet. **4**

I know how to use a s/s application. **6**

I know how to use spreadsheets for a variety of purposes. **8**

I can use them and know ways in which history teachers can make use of them. **10**

I've done some things using spreadsheets in history that have worked really well with pupils. **15**

8.   **Desktop publishing**

I'm not sure what this is. **0**

I know what it is but can't use a DTP application. **1**

I have a basic grasp of a DTP application. **4**

I have a fluent grasp of a DTP application. **6**

I know how to use several DTP packages. **8**

I know how to use DTP applications and have used them successfully in a classroom context. **10**

9.   **CD-rom**

I'm not sure what they are. **0**

I know what CD-rom means/stands for. **2**

I can use a CD-rom. **3**

I am confident in the use of a range of history CD-roms. **5**

I know how to use them and I am aware of a range of activities using CD-roms which can be used to enhance learning outcomes in my subject. **7**

And I have been able to get pupils to do good historical enquiries, productively and autonomously. **10**

10.   **Authoring and presentation packages (PowerPoint/Inspirations/Photostory/Prezi etc)**

I'm not sure what they do. **0**

I can construct a basic PowerPoint presentation. **3**

I am fairly confident and accomplished in my technical grasp of PowerPoint. **7**

I am confident in the use of PowerPoint and some other presentation software packages. **10**

I know how to use presentation software to enhance teaching and learning in my subject. **12**

My use of PowerPoint is generally good, it usually motivates and engages pupils. **15**

And I have been able to get pupils to use presentation software skilfully and effectively. **20**

11. The internet
I'm not sure what it is. **0**
I can find my way around the net reasonably well. **2**
I am pretty good at finding what I want on the net. **4**
I feel confident in teaching pupils about issues relating to the net and history. **6**
I know how to transfer files to my personal webspace. **8**
I know how to put my own stuff up on the web. **10**
I can use the Internet and have several ideas for using it to enhance teaching and learning in history. **15**
I know how to set up a personal or departmental website. **18**
I already have a well designed and educationally useful website. **20**
My use of the net regularly makes a big difference to the quality of my lessons. **24**

12. e-mail
I know what it is. **1**
I know how to send and receive simple e-mail messages. **3**
I know how to send and download attachments. **5**
I know how to do nicknames and pass messages on, set up distribution groups, archive e-mails etc. **10**

13. Scanner
I know what it does. **1**
I know how to use one. **3**
I know how to use scanners and have used them to improve resources for pupils. **6**
I regularly use scanners to improve my lesson resources. **10**

14. Video/DVD recorder
I don't know how to use a video/DVD recorder. **0**
I can use video/DVD recorder to tape and replay TV programmes. **2**
I can use advance timer on VCR/DVD to tape a TV programme. **4**
I can use advance timer to tape several TV programmes at a time. **6**
I can do tape to tape editing of video/DVD programmes. **8**
I can use an editing suite to edit and add my own sound track to video/DVD extracts. **10**
I can do all this and have a developing personal archive of video/DVD extracts which I often use to enhance teaching and learning in my lessons. **14**

15. Video camera
I don't know how to use a video camera. **0**
I think I know how to use a video camera, might need a quick revision session. **4**
I am confident in the use of the video camera. **7**
I can transfer video camera footage to a computer and save it. **10**
I know ways of using the video camera with pupils and have used video cameras to improve the quality of their learning and their enthusiasm for the subject. **20**

16. **Film strip/slide/carousel projector**

I don't know how to use any of them. **0**

I'm OK on ones that I'm familiar with, but not all models. **1**

I feel confident in using any of this equipment. **2**

I even know which way the slides go without having to do it by trial and error. **3**

I know how to use them and how found ways of using slides to improve some of my lessons. **4**

17. **Overhead projector**

I don't know how to use an OHP. **0**

I can use one but I'm not sure about how to do all the adjustments, (focusing etc). **3**

I am completely confident about all aspects of OHP use. **5**

I even know how to change the bulb if one blows. **7**

I know how to use them and have frequently used them to improve the quality of my presentation of lessons to pupils. **10**

18. **Photocopier**

I don't know how to use one. **0**

I can make simple single or multiple copies. **2**

I can also do enlarge/reduce. **3**

I also know how to do back to back copies. **5**

I have made imaginative and effective use of the photocopier to improve the quality of some of my resources and lessons. **10**

19. **Digital video editing**

Don't know what it is. **0**

Know what it does but can't use it. **2**

Can use digital video editing software. **4**

Feel confident using digital video editing applications with real live children. **10**

Can get pupils to use digital video editing activities in history. **20**

20. **Using interactive whiteboards**

I'm vaguely aware of what they are and what they do. **1**

I actually know what sorts of things you can do with them in history. **4**

I can use them successfully as part of my teaching. **7**

I know a wide range of ways that they can be used to enhance teaching and learning in history. **12**

They often make a positive difference to the quality of my lessons. **15**

21. **Data projectors**

What? **0**

I know how to set up and use a data projector. **3**

I sometimes use the data projector as part of my teaching to improve the quality of the lessons. **6**

The use of the data projector has had a big impact on improving my teaching. **10**

Data projectors are great and I feel I use them well but I can get by without them when necessary and am not over-reliant on them – I don't unthinkingly use them in a lazy way in just about every lesson. **12**

22. Wikis
I don't know what they are. **0**
Know what they are but haven't accessed one. **1**
Have accessed one or more wikis. **3**
Know how to incorporate wikis in my teaching. **5**
Can get my pupils involved in work constructing and editing wikis. **8**
Have set up a wiki which is working really well. **15**

23. Blogs
Know what they are. **1**
Have accessed some. **3**
Am familiar with some history blogs. **5**
Have my own blog. **7**
Have my pupils working with blogs and constructing their own history blogs. **10**

24. Podcasts
Know what they are. **1**
Have accessed some. **3**
Can make a podcast. **5**
Use them for homework and they seem to work quite well. **8**
Can get my pupils making podcasts of their own. **12**

25. Web authoring tools
Know what they are. **1**
Can use Flash, Captivate, Audacity, Hot Potatoes etc. **5**
Work with pupils using these applications. **10**

26. Accessing E-resources
Can't use any of them. **0**
Vaguely know what they are but don't use them. **1**
Can use some of them (Metalib, the VLE, History Resource, TTRB, Pathe News etc.). **10**
Use most of them and use RSS feeds to update resources. **15**
I make extensive and effective use of E-resources and have built up a really good archive of resources which regularly help to improve the quality and impact of my lessons. **25**

27. Voting technology
What? **0**
Have seen it used/know if its existence. **2**
Have used a PowerPoint which incorporates voting technology response. **5**
Have devised and used a PowerPoint incorporating voting technology and other resources. **10**
Have used voting technology in a way that has worked really well. **15**

28. Other Web 2.0 applications

I know what Web 2.0 means. **1**

I am familiar with several Web 2.0 applications that can be useful for history teaching. **4**

I have used a range of Web 2.0 applications to do some useful and interesting things in my teaching. **8**

I have used a range of Web 2.0 applications with pupils in ways that have worked quite well. **15**

29. Twitter and other social networking tools

I know what Twitter is and what it does. **1**

I can use Twitter. **2**

I use Twitter to share and access history stuff with colleagues and access history focused Twitter sites. **5**

I have been able to get pupils using Twitter for revision and learning purposes. **12**

30. Visualisers

I know what they are and what they do. **1**

I know how to use them. **3**

I have worked out ways of using them that work really well in my lessons. **8**

I also get pupils using them in ways that seem to work really well. **10**

31. Cloud storage, organisation and sharing

I am aware that the internet (Google Drive, Skydrive, Dropbox, Flickr etc.) can be used to store, organise and share resources. **1**

I sometimes dump stuff and share stuff albeit in a rather haphazard way. **5**

I have a very proactive and well organised system for storing and sharing resources. **15**

32. I-books

I know what they are. **1**

I know how to access them. **2**

I know how to put together an I-book. **5**

I know how to get the pupils making their own history I-books. **12**

Max= 448

Work through the questions and try to give an honest answer as to your current state of competence, according to these criteria. The idea is that when you add up the scores, you get some idea about what there is to think about in terms of history and ICT, and where you are on the continuum between novice and expert levels of competence in various aspects of ICT. It is important to bear in mind that it's not about 'coverage' (acquiring basic proficiency in all applications); the 'bottom line' in terms of new technology is not that you become personally proficient, but that you are able to use new technology to enhance the quality of teaching and learning in your teaching.

Remember that your personal proficiency in ICT is only part of the learning agenda. You also need to think about which of these applications is useful to you as a history teacher, in what ways you can make use of the applications, and what are the classroom management implications of their use. Discuss with your tutor and with other student teachers which ICT applications you should prioritise in terms of developing your ICT competence for the history classroom. (Are there any respects in which the 'weighting' of the scores is 'wrong'?). It can be interesting to do the quotient at the start of your course of education, half way through, and towards the end of the course.

If you are at the start of your course, you may well have a limited grasp of the ways in which some of these applications can be used in the history classroom. An important facet of your development in ICT competence is to investigate how these applications can be used in the context of the history classroom.

Use and abuse of the moving image in the history classroom

Another important 'variable' in the skills of the history teacher is the skill with which moving image extracts are deployed in their teaching. With the advent of the data projector, the wi-fi equipped classroom, the memory stick and moving image archives such as YouTube, showing moving image extracts has become a staple 'component' of the history teacher's repertoire.

Progression in competence

Acquisition: is dimly aware that video/dvd extracts can be used in history lessons.

Novice: is able to operate the machine and play dept. video/dvd resources as part of a lesson.

Advanced beginner: is able to use dept. video and dvd resources selectively and discerningly, intelligently selecting appropriate excerpts, and incorporating them adroitly into the lesson as a whole to enhance the quality of teaching and learning.

Competence: contributes to dept. resources by using initiative and forethought to tape suitable material, is able to plan the lesson to make maximum use of extracts, always watches and selects before use in class and uses to a clear purpose: doesn't use as an 'anaesthetic' or to pass the time.

Proficient: builds up coherent collections on topics/themes and is able to *edit* materials to maximise their efficiency, enhancing dept. resources, can use video camera in the classroom as part of lesson activity to enhance quality of teaching and learning. Handles classroom management implications of such exercises skilfully and without chaos and disruption.

Expert: makes maximum use of material available to build up collections of skilfully edited and effective extracts, and deploys them to maximum effect in the classroom. Accomplished and appropriate use of video camera and able to use editing software to make polished final versions of material. Can teach pupils how to edit film extracts using programmes such as Windows Movie Maker.

Figure 9.6 Use of the moving image in the history classroom

In addition to developing in terms of depth of technical proficiency in the use of television and dvd, you will also become aware of the *breadth and range* of ways of incorporating video and dvd extracts into your lessons. There are more imaginative ways of using video as a resource than simply sticking on a schools broadcast and playing through the whole series, over consecutive lessons. There is also the question of whether and when to use the pause button, to ask questions, and when ICT might be appropriate to give the pupils things to do that will reduce the 'passive' nature of watching the television.

Figure 9.6 gives a summary of some of the reasons for the use of video and dvd extracts in the history classroom.

1   To get the pupils' attention.
2   To cover broad stretches of content quickly.
3   To provide an engaging 'starter' activity.
4   To make a point more vividly or forcefully.
5   To 'break the lesson up'.
6   To provide directed questions for pupils to note and then discuss.
7   To engage pupils' emotions.
8   To get pupils to guess what followed on from the extract shown.
9   To get pupils to supply their own 'script' for an extract.
10 To illustrate a concept.
11 To compare two different versions of events.
12 To help make history interesting and accessible.
13 To enable pupils to watch a video role-play they have made.
14 To help to get you through a lesson with a difficult class.
15 To get out of actually having to teach the pupils yourself.

Figure 9.7 Ways of using the television and video recorder in history

For student teachers in the first stages of their practical teaching, the video and dvd extracts can seem like a godsend, particularly with difficult classes. For understandable reasons, for some, the perfect 40 minute lesson with 9Z on a Friday afternoon would be to show an episode of Blackadder, set a worksheet or homework on it, and for the bell to go. Although part of the agenda of learning to teach is about becoming relaxed and comfortable in the classroom, learning to talk to pupils in an appropriate manner, and learning about 'survival' and coping strategies, even in the early stages of practical teaching, thought needs to be given to the question of using resources so that they maximise effective learning for pupils. DVD extracts can be used as an 'anaesthetic', or to pass the time, but this is clearly bad practice. You need to think about how you use the video extract to promote effective learning by pupils. There may be some excerpts and programmes which 'stand on their own', and do not require follow-up and interpretation. One example of this is the practice of showing the World at War programme on the Holocaust, from start to finish, with no introductory or follow-up remarks from the teacher. Some history teachers feel that this is the most powerful and effective way of getting pupils to think about the Holocaust. Usually, however, the extent to which the video excerpt promotes historical understanding in pupils depends on what is said and done afterwards – on the quality of the follow-up work by you, the teacher, whether this is in the form of teacher exposition and questioning, or pupil activities. It is important to remember that in spite of the claims made for the use of new technology in the classroom, whether involving the use of computers or other forms of new technology, there is no *automatic* learning dividend in using ICT; the use of new technology can have negative as well as positive effects on learning; it depends how adroitly and thoughtfully ICT is used. A computer is like most other things in teaching – the quality and the inspiration comes from you, it is not in the machine.

Task 9.4 *Use of video extracts*

One commonly used extract is the 'What have the Romans ever done for us? extract, from the film, 'The Life of Brian'. Although the pupils may well find the extract amusing, and ICT has hopefully served the purpose of engaging their attention in the past, what might the history teacher do to derive the maximum benefit from the extract after showing it?

Select a video extract which you might use as part of a lesson, and explain what you and/or the pupils would do after you had shown the extract, and what you hope the learning outcomes would be. Discuss the use of moving image resources with your tutor.

Formulating an agenda for the development of ICT competence

The development of personal and classroom proficiency in ICT has time management implications. You cannot have ICT instantly transferred, or injected into you; there is no substitute for spending time becoming familiar with applications and software. As you have to balance developing competence in ICT with other demands, you will probably have to prioritise your agenda for ICT. You cannot reach expert levels in all the above areas. Are there any guidelines or principles on which to construct an agenda for development in ICT?

As you are at different stages in terms of personal expertise in ICT, and work in a variety of school contexts, it is not sensible to lay down a template or formula for developing competence in ICT. Much depends on how the department you are working in is using ICT, which strands of ICT you work with in taught sessions on your course, which aspects of ICT have attracted your interest or that of your tutors. Personal competence in ICT constitutes a necessary but not sufficient part of the requirements for QTS; classroom application and understanding the attributes of ICT applications in relation to teaching and learning history are other important elements.

There are, however, some applications which might be given priority because nearly all schools possess the necessary software. 'Generic' applications (which are not subject specific) such as word processing, PowerPoint, data handling software, and the internet are particularly helpful in that they can be used in a wide variety of contexts. You can devise your own, cost-free activities, and there are an increasing number of examples of activities which can be accessed on the main history and ICT websites.

If you are starting your course with absolutely no knowledge of ICT, the following might be stages of competence to consider over the course of the year in some of these applications;

phases which you might move through if you were determined to become accomplished in ICT by the end of the year.

Novice	To find out about databases and spreadsheets, even if is just at the level of knowing what they are and what sort of things you can do with them in history lessons.
Advanced beginner	To look at the data handling applications which are available in the school you are working in, and if possible, observe someone at school or at the University using a data handling package in order to get a basic idea of how to use it.
Competent	To be able to use a database or data handling package which you are familiar with as part of a lesson.
Proficient	To develop and use in class, a data handling exercise which you have devised and put on disc yourself.
Advanced	To be sufficiently assured and confident in the use of data handling packages that you can use your lessons to teach the pupils how to compile a history data-file and interrogate it.

Figure 9.8 Degrees of ICT competence – Data handling

Task 9.5 *Progression in ICT competence – the internet*

What would a similar continuum of competence on the internet and teaching and learning in history look like, from novice to advanced levels of competence? In what ways can the internet be used to enhance the quality of teaching and learning in history, in relation to the development of pupils' historical knowledge, skills and understanding?

If possible, discuss this with fellow student teachers and the colleagues you work with. (It might also help to look at the section of the ICT quotient relating to the internet and discuss the extent to which you agree with the weighting of the scores.)

For more information on the use of the internet in history teaching, see: http://terryhaydn.wordpress.com/pgce-history-at-uea/ict-in-history-teaching, 'or www.uea.ac.uk/~m242/historypgce/ict

Developing classroom confidence in the use of ICT

Some of your use of ICT is within an 'ordinary' classroom, using a data projector, and (possibly) an interactive whiteboard, but there are also occasions when you want to use an ICT suite because you want the pupils to be working on the computers. However accomplished you are in terms of personal ICT capability, it is not as useful as also having developed your classroom experience, using ICT with real, live pupils. This can only be done in school. One of the most important aspects of competence is being relaxed and confident about using ICT in your teaching. There are some general considerations which make this easier:

1   When they first use ICT in the classroom, most student teachers (and some teachers) do so with a degree of trepidation about how it will go, whether everything will work, whether the pupils will do everything they are supposed to, whether you will get through everything in the time available etc.

    One way to minimise these concerns is to use computers in such a way that they are merely an incidental part of the lesson, rather than the delivery and success of the lesson being entirely dependent on ICT. It is generally more stressful if you have booked the ICT suite for an 'all singing, all dancing' computer extravaganza, rather than simply letting them have a quick look at the timeline on Encarta, or getting them to print off a couple of documents to work on back at their desks.

2   Try to find out about, and use, quick, simple and reliable programs/exercises. Some applications are useful not primarily because they are brilliant at developing children's historical skills and understanding, but because they are easy to use, and therefore build up your confidence and faith in the use of ICT. You can get onto the ambitious stuff when you've (hopefully) got a few successful ICT lessons 'under your belt'.

3   It's not cheating to ask for help and support, even if it's just asking where an ICT literate person will be that lesson in case you need a hand with some technical hiccup. Find out if there are any members of staff or fellow student teachers with an interest in ICT. If there is no one in the department who is seriously into ICT, see if the ICT coordinator is able to help in any way, and talk about your ICT interests with the School Tutor, who may know the right channels and contacts for developing your ICT capability. It may also be possible to observe other members of staff using computers, even if it's not in history.

4   Use ICT with a teaching group that you feel reasonably comfortable with. Not 9Z on a Friday afternoon, and not a class where your control of proceedings might be a bit shaky at the best of times.

5   Have a 'Plan B', so that if there is a problem you can simply say, 'Never mind we'll do something else and get on to that next week', or 'Here's one I printed out earlier'.

6   Try to have mastered the software in rehearsal if possible so that you can concentrate on the classroom management implications of the lesson (throughput of pupils for example).

7   Think carefully about the planning of the non-computer aspects of the lesson. Devise work that is accessible and that lasts a reasonable length of time so that you are making life as easy for yourself as possible.

8   School ICT suites are usually free at some point in the week; try to make use of them, and your fellow students, by 'sub-contracting' the task of finding out about different areas of ICT and sharing the expertise you develop over the course of the year.

9   Make the most of your school placement to develop your ICT experience. This is often a propitious time for working with small groups of pupils, or developing support materials for the software which the school possesses, or simply developing your familiarity with various items of software. In some cases it is an opportunity for the student teacher to repay help and support rendered, by helping the department with its ICT needs and resources.

10 'Throughput' considerations: some ICT applications are excellent but very time consuming. One of the challenges facing history teachers in deploying the use of ICT is to think of activities where the use of the computer can be integrated into the lesson so as to provide quick, effective and eminently practicable activities which do not take up massive amounts of curriculum time.

11 Work out a basic checklist before the lesson such as the one suggested below.

---

1 Are you familiar with the ICT application you will be using?
2 How will you put the ICT exercise into the context of the history topic you're doing (before, during or after the pupils are on the computers)?
3 How long will it take the pupils to do the ICT task?
4 Are you clear, and will they be clear about exactly what they have to do? (will you need support materials?)
5 What will you do if the network is down and the computers aren't working?
6 How will you arrange the groupings?
7 What work will they do/what points will you make after they've been on the computer?
8 Do the pupils have the historical knowledge to undertake the task?

Figure 9.9 Using ICT in a computer suite: classroom management considerations, a checklist

It is important to remember that different applications of ICT are helpful and valuable in different ways. With some applications, the principal benefit might be the enthusiasm it elicits in pupils and the extent to which it draws them into an enthusiasm for learning about the past, even if the extent to which it develops intrinsically historical understanding is marginal. With others, it might be the development of knowledge, skills and understandings which are part of the attainment targets for ICT, with others, the main benefit may be an enhanced understanding of historical processes, concepts, knowledge or skills. Sometimes applications are helpful because they are easy to use, and to incorporate into classroom use, and thus help to develop the teacher's confidence in the use of ICT – in the short term they might benefit the teacher more than the pupils but this may result in a longer term 'pay-off' for pupils who are working with teachers who are comfortable with a broad range of ICT applications. It is unusual to come across an application which possesses all of these attributes; the important thing is to have a clear awareness of what (if any) benefits are being bestowed by the use of ICT.

Differences between individual schools and departments means that ICT will be easier for some student teachers than others to develop ICT competence. Some of you will work in schools where use of computers in the classroom is highly developed, with easy access to computers, others in schools where, for various reasons, this is not the case. Some may well have a subject supervisor who is heavily committed to ICT, and to some extent acts as a 'personal trainer', others have to be very much more reliant on their own initiative and the hardware and software resources of the ICTE institution in order to make progress. If your department, or your tutor isn't heavily 'into' ICT, you have to use your initiative more in order to make progress.

a) Using the internet in the history classroom

With the move towards data projector and wi-fi equipped classrooms, it is now much easier for teachers to make use of the internet in the classroom. There is some evidence to suggest that many teachers make surprisingly little use of these developments, given the wealth of 'impact' resources which can be accessed on the internet (Haydn, 2012). It can be helpful to think about a topic which you have to teach, and spend some time trawling for one or two web-based resources which might improve the lesson.

Task 9.6 *Selecting from and using internet resources*

Look at the list of websites for history teachers listed earlier in this chapter. They have been chosen partly because they are substantial sites. Select one of the sites, and choose some materials which could then be used as part of a lesson. Think through in detail how you would actually *use* the resources in the lesson. This might be as part of a worksheet or group activity for pupils, it might involve using the web pages 'live' using a data projector in your classroom, or with small groups taking it in turns to use a computer. You should be clear about in what ways the material will develop pupils' historical knowledge, skills and understandings, and in what ways the material offers 'value added' in terms of pupils' learning, compared to using textbooks or other resources.

---

b) Extending learning time in history

One of the main problems that history teachers face is that the subject does not get much time on the school timetable and there are a lot to things to get through (not just in terms of subject content) if pupils are to receive a first rate historical education. Making good use of ICT can be a way of getting pupils to (often willingly) do as much work outside the history classroom as inside it. Given the increase in access to computers over the past decade, there are very few pupils who cannot get access to the internet either at school, at the library or at home over a period of several days. Use of the internet can make it much easier to set worthwhile and meaningful tasks for homework. Giving pupils *preparatory* homework, where they find out about topics *before* the lesson, can also make for better discussion and debate in class, and more confident pupil performance in general.

Task 9.7 *Exploring the feasibility of internet-based homeworks*

Discuss with the teachers you are working with the possibilities of using the internet as part of homework activities. Schools vary considerably in terms of pupil access to the internet; if access is limited, it can help to give pupils several days to complete the homework, and to have pupils working in groups, where they are able to 'sub-contract' the work involved. Given the substantial improvements in access to computers in schools over the past decade, in most schools, it is now quite difficult for pupils to say that they have been unable to access the internet if they have been given several days to do the piece of work involved.

c) Keeping in touch with peers and colleagues (and sometimes pupils as well)

Nearly all schools and ITE institutions now have Virtual Learning Environments (VLEs) and content management systems such as *Blackboard, WEbCT, Moodle, Uniservity*, which make possible various forms of 'virtual' communication between groups. This can be a helpful way of sub-contracting tasks and sharing resources, as well as just keeping in touch with your peers when you are on teaching placement. Schools are increasingly using VLEs to help maintain the momentum of revision for external examinations, and to get pupils 'doing history' outside formal timetabled lessons.

d) Using the internet to develop pupils' information literacy

Teaching pupils how to make mature use of the internet should be an essential element of a historical education for the twenty-first century. This means not just being able to search for and locate information efficiently, but to evaluate the status of information, and to make intelligent judgements from analysing a range of information from different sources. In the words of Reuben Moore (2000: 35),

> We (history teachers) must use the internet... it is not a passing trend... young people will use it in their daily lives, no matter what they choose to do with them. And on the internet, they will continue to confront interpretations and representations of history. All adults, no matter what they do with their lives, need to be able to see how and why the historical interpretations that bombard them are constructed. Otherwise they are prey to propaganda and manipulation, not to mention cynicism or a lack of regard for the truth.

The internet is a useful resource for teaching the concept of interpretations and presenting multiple perspectives on events and individuals, and presenting history as 'contested, problematic, and above all else, an argument' (Arnold, 2000: 13). (For some examples of the use of the internet for teaching interpretations, see www.uea.ac.uk/~m242/historypgce/interp/welcome.htm)

There is some evidence to suggest that many pupils do not have a sound grasp of the weaknesses of the internet as a source of information A recent Ofcom survey of 11–15 year olds found that 32 per cent of 12–15 year olds believed that if a search engine listed a result, it must be truthful (and 23 per cent had not considered issues of veracity or accuracy), this has disconcerting implications for the information literacy of young people and for history teachers (Ofcom, 2013). This demonstrates that being able to evaluate the reliability of information from a range of sources is an important part of a historical education, for pupils growing up in the twenty-first century. We need to get across to pupils that 'The internet is wonderful for historians, but you've got to remember that there is absolutely no one between you and the idiot who is putting this stuff on the web' (Church, 2002).

Walsh (2008) makes the point that 'dodgy' internet sources can be invaluable for getting across the point that the internet is not a straightforward or inherently reliable source of information. The vast, confusing and contradictory nature of internet sources can be a major asset in getting across to pupils that history is a construct; that someone has selected, omitted, edited and combined information, not taken a factual 'snapshot' of the past. This means that pupils need to learn about the principles of procedure which a historian would use to try and 'get at the truth' in the face of these difficulties. November (2008) and the Teachers TV programme on Web Literacy (www.tes.co.uk/teaching-resource/Teachers-TV-Secondary-ICT-Web-Literacy-6039011/) offer useful resources and teaching approaches in this area. Teaching pupils about the meaning of URL syntax can be another way of developing pupils' internet literacy (see the ICT section of the website for further detail on this).

e) *Word processing exercises*

Walsh has pointed out that the word processor is not just a typewriter,

> It can search, annotate, organise, classify, draft, reorganise, redraft and save that fundamental of the historian, the written word. When we consider these processes and the difficulties which they represent for so many of our students, the true power and value of the word processor becomes clear. It is not a typewriter, it is an awesome tool for handling information in written form. (Walsh, 1998: 6)

The use of tables, Venn diagrams and writing frames can give pupils tools to sort out the 'vastness' of history and get it under control. Limiting the text length of pupil responses and making them think about reducing the amount of information available (see Chapter 4) can avoid what Walsh (2005) terms 'Encarta Syndrome', where pupils simply copy and paste large chunks of text without reading or understanding it.

 To see some examples of word processing exercises for developing pupils understanding of time and chronology, see: http://terryhaydn.wordpress.com/pgce-history-at-uea/time-and-chronology, or www.uea.ac.uk/~m242/historypgce/time

f) *PowerPoint*

At the time of writing, PowerPoint was still a very common component of history lessons in English classrooms (Haydn, 2012). As with many other teaching approaches, it can be used well or badly. Beswick argues that indifferent use of PowerPoint is caused by users not using the sophisticated and advanced features of the software:

> In the right hands it is an exciting tool that engages the students through multimedia and teachers are doing amazing things with it... When we talk to teachers and students about PowerPoint, we always show them the 'Death by PowerPoint' video [on YouTube]. We show them the different features they could use and they tell us 'I never knew PowerPoint could do that'. (Beswick, 2011: 4).

It is suggested that 'being good at ICT' is about advanced technological skills. We would argue that PowerPoint presentations that are boring are dull not because they fail to use the advanced and sophisticated technical features of the application, but because the authors have lost sight of how to engage the audience with the ideas and content of the presentation. In the words of an Advanced Skills Teacher, 'If you haven't got a good idea in the first place, just shoving up a PowerPoint isn't going to do the job' (OECD, 2010). Many of the outstanding history teachers who do sessions at major history education conferences in the UK make little or no use of the advanced features of PowerPoint or the interactive whiteboard. The quality of the teacher's ideas, resources and subject knowledge matter just as much, if not more than technological expertise (Mishra and Koehler, 2006). When using PowerPoint, the first priority is to think about what the most important ideas and points are that you want to make relating to the topic, how to get those points across in a way which will engage learners and hold their attention, and how to acquire 'impact' resources that will help you to do those things. Further suggestions on the 'do's and don'ts' of PowerPoint can be found on the website and in 'We need to talk about PowerPoint' (Haydn, 2012).

g) Data handling in history

Computers enable us to manipulate, interrogate and test hypotheses on information much more quickly than would be the case of having to read through and take notes on information provided. Once the collection of information has been put on a data-handling package, pupils can create bar charts and pie charts which enable them to see significant patterns in the data, and to explore a range of hypotheses deriving from the data. There are some datasets on the internet; one example is the Commonwealth War Graves Commission site (www.cwgc. org/). This can be used to get pupils to explore local or family connections with the Great War, and the site contains an education section explaining how it might be used. Many history departments purchased copies of the BECTa/Historical Association package (1998) on data handling, *History using IT: searching for patterns in the past using databases and spreadsheets*, and this remains a sound introduction to data handling activities on the history classroom. Walsh (2005: 57–75) also provides a range of suggestions for using census data and other electronically available datasets, and Martin (2003) also provides a range of data handling activities which are practicable and which genuinely develop pupils' historical understanding. It is possible to buy commercially produced history data files; once you know how to use a data handling package, you can put your own data files on to a computer, some pupils can construct a data file and then interrogate it to test hypotheses. As in many other areas of ICT, it is helpful to be able to get to a stage where the pupils can work autonomously and construct meaning for themselves from the sources and applications they are working with.

Task 9.8 *Google Ngram: an example of an online dataset*
(http://ngrams.googlelabs.com/)

An interesting database, which can be used to explore cultural change over time. Ngram can be used to search a digitised collection of books (estimated at around 4 per cent of the books that have been published) for the frequency of appearance of particular words and terms. You can either just put in one word and it will graph it over a selected time span, or you can input up to five words, separated by a comma, to see the changes in the prevalence of the words over time. Some examples:

> To find out about the comparative frequency of occurrence of words describing some left wing movements over the course of the twentieth century, choose the time span 1900-2008 and input socialism, communism, anarchism and syndicalism.

> 'Equality' has become an important and high profile concept in recent years, but how has its popularity or influence as a concept fluctuated over the past few centuries (say, from 1600-2008)? Note the interesting fluctuations within the seventeenth century.

> To what extent has the phenomenon of the 'takeaway' meal become more prevalent over the past century? (Just input 'takeaway' and the date span 1900-2008). Have there been any cultural changes in terms of what *types* of takeaway have become more popular over the past century? (Input 'fish and chips', ' pizza', 'curry', 'Chinese' and 'burger')

> To illustrate the acceleration in the pace of technological change, see what the 'lifespan' of the floppy disk' was. (It might also be interesting to see how many younger pupils can tell what a floppy disk is if you show them one.)

> Do books mainly tell the history of males or females: have there been any changing trends in this area? Type in 'he said' and 'she said' and the timespan 1700-2008 to find out.

> Has there really been a shift from a culture of responsibilities and duty, to one of hedonism and 'I want it now' over the past century? Type in 'I must' and 'I want' and see if there appear to be any changes over the course of the century.

> See if you can come up with any worthwhile enquiries or searches related to something that you will be teaching.

'Pantheon' is another example of a database which can be used to explore issues of 'historical cultural production' (http://pantheon.mediaa.mit.edu).

h) Web quests

A web quest is an inquiry-oriented lesson format in which most or all the information that learners work with comes from the web. The model was developed at San Diego State University in 1995 and the site is a useful resource for templates and examples of web quests (http://webquest.org/index.php). Typing 'History Webquest' into a Google search is another way of finding examples of History Webquests. There is a lot of research which suggests that just letting pupils loose on the internet in an unstructured way is not a time effective way of using ICT, and yet in the longer term, we do want to bring pupils to a point where they can make autonomous use of the internet in a mature and intelligent way.

Good webquests therefore ask questions relating to internet literacy and the reliability of internet sources, as well as the enquiry questions about the topic or person being studied. The basic idea of the webquest is a simple one; that the teacher explores the web first and prepares a path or possible paths for the pupils, which problematise the enquiry question and require the pupils to evaluate the information they are guided through, rather than simply collecting it. Topics of historical controversy (dropping the atom bomb, was General Haig a butcher?, Munich 1938, the wars with Iraq) are therefore fertile territory for webquests. Good webquests require a lot of patient teacher research on the topic in question and intelligent choice of enquiry questions. For more detail on webquests, see Blasszauer (2012).

i) Using the digital archives of newspapers

Perhaps principally for use with older and more able pupils, but even the tabloid press has potentially interesting and useable headlines and lead stories. Although they can seem dull, long and devoid of images, newspapers often contain high quality pieces from some of the world's greatest writers. Introducing pupils to quality writing from the broadsheet newspapers, and getting pupils to read some of these articles can be an important step in moving from the 'bite-size' and 'picture' mentality which prevails in many textbooks, to being able to sustain concentration and persevere with longer and more challenging sections of extended writing. If they are going to go on to university, which some of them will, they need to get into the idea of reading extended text which has no pictures in it. They can also develop pupils' understanding of the important concept of 'polemics', and that not all writing aspires to be 'fair and balanced (see for instance, Glancey's writing on Britain's role in Iraq in the first British war with Iraq in the 1920s at: http://arts.guardian.co.uk/critic/feature/0,,941850,00.html) (for a hyperlinked list of history relevant newspaper articles, see http://historyandict.wikifoundry.com/page/Newspapers).

j) Wikipedia and wikis

A wiki is a website that allows visitors to add, remove and edit content. The most famous and by far the biggest wiki is *wikipedia* (www.wikipedia.org). Many history departments now use the school's virtual learning environment or content management systems to set up wikis that are 'internal' to the school, so that pupils can engage in what might be termed a form of 'knowledge construction', which can also involve argument, debate and the reconciling of different opinions and perspectives. Wikipedia has a history specific section, and just using Wikipedia on its own, without setting up internal wikis, can be an interesting exercise, as the extracts in Figure 9.8 shows. However, in terms of active learning and pupil involvement, wikis where pupils collectively try to construct an encyclopaedia entry for a person, event or concept are a good example of genuinely interactive learning. Of course, pupils need to be educated about the dangers and limitations of Wikipedia as a source of information, particularly in areas which are controversial. However, Wikipedia can sometimes be a time-effective way of developing a sound grasp of the historiography of a topic, or the meaning of a concept or term. You might find it interesting to explore Wikipedia's entry on the historiography of the causes of World War One in order to reach a judgement on its potential as a way of developing subject knowledge.

Russel Tarr's wiki provides a good example of what can be done with a departmental wiki, particularly in terms of 'sub-contracting' enquiry activities for pupils (www.history-wiki. wikispaces.com).

Views on famous people and events from the past are often contested, as is the precise meaning of concepts such as fascism, liberalism or neo-conservatism.

The following extracts from the Wikipedia entry on 'appeasement' gives an example of this:
a) the 'official' wikipedia definition of appeasement:
   'A policy of accepting the imposed conditions of an aggressor in lieu of armed resistance, usually at the sacrifice of principles. Usually it means giving into demands of an aggressor in order to avoid war. Since World War II, the term has gained a negative connotation in the British government, in politics and in general, of weakness, cowardice and self-deception.'
b) (From the section on 'different views of appeasement) 'The meaning of the term "appeasement" has changed throughout the years. According to Paul Kennedy in his *Strategy and Diplomacy*, 1983, appeasement is "the policy of settling international quarrels by admitting and satisfying grievances through rational negotiation and compromise, thereby avoiding the resort to an armed conflict which would be, expensive, bloody and possibly dangerous." It gained its negative reputation for its use in the build up to World War II. It had previously been employed by the British government successfully, see The Treaty with Ireland 1921.' (This is followed by quotes on appeasement from Gilbert, Dilks and Churchill.)

Figure 9.10 Using Wikipedia

k) Blogs

Blogs are online diaries, and given that large numbers of pupils now have some form of online presence through social networking sites such as Myspace, Facebook, MSN Messenger etc., you will be tapping into media that pupils are generally familiar with. Ed Podesta has a good example of what can be done with a teacher-led blog (www.onedamnthing.org.uk/blog/author/ed-podesta/), but blogs can again be 'internal' to the school environment, and can be good for showcasing pupils' work, generating discussion between pupils and giving feedback on pupils' work. To look at a range of examples of history department blogs, just type in a Google search for 'history department blogs'.

l) Podcasts

Podcasts are audiofiles which can be downloaded onto pupils' MP3 players, ipods, or computers. There are hundreds of history podcasts available (just type in 'history podcast' on a Google search), but not all of them are a thrilling and engaging listening experience, and there are issues of age and ability appropriateness. They can be helpful for revision for some pupils who like 'audio' based learning, and the BBC's 'Bitesize' revision site has a large range of audio files for download (www.bbc.co.uk/schools/gcsebitesize/audio/history/index.shtml).

Historians have also started to use the medium of podcasts. BBC History Magazine has a wide range of podcasts (www.historyextra.com/podcasts), as does the Historical Association website (www.history.org.uk/podcasts). Podcasts can be a useful way of augmenting subject knowledge, for pupils and teachers. Again, a step forward in terms of active learning and pupil engagement can be for pupils to produce their own podcasts. The development of downloadable software such as 'Audacity' (http://audacity.sourceforge.net) which makes it easy to make and save audiofiles, has made this a relatively straightforward exercise.

m) Web interactivities and toolkits

Given that some schools now have wireless technology, it is now possible to get pupils using a wide range of the interactive features of history websites. Sometimes these are fairly 'light' starter activities or end of lesson games and quizzes, but they are not all limited to 'just a bit of fun' type activities. They can range from PowerPoint presentations to 'virtual interviews' with historical figures, and simulations and decision-making exercises. Russel Tarr's Active History site (www.activehistory.co.uk) has a large range of such activities. Although it is a subscription site, it usually has a 'free' section as well. Further examples are given in the ICT section of the website (http://terryhaydn.wordpress.com/pgce-history-at-uea/ict-in-history-teaching/). Tarr also hosts 'Classtools', which provides templates for history teachers to design their own ICT-based activities for pupils (www.classtools.net). 'Hot Potatoes' is another site which provides such activities (http://hotpot.uvic.ca/). See the discussion at the School History site for further detail about online simulation activities in history: www.schoolhistory.co.uk/forum/index.php?showtopic=1876. (You might also want to explore the potential of Googlefight (www.googlefight.com) as a 'starter' for discussions about historical significance.)

n) Departmental websites

Richard Jones (2007) makes the point that a departmental website can help you to keep your resources organised, and engage both pupils and parents in making progress in history, and his site is a powerful example of what departmental websites can aspire to (see reference below). They can be particularly helpful for revision activities. Further details of history department websites are given on the ICT section of the website, and Chris Higgins' e-help seminar talks about how to create and maintain a departmental website: (http://educationforum.ipbhost.com/index.php?showforum=246.

o) Interactive whiteboards

There is evidence to suggest that skilful use of interactive whiteboards can aid pupil learning. A Becta review of research evidence about the use of interactive whiteboards suggested that their use:

> increases enjoyment of lessons for both students and teachers through more varied and dynamic use of resources, with associated gains in motivation... and offers greater

opportunities for participation and collaboration, developing students' personal and social skills (BECTa, 2007: 2).

Particular attention has focused on their potential for aiding discussion and 'dialogic learning', with pupils using interactive whiteboards as part of small group activities, and a majority of students reporting that they felt that they learned more from such discussions than from written tasks (Brown, 2014; Hennessy *et al.*, 2014). Hennessy *et al.* describe an activity where pupils annotate a portrait of Queen Elizabeth I, and do a 'think-aloud' of their reflections on the portrait. A digital clip of the activity, and others, which illustrates this way of working with whiteboards is available at http://t-media.educ.cam.ac.uk.

It should be stressed that not all history teachers are enthusiastic devotees of IWBs, and they are still not universally available in classrooms. It does take some time to become 'fluent' in using an IWB, but there are commercially available resources for IWBs which can provide models and ideas for use, and which can save teachers the time of having to devise their own whiteboard activities. Keep in mind that it can be helpful to be able to use an IWB in an interview lesson (see Chapter 12). You should try to ensure that you at least explore the world of whiteboards so that you can make your own mind up on this. An e-help seminar by Roy Huggins on the use of interactive whiteboards can be accessed at www.e-help.eu/seminars/huggins.htm.

p) Voting technology

Not all history departments have access to voting sets but they are becoming increasingly common in schools, even if the history department does not have their own set. If you are working in a school where there is access to such technology, try to talk to some of the teachers who use it. Walsh (2006) warns of the danger of just using them for banks of multiple choice tests, and suggests a range of ways of using voting technology to promote discussion and debate in the history classroom. Although the technology is not cheap, it does have the potential to make learning genuinely interactive, and to make pupils think. As with many other aspects of ICT in history, there is an e-help seminar on this (see URL above) as well as a section on the Historical Association's website (www.history.org.uk/resources/primary_resource_1177_2.html). See also, Diana Laffin's article in *Teaching History* (Laffin, 2008). If the department you are working in does not have voting technology, the Web 2.0 application, www.polleverywhere.com offers an alternative.

q) Digital video

This is perhaps one of the most exciting recent developments relating to school history and ICT. The incorporation of easy to use moving image editing software (such as, for example, Windows Movie Maker) into the standard 'package' for personal computers, and the accessibility of moving image files on the internet and video cameras within history departments has made it easy for pupils to make and edit films, and to put their own subtitles and commentary on them. There are also three e-help seminars on digital video (by Ben Walsh, Richard Jones and Peter Tollmar), and a section on the use of digital video (pages 133-56) in Ben Walsh's book, *Exciting ICT in History* (2005). Richard Jones Nerzic's chapter, 'Documentary film making in the history classroom' provides a more recent resource on using digital video, and the film which his pupils made about Nicholas Winton, sometimes called 'The English Schindler', is a good example of what can be done with digital video in the history classroom (www.internationalschoolhistory.net/BHP/index.htm).

r) Twitter

Twitter has become an influential mode of professional development for teachers. The 140 character limit on the length of 'tweets' makes it quick to use, and follow the tweets of others. A common way of using it is to post a link to 'impact resources', and to 'favourite' incoming tweets that are useful. An important point to keep in mind is that it can pay to be discerning in terms of who you 'follow', or it can become time consuming with limited reward. The use of 'lists' can also help you to organise and prioritise incoming tweets. Figure 9.11 contains some suggestions for history education feeds which were suggested by some history teachers and teacher educators who are interested in the use of new technology in history teaching.

@russeltarr	@kenradical	@HistoryResource	@UkNatArchives
@History_Ben	@nwatkin	@ahrenfelt	@northernhistory
@johnsimkin	@nickdennis	@dale_banham	@andyfield
@LA_McDermott	@MrsThorne	@Jivespin	@apf102
@mfordhamhistory	@HFletcherWood?	@tothechalkface	@ histexplore
@ActiveHist.ca	@SHEG_Stanford	@DTWillingham	@HolocaustUK
@RealTime WWII	@tutor2uhistory	@teachit.co.uk	@MassObsArchive

Figure 9.11 Twitter feeds which have been suggested as being potentially useful for history teachers by a number of history teachers and teacher educators with an interest in social media

Sue Beckingham provides an excellent guide to 'Getting started with Twitter' at www.slideshare.net/suebeckingham/getting-started-with-twitter-23557615.

s) Other Web 2.0 applications

There are now lots of Web 2.0 applications that can be used for teaching history, many of them useful in terms of enabling learners to do history outside the confines of taught sessions. A few examples are given here; more can be accessed at http://historyandict. wikifoundry.com/page/Web+2.0+apps+that+might+be+useful+to+history+teachers.

Pinterest www.pinterest.com	Allows pupils (or teacher) to set up a 'digital pinboard' and 'pin' images, videos and other objects to their pinboard. Interesting to compare pinboards which have been made previously – striking differences between pinboards on the Tudors and the Stuarts, Victorians and Edwardians.
Scoop.it www.scoop.it	A tool for quickly 'curating' collections of resources in different media forms on particular topics. Can be used by teachers and pupils.
Padlet http://padlet.com	Enables pupils to contribute a 'digital post-it' before or after a lesson, for example, to say what they thought was 'the golden nugget' of the lesson, or to answer a question posed for a homework.
Slideshare www.slideshare.net	Gives you access to thousands of other people's PowerPoint presentations which you can search by topic, keyword etc. Can be great for getting ideas. There are some really interesting ones on Web 2.0.
Bubbl.us https://bubbl.us	Free mind mapping software.
Mural/ly https://mural.ly	A more layered and perhaps sophisticated version of Padlet.
Timerime www.timerime.com	A template which enables pupils to construct their own timelines, including text, images and links to music and YouTube clips.
Museum Box http://museumbox. e2bn.org	This site provides the tools for you to build up an argument or description of an event, person or historical period by placing items in a virtual box. What items, for example, would you put in a box to describe your life; the life of a Victorian Servant or Roman soldier; or to show that slavery was wrong and unnecessary? You can display anything from a text file to a movie. You can also view and comment on the museum boxes submitted by others.

Figure 9.12 Web 2.0 applications which can be used in history teaching

t) Using tablet computers in the classroom

Increasingly, schools are acquiring sets of tablet computers (ipads or other models) which can be used so that pupils can have one-to-one use of a tablet computer during the lesson. One of the key advantages of this is that tablets provide (at least in theory) a very quick and convenient way for pupils to access internet resources in the history classroom, and are less 'clunky' than manoeuvring laptop trolleys around the school. However, you usually need to have a clear idea of how you want pupils to use this facility, rather than just asking them to 'find out about something' on the internet. As with voting technology, they are often best use in conjunction with other resources rather than always basing the whole lesson around the tablets. They are particularly useful for 'sub-contracting' aspects of a (carefully structured) enquiry, so that pupils find out about different facets of a historical issue or problem (see Chapter 5 for two examples).

Don't just carry on collecting more and more web addresses without thinking about how you might use them in your teaching. It is important to achieve a balance between acquiring more resources, and deploying them effectively in your teaching. It is possible to browse the web for hours, and encounter fascinating material, but end up with nothing that you will use in a lesson.

Figure 9.13 Use, don't just collect

Summary and key points

Developing competence in ICT in a way that fulfils the requirements for QTS means that you not only need to develop personal proficiency in ICT, you must also have a clear grasp of the ways in which ICT can contribute to effective learning in history. You must make every effort, whatever the circumstances of your school placements, to get as much experience in the use of ICT applications as possible; *classroom* experience is particularly helpful. You also need to consider the classroom management factors which influence the successful use of ICT, and to be able to evaluate the impact of the use of computers in the classroom. It is not a question of how much you use computers, or the breadth of applications used; what matters most is how effectively you are able to use new technology to improve the quality of your lessons. With many applications, it is not a question of competence, but of *levels* of expertise, in terms of your understanding of both the technology, and the pedagogy of the subject you are teaching. Investing time and thought into how you can harness the use of ICT and take full advantage of the rich resources of the internet can have massive benefits in terms of making it much easier to motivate and engage pupils in learning.

For further reading and resources on the use of ICT in history teaching, and examples of some of the uses of ICT mentioned in this chapter see:
http://terryhaydn.wordpress.com/pgce-history-at-uea/ict-in-history-teaching

References

Arnold, J. (2000) *History: A very short introduction*, Oxford: Oxford University Press.

BECTa (2007) *Key Research Evidence About Interactive Whiteboards*, Coventry: BECTa.

Beswick, S. (2011) Quoted in L. Lightfoot, 'Are your pupils bored by the whiteboard?', *Times Educational Supplement*, propedagogy section, 16 December: 4.

Blasszauer, J. (2012) History webquests, in T.Haydn (ed.) *Using New Technologies to Enhance Teaching and Learning in History*, London: Routledge: 171-84.

Brown, L. (2014) Using the interactive whiteboard to support dialogic teaching in history: the student perspective, in S. Hennessy, P. Warwick, L. Brown, D. Rawlins and C. Neale, *Developing interactive teaching and learning using the IWB*, Maidenhead: Open University Press: 51-6.

Church, S. (2002) Seminar, University of East Anglia, 29 January.

DfE (2012) Teachers' Standards, London: DfE.

Dickinson, A. (1998) History using IT: past, present and future, *Teaching History*, No. 93: 16-20.

Easdown, G. (1997) IT in initial teacher education: a survey of feelings and preconceptions, in A. Pendry and C. O'Neill (eds) *Principles and Practice: Analytical perspectives on curriculum reform and changing pedagogy for history teacher educators*, Lancaster: Standing Conference of History Teacher Educators (SCHTE): 102-12.

Easdown, E. (2000) History teachers and ICT, in G. Easdown (ed.) *Innovation and Methodology: Opportunities and constraints in history teacher education*, Lancaster: HTEN: 19-35.

Haydn, T. (2003) 'What do they do with the information? Working towards genuine interactivity with history and ICT', in T. Haydn and C. Counsell (eds) *History, ICT and Learning*, London: RoutledgeFalmer: 192-224.

Haydn, T. (ed.) (2012) *Using New Technologies to Enhance Teaching and Learning in History*, London: Routledge.

Heath, D. and Heath C. (2008) *Made to Stick: Why some ideas take hold and others come unstuck*, London: Arrow.

Hennessy, S., Warwick, P., Brown, L., Rawlins, D. and Neale C. (2014) *Developing Interactive Teaching and Learning using the IWB*, Maidenhead: Open University Press.

Jones-Nerzic, R. (2007) Unpublished seminar, 'The creative use of ICT in history teaching', University of East Anglia, Norwich, 30 May.

Jones-Nerzic, R. (2012) Documentary film making in the history classroom, in T. Haydn (ed.) *Using New Technologies to Enhance Teaching and Learning in History*, London: Routledge: 95-114.

Laffin, D. (2008) 'If everyone's got to vote, then obviously, everyone's got to think': using remote voting to involve everyone in classroom thinking at AS and A2, *Teaching History*, No. 133: 18-21.

Martin, D. (2003) 'Relating the general to the particular: data handling and historical learning', in T. Haydn and C. Counsell (eds) *History, ICT and Learning*, London: RoutledgeFalmer: 134-51.

Mishra, P. And Koehler, M. (2006) Technological pedagogical content knowledge: a framework for teacher knowledge, Teachers College Record, Vol. 106, No. 6: 1017-54, online at http://punya.educ.msu.edu/publications/journal_articles/mishra-koehler-tcr2006.pdf, accessed 18 November 2011.

Moore, R. (2000) Using the internet to teach about interpretations in years 9 and 12, *Teaching History*, No. 101: 35-9.

November, A. (2008) *Web Literacy for Educators*, Thousand Oaks CA: Corwin Press.

Ofcom (2013) *Children and Parents: Media Use and Attitudes*, London: Ofcom.

Ofsted (2011) *History for All*, London: Ofsted.

OECD (2010) *Case studies of the ways in which initial teacher education providers in England prepare student teachers to use ICT effectively in their subject teaching*, Paris: OECD, online at www.oecd.org/dataoecd/42/39/45046837.pdf, accessed 19 August 2014.

Rollason, D. (1998) Quoted in *Daily Telegraph*, 29 October.

Rusen, J. (1993) 'The development of narrative competence in historical learning: an ontogenetical hypothesis concerning moral consciousness'; 'Experience, interpretation, orientation: three dimensions of historical learning'; 'Paradigm shift and theoretical reflection in Western German historical studies', in P. Duvenage (ed.) Studies in Metahistory (Pretoria: Human Sciences Research Council), 63-84.

Walsh, B. (1998) Why Gerry likes history now: the power of the word processor, *Teaching History*, No. 93: 6-15.

Walsh, B. (2003) Building learning packages: integrating virtual resources with the real world of teaching and learning, in T. Haydn and C. Counsell (eds) *History, ICT and Learning*, London: RoutledgeFalmer: 109-33.

Walsh, B. (2005) *Exciting ICT in history*, Stafford: Network Educational Press.

Walsh, B. (2008) Stories and their sources, *Teaching History*, No. 133: 4-9.

Walsh, B. (2006) *Beyond multiple choice: voting technology in the history classroom*, seminar presentation at e-help conference, Stockholm, October, online at: http://educationforum.ipbhost.com/index.php?showforum=246, accessed 13 October 2007.

10 Assessment in the classroom

The right answer approach is deeply ingrained in our thinking. This might be fine for some mathematical problems which do indeed have one right answer. The difficulty is that most of life isn't that way, it is deeply ambiguous. (Richard Van Oech, *A whack on the side of the head*, 1990)

Introduction

Assessment is an ongoing dialogue between pupils and their teacher. Its purpose is not only to gain information on how much progress each pupil has made, but also to learn about the best ways forward in teaching and learning. Feedback to pupils can be given and received in many different ways. The key is that it should lead to thinking on the part of the pupil (Wiliam, 2011).

Under pressure of a heavy workload, it can be difficult to strike the right balance between planning lessons and assessing work. Some student teachers are tempted to evaluate their own progress far more in terms of what they deliver than what their pupils achieve. Assessment of pupil progress is crucial to your own evaluation of your teaching. It must be integrated within the whole process of planning. Using formative and summative assessment to secure pupils' progress, as well as target setting, giving feedback and encouraging pupils to respond to it, are a statutory requirement (see Teachers' Standard 6, DfE, 2012). This chapter will consider what we are assessing in the history classroom and how we measure progress. We will review a range of approaches to assessment relating them, where appropriate, to the principles underpinning 'assessment for learning'.

Objectives

At the end of this chapter you should be able to:

- identify some of the key issues which affect the assessment of history;
- understand and deploy the recent recommendations for the use of both the formative and summative assessment of pupils' progress at KS3; and
- set and mark tasks for pupils and record and report on pupils' progress in an appropriate and effective way.

Key issues in the assessment of history – how do we measure progress?

This important relationship between planning, methods and assessment means that the vast changes in the teaching of history in the last 30 years have also had a considerable impact on how learning in history is assessed. More than a generation ago the principal concerns were to assess the recall of knowledge, to reward the ability to select information relevant to a question and to deploy that knowledge in Standard English. Differentiation was achieved in the quantity and quality of the answers.

With the evolution of the 'new' history, teachers and examiners had to consider how to assess pupils' progress in their use of sources, their understanding of key concepts, of past ideas and attitudes and, more recently, of historical interpretations and representations. Such changes made it even more imperative that the concept of progression in historical understanding was researched and applied to the assessment of that understanding. The development of 'levels' marking schemes at 14+, and the later Attainment Target model enshrined by the NC, implied the existence of some acceptable theory of how pupils' historical understanding progresses. It may be argued that the problems experienced of both the GCSE and the NC are in part related to the limited and inconsistent application of any theoretical basis, and the lack of a universally acceptable model, which would explain pupils' progression in historical understanding. It could be argued that policymakers' (understandable) concern that teachers and schools should be accountable for their teaching meant that under the 'levels' system, validity in assessment was sacrificed on the altar of 'accountability'. The June 2004 issue of *Teaching History*, entitled 'Assessment without levels', included several articles, which highlighted the limitations and frustrations of using the NC level descriptions. Burnham and Brown (2004) felt that the descriptions 'do not define the changing ideas, patterns of reasoning and layers of knowledge that make up progression in historical learning.' The tension arises when teachers are asked to produce regular reports on pupils using levels or part-levels, yet pupils do not make uniform progress through the levels. It is correctly stated that the level descriptions were never intended to be used in this way. Burnham and Brown found them 'too blunt' for individual pieces of work and Ofsted (2011) agreed that there was often too much superficial focus on NC level, with 'sweeping judgements on what level students might have achieved in class, often based on flimsy evidence'. This Ofsted report also found division of levels into sub-levels to be 'unhelpful'. Use of level descriptions was found to be useful for pupils, however, where they understood how to improve. The new National Curriculum for 2014 (DfE, 2013a) dispenses with levels, putting responsibility for measuring progress back with schools. Consequently, there is more necessity for history teachers to develop a firm understanding of what progression might look like.

These changes in the form of school history and in ideas about assessment over the past few decades have raised important and difficult questions about what it means 'to get better' at history, and how we make sure that the time that we invest in assessment is of maximum benefit to all parties involved in the process. Issues include: (1) the use of knowledge; (2) progression; (3) forms of assessment (4) the validity and reliability of your assessment; and (5) differentiating assessment.

The role of knowledge

The role of historical knowledge in assessment has become the subject of much debate. It has been prominent in the media as revisions have been made to the NC by the Coalition government. To many historians, this would seem to have been a rather artificial debate which sought to place the advocates of knowledge (traditional history) against those of skills (new history), what Counsell has called 'a distracting dichotomy' (Counsell, 2000). Most history teachers accepted that the learning of history required both skills and knowledge. Assessment which attempted to test skills without reference to the historical context was as arid and unhelpful as the recall of information without understanding.

The challenge for you is to determine how that knowledge is to be used. Some pupils gain great satisfaction when they are able to recall information and there is a place for this in your assessment, particularly with the younger pupils. The danger is, of course, that history is once more seen as a subject whose prime objective is the memorisation of facts.

Two issues may be highlighted:

- What is historical knowledge?
- Are there gradations of historical knowledge?

How you respond to these questions will influence your thinking about how you assess your pupils.

What is historical knowledge?

If you are trying to assess historical knowledge, you need to have a clear understanding of what this means (see Lee and Ashby, 2000: 199-201 for a helpful discussion of this issue).

It is now generally accepted that historical knowledge is much more than factual knowledge or description of events. It also includes knowledge of explanations of events, changes and issues; and knowledge of the historical process, for example, what procedures do you adopt for analysing evidence or what questions should you ask when confronted by differing interpretations? The issue then is – how can you assess such aspects of historical knowledge and understanding, while still rewarding factual knowledge?

Are there gradations in historical knowledge?

Lee and Shemilt (2003) note the limitations of gradations of knowledge based upon substantive concepts such as 'peasant', 'parliament' in contrast to ideas that shape history such as key concepts such as that of evidence. The 2008 NC was based on 'key concepts' and 'key processes' with the attainment target implying a model of progression for each of these (QCA, 2007).

But can we be so dismissive about the relative value of historical knowledge? It is possible to argue that knowledge will be rewarded either *for the way in which it is acquired* or *for the way in which it is used*. Your pupils' historical knowledge is likely to be worthy of praise if it has been acquired as a result of the use of initiative and the use of enquiry and reference skills: enquiry was one of the 'key processes' in the 2008 history curriculum. Higher rewards are also likely to be available for knowledge not immediately available to the pupil or candidates in sources or descriptions of a context. Should that knowledge be used to demonstrate the wider significance of a topic, to make links, connections and perhaps well-founded generalisations then again this is likely to be graded more highly. Within a levels marking scheme, what often pushes a mark to the top of a level is the extent knowledge is used to support that level of understanding. GCSE markschemes reward the use of 'contextual knowledge' to inform source analysis, for example. The real requirement is for pupils to be able to *apply* their knowledge to inform their opinions and judgements.

It is important that you continue to think carefully about the relationship between knowledge and understanding. For example, supposing you were to set a task, the main purpose of which was to assess the pupils' understanding of historical interpretations. Pupil A *described* in detail the differences between the two interpretations and used plenty of factual information to support the answer. Pupil B was able to make some attempt at *explaining* the differences with some, but not a lot, of factual support. Who gets the higher mark? This question of balance has again been a feature of the debate over the last ten years and remains a key issue. Lee points out that learning history is difficult, and does not take place in a flash at 18 or even at 25. It is a gradual process of developing ideas, in which pupils need a great deal of help. A substantial part of what is learned has to be *knowing-how*, not just *knowing-that*. Some of what children have to learn is not itself historical knowledge at all, but provides crutches and tools for assisting them to acquire that knowledge (Lee, 1994: 44).

Task 10.1 *The role of historical knowledge*

1   Discuss with the subject teachers in your school how they encourage their pupils to recall and use their historical knowledge. On what occasions are the pupils required to recall their historical knowledge (a) orally and (b) in writing? Do they have a different emphasis for the ability to recall and use historical knowledge for KS3 pupils in comparison to GCSE pupils? Consider how the responses might influence the objectives you formulate and the tasks you set.

2   With two different age groups (e.g. Year 7 or 8 and Year 10), ask the pupils the following question: 'If a pupil is "good at history", how do we know?' Compare their answers with your own answer to this question. What do the pupils' answers tell you about their understanding of history?

3   Present a group of Year 7 or 8 pupils with two pictures, related to a topic they have covered, for comparison, e.g. a motte and bailey castle and a concentric castle. Ask the pupils to draw two columns, one headed 'How they differ' and the other 'Why they differ'. Ask them to try to complete the columns. When assessing their responses, consider the role of knowledge in your final judgement. Are you rewarding the quantity or the quality of the knowledge used?

For further consideration of the nature and role of historical knowledge, see http://terryhaydn.wordpress.com/pgce-history-at-uea/pgce-student-teacher/subject-knowledge/.

Progression

The issue of progression raises fundamental questions, which will influence your whole approach to teaching and designing work for pupils. Teachers' standard 2.2 requires you to 'be accountable for pupils' attainment, progress and outcomes' and to 'be aware of pupils' capabilities and their prior knowledge, and plan teaching to build on these' (DfE, 2012).

Without an understanding of progression you are likely to make assumptions about what your pupils can do and understand, or to ignore obstacles to their progress. You might repeat tasks that do not offer sufficient challenge because you are unsure about how to encourage a deeper understanding of the subject.

So what does the concept of progression mean in the context of learning history? What characterises better understanding of key concepts such as causation, change and the attitudes of differing past societies? How can we identify progression in the development of source skills and in the ability to handle historical interpretations? Much has been written to help you to understand the basis for progression in the learning of history. The work of Hallam (1972), Watts (1973), Shemilt (1976), Booth (1983), Dickinson and Lee (1984), Lomas (1989) and Lee and Ashby (2000) covers some of the debate about how children's historical understanding develops and its implications for teachers. More recently QCA (2007) have stated that progression at Key Stage 3 is characterised by:

- the acquisition of an increasing range and depth of historical knowledge, and the ability to make links and connections within and across historical periods;
- deepening understanding of general and specific historical concepts;
- greater understanding of and proficiency in the use of historical skills;
- an increasing ability to apply skills and conceptual understanding across a variety of historical contexts;
- an increasing ability to communicate knowledge and understanding using language appropriately and accurately; and
- becoming independent in learning across a variety of situations.

The challenge is to translate these characteristics into detailed, specific mark schemes. For over two decades now progression in history has often taken the form of levels and levels mark schemes with the assumption that a pupil progresses up a 'ladder of progress'. The task then, has until recently been to identify which level statement most closely fits the work produced by the pupil. This is the model of progression used by the National Attainment Target (NCAT), which presents you with levels of attainment, each of which have a collection of statements covering the range of second order concepts. The theory is that these statements can be applied to indicate the level of progress an individual pupil has made.

But, as indicated earlier, many teachers have misgivings about the NCAT model of progression. These are voiced in many places and are effectively expressed by Lee and Shemilt. Their concerns about the NCAT model include:

1   Pupils' understanding does not necessarily follow this linear approach. It does not necessarily move up this step-ladder one rung at a time.
2   The use of phrases such as 'beginning to identify' are *weasel* phrases, which in their use, seem to admit the limitations of levels and to encourage the use of sub-levels. They also challenge the evenness of the levels as you cannot really say the gaps between levels are equal.
3   The use of history specific language within the documentation, for example the failure to distinguish between what constitutes 'evidence' and what is 'information'.
4   It is not possible to state that a particular pupil is at say level 5 because progress in one area of the statement is not necessarily balanced by similar progress in another.
5   Possibly one of the most telling points they make is the assumption within the model that the skill of evaluation is a higher level activity and so limited to a few pupils. Many teachers will see the rigidity here does not equate to their classroom experience, where, depending on the context and how the task is set up, many pupils are capable of making evaluations. (This has a familiar ring about it as for many decades hierarchies of types of questions have listed comprehension as a low order activity whereas in practice it depends on the context, as similarly evaluation questions are not necessarily higher order ones.)
6   The use of 'best fit' practice for matching pupils' work to levels seems highly hit and miss; a compromise to produce data which could obscure the detail needed to help pupils make progress (Lee and Shemilt, 2003).

Where there does seem to be general agreement is that progression in history should be based upon the development of pupils' understanding of its key concepts. Thus, instead of assembling a collection of disparate statements in an arbitrary manner, as Cottingham (2004) concluded, 'the clear implication is that separate progression models are needed for different concepts.' Much work is still needed in their development, then, given such models, departments could then use them to assess pupil progress for each concept across topics, years and key stages. In being able to do this, what is clear is that such models need to be secure enough to be applicable to a range of contexts but most of all they need to be user-friendly, unambiguous and not unduly time-consuming in their application. Lee and Shemilt find that there is much to be gained from teachers having a good understanding of the likely misconceptions which pupils may hold about a concept (of the sort indicated in previous chapters) and also of the nature of any barriers they need to overcome in order to make progress in their understanding of a key concept.

Clearly it is far easier to criticise existing models than it is to create better ones. For the student teacher it is therefore important that you are aware of the difficulties and the possibilities of progression and use this information when constructing specific objectives for the learning of a concept and in devising your own mark schemes.

Task 10.2 *Identifying progression in history*

You will find it useful to see how various notions of progression have influenced the NC and the GCSE.

1   Ask the history department in which you are placed if they have a copy of the original documentation for the 1991 NC specifications for history. Look carefully at all three Attainment Targets and try to identify any principles that underpin the level statements.
2   Compare these statements with those in the 2007 Attainment Target for History (online at www.education.gov.uk/schools/teachingandlearning/curriculum/secondary/b00199545/ history/attainment). Extract those sentences which are comparable e.g. causation, interpretations, use of sources. How much do they differ? Note the key words 'describe', explain' etc. in the latest version.
3   Again analyse GCSE mark schemes to identify any principles of progression, which underpin the levels of response. (Alternatively, you should be able to access examples from the Awarding Body websites: www.ocr.org.uk, www.edexcel.org.uk, www.aqa.org.uk.)

Assessment for learning

Assessment is more effectively used when it is integrated within the teaching of a topic; planned for, not bolted on at the end as an afterthought. Keep in your mind the idea that the prime objective of assessment is to support learning not just to test it. Trying to achieve this is quite a sophisticated skill as you try to choose assessment strategies which are appropriate to the learning activities in which the pupils are engaged. Acknowledging that assessment is part of effective learning is central to the *Assessment for Learning* initiative now becoming well established in schools. The thinking behind assessment for learning, articulated in the seminal paper by Black and Wiliam (1998) and enshrined in the 2003 National Strategy (DfE 2003), is that pupils and teachers work in partnership to fulfil learning objectives. Assessment for learning is a formative strategy. Assessment is formative when the evidence gained through assessment is used to shape the teaching and learning programme. Black and Wiliam, amongst other writers, refer to numerous studies, which show that strengthening formative assessment procedures produce significant gains in learning, particularly for lower attaining students or those with learning disabilities. Wiliam (2011: 39) states that there are five qualities needed for assessment to improve learning. These are:

1   effective feedback for students;
2   active involvement of students in their own learning;
3   the adjustment of teaching to take into account the results of assessment;
4   the recognition of the profound effects of assessment on student motivation; and
5   the need for students to be able to assess themselves and understand how to improve.

This is a complex agenda, and it takes time for you to acquire a solid grounding in all aspects of assessment. It is perhaps better as a student teacher to adopt the policy of gradualism and not expect to fulfil all aspects at once. This section aims to offer a few starting points.

Further resources and information on assessment in history can be accessed at: http://terryhaydn.wordpress.com/pgce-history-at-uea/assessment.

Further information about assessment more generally, including the use of 'value added' data, can be found at the website for the Association for Achievement and Improvement through Assessment (AAIA): www.aaia.org.uk/index800.htm.

Task 10.3 *Applying principles of assessment*

The following questions are derived from the principles of assessment defined by the Association for Achievement and Improvement through Assessment (AAIA).

(i)   How can assessment reflect the academic, social, emotional and moral development of the pupils?

(ii) How can pupils be fully involved in assessment processes so that they can understand how to improve and become independent learners?

(iii) How can assessment be organised so that pupils work towards long-term as well as short-term goals?

(iv) How can assessment be used to encourage motivation and enhance pupils' self-esteem?

(v)   How can I employ a range of assessment strategies in my day-to-day teaching and base my judgements on a wide range of evidence in order to obtain a holistic view of pupils' achievements.

(vi) What opportunities exist for my assessments to be moderated and discussed?

(vii) How can I present my assessments in way that is useful to the pupils, the school's assessment policies and also to parents?

1   Using your department's schemes of work for KS3 consider where and when these principles are likely to be applied.

2   Decide which principles are relevant to your own planning and how you would incorporate them into your schemes.

3   Discuss with your tutor or HOD how the department seeks to apply these principles to the teaching of history at KS3.

The range of approaches listed below, in which the principles of Task 10.4 are implicit, show the variety of possibilities for the integration of assessment in both your planning and the delivery of your lessons.

Day-to-day assessment

Ongoing assessment seems to be one of the hardest things the beginning teacher needs to master. For example, it is found that often a student teacher cannot see that a lesson was wrongly pitched, sometimes too low, frequently too high. That miscalculation could be based on the fact that some pupils have provided correct answers to oral questions even though the answering may have been limited to a few pupils and many may not have been keeping up. Some suggestions towards getting a better idea whether all or most pupils have grasped the points and met your objectives are as follows:

Questioning techniques. The disadvantages of traditional whole-class question and answer sessions are that they often do not inform the teacher about the learning of all pupils, and can also encourage pupils to switch off in the knowledge that participation is voluntary. Many teachers have turned to 'no hands up' question and answer sessions. Targeted questioning whereby a pupil gives an answer, which is then 'bounced' to another pupil for comment (such as 'do you agree with that answer?' 'Can you add anything to that?') will help to ensure that everyone is concentrating and thinking. Pupils have to become more active in the process of learning. Other techniques are use of a random name generator (found on various websites) or the drawing of lollipop sticks with pupil names written on them. Pupils who answer 'I don't know', even after a thinking space, could be called upon later to comment on the next pupil's answer, or to decide which other class member they agree with.

Encouraging progress against learning objectives. Claire Gadsby (2012) suggests reinforcing learning objectives by asking pupils to annotate or highlight key words in them, rearranging words in the correct order, or leaving out verbs for example and asking pupils to decide on what they should be. Learning objectives need to be 'kept live' throughout the lesson by inviting pupils to reflect on their learning at opportune moments, as well as in a plenary at the end of the lesson.

Techniques where pupils give instant feedback.

- Use of *mini whiteboards* in class sets in folders with pen and rubber. They can be used to write very brief answers to questions, e.g. factual recall, key words or simple understanding. 'Give me a date in the twelfth century' is a question many Year 7 pupils can find difficult. This kind of instant feedback can assess factual recall skills or simple understanding, rather than demonstrating any depth of understanding.
- Use of true/false cards to show simple understanding after reading a text or A, B, C, D cards to give answers to multi-choice questions. Various voting technologies are now available to serve this purpose electronically.
- Plenaries involving active participation by everyone, e.g. giving each pupil a card with a key word on it and a pupil has to stand up when the teacher calls out the meaning to match their word.
- Wiliam (2011) refers to 'exit passes', whereby each pupil has to record an answer to a question related to the learning objectives on a slip of paper. The teacher checks these, and can either dispose of them if pupils have understood the learning, or adapt the next lesson to address any gaps in understanding.
- Sticky notes could also be used for a plenary where students write down one main point of their learning, and one remaining question. These could be dealt with next lesson either by the teacher or by their peers.
- Pupils could be divided into three groups: those who are confident with their learning; those who feel they only partly understand; and those who feel they do not understand.

The teacher can then work with third group, whilst pupils in the first and second groups pair up to help each other.

- Use of coloured cards on the desk – red, amber, green – students can display one of the cards on their desk as they work to indicate if they need further support. Pupils who are showing green could be asked to offer that support.
- Given that pupils' self-reports on their own understanding (e.g. colours, thumbs up or down) can be unreliable, Wiliam suggests testing understanding by asking one pupil who is confident to make a change to an incorrect point on the whiteboard, then asking the rest to use thumbs or colours to indicate whether they think the change is correct.
- Dominoes as a starter or plenary, i.e. cards telling a story. The pupil with the first card begins a sentence, the next card completes the sentence and starts the next one. Each pupil has a card. Repeat as a class exercise a couple of times, the second time is much easier. Pupils can help each other to make it easier.
- As a plenary, or a starter to reinforce learning from prior learning, pupils could be given a card with a question or answer on it. They have to find their partner who has the correct match.
- Use of factual recall exercises. The important role of knowledge has already been discussed. There remains a place for encouraging and checking factual recall as part of your instant feedback. Again mini white boards are useful. Simple 'pencil and paper' tests can be a time-effective way of finding out what pupils have learned.

Self assessment. Teachers are increasingly finding value in encouraging their pupils in the use of self-assessment. Black and Wiliam (1998, 2002) have been advocating the use of this type of formative assessment for some time. Very much a feature of 'assessment for learning', self-assessment is seen to carry many benefits for the pupils. It encourages a more positive classroom climate by reducing the fear of failure and emphasising what has been achieved, thereby improving the pupil's self-esteem. Pupils benefit from being involved in using and at times creating the 'success' criteria to be used and have a clear idea of what it is they are expected to learn. When applying the criteria they can work out how well they are doing and what they now need to do in order to improve as they reflect upon their own assessment.

Robin Conway's article (2011) explains a project where his students were asked to devise their own enquiry questions for a unit of work on the Holocaust. They were involved in setting the success criteria and deciding the learning outcomes, assessing their own work against the learning objectives periodically throughout the project.

Task 10.4 is designed to help you in your earliest efforts with self-assessment. You will see just how important it is that you have a precise understanding of what it is you want your pupils to learn. Note too the importance of giving *all* pupils a chance to succeed and to be able to reflect on their own assessment. From more simple approaches you may be able to move on to using some forms of progression models, possibly including concept and context-specific levels.

Task 10.4 *Beginning to use pupil self-assessment*

1   In planning a sequence of lessons, think about how you can find out whether all your pupils have achieved the objectives. What forms of assessment will you use? When will they take place? At what point will you inform pupils of the ways in which they will be assessed?

2   Include in your planning a piece of work which concludes a set of lessons. Before the pupils attempt it, work with the pupils to create the criteria to be used in the assessment.

3   After completion of the piece of work, ask the pupils to create a grid with the criteria down the left-hand side and 'Have I done it?' across the top. Then ask the pupils to go through their work and tick the criteria, which they think they have met.

4   Field the responses. What criteria have been met and what has proved the most difficult? Ask the pupils to indicate what should be the next thing they could do to improve.

Peer assessment. The Ofsted *History for all* report (Ofsted, 2011) found that self and peer assessment, done effectively, 'markedly enhanced students' learning'. The advantages of peer assessment include giving the pupils an opportunity to talk about their work in a constructive manner, which would involve trying to accommodate subject-specific language into their exchanges; they can learn from each other and benefit from examining each other's work. Opinions might vary about how you pair up the pupils but some, but not all teachers often find it helps if you put together pupils of a similar ability. Again the follow-up to the paired discussion is crucial, ensuring all pupils have reflected on the assessment and have a clear idea of how to progress. Effective peer assessment needs to be based on clear learning objectives, where pupils understand how to show progression in learning, regardless of whether this is linked to national curriculum levels. Students could be given a progression grid by which to measure attainment, or could simply use 'two stars and a wish' to guide their peers about strengths and areas for improvement. Laminated cards can be a useful classroom tool to aid pupil assessment of a piece of work. These could remind pupils of generic targets in their learning, such as PEEL (Point, Evidence, Explanation, Link to question) for a piece of writing, or simple progression points in source work such as 'takes information from a source, uses a range of sources as evidence, selects useful sources for an enquiry, uses source criticism to help evaluate an argument'.

Peer assessment often works well for group presentations, where other pupils are asked to comment on the work presented. This also serves the purpose of encouraging active listening to pupil presentations. Wiliam suggests an 'I-You-We' checklist for groups to assess their own work, whereby each member records something about their own contribution to the learning outcome, then about other individuals' contributions, then gives an evaluation of the work of the whole group.

Whilst it is not usually used for marking summative tests, peer assessment may have a valid place in the preparation or feedback on a test, for example by devising or asking questions of each other in revision, or by working together in a group after the test has been done to devise a better answer to some of the questions. This is sometimes called 'formative use of summative assessment'.

Modelling. Closely linked to the use of self and peer assessment is the use of modelling. This is use of examples of completed work. The model work does not have to be perfect. Modelling can be used at different stages throughout a set of lessons: at the beginning of a unit of work by showing the pupils an example of a piece of work and by comparing this with the written learning objectives. The visualiser can be a very helpful tool for modelling responses to written tasks, or providing an example of a good piece of work. With some pupils you may find they need to be shown exactly how to set out their work or begin their work. Presenting model answers, then asking pupils to comment on or improve those answers, is a valuable aid. As their work develops the pupils can use the model as a guide in order to improve and modify their work. Another modelling activity involves presenting pupils with four different answers to a question and using these to discuss which is the best and for what reasons, considering to what extent do they answer the question and meet the assessment objectives.

For an example of this approach, go to: www.uea.ac.uk/~m242/historypgce/assess/welcome.htm or http://terryhaydn.wordpress.com/pgce-history-at-uea/assessment.

The form of assessment

Using levels. In spite of all the misgivings about and limitations of the NCAT levels discussed earlier, and despite their omission from the new National Curriculum for 2014, there is every probability that you could find yourself in a school where the history department is required to produce, even on an interim basis, data which indicates the level which the pupil is said to have reached. An important part of your placement would be to find out how the history department uses the NCAT levels and builds them into its schemes of work. It should be remembered that the levels were intended to be used as 'best-fit' end of key stage descriptors for pupils' progress, but departments are not always 'free agents' in terms of school policy on the use of NCAT levels.

As a student teacher you will begin to formulate your own assessment criteria and devise your own mark schemes. For this, most teachers would advise making such schemes specific to your precise learning objectives and also very much related to the topic taught. Harrison (2004) confirmed the value of devising precise contextualised diagnostic tasks with mark schemes on specific skills with indicative content knowledge together with annotated examples of pupil responses. This was found to be particularly valuable when tried and tested tasks were used across schools.

When assessing pupils' work a basic but very important question to keep asking yourself is, 'Am I assessing what I think I am assessing?' Also, you need to ensure your marking scheme really does reflect the question or the task set and that you are not asking the pupils to guess what you really had in mind. For example, does a question asking the consequences of an event necessarily imply that the pupil should analyse the different types of consequence to achieve the best reward or the highest level?

Task 10.5 *Experiment with using levels*

1   Ask your tutor or HOD for a set of unmarked pieces of work together with the associated assessment objectives.
2   Read through the pupils' work and try to place the pieces in rank order. Teachers generally find it easier to find agreement over rank order than in the allocating marks or levels.
3   With the work in rank order, try to identify the reasons for your decisions. Reflect on what has informed your decisions.
4   Translate these reasons into a marking grid with statements for marks.
5   Check once more your statements against the assessment objectives and the task description.
6   Work out what feedback you would give to (i) the class and (ii) a sample of individual pupils.
7   Compare your results with the conclusions of the teacher who set and marked the work.

Adding variety. Assessment tasks in history should not be a seemingly unending and demotivating diet of tasks replicating the types of questions to be found on GCSE papers. Much is to be gained by adding variety to your use of assessment. As different individuals perform better on different tasks, it is fair, at least at Key Stage 3, to measure their progress and understanding in different ways. There are aspects of historical understanding that do not fit easily into a narrow examination format, for example the key concept requiring understanding of attitudes and beliefs of different times as well as the skills employed in well-constructed enquiries. The squeezing of coursework at GCSE has led to a narrowing of assessment formats and a limitation on the range of what studying history entails. However, as Luff (2003) has argued, this need not affect your teaching and formative assessment. He shows with a range of role play activities how they can be used to cover effectively a range of external examination objectives (for some examples, see www.uea.ac.uk/~m242/historypgce/drama/welcome.htm). Guscott (2006) sets out his own guidelines for using role play for assessment in which a range of key concepts are covered. Both emphasise the importance of motivation and enjoyment together with the need to provide learning and assessment opportunities for pupils with differing learning styles. Conway (2011) demonstrates how a range of learning outcomes was effectively used to illustrate depth of learning as well as to improve motivation in a project on the Holocaust. Nemko (2009) presents ideas about use of visual assessment, through photographic displays, to measure pupil progress in historical interpretations following a visit to the World War One battlefields. Issue 131 of *Teaching History* (2011), entitled 'Assessing differently', presents a variety of non-verbal learning outcomes which are used to assess progress, while Stanford (2008), also in *Teaching History* describes non-verbal methods of assessing Year 7 work, where they created pictures to show their understanding of the Renaissance.

Further variety in assessment may be found in the use of oral presentations either by individuals or by groups. The use of technology such as PowerPoint has added to the attraction of this approach. Such a method, apart from encouraging research skills and the use of the internet, can be used to involve peer assessment as outlined above. Cain and Neal (2004) combined presentations, role play and display as part of continual assessment for

Year 8. All groups, given set questions for enquiry, presented their findings in different ways, yet all were subjected to the class's success criteria for what a high quality enquiry should contain. In this way, many facets of learning history were covered in an enjoyable way, developing key historical skills not always covered by conventional examinations.

The validity and reliability of your assessment

In assessing your pupils you need to be constantly aware of the factors that can affect the validity and reliability of the information you acquire. A task may be said to be valid if it achieves what it is intended to do, if it clearly addresses the assessment targets you have in mind. Several factors can limit validity.

First, a most frequent reason for a test being of limited validity is *because the question has been poorly formulated*, that could mean the pupils are confused about what they have to do, it is ambiguous and your instructions are unclear and you may be asking the pupils to try to read your mind and guess what it is you want. Alternatively the question you have devised is actually testing a different set of objectives than you thought. Finding the best words and phrases for a question or task is much harder than you might initially believe and usually needs plenty of thought and time.

Second, if the tasks are dependent on sources, as many are, then you need to make sure the sources are accessible, and are appropriate for the parameters of the ability levels of the pupils they are designed for.

Third, you also need to consider whether the pupils have access to the *amount of knowledge* they will require for a good answer. A test loses validity if the pupils are being assessed on content, skills or concepts which they have not been taught. There are implications here for situations where there are several history teachers teaching different classes who are all given the same test or examination. Should your pupils not be given sufficient time to complete a task, this again affects the validity of any assessment made.

A task is potentially less reliable if there are several teachers involved in the marking. Hence the need for clear mark schemes, which can be consistently interpreted and the identification of clear criteria for the marking. Many departments consider the assessment of key pieces of work across the year and the key stage as a team. The discussion of the mark schemes, the principles behind them and examples of pupil responses is likely to increase reliability. As a student teacher you will find involvement in such discussions makes a valuable contribution to your understanding of good practice in teaching and assessment.

Applying differentiation to your assessment

Your methods of assessing pupils' achievement in history should keep in mind whether differentiation is necessary. There is some guidance on when and how differentiation might be practised in teaching in Chapter 7. When you are setting written assessments for pupils of different abilities will need to consider the points below.

1   *Making sure your pupils write as fully as they can*. This can be helped by giving *precise indications* of your expectations. For example, instead of 'give reasons for' ask 'Give at

least *five* reasons for'. With younger pupils you might, where appropriate, suggest they write 'at least ten lines' for their answer.

2   The extent to which *you will provide a structure* for the pupils' answers, for example by helping the pupil by breaking down the task into manageable parts or providing the first sentence of a response. An issue of differentiation arises if you give too much help to the more able pupils, who would be better assessed with a more general or open-ended task.

3   The *format of the tasks* can involve differentiation. For example, as an alternative to extended writing, you might ask some pupils to make lists, label diagrams or sources, or complete sentences or sequencing exercises. All of these considerably reduce the amount of writing, but also prompt you to keep asking what you are assessing. A 'rule of thumb' is that the more you reduce the number of sources and 'variables' involved in a task, the more likely you make it more accessible to pupils of lower abilities. However, you need to give all pupils the opportunity to use their knowledge to inform their answers, possibly with one or two more open-ended questions.

4   A further issue is the relationship between the use of differentiated assessment and norm-referencing. If pupils are set tasks according to their ability so that they can demonstrate what they can do, you may need to have some sensitivity in making the less able pupils aware of the limitations of their success. Otherwise they may hold unrealistic notions about their level of performance when compared with others. Similarly, you need to take into account the level of intervention provided when assessing the quality of your pupils' responses.

Task 10.6 *Assessment and differentiation*

Choose a topic, which you know you will be teaching on your placement to a class with a wide range of ability. When you have familiarised yourself with the content and the available resources, select as a target, an element of the knowledge, skills and understanding in the NC for History, for which that content and those resources presents an appropriate vehicle.

Plan *three* different task-sheets for the different abilities, taking into account the following:

(a)   the use of language involved for both the instructions and any sources;
(b)   the appearance of the sheet (where possible making use of ICT facilities);
(c)   the use of abstract concepts;
(d)   the variety and nature of any sources used;
(e)   the range and progression of skills you wish the pupils to employ;
(f)   your expectations about the amount of knowledge you wish them to use; and
(g)   your expectations about the length and format of their responses.

Try to ensure that there is a very noticeable difference in demand between the tasks for the most able and the least able pupils.

Discuss your task sheets with the teacher and, if convenient to the department, use them.

Written feedback: marking, recording and reporting on pupils' progress

'Assessment occupies such a central position in good teaching because we cannot predict what students will learn, no matter how we design our teaching (Wiliam, 2011: 46). Marking pupils' work helps you diagnose what they have learned. Because marking takes up a significant amount of your time, you will need to give plenty of thought to how you can make the best use of that time. Marking should be done as regularly as possible, both to check pupil work and to prevent the task from becoming unmanageable. When purposeful, it can be a rewarding experience, as over time you observe pupils acting on feedback and making progress as a result. To make the task practicable, you might consider marking pieces of work in terms of specific objectives without commenting or correcting on everything every time (making sure all realise what is the basis of your marking). As a student teacher you will be required to follow your department's marking policy, it is useful to be involved in any discussion that takes place about marking strategies and moderating and standardisation procedures. Often codes are used to indicate spelling errors or the need to develop points and so on. Remember that the purpose of written feedback is to provoke thought rather than an emotional response. This is where comment marking can be more effective than use of grades, which often lead pupils to compare themselves with others. Wiliam's research (2011) found that the effects of giving feedback in the form of scores with comments was very similar to the effect of providing scores only, that is it was motivating to students with high scores, but de-motivating to those with lower scores. In one study, students who were given comments only scored on average 30 per cent higher on work done in the second lesson than in the first. Once a score is given, it can distract the pupils from the comments. To be purposeful, comments should be focused and related to learning goals which have been shared with the students. Too much praise can be demotivating for able pupils who are inclined to coast, settling for less than their best just as long as they know it is as good as the work done by their peers and has left the teacher reasonably happy. In order to ensure that your pupils read and understand the comments, especially where grades are given as well, you might ask them to summarise your comments on a feedback sheet, give their own response (see Figure 10.1) to those comments, or even to pick out and copy out the comments meant for them from a list of several given to the class.

In issue 98 of *Teaching History*, the 'Move me on' section, for history student teachers and their tutors, focuses on marking and assessment (*Teaching History*, No. 98, February, 41-45). As well as identifying common problems and difficulties, the article provides practical strategies for moving forward in marking and assessment.

Individual target setting is a key aspect of assessment, although with the number of pupils a history teacher meets during the course of a week it is not easy to achieve.

The Ofsted, *History for all* report (Ofsted, 2011: 28) judged that assessment had improved in secondary schools between the years 2007-2010, although it was better at Key Stage 4 than at Key Stage 3. It stated that 'too often teachers made too little use of performance data in class work and examination work to determine the next steps in students' learning'. Other weaknesses in marking at Key Stage 3 were irregular marking, too much focus on presentation, 'assessment which was neither frequent enough nor specific enough to ensure that targets were always adequately challenging, little evidence of dialogue in books about work that had been marked, for example pupils' responses to a teacher's comments'. It is important that any targets set are periodically reviewed and it is worth spending time to do this. When this becomes habitual, most pupils will see this as an important part of their learning, so that they begin to become active participants in the process of learning rather than passive recipients. History departments use various systems to achieve this. Such systems might include the use of a target sheet, which the pupils stick in their book. Initial targets are selected by the teacher or pupil, then reviewed every so often by the pupil. Some departments use traffic light signals for specific skills. Another method is to use large printed target cards, which pupils place in a wallet stuck in the back of the exercise book. Pupils replace them with a new one when they have been achieved. Alternatively, a simple table could be provided for pupil books to record targets, when they are achieved and next steps.

Teaching standard 6 requires all teachers to 'give pupils regular feedback, both orally and through accurate marking, and encourage pupils to respond to the feedback' (DfE, 2012: 12). Opportunities for dialogue with pupils could be provided through writing questions at the end of their work rather than comments. Their responses here might actually improve the quality of their work, and grades if appropriate. Learning journals might be used on occasion for pupils to record information including comments on their progress in learning, how much has been achieved towards targets or long-term projects, and how much time has been spent, or levels of confidence. Whilst this method is more manageable with older students in a smaller class, there are simpler ways of recording the same information with large groups. One example provided by Claire Gadsby (2012) might be use of codes 'www' (what went well) and 'ebi' (even better if) by the teacher, followed by 'mri' (my response is) by the pupil. This is a simple extension of a process long used by advocates of assessment for learning. Another simple idea is a comment sheet on A4 stuck into the back of the book. The left hand column is used for teacher comments, with the right hand side for pupil comments and references to pages in their books where they have demonstrated certain points of learning (Black and Wiliam, 1998). Useful comments can be gathered through pupil voice questionnaires with multi-choice questions and an opportunity to respond in an open-ended fashion, such as 'I would like it if...'

Schools and history departments use various methods of recording, tracking and reporting on pupil progress. You will need to find a way of tracking the progress of each individual in a markbook or electronic gradebook. Data such as whether homework was completed, and grades awarded are usually recorded. A traffic light system, completed with highlighter pens in a book, or with a coloured spreadsheet, can give clear indication of whether a pupil has made the expected progress. This can easily be shared with the pupil or parents. Many schools use electronic systems such as sims where grades and target grades can be recorded. This might feed into a national system of tracking progress against national expectations such as SISRA or Fischer Family Trust (FFT). Such systems predict targets for pupils in each subject using attainment data in core subjects at the end of Key Stages 2 and 3. These systems are used by school leaders for monitoring teaching and learning. They can be useful to identify patterns of underachievement, or special educational needs, and interventions required. Teacher expertise is needed to diagnose why individuals identified may be struggling with learning or personal issues or attendance. One particular difficulty in predicting progress in history is that much of assessment at GCSE in history is based on memorisation and revision skills which are not measured by the baseline data used, such as English SATS. They are also inaccurate for students with very low levels at Key Stage 2, since the levels of progress expected are unrealistic. Datasets will be incomplete for pupils who have moved around a lot or have arrived from different countries.

Within history departments, the recording of pupil progress has its uses for the planning of learning but also to meet school requirements about that progress. Often history departments set pieces of work which over time cover the range of key skills and concepts. Such work is placed in a folder for moderation and comparison with previous work. Figure 10.1 is an example of an assessment record sheet used with Year 9, showing the use of set tasks, grades, teacher comments and targets for improvement. The information on such a sheet would be the basis for reporting to senior management, discussion with parents and to facilitate continuity.

Grade Awarded at end of Year 8:

Assessment title	Attainment grade	Effort grade	Teacher comment / targets for improvement	Pupil response
Slavery sources (source skills)				
Slavery essay (causation, understanding, extended writing)				
Holocaust memorial (knowledge and understanding, significance)				
Dunkirk sources (sources, interpretations)				
Other				

Grade awarded on Year 9 report:

Figure 10.1 Example of an assessment Record Sheet for a Year 9 pupil

Reporting to parents. As a student teacher, you may be required to assist in this process. It is a critical channel of communication with parents. All written reports should be personal, objective and meaningful, with an explanation of strengths and areas for improvement in language that parents will understand. On a parents' evening, there will be more opportunity to discuss the child's progress in depth. A 'rule of thumb' is to make positive comments, remembering that it can be very disheartening to hear repeated reports of weaknesses, but to be frank where improvement is needed.

Continuity. Assessment and records of assessment are useful tools to aid a smooth transition from year to year and also from one key stage to another. Within the secondary school, it is instructive to find out how history departments seek to prepare pupils for the expectations and demands of Key Stage 4. Given the pressures to recruit for the GCSE, consider how this can be achieved in a positive manner. The more pupils see that much of the preparation for Key Stage 4 has been done within Key Stage 3, the more comfortable they will be in opting for history. This could be reinforced by showing pupils the Grade C description for the GCSE, when they would realise how much it reflects that KS3 work and connects with their records of that work.

Task 10.7　*Marking, recording and reporting on pupils' progress*

In your placement schools, find out if there is a policy for marking and recording in:

(a) the whole school;
(b) the Faculty; and
(c) the history department.

Discuss with your tutors the main features of any policy - purposes and procedures. Does the school use profiling, individual pupil targets, review and self-assessment. Make notes on the procedures and ask to talk to pupils about their progress records.

History subject marking

How is this achieved? What use is made of pupils' exercise books? How do the teachers organise and use their mark book? Do they reflect the main areas of the NC? Is it possible to identify the strengths and weaknesses of individual pupils in their ability to apply knowledge, use skills and understand concepts?

What use is made of ephemeral evidence - oral responses, contribution to group work, use of initiative in historical enquiries?

Reporting

How is the recorded information translated into material for reporting?

(a) to pupils;
(b) for the school records; and
(c) to parents.

What are the means by which the parents are informed of their child's progress?

Summary and key points

There is more to getting better at history than simply accumulating factual information about the past. Concentration on a range of skills and understanding helps to define some of the ways in which pupils make progress in history. The assessment of pupils' progress in history is a highly sophisticated and extremely challenging aspect of your teaching. Although it is acknowledged that assessment is always an imperfect procedure, it is important that you are familiar with some of the pitfalls and are aware of some of the strategies to improve the validity and reliability of your assessment. You benefit from having a good understanding of the key issues involved in the assessment of history, and of the need to integrate assessment into your planning. Such planning should make sure that all the prescribed aspects of knowledge, skills and understanding are covered by the range and diversity of the tasks you offer to cater for the different abilities and aptitudes of your pupils.

It helps if you make sure you are assessing what you think you are assessing, if you have a clear idea about your expectations and these in turn are clearly communicated to the pupils. By working out in advance the kind of responses you are expecting and checking these against your objectives for the exercise, you are more likely to concentrate on these criteria when you come to mark your pupils' work. This adds to the reliability of your assessment by making it more objective and less dependent on 'impression' marking. As far as possible, your pupils should be active participants in the process of learning, and of assessing their own progress towards shared learning objectives.

The announcement by the Department for Education that 'The current system of "levels" used to report children's attainment and progress will be removed. It will not be replaced' (DfE, 2013b), marks a radical change in assessment practice for all subjects in English schools. This move is complicated by the fact that the National Association of Head Teachers has announced that 'schools should retain the use of levels while designing a new system' (NAHT, 2014), and also because academies and free schools are not obliged to comply with the National Curriculum. This means that schools may pursue very different paths with regard to assessment practice.

As Burn points out, these are 'interesting times' for assessment practice in history:

> The effective revocation of the previous attainment target is radical indeed. When these changes are considered alongside the fact that more than half of maintained secondary schools (all academies and free schools) now have no obligation at all to adhere to any prescribed curriculum, the revolutionary potential of current curriculum reforms is readily apparent. The word 'potential' is deliberately chosen, because there is no guarantee that history departments will capitalise on these new-found freedoms to shape their own curricula and assessment policies in response to their professional understandings of their subject discipline and the needs of their pupils. Heads of history may well find their options curtailed or constrained by whole-school policies and decisions made by senior leadership teams. (Burn, 2013: 1)

How should student teachers respond to this challenge? A sensible way forward is to ensure that you are aware of what constitutes 'good practice' in assessment. Assessment, testing and feedback are not necessarily helpful, and can do more harm than good (Haydn, 2013). You need to ensure that you use assessment methods 'that enhance learning as well as test it' (Alexander, 2014: 161). Assigning marks, grades or 'levels' to pupils is not unproblematic, but it is not the most difficult part of classroom assessment. The most challenging and important part of assessment is saying and doing things which help pupils to make progress in history.

In an effort to draw attention to the wider dimensions of learning, the Education Committee of the Inner London Education Authority (abolished in the 1980s) drafted a broad set of aims for schools called Aspects of Achievement (Hargreaves, 1984). The aims were published in an attempt to counter the emphasis placed on examination success to the exclusion of other important pupil achievements. Hargreaves' idea should be a strong reminder to teachers that there should be more to assessment than just measuring the cognitive development of pupils. Hargreaves argued that assessment should also attempt to measure the development of pupils' personal and social skills: 'The capacity to work with others... to work cooperatively in the interests of a wider group; initiative, self-reliance and skills of leadership.' And also, pupils' motivation and commitment to learning: 'The willingness to accept failure without destructive consequences; readiness to persevere and the self-confidence to learn despite the difficulty of the task' (Hargreaves, 1984: 2). Hargreaves makes the point that application, and willingness to learn are considered to be valuable qualities in most spheres of public life, and have an important influence on other aspects of attainment. These broader aspects of achievement in our assessment practice can also be very helpful in providing positive and encouraging feedback to pupils who are not 'high-fliers' in a subject, so that they maintain their commitment to learning rather than giving up. Keep in mind the question 'what is the full breadth of benefits which this pupil might derive from the study of my subject and being in my classroom?' and try to ensure that your assessment practices reflect this breadth.

It is also important that you keep up to date with developments in practice in assessment in history, while working constructively and professionally within the policies and practice of the department and the school you are working in.

Further reading

Breakstone, J., Smith, M. and Wineburg, S. (2013) Beyond the bubble: new history/social studies assessments for the Common Core, *Phi Delta Kappan*, *94* (5): 53-7, online at https://ed.stanford.edu/sites/default/files/breakstone_smith_wineburg.pdf, accessed 32 March 2014. (See 'Beyond the Bubble' weblink below.)

Fordham, M. (2013) O brave new world without those levels in't: where now for Key Stage 3 assessment in history, *Teaching History: Curriculum Supplement*, December 2013: 16-23.

Freeman, J. and Philpott, J. (2009) 'Assessing Pupil Progress': transforming teacher assessment in Key Stage 3 history, *Teaching History*, No. 137: 4-13. APP has 'gone out of fashion', but the 'portfolio' approach still has some things to commend it.

Harrison, S. (2009) Rigorous, meaningful and robust: practical ways forward for assessment, *Teaching History*, No. 115: 26-30.

History Resource Cupboard (2013) *What is good assessment practice at Key Stage 3?*, online at www.historyresourcecupboard.co.uk/content/?page_id=274, accessed 13 February 2014. A package of resources to help improve assessment practice at KS3. Some of the resources on this site are free, but this one costs £5.49.

Husbands, C. (2012) Using assessment data to support pupil achievement, in V. Brooks, I. Abbott and P. Huddleston (eds) *Preparing to Teach in the Secondary School*, Maidenhead, Open University Press: 132-45. One of the most lucid and succinct guides to what can be a quite complex area.

Stanford History Education Group (2012) 'Beyond the bubble', online at https://beyondthebubble.stanford.edu, accessed 15 March 2014. Although the context is mainly US history, this working group formed to devise more valid and appropriate assessment approaches for school history has ideas that could be applied to NC content. Some interesting ideas.

VanSledright, B. (2014) *Assessing historical thinking and understanding: innovative designs for new standards*, London, Routledge. VanSledright's ideas about the use of weighted multiple choice questions are particularly interesting.

References

Alexander, R. (2014) The best that has been thought and said, *Forum, 56* (1): 157–66.

Association for Achievement and Improvement through Assessment (AAIA) www.aaia.org.uk, accessed 13 October 2007.

Black P. and Wiliam D. (1998) *Inside the Black Box*, London: Nelson Publishing, online article found at http://blog.discoveryeducation.com/assessment/files/2009/02/blackbox_article.pdf, accessed 5 June 2013

Black, P.J., Harrison, C., Lee, C., Marshall, B. and Wiliam. B. (2002) *Working inside the black box: assessment for learning in the classroom 2002*. King's College London.

Booth, M. (1983) Skills, concepts and attitudes: the development of adolescent children's historical thinking, *History and Theory*, Vol. 22.

Booth, M. and Husbands, C. (1993) 'The History National Curriculum in England and Wales: Assessment at Key Stage 3', *The Curriculum Journal, 4* (1): 21–36.

Burnham, S. and Brown, G. (2004) Assessment without level descriptions, *Teaching History*, No. 115: 5–15.

Burn, K. (2013) Editorial, *Teaching History: Curriculum Supplement*, December 2013: 1.

Cain, K. and Neal, C. (2004) 'Opportunities, challenges and questions; continual assessment in Year 8', *Teaching History*, No. 115: 31–6.

Checketts, J. (1996) 'GCSE History: A Case for Revolution', *Teaching History*, No. 82: 20–22.

Cottingham, M. (2004) Dr Black Box or How I learned to stop worrying and love assessment, *Teaching History*, No. 115: 16–23.

Conway, R. (2011) Owning their learning: using 'Assessment for Learning' to help students assume responsibility for planning, (some) teaching and evaluation, *Teaching History*, No. 144: 51–57.

Counsell, C. (2000) 'Historical knowledge and historical skills: a distracting dichotomy', Chapter 5 in J. Arthur and R. Phillips (eds) *Issues in History Teaching*, London: Routledge.

Dicksee, I. (2006) 'Peer Assessment', Chapter 10 in M. Hunt (ed.) *A Practical Guide to Teaching History in the Secondary School*, London: RoutledgeFalmer.

DfE (1995) *History in the National Curriculum*, London: HMSO.

DfE (2003) *The Assessment for Learning (AfI) strategy* – this has now been archived online at http://webarchive.nationalarchives.gov.uk/20110113104120/http://nationalstrategies.standards.dcsf.gov.uk/node/182275, accessed 5 June 2013.

DfE (2012) *Teachers' Standards, May 2012* found online at www.education.gov.uk/publications/eOrderingDownload/teachers%20standards.pdf, accessed 19 August 2014

DfE (2013a) *The National Curriculum in England Framework for key stages 1–4, September 2013*, online at www.gov.uk/government/collections/national-curriculum, accessed 18 December 2013.

DfE (2013b) 'Assessing without levels', press release, 14 June. Online at www.education.gov.uk/a00225864. Online, accessed 14 August 2013.

DfE/QCA (1999) *History: The national Curriculum for England*, London: DFEE/QCA.

Dickinson, A. and Lee, P. (1984) Making sense of history, in A. Dickinson, P. Lee and P. Rogers, *Learning History*, Oxford: Heinemann: 117–53.

Frith, D.S. and Macintosh, H.G. (1984) *A Teacher's Guide to Assessment*, London: Stanley Thornes.

Gadsby C. (2012) *Perfect Assessment for Learning*, Carmarthen: Independent Thinking Press.

Guscott, S. (2006) 'Role Play as Active History', Chapter 5 in M. Hunt (ed.) *A Practical Guide to Teaching History in the Secondary School*, London: RoutledgeFalmer.

Hallam, R.N. (1972) Thinking and learning in History, *Teaching History*, 2 (8): 337–46.

Hallam, S. (1996) *Pupil Learning and Differentiation*, unpublished lecture: Institute of Education, University of London, 17 January.

Hammond, K. (2001) From horror to history: teaching pupils to reflect on significance, *Teaching History*, No. 104: 15–23.

Hargreaves, D. (1984) Improving secondary schools, London: ILEA.

Harrison, S. (2004) Rigorous, meaningful and robust: practical ways forward for assessment, *Teaching History*, No. 115: 26–30.

Haydn, T. (2013) 'First do no harm: assessment, motivation and learning', in S. Capel, M. Leask and T. Turner (eds), *Learning to Teach in the Secondary School*, London: Routledge: 417–38.

Historical Association, (2011) *Teaching History No. 131: Assessing Differently*, London: Historical Association.

Husbands, C. (2012) Using assessment data to support pupil achievement, in V. Brooks, I. Abbott and P. Huddleston (eds) *Preparing to Teach in the Secondary School*, Maidenhead: Open University Press: 132–45.

Lee, P. (1994) 'Historical Knowledge and the National Curriculum', in H. Bourdillon (ed.) *Teaching History*, London: Routledge: 41–52.

Lee, P. and Ashby, R. (2000) 'Progression on historical understanding 7-14', in P. Stearns, P. Seixas and S. Wineburg, *Teaching, Knowing and Learning History*, New York: New York University Press: 199–222.

Lee, P. and Shemilt, D. (2003) A scaffold, not a cage: progression and progression models in history, *Teaching History*, No. 113: 13–23.

Lewis, A. (1992) From Planning to Practice, *British Journal of Special Education*, 19 (1): 24–7.

Lomas, T. (1989) *Teaching and Assessing Historical Understanding*, London: Historical Association.

Luff, I. (2003) Stretching the strait jacket of assessment: use of role play and practical demonstration to enrich pupils' experience of history and beyond, *Teaching History*, No. 113: 26–35.

National Association of Head Teachers (2014) *Press release: Profession takes lead on assessment after the end of levels*, 13 February, online at www.naht.org.uk/welcome/news-and-media/key-topics/assessment/profession-takes-lead-on-assessment-after-the-end-of-levels, accessed 25 March 2014.

Nemko, B. (2009) Visual assessment as a means of measuring pupils' progress in historical interpretation, *Teaching History*, No. 137, London: Historical Association.

Ofsted (2011) *History for All*, London: OFSTED.

QCA (2005) *History, Annual Report on Curriculum and assessment*, London: QCA.

QCA (2007) *History Programme of Study, key stage 3*, London, QCA, found online at www.education.gov.uk/schools/teachingandlearning/curriculum/secondary/b00199545/history/programme, accessed 5 June 2013.

Shemilt, D. (1976) Formal Operational Thought in History, *Teaching History*, 4 (15): 237–43, London: Historical Association.

Spendlove, D. (2009) *Putting Assessment for Learning into Practice*, London: Continuum.

Stanford, M. (2008) 'Redrawing the Renaissance: non-verbal assessment in Year 7' in *Teaching History*, No. 130: 4–11, London: Historical Association.

Stephen, A. (2006) 'Ensuring inclusion in the classroom', Chapter 8 in M. Hunt (ed.), *A Practical Guide to Teaching History in the Secondary School*, London: RoutledgeFalmer.

Vermeulen, E. (2000) What is progress in history? *Teaching History*, No. 98: 35–41.

von Oech, R. (1990) *A Whack on the Side of the Head*, London: Thorsons.

Watts D.G. (1973) *The Learning of History*, London: RKP.

White, C. (1992) *Strategies for the Assessment and Teaching of History*, London: Longman.

Wiliam, D. (2011) *Embedded Formative Assessment*, Bloomington IN: Solution Tree Press.

11 Teaching for external examinations

Introduction

Although the balance of your teaching experience during your course is likely to be with Key Stage 3 classes, even within your course, you will almost certainly have responsibility for teaching some classes with examination groups. If your course of initial teacher education is qualifying you to teach pupils aged 11–18, this will include some teaching of GCE AS and A2 classes, as well as GCSE classes. What's different about teaching examination classes – and what is the same?

Teachers care about the progress of all their classes, and are concerned about handing them over for you to 'practise on', whether they are in Year 7 or Year 12. But whereas slow content coverage with a Key Stage 3 class can be 'retrieved', lessons with exam classes are particularly precious; pupils generally only get one chance to do well in an external examination, and you have to take the gravity of this responsibility on board in your preparation and planning. Time is precious, there is a specification to be covered (and time left for revision towards the end of the course), and pupils do have to remember things and have strong subject content knowledge to do well in history examinations: 'recall' is an important skill both at GCSE and GCE A Level. There is less scope for eclectic approaches with exam classes, and interesting but not strictly relevant diversions. You have to have a clear grasp of the detail of the exam specification (including the assessment objectives and the nature and format of the questions that pupils will be asked), and stick to these things in your teaching, whilst avoiding the danger of making the learning dry, dull or repetitive. There is a much stricter 'compliance' agenda than with Key Stage 3 teaching, where the teacher has much more autonomy in terms of what topics are covered, in what way, and at what length. Retention of knowledge and revision play a larger part in the learning. At the same time, imagination, initiative and varying your approaches is just as important with exam classes as with Key Stage 3 groups.

Another difference is that you may well be teaching exam groups 'alongside' their regular teacher, either team teaching, with you sub-contracting responsibility for planning teaching parts of the lesson, or planning and teaching collaboratively, or working with sub-groups of pupils or even individual pupils, to support the regular class teacher. This requires you to be extremely conscientious, flexible and adaptable in your approach.

You are unlikely to be given sole responsibility for teaching groups in the year of their external examination over a long period. If some of this seems rather daunting, you should keep in mind that working with examination classes is one of the most purposeful, enjoyable and exciting aspects of being a teacher. You see much more of the pupils over the two years of the course and consequently get to know them much better. To at least some extent, you are working with pupils who have chosen to do the subject in preference to other subjects. It is easier to get to the stage of feeling that you are all on the same side, working together towards shared objectives, and when it is your own exam class, you care very much about how well they do in the exam.

Objectives

At the end of this chapter you should be able to:

- locate and be familiar with examination options available at GCSE and GCE A Level;
- locate and understand the assessment objectives for GCSE and GCE A Level examinations;
- identify approaches you may adopt when given a GCSE class to teach;
- list possible approaches you may use when asked to teach an A Level class;
- obtain and use relevant information and resources to approach your teaching for examination classes.

Using information from awarding bodies

There has been a revolution in the amount of information and guidance for teachers provided by awarding bodies over the past three decades. The three main awarding bodies now provide a wide range of materials to support teachers in preparing their pupils for external examination. In addition to specifications, past papers, and examiners' reports for particular exams, there are resources guides, teachers' handbooks, notice boards, samples of candidates' work with examiner comments, sample schemes of work, as well as textbooks designed for each particular specification, written by senior examiners. Following recent media controversy, there are now fewer opportunities for face-to-face meetings with examiners.

You need to familiarise yourself with the examination specifications for the courses you will be teaching in the course of your school experience by discussion with colleagues. You must also be proactive in accessing the full range of resources made available by the relevant awarding body.

Task 11.1 *Familiarising yourself with the range of support materials available from awarding bodies*

Your first priority is to acquire 'a grounding' in the exam courses that you are teaching on placement and to prepare as conscientiously and effectively as possible for the pupils who are in your care; you can develop your grasp of the range of exams available at GCSE and A Level at a later stage.

As soon as you know which exam groups you will be teaching, access the relevant awarding body website, download the materials and resources which are available for the particular exam you will be teaching, and then explore the site to familiarise yourself with the full range of services which the awarding body offers.

The web addresses of the three main awarding bodies are:
Exexcel: www.edexcel.org.uk
OCR: www.ocr.org.uk.
AQA: www.aqa.org.uk.

Teaching GCSE history

Background

GCSE was introduced in 1986, replacing the earlier GCE 'O' level examination, intended for the most able 20 per cent, and the C.S.E., which targeted the next 40 per cent of ability. The hope was expressed that GCSE would not just amalgamate the two existing examinations but would extend examination opportunities for candidates of *all* abilities. The GCSE examination also introduced the idea that not all the assessment of a pupils' progress in the subject would be based on the final written examination. All candidates would produce coursework, which had to meet precise assessment objectives, and which would be carefully moderated by Examination Boards (now 'awarding bodies'). More recently, concerns over internet based plagiarism and parental assistance have led to insistence that coursework, now called 'controlled assessment' be completed under supervised conditions in school. ('Coursework axed to beat GCSE cheats', *Guardian*, 14 June 2007).

Since the inception of GCSE, there have been a number of changes to the subject criteria. The proportion of the specification to be devoted to British history has been set at 25 per cent, because of concerns in some quarters that pupils could 'escape' doing any British history between the ages of 14 and 16. In the draft proposals for teaching from 2015, the requirement for English, Scottish, Welsh or Irish history has been raised to 40 per cent (DfE, 2013). The original GCSE exam saw a massive reduction in the amount of marks allocated to essay type questions, but more recently, the importance of pupils being able to express their knowledge and understanding in the form of extended writing has been acknowledged and the examination now has a more even balance between short 'source-based' questions, and questions involving extended writing. Another area of controversy was the inclusion of historical empathy in the original assessment objectives, in the form of 'an ability to look at events and issues from the perspectives of people of the past'. This has disappeared in the light of concern over the way in which empathetic understanding would be assessed.

History is one of a very small number of subjects which has always had one set of examination papers for the full range of GCSE grades. Tiered examination papers (papers targeted at a narrow range of GCSE grades) have been a feature of examinations in some subjects since GCSE was first introduced. Other subjects, including geography, introduced tiered papers in the context of the 1995 revisions to GCSE. From 2016, tiering is likely to be dropped in nearly every subject except for mathematics. The main argument against tiering is that it can limit the achievement of candidates in the middle band who are prepared for a foundation paper where their attainment is capped at Grade C, and for which their learning is limited to the essentials to achieve this 'pass' grade. The difficulties with un-tiered papers are that the source material and language of the questions can be confusing for less able pupils or for those with English as an additional language. Whilst the mark schemes may seek to discriminate across the full ability range, sources in the history exam papers may be designed for candidates with a reading level of 15+, making it difficult for some of the candidates, who have a lower reading age, to make sufficient sense of the materials to achieve even the lowest grades.

Proposed changes to GCSE for teaching from September 2016

The current government is planning a radical overhaul of the GCSE qualification. The overall aim is to achieve a more stretching, essay-based system with an increase in demand at the level currently considered a pass (Grade C). Controlled assessment will be dropped in nearly every subject, including history, with grading by numbers 1–8 rather than letters.

Under the plans for history GCSE, pupils must undertake at least one piece of in-depth study covering either the Medieval (500 to 1500), Early Modern (1450 to 1750) or Modern period (1700 to the present day). There will be a requirement to study a range of eras, to avoid a perceived concentration on the twentieth century. Whilst 40 per cent of the course will comprise British or Irish history, at least a quarter of the course will have to cover the history of the wider world (DfE, 2013).

The assessment objectives for GCSE history

Given the 'high stakes' nature of external examinations, it is important that there is clarity about exactly what we are measuring when we make judgements on pupils' achievements in the subject. In the examination specifications, this is indicated in the form of assessment objectives. These are the same for all the awarding bodies and all the specification options (the three main boards all offer GCSE courses Modern World History, and the Schools History Project).

Under current GCSE regulations, candidates have to be able to:

(Assessment Objective 1): recall, select, organise and communicate their knowledge and understanding of history.

(Assessment Objective 2): demonstrate their understanding of the past through explanation and analysis of:

- key concepts: causation, consequence, change and significance within a historical context; and
- key features and characteristics of the periods studied and the relationships between them.

(Assessment Objective 3): Understand, analyse and evaluate:

- a range of source materials as part of an enquiry; and
- how aspects of the past have been interpreted and represented in different ways as part of an historical enquiry.

The draft proposals for the new GCSE history (for first teaching from September 2016) are very similar to the above, as are those for International GCSE history qualifications.

Task 11.2 *Thinking about progression from Key Stage 3*

How do the three assessment objectives above compare to the Attainment Target in the NC at Key Stage 3? Look for the concepts and skills expected for Key Stage 3 and compare them with the GCSE assessment objectives. To what extent is there continuity in terms of how we are attempting to measure progression in history? Are there any differences?

Planning, teaching and learning approaches for GCSE

On at least one of your school placements you should find that you are responsible for a series of GCSE lessons. You need to think about how to prepare a 'medium term' plan for the topic or topics you have to teach. Here are some suggestions for the preparations you can make for such teaching.

- Study carefully the specific specifications for which the pupils are to be entered.
- Find out in which examination paper the content you have to teach is to be used. Find out what are the chief emphases of that particular examination paper – concepts, interpretations, sources. This influences to some extent the way you approach the teaching of the topics you have been given.
- Examine the resources which the department uses for the teaching of that content; find out which books the pupils may take home.
- If the content area is one you have not recently studied, complete some background reading to ensure that you are not only familiar with the detail but also your knowledge is wide enough to consider associated causes, consequences and the significance of events.
- With guidance from the teacher, begin to create a scheme of work for the series of lessons. Make sure that the main emphases of that element of the examination to which the content contributes, is well represented in your scheme. If sources form a major feature, include source work within the scheme.
- Whatever the paper, your pupils need to support their answers with relevant knowledge. To this end there will be some lessons, usually the earlier ones in a scheme, when you will need to consider how the pupils are to gather and record that knowledge.

The critical issue is to strike a balance between stimulating learning and preparation for external examinations. The knowledge and understanding can be built up in the same ways as it is at Key Stage 3. Often it is helpful to frame learning within enquiry questions, following or adapting those used by the awarding bodies. An article on planning and teaching linear GCSE by Burn, McCrory and Fordham (2013) is informative about approaches here. This article stresses the need to build factual knowledge within a clear conceptual framework as an organising structure. Historical understanding at GCSE is framed within the same key concepts as at KS3.

Remember, there are many ways of gathering knowledge and recording information. Your approaches should not be merely didactic (in the sense of *always* teaching by telling); you need to actively engage your learners to help reinforce the learning. Suggestions are use of mystery cards as initial stimulus for a new topic, where students have to use several clues to piece together events in a story; or research using a variety of books or the internet, or a webtrail; or making group presentations which might argue the case for the significance of an event or its relative importance within a web of causes. As at KS3, focused exploratory talk remains an important part of learning, and this should include some pupil to pupil talk. Market place activities involve teams of pupils whose role is to summarise one aspect of new learning. One member of the group then stays at their market stall to explain their learning to others who visit, whilst the other team members collect information from the other market stalls. Pupils might also consider unfolding events in role as one individual or country. An example of an extended simulation activity is provided by Chapman and Woodcock (2006). Pupils researched countries that were members of the UN, taking on a role in order to explain the complex decisions taken at the time of the Abyssinia Crisis. The 'Marble Maze' game was used in order to encourage thinking about possibilities for different actions within the historical situation. Chapman and Woodcock also suggested use of the Buckaroo or Jenga games. Worth (2012) has written about the use of a game to improve causal reasoning with Year 10. Various techniques such as roleplay, or use of movie maker software can be used by GCSE students at a more complex level than for younger pupils. See Clements' (2010) article for ideas about using creative play toys to teach historical skills. Osowiecki (2006) explains how top trump cards, created by pupils using PowerPoint software, were used by GCSE students to analyse and compare key points. Teachers who are experienced at working with exam classes are often accomplished at 'activating learners as instructional resources for one another (Wiliam, 2011: 46). This involves getting pupils to talk, discuss, argue, develop their thinking, and reinforce their subject knowledge. However, it is important to keep in mind that although groupwork and collaborative learning can be helpful, there is still a place for high quality teacher exposition, with the teacher 'leading the learning', from the front of the class. Philpott (2009) makes the point that experienced and effective A level teachers are accomplished in getting pupils to participate actively in the lessons, *and* in getting pupils to work outside the confines of the taught sessions, by the adroit use of ICT.

It is worth practising cartoon analysis, as examiners often use cartoons, which are not regularly used at KS3. There are ideas for using pictures in Chapter 7. Some of these might provide a welcome break from writing about text-based sources, as well as requiring pupils to look closely at the subtleties of the drawing and any captions.

Whilst historical knowledge may have been acquired independently, some history departments chose to give out school-produced work booklets to supplement this, and to use for revision. Such booklets might contain homework activities. Homework is often a critical factor in determining success at GCSE. As you plan your teaching, try to ensure that homework is built into the scheme of work, using a variety of tasks in line with the departmental homework policy. Non-written tasks might be revision for short tests, web research or additional reading, making cartoons or drawings about topics studied in class, finding a song connected with the current topic. You might ask pupils to take more responsibility for their learning by keeping a record of when they complete tasks and how long they spend each week doing history homework.

In terms of application and deployment of their knowledge, you will need to look carefully at past papers, and other materials from the awarding body in order to gain a clear picture of expectations. As indicated in the previous chapter, the challenge to both teachers and examiners is how to accommodate knowledge within levels of response marking schemes. The specifications include 'extended writing' as one form of assessment of candidates' achievements. The presence of such questions, carrying a substantial percentage of the marks for the paper, influences the way you prepare your pupils for the examination. They will benefit from the occasional class essay on a prescribed topic, in which they are given about 25 minutes to complete an answer without reference to books or notes. As Husbands notes,

> It is not primarily the length of the written work which matters, but the provision of written tasks as culminations of historical enquiries which extend pupils' capacity to think historically... they should be challenging in the ways they ask pupils to complete the move from the accumulation of material, through the sketching of relationships, to the presentation of a statement about the historical material which they have explored.
> (Husbands, 1996: 109-10)

In the early stages of their GCSE course, many pupils need help in structuring their written work. Even if their analytical and writing skills are strong, they will need practice in understanding expectations. Differentiated resources, and scaffolding writing may help, although these will need to be withdrawn at a later stage, given the demands of an un-tiered external exam paper. Modelling answers may be a helpful approach. Often the awarding bodies provide model work on their websites. Practice questions from an early stage will be helpful, perhaps starting with more accessible source material or simpler questions, so that the pupils feel a sense of progress. Pupils could engage in peer marking exercises using simplified extracts from examiners' mark schemes. Again these can be found on the websites of the awarding bodies. One effective technique is for the class to mark a short answer to a question, displayed on the class whiteboard or visualiser, pointing out strengths and weaknesses. Pupils could then try to improve upon the answer in pairs. Alternatively, they could attempt to refine their answers in groups after the teacher has marked them. Many schools now require progress of individual pupils to be tracked from early in year 10, and the history department in which you are placed is likely to have its own system of tracking. Mock tests and exams are likely to be used periodically, with revision periods leading up to them.

Since 2013, awarding bodies have been required to allocate additional marks (5 per cent of the total) in history GCSE papers for quality of written communication and spelling, punctuation and grammar. These attributes cannot be taught in isolation, but pupils should be reminded of the need to use formal English. Again use of model answers might be helpful. Team games based on correcting common spelling errors or thinking of more expressive verbs than 'did' to improve a piece of writing, can also be very popular with GCSE pupils.

As with knowledge acquisition, approaches to revision needs to involve pupils actively rather than simply providing them with topic summaries. Some ideas would be to include class quizzes, recording podcasts, matching exercises, devising quiz questions, board games, mnemonics, mind maps, tables, summary cards, designing, or revision guides for classmates. In class, pupils could be given a choice of activities so that they begin to understand that a variety of approaches other than simply reading notes. Revision can become a shared exercise in class. Short stimuli such as video clips (see BBC broadband clips or the BBC bitesize website for examples). Then pupils could be given time to present their knowledge in some form such as a mind map, which could then be added to, after another short input from the teacher or a class member, by classmates in a different colour. This should be complemented by application of knowledge to exam type questions.

Task 11.3 *Studying past papers*

Another useful preparatory task is to study the past or specimen papers of the specifications you are to teach. Look closely at the questions and the associated marking schemes. Consider what teaching and learning strategies you could employ to enable you to be able to tackle such questions.

- What do the pupils need to know?
- What skills do they need to employ?

How do your answers to these two questions affect your planning and choice of teaching strategies?

- Devise a question of your own that you feel would be appropriate for a GCSE exam. With the permission of your tutor, set the question for a class and think about its effectiveness and limitations, and how you will assess it.

Common mistakes and misconceptions of GCSE candidates

Technique

As a result of your own experience of examinations, you are already familiar with some of the guidance teachers need to give to candidates for external examinations. Advice about **the need to look carefully at the precise wording** of a question and to note that the number of marks available for question determines how much time should be spent on it. Your pupils should be familiar with the requirements of the paper and its rubric by working on an earlier paper. Encourage them to look for and understand the *meaning of the command words in a question* such as 'explain', 'compare', 'useful', 'reliable' and 'give reasons for'. They should clearly understand how such words will guide their answers.

Source skills

A common practice with some weaker candidates is to paraphrase the sources on the paper in the hope that such words will contain the answer. This may result from a limited understanding of the content of the source or from familiarity with rather undemanding worksheets, which allow pupils to copy or paraphrase without showing much thought.

There are times when pupils faced with a requirement to compare sources, will, nevertheless, paraphrase or describe each source in turn but without making any comparison. It may be helpful *to encourage such pupils to develop certain routines* such as completing a table.

	SIMILARITIES	DIFFERENCES	REASONS FOR DIFFERENCES
SOURCE A			
SOURCE B			

There are some candidates, who, in the belief that the more they write the greater will be the mark awarded, devote much of an answer that requires the interpretations of sources to their description. Some give the impression that they think that assessing a source's utility means describing it. Practise assessing answers of this type against a mark scheme might help to avoid this pitfall.

Another common difficulty is *the inability to differentiate between the 'utility' of a source and its 'reliability'*. You might find it helpful if the pupils are encouraged to ask questions such as 'Useful for what?', 'Useful for whom?', and to realise that some sources, which contain some inaccuracies, still have their uses for certain enquiries. Some candidates can be too dismissive of such sources. Analogies to everyday objects might help convey a message here. For example, you might ask the whether a school shirt is a useful item of clothing, you would expect the answer to be yes. You might then ask if it is a reliable source of evidence about school life in the early twenty-first century, you would again expect an affirmative answer. However, if you ask whether it is useful to tell us about fashion in the early twenty-first century, you would expect a range of answers.

Again, with reliability, your pupils benefit from being encouraged to ask 'Reliable for what?', which again may not always be determined by the accuracy of some of the details in the source.

Your pupils benefit from having set procedures for tackling both source questions and also different interpretations

Whilst examiners discourage formulaic answers, your pupils might practise source analysis using tables or question cards based on mnemonics such as CAP (Content, Author, Purpose), or PACK (Purpose, Author, Contextual Knowledge) and so on.

Less common now is the misconception that because a source is a 'primary' source it must be more reliable than a secondary source. It may still be worthwhile to pose a question which might explore this idea. (For example, 'Would it be possible for a secondary school pupil in this school to have better knowledge and understanding of what happened at the Battle of Waterloo than a soldier who fought in that battle? Give reasons for your answer.)

Use of knowledge

As discussed in Chapter 10, the role of knowledge has generated considerable debate since the introduction of GCSE. One of your tasks is to try to encourage your pupils to think about how they use their historical knowledge. In this they should be aware of *not relying too much on the information available on the paper but being able to support their opinions with other relevant, accurate information.* Such knowledge is likely to push a mark to the top of the level in a mark scheme. The revised GCSE places more emphasis on knowledge and so those candidates who not only display a certain level of conceptual understanding but can also support the answer with knowledge will be rewarded. The more you can encourage your pupils to make use of knowledge to *back up* their statements and judgements the better. The more this is done at KS3, before the GCSE course, again the better. Breaking down and highlighting model answers is helpful in practising technique. Use of the acronym PEEL (Point, Evidence, Explanation, Link to question) is a tool used in some schools to help pupils to structure paragraphs.

Concepts

While it is important to encourage candidates to use their historical knowledge intelligently, there are times when questions dealing with concepts such as causation and change are seen by some pupils as requests for lists. This illustrates one of your problems in teaching GCSE history, namely, how to achieve a balance between teaching a body of knowledge but not giving sets of prepared answers, which may or may not answer the specific question set. Such a balance is often the case with, for example, causation, where a good candidate not only recalls the causes of an event but is able to use them to construct a well substantiated explanation which assesses the comparative importance of the various causes, and the interrelationships between them. A recurrent comment from examiners is that candidates need more *practice in evaluating the relative merits of different causes of events and of explaining the links between them.* In other words, try to encourage your pupils to assess and evaluate rather than merely list, thus, some of the approaches to the teaching of concepts discussed in Chapter 5, are equally applicable to your teaching for the GCSE. In the classroom, this might be done by setting up a trial of different causes, where groups of pupils have to argue the relative merits of each one, or similar activities. So, in this way your pupils will not, for example, recount lists of results without making any attempt to assess and evaluate explicitly whether the changes they mentioned were important.

Task 11.4 *Resources to support GCSE teaching*

You don't have to limit yourself to departmental resources and your own ideas for teaching GCSE. There are many websites which have substantial sections on teaching GCSE. Explore some of the sites listed below and consider how you would use or adapt some of the ideas and resources available for topics which you have to teach. There are so many resources available that there is always a danger that you can just 'browse' and not collect, organise and deploy resources effectively. Try to make sure that you put together a powerful 'learning package' (see Chapter 8) on at least one of the topics that you are teaching using internet resources, together with material from other sources. (This is just a small selection of what is available, try a Google search on 'History GCSE' for further options):

www.bbc.co.uk/schools/gcsebitesize/history/
www.historygcse.org
www.schoolhistory.co.uk/revision
www.schoolhistory.co.uk/gcse.html

---

www.johndclare.net
www.schoolshistory.org.uk/gcse.htm
www.schoolshistoryproject.org.uk/Teaching/GCSE/Index.htm
www.activehistory.co.uk/Miscellaneous/menus/GCSE/menu.htm
www.redhotscott.co.uk/revision/
www.revisioncentre.co.uk/gcse/history/index.html
www.teachithistory.co.uk/ks4alphabetical

Valuable advice on preparing pupils for GCSE examinations can also be found in the following articles in *Teaching History*:

- Angela Leonard, 'Exceptional performance at GCSE: what makes a starred A?' (1999) No. 95, May: 20-23.
- Diana Laffin, 'My essays could go on forever': using Key Stage 3 to improve pupil performance at GCSE', (2000) No. 98, February: 14-21.
- Chris Culpin 'Breaking the 20 year rule: very modern history at GCSE' (2005) No. 120: 11-14.

Task 11.5 *Analysis and commentary on GCSE questions*

Go to www.uea.ac.uk/~m242/historypgce/exams/welcome.htm or http://terryhaydn. wordpress.com/pgce-history-at-uea/teaching-exam-classes.

Read through the analysis and commentary on the two GCSE questions detailed on the website. How would you use this information to devise your own levels of response mark scheme for a GCSE type question for your pupils?

Non-GCSE courses in history

Entry level certificate

This qualification was introduced to meet the needs of pupils for whom the GCSE history courses were too demanding, both in terms of their assessment requirements and in the amount of material to be covered.

There are three pass grades: Entry 1, Entry 2 and Entry 3, which are intended to recognise a level of achievement below that of a grade G at GCSE, but candidates who are entered for the Entry Level Certificate qualification may also be entered for GCSE history courses The courses give teachers considerable flexibility in selecting content to study from within the specifications. Pupils complete around four assessed tasks, usually set by the awarding body. These are designed to match with GCSE topics so that the course can be completed by some pupils within a GCSE class. Some history departments like the entry level certificate because it gives some students a chance to gain a qualification where they might otherwise have ended up with nothing, but take-up has thus far been modest.

Other courses include the ASDAN history short course. This can be completed as a standalone certificate, or may form part of the wider portfolio for the Certificate of Personal Effectiveness (CoPE), which has GCSE equivalence at Levels 1 and 2 (see www.asdan.org.uk/Award_Programmes/history). The OCR Level 1/2 Certificate in Applied History is an alternative qualification. It is adapted from the previous OCR Pilot GCSE course, and is graded, A* to G, to the same standard. Whilst it has equivalence at Levels 1 and 2, unlike the GCSE course, it does not count towards school league tables or towards the current e-bacc qualification. However, some schools have considered it an appropriate alternative, firstly because of the form of assessment, with 75 per cent done by coursework and teacher assessment, and secondly because there is more choice over topics studied, with local, heritage, and multi-media options for example. Four units are studied in total, allowing opportunities to go into more depth than the GCSE courses, which require a greater spread of content.

Task 11.6 *Developing insight into tasks for less able pupils post Key Stage 3*

The suggested frameworks for the Entry Level Certificate in History provide interesting insights into 'official' versions of differentiation in history. Course specification and examples of the sort of work which Entry Level Certificate pupils are asked to undertake can be accessed at:

Edexcel: www.edexcel.com/quals/elc/8916/Pages/default.aspx
OCR: www.ocr.org.uk/qualifications/entry-level-history-r434-from-2010/
AQA: www.aqa.org.uk/subjects/history/elc/history-5904

Examine a range of the tasks which pupils are asked to undertake. What insights do these tasks provide for ways of providing meaningful, worthwhile and genuinely historical activities for less able pupils? Does this provide any ideas for types of learning pupils of this ability might engage in if they were studying for a traditional GCSE course.

Take-up for 'Entry Level' qualifications has not traditionally been high. Talk to the history teachers you work with about the pros and cons of entering pupils for the Entry Level Certificate.

Teaching Advanced Level History

Background

When GCE A Levels were first introduced, sixth form education had been a 'prize' won only by the most able, most of whom were destined for university but by the mid-1990s more than 60 per cent of pupils stayed on at school beyond the statutory leaving age and full-time education post-16 was generally perceived to be desirable and an entitlement for all those who wanted it. However, a result of the move to an open access sixth form led to concern about the large number of students who, after two years in the sixth form left school with no qualification to show for their efforts. Initiatives intended to broaden the sixth form curriculum to make it appropriate to students with a variety of career goals had been less successful than hoped and concerns to improve this situation led to the setting up of an enquiry into Qualifications 16-19, which was published as the Dearing Report (Dearing, 1997).

The recommendations of the Dearing Report were reviewed and refined by the New Labour administration in 1997 and by September 2000 far reaching changes to the system of qualifications post-16 were finally implemented. In an attempt to ensure parity of esteem of General National Vocational Qualifications (GNVQ) with GCE A level qualifications all qualifications, including GCSE were accredited within a common qualifications framework, whereby GCSE (Grades A-C) is a Level 2 award and a pass grade at GCE A level or in an advanced vocational qualification is a Level 3 award. A modular structure was introduced for all post-16 qualifications and a grading scale of A-E was to be used.

Perhaps the most radical of the changes implemented in 2000 was the introduction of what was, in effect, an entirely new qualification which could be taken at 17+ and is called the Advanced Subsidiary (AS). This new qualification is gained at the midway point between GCSE and 'A2' level and recognises achievement at a standard reflecting the progress students have made at that midway point in an advanced level course. A full GCE A Level constitutes an AS in the subject (three modules of study) plus three additional modules usually taken in the second year of the sixth form and assessed at the A level standard. The QCA is currently undertaking a review of GCE A Levels across all subjects. For further detail on this, follow the URL given below.

For commentary offering some insights into the challenges and opportunities of the AS/A2 model, and the rationale behind the introduction of AS levels, see www.uea.ac.uk/~m242/historypgce/exams/as.htm

The new specifications continue to offer schools or colleges a good deal of autonomy in terms of what areas of historical content can be taught. There is scope to teach from medieval to modern and the history of a wide range of countries, although the scope for teaching the history of countries in Africa, Asia and Australasia is somewhat limited. At present, there is still opportunity for centres to offer candidates the chance to carry out a personal study which can be selected to meet an individual candidate's own area of interest, but the 'coursework' or personal study component of GCE A Level is one of the elements currently under review. From 1998, additional requirements were placed on awarding bodies in the development of the new specifications. There is now in place a set of nationally agreed criteria for each of the major GCE AS/A Level subjects, including history. These criteria provide the basis for the approval of new specifications at advanced level by QCA, ACCAC and CCEA, the regulatory bodies for England, Wales and Northern Ireland respectively who have the responsibility for ensuring the maintenance of standards and rigour of public examinations. Many of the criteria are common to all subjects at GCE Level. For example at GCE A Level, all subjects need to provide opportunities for the development of the six key skills and to indicate what aspects assist candidates in their spiritual, moral, social and cultural development as well as the provision at the end of the full advanced level course for the candidates to sit an examination that tests their understanding of the course of study as a whole, a synoptic assessment.

There are also content criteria that are different for each subject. Two aspects of the history content criteria proved to be controversial with the subject officers at the awarding bodies and within the subject community more widely, as they had significant implications for the structure of the current specifications. The first of these was the requirement for all GCE A Level specifications (but not AS specifications) to include a 'substantial element of British history'. A substantial element was subsequently interpreted as one module of the six leading to the full A Level award. The criteria also required the study of change over time of at least 100 years. The requirement to study change over time had been included in the original draft criteria and was a response to a perception from the history community, particularly historians in university departments, that A Level courses had become too narrow, with some only requiring the study of a period of 30-50 years over what was typically a two-year period of study. More recently, concern has been expressed about the trend towards many pupils' diet of history being limited post 14 to the study of 'Hitler and the Henries', and repeating the same content at KS3, KS4 and GCE A Level. This narrowing of A level courses had been the major issue emerging from the deliberations of the tribunal of subject experts on the outcomes of the 'Five yearly review of standards in A level history'.

Task 11.7 *Preparing to teach GCE A Level history*

1   History A Level specifications that are taught in schools are usually selected by the Head of Department based on three considerations: their personal preference, their expertise and the resources available to them. You no doubt wish to share in the selection but you first need to familiarise yourself with the variety of specifications available. Send for a copy of two separate specifications from two different awarding bodies. You may also send for the examiners report for that particular specification. After studying each specification, comment on the following:
    a)   Which publishers produce the appropriate course textbooks? Are they useful?
    b)   What assessment arrangements does the awarding body make?
    c)   Do the assessment procedures require resources? What are they?
    d)   Would the content of the course appeal to both teacher and student?
    e)   What teaching strategies are necessary for the course?
    f)   What skills are demanded from the students and how do you prepare them for the examination?
    g)   Does the examiner's report help you to decide whether to recommend the specifications?
    h)   How would the course work/personal study be marked?
    i)   Do you need to train the students in new assessment techniques?
    j)   Is the course 'objectives led'?
2   There is an art to asking questions of documentary sources of the type which are used in the GCE A Level examinations. Pick out some A level textbooks which have examples of documentary sources and look at the sorts of questions which are posed of them. Look at the document questions from past examination papers and then try setting your own set of questions of a small collection of documents which are appropriate for A level pupils.

Preparations for teaching a GCE A Level group

Most secondary courses are 11–18 courses so that you find yourself teaching not only KS3 and the GCSE but also some post-16 history classes. Even if you are teaching in an 11–18 school, opportunities to teach whole A Level groups for sustained periods of time are often limited. However accomplished and conscientious you may be, schools have to be careful that involvement in ITE does not compromise the examination preparations of pupils, and have to reassure parents on this point. Because opportunities are limited, you need to take advantage of any offers available to become involved in A Level teaching. This can often include observation, work with small groups, or team and collaborative teaching with the teacher responsible for the group. Often, exposure to A Level classes comes later in your school placement, when you have (hopefully) become more comfortable in the classroom and have had some time to think about the challenges of teaching A Level. Experienced teachers can often make A Level teaching look deceptively easy. Many student teachers find A Level preparation and teaching quite challenging at first, and an illuminating experience. If you do find that it is 'hard going' at first, in terms of both preparation and teaching, remember that many teachers find it to be one of the most enjoyable and rewarding aspects of teaching.

Because you are learning so much with all ages and abilities in such a short space of time, it can be helpful if the topic you are asked to teach is one with which you have considerable familiarity from your own higher education or A Level experience, but as with so many facets of school experience, it is important that you try to fit in with the needs of the department. It may be possible to negotiate A Level experience which ties in with your subject knowledge strengths and the convenience of the department, but if this is not possible, do not eschew the opportunity to get as much experience of A Level as possible. You have to accept that preparation time will be increased if you have to work on subject knowledge in addition to subject application.

Task 11.8 *NC and GCSE as a preparation for A level*

Before considering your preparation for teaching, it may be instructive to consider the extent to which NC History and the GCSE might have prepared your A level students for their history course.

1   Ask the Head of History for the appropriate documentation related to the A Level course you are to teach. This involves details of the syllabus, the department scheme of work, the assessment procedures and the examiners' reports. What are the assessment objectives for the A Level course? What are the characteristics of the work of a good A Level candidate?

2   Make a list of the principal characteristics and objectives and then consider the extent to which the study of NC History and the revised GCSE has already developed the students' understanding of history in a way that the A Level course can extend. Compare the A Level assessment objectives with the NC Key Concepts and Processes and the revised GCSE assessment objectives.

---

3   Consider (a) the development of pupils' skills in reading history; and (b) their ability to produce extended writing. How much opportunity did pupils have to develop these skills before the A Level course?

Discuss your answers to these questions with the history teachers and ask how such considerations influence their approaches to A Level teaching.

Preparation for A level teaching can be onerous and time-consuming. Because you are so conscious of the need to do your best for the students, knowing from first-hand experience the importance of grades, *there may be a danger that you allocate too much time to your A level preparation at the expense of the younger pupils.* To reduce this kind of pressure, if possible, *try to ensure that you are given as much prior notice as possible of any A level teaching commitments.* It is often better to begin your A level teaching a few weeks after the rest of your teaching and very useful to have spent time observing the class for several lessons before you take over. In this way you become more familiar with the prior content and with the teacher's style and approaches. There is a case for greater observation before taking external examination classes.

Your own knowledge of the topic

Your first concern is to gather together as much background information for yourself. Secure subject knowledge helps you to feel more relaxed and confident about teaching the class, and in responding confidently to pupils' questions. Dig out your own notes if you have them, but be prepared to discuss your preparation with the teachers. They appreciate the pressures on your time and can be very helpful in indicating useful chapters and articles for you to read. Make sure you do not confine your reading too exclusively to the topic you are to teach but read around it as well. In this respect, you should pursue what is also good practice for pupils; that is to read around the subject at several levels, studying general texts, books more specifically related to the topic in question, and also articles and monographs from journals written specifically to support A Level history, (see 'Further reading' at the end of this chapter). You may need to extend your reading as your preparation develops, and as your involvement with A Level classes extends.

Be clear about your objectives

This is just as important as for your teaching of younger pupils. In the same way as your schemes of work covered a variety of objectives and approaches with, say, KS3, the same applies to A level teaching. Different lessons will have different purposes. You need to be clear what these are and they could include:

• to contextualise, to present a general framework of the topic;
• to identify the key issues/concepts/attitudes;

- to discuss differing interpretations;
- to develop further the students' study skills
- in communication, oral, written, essay-writing;
- in expressing their opinions with confidence, substantiated by use of knowledge;
- in reading , pursuing enquiries and note-making;
- to develop further the students' historical understanding;
- in the analysis, interpretation and evaluation of primary and secondary sources;
- in the application of key concepts in history;
- in assessing the significance of events;
- to develop an informed scepticism and an acceptance of uncertainty.

Check the students' previous knowledge

As you are taking over a group during the course of the academic year, familiarise yourself with the content they have already covered. This gives you some idea about what the students may be expected to contribute and helps you to link your topic to others. You also need to find out about the abilities and attitudes of the students. With the great increase in the numbers continuing in full-time education beyond the statutory school-leaving age, *you meet a quite wide range of ability in A level groups with the result that differentiation* continues to be a significant factor in your planning and teaching.

Resources

You need to find out what books and other reading materials are in the possession of the students and what other books, articles and source material are within easy access to the students. Limitations on resources can be one of the more frustrating aspects of A level teaching and you need to find out how the department tries to manage, especially if there are large groups. Try as much as you can to resist the temptation to rely on an untransformed version of your own notes from previous study because of the limited availability of books. Your undergraduate notes, however assiduously compiled, may well be wildly inappropriate for the purposes of A Level teaching. Find out what scope there is for the students to use their own initiative, local libraries and information technology resources such as history magazines and the internet; whether some purchase their own paperbacks, and the extent to which they cooperate in the effective sharing of resources.

Choice of approaches

As with your teaching of the younger pupils, you need to include a variety of approaches and styles in the planning and delivery of your A level lessons. Indeed, many of the methods recommended elsewhere in this book can be applied with equal effectiveness in the A level classroom. Your choice of approach is, as ever, determined by your learning objectives for a particular lesson. You still need to think precisely about the outcomes for the students and try to avoid the notion that your preparation is only concerned with the historical content.

Teacher presentation

You will find that there are times when you have to do quite a lot of the talking in some lessons. It is useful to think about what aspects of the scheme is most appropriate for teacher presentation. Yet it can be an interesting challenge to try to reduce the amount of teacher talk in teaching A level history. There is a good case for teacher exposition at the beginning of a topic, to set the framework of the topic in its general context, to draw out the main issues and events and to indicate, where appropriate, the different interpretations that have emerged. Given the range of ability you are likely to encounter there remains a good case for the use of visual aids, charts, diagrams or duplicated handouts to assist your presentation. There is a good case for then presenting the students with task sheets and book references to help them to research the details for themselves rather than you pursuing such detail in a lengthy monologue while the students attempt to transfer your exposition to their notes.

Reading and note-making

Be prepared to allocate time in the classroom for the students to do their individual reading and note-making. This could give you time to talk to individuals, review their progress and apply some differentiation. The reading and note-making usually needs to be done within a prescribed framework and time limit *with clear indication about the purposes of the reading. The History Manual* (1985) by J.A. Cloake, V.A. Crinnion and S.A. Harrison remains one of the best and most detailed guides for A level students and is particularly helpful on the key activities of reading and note-making. They make the point that often students read inefficiently and ineffectively and so much thought needs to be given to helping them to make the most of their reading, especially as reading can be a neglected feature of the learning of history lower down the school. The new entrant to the A level course needs plenty of help and encouragement. There is a case for spending some time analysing some texts together, deciding what are the key points, what is noteworthy and how one might set out such notes. What students decide is noteworthy is often an indicator of their historical understanding. Inspection of pupils' notes can produce a useful dialogue. Cloake, Crinnion and Harrison also emphasise the need for the pupils to be involved in 'active' reading, questioning and consciously assimilating what is being read, with reference to their previous understanding of the topic. Diana Laffin's *Better lessons in A level history* is a more recently published book to support A level history teaching, which many student teachers have found to be helpful (Laffin, 2009). Jo Philpott's (2009) *Captivating your class* has a substantial section on approaches to A level teaching.

Source skills

The extent to which this might feature in your scheme depends on the topic you have been asked to teach and the syllabus for which you are preparing students. With a background of the GCSE pupils have a familiarity with source skills in a way that many former 'O' level candidates did not. This needs to be built upon with more advanced text and language and greater emphasis on the significance of the sources and their relationship to the wider issues. Again it is much better that such source activities are placed in the context of a genuine historical enquiry, debate or problem rather than a rather sterile skills exercise. It can be helpful to use case studies with the students being given initially a general context and framework, as advocated earlier, and then provided with a selected body of primary sources with which to analyse the historical correctness of a given statement or to discover the solution to a particular problem. Howells (2000) offers practical suggestions for the use of documents with A level pupils.

Variety of activities

Teaching A level history can offer plenty of opportunities for pair work and group work. Different groups can be set different tasks, particularly if there are limitations of resources, as a preparation for a plenary feedback. You can try to be imaginative in creating situations where the students have to make decisions, e.g. comparing the treatment of a topic by different authors, evaluating interpretations or deciding what of two written responses to a question is the better. Getting the students to be able to communicate and discuss *from an informed position* requires thought and preparation, but can be both rewarding and enjoyable to properly set up and implement.

There is a good case for using role play in A level history teaching. It will differ from similar activities with younger pupils in that it is much more firmly rooted in the sources, secondary and primary. Role play could be used effectively to draw explanations of why different historians produce different interpretations. The nature of the subject also encourages the use of set debates for which the students need to use their reading to prepare a case. They can be asked to devise and explain charts and diagrams to summarise ideas.

Essay writing

Setting essays, marking them and giving detailed feedback is another important part of A level teaching, especially as there may have been limited opportunities for extended writing in the GCSE. Many students find essay writing to be one of the most difficult features of their study and usually need detailed guidance and feedback, as well as encouragement. Study the examiner's reports for indications of the qualities that should be encouraged. They often give examples of good answers. Students can be encouraged to devise, perhaps in pairs, skeleton answers to questions as a basis for discussion.

Reviewing

As indicated above, setting reading and other tasks can free you to talk to individuals and review their progress. With a range of ability, you can try to match their individual study to their ability, suggest appropriate reading, check understanding, consider written work, including essays, and set targets. It is useful to keep your own records of such meetings.

'Flipped' classes

Laffin (2009) suggests that it can be helpful to set 'homework' for A level pupils to be done in preparation for a lesson, rather than in the aftermath of a lesson. Sometimes termed 'flipped learning', this means that pupils come into the lesson already having researched and learned about the topic in question, and this means that discussion and debate about the topic can be much richer and more focused, as the teacher is having to spend less time 'spoon feeding' the pupils with information. This approach can make for more effective use of precious lesson contact time, but of course, it depends on pupils having done the pre-session work diligently, and the teacher's skills in developing pupils' knowledge and understanding further within the lesson itself.

Team teaching

There are times when there is much to gained by team-teaching an A Level topic with the students' usual teacher. There are many ways in which together you can present differing viewpoints and stimulate debate. There are other occasions when you and a fellow student can work effectively as a pair in teaching an A level topic.

The following list is taken from a lecture to history student teachers by Bernadette Josclin of Richmond Tertiary College, which many students found helpful.

Things to try to do:
1   Plan your classes carefully within the framework of a topic and then the overall scheme of work. Keep a close eye on *timing*. Know how long you've got for each topic.
2   Ensure that students have a clear idea of where they are going in a topic/scheme of work. (Give out a typed scheme, or plan of the topic.)
3   Remember, topics take longer at the start of the course than at the end.
4   Prepare your notes using past papers, syllabuses, key texts etc.
5   *You* set the agenda in class, i.e. deadlines, work rate etc.
6   Remember to explain key concepts – particularly at the start of the course.
7   Build in a variety of activities to the sessions.
8   Start from *their* knowledge and work back.
9   Build in study skills sessions – time management, essay writing etc.
10 Organise some low energy sessions for yourself – sessions where *they* have to do most of the work.
11 Think carefully about how the work which you do in class will translate into effective revision notes for them – clear headings etc.
12 Set them work which they can bring *to* the lesson, so they know something about the lesson beforehand.
13 Check their notes/files; keeps pupils on their toes and gives you an idea of how they are translating the work you set for them.
14 Build in *regular* checks on understanding – not just essays.
15 Constant reminders of key issues.
16 Recognise and remember that most groups are mixed ability; identify learning difficulties.

17 Be clear about deadlines and stick to them, even if this is unpopular!

18 Use the blackboard (or whatever) to emphasise key words, points etc.

19 Look in GCSE and Key Stage 3 resources to see it there are good teaching ideas and resources which can be adapted.

20 Use source material wherever possible – try to develop historical skills.

21 Try and create situations where the pupils work/talk rather than you.

22 Be positive in the comments you make in response to pupils' efforts.

23 Give pupils lists of past questions at the end of a topic – useful for revision.

24 Always prepare a fall-back activity in case you run out of material.

Try not to:

1 Talk too much; what are the pupils doing?

2 Do all the work – the pupils must do some things for themselves.

3 Always have 'high energy' sessions on your part. They are not always what is educationally best for your pupils.

4 Always prioritise transmission of content at the expense of other learning objectives.

5 Be sloppy in your time keeping – punctuality to lessons, giving work back – this will only encourage the same traits in them.

6 Assume that all pupils are highly motivated budding historians. Like all other teaching groups, they need motivating and encouraging.

7 Waffle in class – be prepared! Admit mistakes if you don't know.

8 Assume too much about pupils' knowledge and vocabulary.

(Josclin, 1995)

Resources to help with A level teaching

● The major history websites for history teachers (see Chapter 10 for a list of some of these sites) have been invaluable in enabling student history teachers to quickly develop a wide range of teaching approaches and materials for A level classes, see for instance:
>   www.schoolhistory.co.uk/alevel.shtml
>   www.schoolshistory.org.uk/ASLevel_History/index.htm
>   www.activehistory.co.uk/Miscellaneous/menus/A_Level/menu.htm
>   www.thinkinghistory.co.uk/ActivityKS/ActivityALevel.html

● There are also journals specifically targeted at history teaching for examination classes (see Chapter 10), and the popular history magazines mentioned in Chapter 10 also contain articles on current historiographical controversies and issues which are appropriate for A level pupils. *History Today* has recently provided free access to articles about the A level examination from its online archive of such articles (www.historytoday.com/students).

● Diana Laffin's book *Better lessons in A level history* (London, Hodder, 2009) has a wide range of suggestions for varying teaching approaches in A level lessons.

● Teaching history also regularly has articles relevant to teaching A level (see www.uea.ac.uk/~m242/historypgce/exams/as.htm).

- Dale Banham and Russell Hall have compiled a package of resources to support history teachers in raising attainment at GCSE and A level, which can be accessed on the SHP website at www.schoolshistoryproject.org.uk/ResourceBase/BanhamHallGCSE.htm.
- Joanne Philpott's book, *Captivating your class: effective teaching skills*, (London, Continuum, 2009), has several chapters which are particularly helpful for teaching A level classes.
- See also, Gershon, M. (2014) Classroom practice – Five simple steps for raising achievement, *Times Educational Supplement*, 28 March: 34, online at www.tes.co.uk/article.aspx?storyCode=6420273, accessed 30 March 2014.
- Details of the proposed revisions to the subject content of GCSE examinations can be accessed at www.gov.uk/government/uploads/system/uploads/attachment_data/file/302157/GCSE_history.pdf, accessed 13 April 2014.
- Details of the proposed revisions to GCE AS and A level subject content can be accessed at: www.gov.uk/government/uploads/system/uploads/attachment_data/file/252939/History_subject_content.pdf, accessed 14 April 2014.

Summary and key points

Assessment in history has experienced enormous changes in the last 30 years. Much of what is now established as common practice would be unrecognisable to the history teacher of a generation ago. Such changes in assessment have resulted from the acceptance that what constitutes historical understanding involves a combination of skills, concepts, and attitudes allied to knowledge. Attempts to assess these various elements have led to the use of varied types of assessment and much debate about their validity. The recent moves away from the targeting of a precise skill towards a less compartmentalised and more holistic approach indicates a probable resolution of some of the difficulties surrounding an achievement of balance between historical understanding and knowledge.

References

Biddulph, M. and Adey, K. (2003) Perceptions v. reality: pupils' experiences of learning in history and geography at Key Stage 4, *The Curriculum Journal*, 14 (3), 292-303.

Boston, K. (2006) *QCA awards contract to develop GCSE history pilot*, Press Release, London: QCA.

Burn, K., McCrory. C and Fordham, M (2013) Planning and teaching linear GCSE: inspiring interest, maximising memory and practising productively, *Teaching History*, No. 150: 38-43.

Chapman, A. and Woodcock, J. (2006) Mussolini's missing marbles: simulating history at GCSE, *Teaching History*, No. 124: 17-36.

Clements, P. (2010) 'Picture This': A simple technique through which to teach relatively complex historical concepts, *Teaching History*, No. 140: 30-36.

Culpin, C. (2002) Why we must change history GCSE, *Teaching History*, No. 109: 6-9.

Dearing, R. (1997) *National Committee of Inquiry into Higher Education*, London: DfEE.

DfE (2013) *Reformed GCSE subject content consultation,* found at www.education.gov.uk/consultations/index.cfm?action=consultationDetails&consultationId=1911&external=no&menu=1 - last accessed 6 August 2013.

Howells, G. (2000) 'Glastone spiritual or Gladstone material? A rationale for using documents at AS and A2', *Teaching History*, No. 100: 26-31.

Husbands, C. (1996) *Why teach History?*, Buckingham: Open University Press.

Josclin, B. (1995) Unpublished lecture, Institute of Education, University of London.

Laffin, D. (2009) *Better lessons in A level history*, London: Hodder.

Osowiecki, M. (2006) 'Miss, now I can see why that was so important:' using ICT to enrich overview at GCSE, *Teaching History*, No. 125: 37–42.

Philpott, J. (2009) *Captivating Your Class: Effective teaching skills*, London: Continuum.

Wiliam, D. (2011) *Embedded formative Assessment*, Bloomington IN, Solution Tree Press.

Worth, P. (2012) Competition and counterfactuals without confusion: Year 10 play a game about the fall of the Tsarist empire to improve their causal reasoning, *Teaching History*, No. 149: 28–35.

12 Continuing professional development

Introduction

The final chapter encompasses two elements of teaching history which are not part of the competences outlined in the *Teachers' Standards* (DfE, 2012) which define the capabilities that student teachers must possess if they are to be granted Qualified Teacher Status (QTS) in England. The first is the question of applying for your first post in teaching. It is important to realise that effective preparation for this is a separate area of competence. There is no necessary correlation between teachers' classroom teaching abilities and their skills in self-promotion and preparation for job applications. There are many excellent teachers and student teachers who do not do themselves justice in terms of job applications because they have not applied the same degree of thought and rigour to the process of application as to their classroom competence in teaching history.

The second area returns us to questions which were broached in the first chapter: how do history teachers get better at teaching, and why do some progress to higher levels of competence than others?

What can you do to ensure that you are successful in your applications for teaching posts, and to ensure that your Newly Qualified Teacher (NQT) year marks the start of your progress towards becoming an inspirational history teacher rather than a competent one. You didn't go into teaching with the aspiration of becoming merely 'competent', and your school experience will quickly make you realise that a substantial part of the pleasure to be derived from a career in teaching is knowing that you are getting better at it. It is probably true to at least some extent that the better teachers become at their job, the more they enjoy their work, and in teaching, you can always get better, this is why the job does not lose its interest and challenge.

Objectives

At the end of this chapter you should be able to:

- draft a letter of application or personal statement for a first post;
- identify a range of questions which might be asked at an interview for a first post in history;
- approach your first teaching post in a manner conducive to assisting your continuing professional development and prospects for career success and job satisfaction.

Applying for your first teaching post

Advice on job applications and interviews for student teachers for all subjects is provided in Chapter 8 of *Learning to Teach in the Secondary School* (Capel, Leask and Turner, 2013). This includes sections on 'Getting your first post', and 'Developing further as a teacher'. To a large extent, this chapter confines itself to information relevant to student teachers of history.

The word processor has made it much easier and quicker to adapt personal statements and letters of application to the particular school you are applying to, and the job and person specifications to which you are directing your application. There is a tension here between simply constructing one version and sending it to all the schools you apply for, and 'customising' the content of your letter or statement in order to fit the post advertised. This is a question of judgement. If there has been no effort to direct your response to the post as specified, this might smack of laziness or a casual attitude. There is, however, the danger that if you attempt to tailor your writing to suggest that you have always dreamed of teaching in St. Swithin's, Bolton, teaching SHP GCSE syllabuses, and Edexcel 'Syllabus E' A Level, your sincerity might be called into question. Most schools accept the reality that you are applying for a range of schools; there is therefore no need to dissemble over your reasons for applying, but it is helpful at interview if it is apparent that you have made some efforts to find out about the school you are hoping to work in. At the very least, you should look at the Ofsted report on the school. Most schools now have a website, and it can be helpful to explore the school site, and see if the history department has its own website. If the departmental website is limited or non-existent, it is an area that you could (diplomatically) declare an interest in and enthusiasm for at interview if you possess the capability to make and maintain a website.

	The URL for accessing Ofsted school inspection reports is: www.ofsted.gov. uk/reports/

The schemes of work which the department has developed, and the department's choices in terms of GCSE and A level examination entry, pose questions about how to approach the issue of subject knowledge which perhaps go beyond those pertaining to other subjects. Very few applicants have expert levels of subject knowledge of all optional elements of the NC, and are familiar with all examination alternatives. You can however, 'do your homework', in terms of studying the information which the school sends to you, looking at the exam syllabuses which the school subscribes to, and considering what you would suggest as your present strengths and developing interests in terms of subject knowledge. As well as being able to talk confidently about areas of history which you think you are particularly well equipped to teach, you should be prepared to talk about the ways in which you have augmented your subject knowledge in the course of your training, and your agenda for developing your subject knowledge further. Capel *et al.* (2013) make the point that there are several ways of developing subject knowledge other than reading. This might include observation in schools, talking to fellow student teachers, watching video recordings, exploring history websites and history podcasts, and peer or collaborative teaching. Capel *et al.* also stress the importance of keeping a record of your developing breadth of competence, in subject knowledge and other areas. If you have kept a thorough record of your experiences in the course of training, it can streamline the process of constructing your letters of application and preparation for interview. If you are well organised, and make the time to record your observations, experiences and evaluations, this can also make your NQT year much easier, and save you from having to redraft lessons from scratch, instead of simply refining and adjusting what you have tried out in the course of your training.

Letters of application

Some schools require you to fill in an application form, part of which is a personal statement in support of your application, other schools simply ask for a letter of application. It is important that you do not repeat yourself and reiterate statements that have been made elsewhere in your response, for instance, in talking about your degree details in the personal statement, when they are appended in a curriculum vitae. The construction of curriculum vitae and letters of application in general are described in depth in Chapter 8 of Capel, Leask and Turner (2013).

It may be salutary to remind yourself of what schools are looking for when they seek to appoint a new member of staff. Although not all schools send out both a job description and a person specification with the details for a post, it is helpful to keep in mind that there are two ways of looking at what schools want when they advertise a post. One way of looking at this in terms of an 'audit' of various aspects of the job which need to be done – 'What is this person required to do?' Another way of looking at the vacancy is to think of what qualities a person would need in order to do the job effectively. Your letter of application should bear in mind both these considerations. Few student teachers find writing letters of application an easy or edifying process. How do you indicate that you are good without coming over as bumptious or arrogant? Many applications suffer from an inability to make clear that the candidate has not merely undergone teaching practice, but has done so successfully, and in a way which has developed their teaching skills and reinforced their commitment to entering the profession.

As in writing history, you should attempt to provide supporting evidence for your claims, but in a carefully measured and (if anything) understated manner. One way of doing this is to incorporate *brief* extracts of summary reports and lesson observation notes which have been produced in the course of your placement. This is a way of avoiding having to rely solely on personal claims about your teaching competence, and can be balanced with statements indicating that you felt or believed that certain aspects of your teaching competence developed and improved as your practice progressed. If you look carefully at all the written comments which have emanated from your school experience, it should be possible to marshal the comments in such a way as to give a clear indication of the ways in which you have done well and proved to be successful, or demonstrated the potential to be a good, or very good history teacher. So, phrases such as:

- 'My mentor noted that "Over the course of the placement Melanie developed excellent working relations with all her teaching groups"';
- 'The final summary report on my progress stated that "Alan has demonstrated exemplary professionalism in all aspect of his work in the placement"'; and
- 'My university tutor reported that "Over the course of the placement, Susan became increasingly adept at providing access and challenges for all the pupils in her teaching groups."'

There are obvious connections between the competences stipulated by the *Teachers' Standards* (DfE, 2012), and the prerequisites outlined in Figure 12.1, but schools are looking for more than a teacher who can 'adequately' fulfil the demands of the Standards. The eight domains of competence specified in Section 1 of the Standards are central to teaching competence, and schools are looking for teachers who have reached high levels in these areas of competence, but there are attributes which lie beyond this central core which can often be decisive in interview situations where more than one candidate convinces the interview panel that they possess the fundamental competences of classroom teaching.

The following list may not be comprehensive, but gives some indication of what most Heads of History would be looking for when seeking to appoint a new member of staff. The first four criteria are particularly important.

1   Secure a purposeful and controlled atmosphere in the classroom and establish positive working relations with pupils.
2   Arrive at lessons equipped with materials and ideas which provide worthwhile, stimulating and challenging learning experiences for pupils.
3   Work with colleagues in a co-operative and helpful manner and be prepared to play a full part in the life and work of the department.
4   Get good results with their examination groups.
5   Make effective use of assessment to improve pupils' learning.
6   Set and mark purposeful and worthwhile homeworks according to school policy.
7   Keep an effective record of pupil attainment and progress.
8   Liaise effectively with parents, heads of year, form teachers, other members of your department and the school's senior management team.
9   Develop and maintain the state of classrooms, prepare display work etc.
10 Contribute to the department's teaching resources and take care of resources used.
11 Be aware of, and make a positive contribution to school policies and the life of the school in general.

Figure 12.1 What do Heads of History want from a prospective member of their department?

There are other facets of classroom teaching to which departments might attach particular importance, in the light of their circumstances; the department may be looking for a new appointment who can provide a lead in the development of ICT, citizenship, or equal opportunities, but the attributes outlined in Figure 12.1 are at the heart of the work of all history departments, and the first four items on the list are of particular importance. Your letter of application, and your performance at interview should bear in mind that these are the considerations which are central to the head of history's concerns. Are you the sort of teacher who can do these things well?

In view of this question, many schools draw up a person specification as well as a job description. Even where this is not the case, in addition to teaching competences, schools are looking for teachers who possess personal and professional qualities which will complement technical classroom competence and subject knowledge. Your letter of application and your performance at interview needs to convince the panel that you are intelligent, conscientious, committed to working with young people, well organised and able to work to deadlines, with a sense of initiative and imagination, and that you are a 'reasonable human being', who has the interpersonal skills to work as part of a team. Probably the most important paragraph of your letter of application, and the one which should be longest, is the one which relates to your performances on school placement, and in composing it, you should attempt to convey these professional attributes, as well as your classroom competence in planning, assessment, and subject knowledge. It is also important to keep in mind the importance which schools attach to the life of the school beyond the classroom. It is not unknown for one of the questions at interview to be about what you could bring to the school in addition to your abilities as a history teacher.

One of the most important things when you start your school experience is to demonstrate your overall professional attitude and approach, and demonstrate to the colleagues you work with that you are conscientious, dependable, quick to learn, a pleasure to work with and keen to do the best for the pupils in your care. A further skill is to prepare and teach a series of good, well planned lessons to the classes you are responsible for, and try to establish a good working atmosphere in your classes.

Once you are (hopefully) established in these ways, you should give some thought to what else you might be able to contribute to the department and the school you are working in. Before the end of the placement, try to make sure that you make at least some contribution (preferably something you are genuinely interested in and have a real enthusiasm for) beyond the history classroom, such as extra curricular activities, ICT or SEN support, clubs, trips, sport, drama, departmental development. As well as being rewarding and worthwhile in its own right, particularly in terms of helping your relations with pupils inside the classroom, it is invaluable for your CV. Most inspirational teachers are 'givers'; they have a generosity of spirit as well as being expert practitioners.

This thought might come at a bad time when you are on your knees with the burdens of preparation, teaching, marking etc., and crawling towards Easter desperately looking forward to the break, but even if you are feeling tired, give some thought to this for action at some point in your NQT year: what would be the best way (for you as an individual) to contribute to the department or school beyond 'just' being good in the history classroom?

One final point about interview; although you are judged to some extent on the quality of your answers to the specific questions posed by the panel, your general manner and approach can have an important bearing on the outcome. If you come over as sincere, composed, intelligent, personable and committed, this may outweigh a less than perfect answer to one or more questions. Often student teachers who have been unsuccessful at interview blame their fate on the content of their response to a particular question, and underestimate the importance of their general demeanour. Although you may feel self conscious about the exercise, it can be helpful to tape record your answers to some possible interview questions, and play them back to see whether you are answering at inordinate length, whether your responses come over as glib or ponderous, faltering or garbled, or simply boring.

The following details are an exemplar of a job description for a history post. Read them and then draft a letter of application which attempts to address the demands of this particular post.

'In the first instance, the successful candidate will be required to teach across the 11–16 age and ability range, at this mixed, split-site 11–18 high school. Opportunity for 'A' level work would be considered for candidates with appropriate experience and qualifications. The person appointed would be expected to take responsibility for the teaching and organisation of history in the Lower School, under the overall supervision of the Head of History. They will also be expected to teach GCSE classes, and contribute to the department's impressive academic record in public examinations. An ability to contribute to extracurricular activities, particularly in the areas of sport and drama would also be welcomed. The ability to promote the development of information technology in the history department would also be helpful. Pupils study Modern World History at GCSE, and nineteenth-century British and European history at 'A' level. History classes are setted according to ability at the end of year 7.

The successful candidate will be expected to possess the following attributes:

- A determination to aspire to the highest academic standards for pupils.
- The ability to take responsibility and initiative in the field of curriculum development.
- Willingness to play a full part in the whole life and activities of the school.
- The ability to contribute effectively to the school's pastoral system by involvement as a form tutor.
- Expertise in information technology and its application to the history curriculum.
- Health, stamina, energy and determination.'

Figure 12.2 Composing letters of application

Task 12.1 *Adapting letters of application*

What changes would you make to your letter of application in the light of the following job specification:

'The school is seeking to appoint a candidate who will be able to teach across the age and ability range at this 11-16 inner-city comprehensive school. An ability to teach the subject in a way that will stimulate the interest and enthusiasm of all pupils is an important prerequisite for the post, as is the ability to establish good working relations with pupils. The department enters pupils for Schools Council History syllabus; pupils are in mixed ability groups from year 7 to year 9. The ability to teach some key stage 3 Geography or R.E. would be welcomed, as would a willingness to contribute to the school's extracurricular activities.

The following would be considered to be particularly important attributes for the post in question:

- Liveliness of approach and variety of teaching methodologies.
- Relationships with students and colleagues.
- Commitment to working with pupils of all abilities.
- Contribution to activities outside the classroom.
- Flexibility and resilience.'

Interview questions

Although the details of the post which you receive along with the application form may provide some clues as to what questions might be asked, and what are the most urgent concerns and priorities of the school, question spotting is as speculative an activity in the context of interviews as in attempting to predict what questions will be asked in written examinations. There may be general trends underlying which questions are 'fashionable' or prevalent, and it can be helpful to talk to peers to get a feel for the range of questions which seem to be 'current' (ICT, 'Narrowing the gap', Assessment for Learning, exam performance, differentiation, 'stretching' able pupils, literacy, independent learning, boys' underachievement) but it is probably more helpful to practice answering interview questions in general, rather than rehearse a 'set piece' answer to particular ones in the hope that you can then trot out a pre-rehearsed formula, if one crops up at interview. You should also beware of trying to say what you think the panel wants to hear rather than what you feel. Interviews are not generally a test of political or pedagogical correctness, and you are more likely to talk fluently and convincingly if you believe what you are saying. It is also advisable to be measured and careful in what you claim, rather than lurching beyond what you can plausibly claim from your limited experience. You do not want to come over as dogmatic and inflexible, but neither do you want to be seen as an empty minded opportunist.

The short list for a first appointment in history is unlikely to be fewer than four candidates, and may be as many as ten. Given that part of the day is generally given over to showing candidates round the school, introducing them to the senior management team, and meeting members of the history department, this usually leaves time for an interview of no more than 25 to 45 minutes. The former length would usually leave time for no more than five or six questions; you should be aware of these constraints, not feel the need to talk for the same length on all of them, and keep answers short if you feel you have nothing further of value to say. Another factor which you should keep in mind is that in the course of the day, the head of history will be considering whether you would be a pleasure to work with, and whether you would 'fit in' to the department, both socially and professionally. 'Reasonable human being' qualities are not central to the demands of the *Teachers' Standards*, but at this point in the process of entering the teaching profession, they are an important factor.

The following list of questions was drawn up by Heads of History who work with student teachers as examples of the sort of questions they have used at interview:

- How do you assess pupils' learning in your classes?
- Why should we give time and space to history on the school curriculum?
- How would you be able to contribute to a collaborative approach to curriculum development?
- How would you monitor and assess your own delivery of the curriculum?
- What do you feel are the most important issues in history teaching and learning?
- Using specific examples, what principles would you apply when designing resources for mixed ability classes?
- Describe a lesson that you were responsible for that you feel was particularly successful and explain why?
- If appointed to the post, what evidence might you point to in a year's time to show that you had executed the job description successfully?
- How can we maximise the achievements of our students?
- What are your principal strengths and weaknesses as a teacher, how will you ensure that the effects of your weaknesses are limited?

- How do you engage the interest and enthusiasm of the pupils for the study of history? Give some examples of ways in which you have done this.
- What can you say to persuade us that you will be successful in securing good results with examination classes?
- How can you ensure that all pupils make good progress in your lessons?
- In what ways might history teachers use ICT successfully in the classroom... can you give some examples from your own practice?
- In what ways will pupils have benefited if they have been in your history lessons from year 7 to year 9?
- What are your views on the use of *Blackadder* extracts when teaching World War One?

Figure 12.3 Interview questions

Task 12.2 *Practising for interview*

Together with two fellow student teachers, conduct a practice interview using some of the above questions, or others which you might devise. One of you should act as observer, commenting on what they felt were the strengths and weaknesses of your responses and any idiosyncrasies/ habits which might adversely influence performance at interview, such as a tendency to say 'you know' at intervals, scratching the back of your neck, looking too gloomy, or evasive eye contact.

Task 12.3 *Finding out about interview procedures and questions*

Ask your subject mentor about the general procedures for interview at the school you are working in, what questions are commonly asked at history interviews, what heads of history look for in candidates, what mistakes candidates sometimes make in answering questions, and what advice he or she would give you in terms of preparation for the interview.

Teaching at interview

It has become increasingly common in recent years to incorporate some element of presentation or teaching into the selection process. Although this introduces an extra hurdle, and possibly an element of pressure and concern into the procedures, in many ways it is easier to prepare for this element of the selection process. Unlike the interview, where you do not know exactly what will be asked of you, it is usual to give candidates a clear brief of what is to be taught, and to what class. It is not likely to be the class from hell on Friday afternoon, and there will usually be someone observing the class, so classroom management should not be a major concern. You are usually told what topic to teach but are given a degree of latitude in how to approach it. In effect, you should have a reasonable amount of time to prepare a single lesson; most applicants find that this can be a comparatively straightforward and surprisingly enjoyable aspect of the selection process, given the extent to which the candidate is informed beforehand what is required (whereas interviewees do not normally know what questions will be asked at interview). You often only have 'half a lesson', and have to plan a lesson for 20-30 minutes rather than an hour or longer, and you should take account of this in your planning rather than try and squeeze too much in and rushing your delivery. In terms of 'components', you need to show that you can teach 'from the front of the class', succinctly explaining the purposes and aims of the session, demonstrating that you have a relaxed, assured and unselfconscious presence in the classroom, that you have good skills of exposition and questioning and can interact with pupils in an accomplished way, even if this is just for a few minutes. There should generally be some 'active learning experience' for pupils, where they 'do the work', and are made to think and learn through some skilfully designed task. It can also be helpful if you can come up with at least one 'impact' resource (see Chapters 4 and 10) that evinces the pupils' interest or sticks in their minds. You should also leave at least a couple of minutes to 'construct meaning' from the encounter; to draw things together, summarise what has been learned (look for a 'golden nugget' for example – see Chapter 4), preferably in a way that makes explicit the purposes and benefits of studying and learning from the past, and a good last line to finish on. All this without rushing it! Do try to be realistic about how much you can fit in to the time available; feedback from Heads of History about the performance of students on their 'interview lesson' suggests that this is sometimes misjudged as this extract from a mentor email notes – 'We found that all the candidates today tried to cram far too much into their lessons and as a result the quality suffered as they were rushing to get through things. In all cases today it would have been better to see less done and the proper time given to each activity.' (Email from a partnership Head of Department).

The induction statement

The induction statement (formerly termed the Career Entry Development Profile) provides a formal plan for mapping your professional career development when you enter the profession. All newly qualified teachers are required to bring with them to their first post an audit of 'strengths and needs' which can serve as a basis to negotiate a programme of continuing support and professional development. You still need to work on weaker areas of your teaching, but you should also give some thought to thinking about which strengths to develop to higher levels, in order to further your career and ensure that you continue to find the business of teaching rewarding.

Some history teachers choose to focus on the consolidation of their subject knowledge, others on progressing to more sophisticated levels of expertise in ICT. Many find that involvement in the mentoring of student teachers is an interesting and helpful area for developing professional expertise. INSET courses, whether accredited and leading to advanced diplomas and masters degrees, or simply one day workshops to develop new schemes of work, do not magic away all your problems and limitations in the classroom, but can serve to sustain your interest and offer some practical ways forward.

The choice of ways forward needs to be negotiated with the school and department you work in, but it is important to be proactive in terms of your professional development;

initiative and drive are as important after QTS (Qualified Teacher Status) as before. When you start in your first teaching post, your induction statement should be given to the teacher in charge of staff development. It should be used as a basis for setting short, medium and longer term targets for your professional development. The extent to which you make the most of opportunities for development and advancement as a teacher can depend to some extent on the thought which goes into this process.

The induction statement is important, not least because it says something about you as you start in your new school, it conveys a 'first impression' of your professionalism. Some student teachers produce thoughtful and thorough induction statements, others can be careless, vague and minimalist. It is interesting to note that in the annual survey of NQTs produced by the Teacher Development Agency (TDA), only 10 per cent of NQTs felt that their preparation for completing (what was) the CEDP was 'very good'. This survey can in itself be helpful in thinking about what to put in your induction statement, as it details over 20 aspects of teaching which might be considered as areas for development (use of ICT, using assessment, managing pupil behaviour, working with pupils with SEN or EAL, teaching pupils of differing abilities and so on). The survey is available at www.gov.uk/government/publications/newly-qualified-teachers-annual-survey-2013 (or do a Google search for 'NQT survey'). One of the key things about the induction statement is not to leave it to the very end of your course of training. It should be formulated in draft form over the latter half of your training, in consultation with the teachers and tutors you work with, and should be based on the feedback you receive from them, as well as on your own ideas and priorities for development.

There should be funding available to support you in your induction year, and it helps to be aware of the range of CPD opportunities available for history teachers (see below). Although support in this area is negotiated rather than demanded of the school you will be working in, it can be helpful to them if you have clear and specific ideas about your priorities for development. This might be in the area of support for your A level teaching commitments, particular GCSE exam courses, ICT or SEN development, or help with behaviour for learning strategies. It might be as specific as indicating that it would be helpful to have departmental or personal access to *Teaching History*, or a wish to attend the School History Project Annual Conference.

Well before the end of your course, you should, in consultation with your mentor and university tutor, discuss your progress with reference to developing strengths and areas of particular interest, and aspect of your teaching which you need to prioritise in terms of the need to develop and improve. An example of a possible framework for such a discussion, in a format which might inform your induction statement, is given in Figure 12.4.

Should the requirement to complete a formal induction statement for your first post change, it would still be useful for the colleague or colleagues responsible for your professional development in your first post to have some indication of your interests, your concerns, and your comparative strengths and weaknesses when you start the job.

> **Preparation for induction statement – Questions to consider**
>
> (i) At this stage, which aspect(s) of teaching do you find most interesting and rewarding?
>   - What has led to your interest in these areas?
>   - How would you like to develop these interests?
>
> (ii) As you approach the award of QTS, what do you consider to be your main strengths and achievements as a teacher?
>   - Why do you think this?
>   - Give examples of your achievements in these areas.
>
> (iii) In which aspects of teaching would you value further experience?
>   - Are there aspects of teaching about which you feel less confident, or where you have had limited opportunities to gain experience? Do you have areas of particular strength or interest that you would like to build on further?
>   - Which of these areas do you particularly hope to develop during your induction period?

Figure 12.4 The induction statement

Getting better at teaching history

In Chapter 1, we posed the question of how people get better at teaching. It is generally accepted that it is not simply a matter of accumulated experience, and that several factors are involved, including learning from doing it, watching it being done, being instructed in it, reading about it and talking about it with fellow practitioners. Matthew Arnold, commenting on a school inspector who boasted of being an inspector of 13 years' experience, remarked that he was an inspector of one year's experience, repeated 13 times over. How can you avoid similar accusations being made of your own teaching career? Although the idea of reflective practice has become an influential one in recent years – the idea that teachers improve through the quality of their reflection on doing it, reading about it and so on – reflection on practice might not *per se* enable teachers to develop to expert levels. Part of the definition of being professional is that you want to improve and are determined to do whatever is necessary to effect improvement. Initiative, determination and ambition (to aspire to the highest possible professional standards) are as important as reflection in making progress as a teacher.

Other agendas include the question of developing ownership of your own teaching. Whilst working within the framework of your department, you will hopefully develop your own ideas and style of history teaching, and generate ideas as well as assimilating those of other history teachers and tutors; one of the pleasures of teaching as a profession is that it offers the opportunity for genuinely creative and innovative practice. There is, however, the danger of what MacDonald has termed 'induction into bad practice' (MacDonald, 1984), and of being socialised into a particular brand of professional practice, rather than remaining open to new ideas and suggestions (Calderhead, 1994). This is why it is so important to look for opportunities to meet up with and work with history teachers outside your own department, and become part of a broader 'community of practice'. As well as being useful, this is also one of the most enjoyable facets of being a teacher; teaching tends to attract 'reasonable human beings', and getting to know other history teachers is one of the 'perks' of the job. The Schools History Project Annual Conference is a good example of this (see www.schoolshistoryproject.org.uk/index.php for details).

The demands of your course, and your observations and experiences in the course of your training, will have made you fully aware that however diligent and accomplished you have been, you do not emerge from your training as the perfect, fully equipped 'expert' teacher. As in so many aspects of teaching, the idea of a continuum can be extremely helpful. The best teachers are aware of the continuums involved on the journey towards becoming an expert teacher and are constantly seeking to aspire to the highest possible professional standards. Progression is an issue that pertains to teachers as well as pupils.

Even as an NQT, you may have the opportunity to be involved in some way with working with students on their course of initial training, and as someone who has recently been through this process, you are well placed to offer support. Many mentors who are involved with working with student teachers say that they benefit from this involvement because it makes them think about their own teaching. Figure 12.5 gives a list of the qualities which the Teacher Training Agency noted as being desirable for someone mentoring student teachers.

'The ideal contributor to ITT (Initial Teacher Training) might, amongst other things, be:

- knowledgeable about teaching and learning, and still curious about them;
- knowledgeable about a subject and how to teach it;
- knowledgeable about a range of teaching methods and when and how to use them;
- always ready to reassess teaching methods in the light of research, experience and feedback (a 'reflective practitioner');
- an active listener;
- good at giving clear and constructive feedback;
- a skilful planner;
- a skilful manager of time;
- someone with plenty of enthusiasm, energy and imagination;
- someone who goes on learning throughout their career.'

(TTA, 1996)

Figure 12.5 Qualities desirable in subject mentors

At one level, this is about continuing to develop and refining your classroom teaching skills, as defined in the specifications for acquiring QTS. You *must* develop to adequate levels of competence in the areas stipulated by the QTS Standards, but you *should* aspire to excellence in all these areas, rather than settling for 'baseline' or minimum levels of competence. The framework of competences outlined for the acquisition of QTS has a continued relevance, but you should now be focusing on expert levels of competence, rather than adequacy. Thus, for instance, with regard to your ability to maintain pupils' interest and motivation, there is the question of the *range and percentage* of lessons in which you are able to arouse the interest and engagement of pupils, and get them all to commit wholeheartedly to learning, and there is also the *degree* of interest and engagement which you are able to elicit from your teaching groups – the *intensity* of pupils' commitment to doing their best in the subject. In what percentage of your lessons do pupils leave the room still talking about what they have learned? As your experience and classroom knowledge increase, there should be more and more historical topics which you are able to present in a way which elicits the engagement and enthusiasm of pupils.

If teaching is to continue to be a rewarding, enjoyable and fulfilling profession, you need to feel that you are getting better at it and learning new skills, or acquiring higher level skills in your teaching. The range of factors involved in developing into the expert teacher, and the 'complete' history person are such that as in your training, you have to make difficult choices in terms of prioritising some areas of professional development over others; this requires thought, professional dialogue with colleagues, and intelligent judgement.

The induction year

All teachers who obtain QTS have to successfully complete an induction period. If you are working part-time, this period could be up to two years. NQTs have a reduced timetable of 90 per cent of the teaching duties of staff without posts of responsibility during this period. Formative assessment of the NQT's progress involves regular observation and monitoring, and targets for progress and development are usually set as part of this process.

All this is within a professional culture of 'performance management' where the professional performance of all teachers is subject to review and development, with the intention of raising standards in schools, and enabling all teachers to fulfil their professional potential in full.

There are many areas of history teaching where student teachers develop to basic levels of competence in the course of their training, but not to higher levels of competence. The following are 'prompt' questions, which you might consider in thinking about where you are on the continuum between adequate and expert levels of proficiency in various aspects of teaching history. With all these questions, you might consider both the percentage of lessons in which ..., and the extent to which...

How effective are you at explaining to pupils what happened in the past in a way that interests them and in a way which they can understand?

How effective are the homeworks which you set in terms of advancing pupils' learning, and reinforcing their motivation to do well in history?

How effective are you in using new technology to enhance the quality of teaching and learning in history?

How effectively do you differentiate your planning for learning in a way that provides both access and challenge for pupils in your history lessons?

How broad and accomplished is your range of teaching approaches in the history classroom?

How good are you at working cooperatively with colleagues to share ideas and good practice?

How assured is your subject knowledge in the areas you are obliged to teach?

Figure 12.6 Questions to think about in terms of degrees of competence

These are but a handful of many questions/continuums which you should consider in the course of your continuing professional development. As you aspire to subject leadership, there are also agendas such as time management, administrative efficiency, professional relationships and effective communication which complement those of classroom teaching. You also need to continue to develop your subject knowledge, keep abreast of new developments in ICT, keep up to date with new ideas for teaching history, and ensure that you have an up-to-date knowledge of official documents relating to assessment arrangements and changing syllabuses.

Proposition: There are not enough hours in the day to do everything which might be done to become the perfect or complete history teacher (and keep a sliver of life apart from your teaching).

However, if you do at least some of the following things, the improvements in your effectiveness as a teacher is sufficiently rewarding to justify the time and effort involved:

- They continue to read history books for pleasure and pass on some of the fruits of their reading to pupils.
- They read books, and journal and newspaper articles about current debates about history, history teaching. and the nature and purposes of school history.
- They read review articles about new publications in history.
- They attend INSET courses and history conferences to keep abreast of new ideas and to develop a broader repertoire of teaching skills.
- They talk to other history teachers about their teaching, and exchange ideas and resources.
- They find time to read history journals such as *Teaching History*, *Modern History Review*, *History Today*, *BBC History Magazine*.
- They make changes and refinements to lessons even when they have worked quite well first time with classes.

- They keep abreast of broader educational debates by reading the Times Educational Supplement, and the weekly Education sections in the newspapers.
- They are familiar with and make regular use of good internet sites for history teachers to improve their practice.
- They continue to try out new ideas and methods in their teaching.
- They display initiative in 'scavenging' for resources which help to make lessons more vivid and enjoyable for pupils.
- Their relations with teaching groups improve as the teaching year progresses.
- They make time to talk to and work with pupils outside formal lesson time.
- They make strenuous efforts to get the best results possible for pupils taking external examinations.
- They enjoy their teaching.
- They learn to balance their personal and professional lives to the advantage of both.

Figure 12.7 Some characteristics of improving history teachers

It might also be added that at the end of term, they are tired; but in recent years, intrinsic enjoyment of employment has been increasingly regarded as an important element of job satisfaction. It is much more likely that you will enjoy teaching if you believe you are doing it effectively, and getting better at it.

The areas of competence defined by the regulations for acquiring QTS – professional attributes, professional knowledge and understanding, and professional skills – remain just as central to your development as a teacher after you have gained QTS. There are however other models of competence which might provide insight into which teachers are likely to progress towards mastery of teaching skills and expertise. John Elliott's work on action research as an agent for teacher development has been influential (Elliott, 1991, 2007). Another source of insight might be to study the weekly feature on 'My best teacher', which is now included in both the *Times Educational Supplement*, and *The Guardian*'s education section. As well as demonstrating that there are very different types of expert teacher, it is heartening to be reminded of the impact and difference that a good teacher can make.

What forms of Continuing Professional Development (CPD) are available to history teachers?

Ofsted (2006: 4) described opportunities for CPD for history teachers as 'wholly unsatisfactory... far more needs to be made available'. Research commissioned by the TDA suggested that although provision was variable, both across and within LEAs, there was a wide range of CPD opportunity for history teachers, some of which was felt to be of high quality. If you use your initiative, there are plenty of things 'out there' which can help you to develop and improve as a history teacher.

Probably the single most important thing you can do to ensure that you continue to develop and improve as a history teacher is to make sure that you continue to read *Teaching History*. Membership of the Historical Association also gives you access to the Historical Association's website, which is an excellent resource for keeping up to date with developments in the subject (see, in particular, the *history in the news* page - www.history. org.uk/resources/secondary_news_1724.html). Membership of the Historical Association also provided access to the Association's E-CPD courses and resources (www.history.org. uk/resources/secondary_page_1845.html).

Another step which we would strongly recommend is to register for the major national history conferences run by the School History Project (SHP), and the Historical Association. These conferences bring together experts in history education and large groups of dedicated and enthusiastic history teachers. The main annual SHP conference in July attracts large numbers of history teachers over the three days of the conference (Friday, Saturday and Sunday morning), and as well as providing a plethora of ideas and resources from some of the most inspirational and experienced history teachers in the country, it also makes you a part of a very uplifting and professionally affirming community of practice. As well as the ideas and resources, it is good for morale, and it can make you feel that it was a really good decision to dedicate your professional life to being a history teacher (the same benefits apply to attending Historical Association conferences).

The Prince's Teaching Institute also provides subject days for new teachers, with a particular emphasis on developing substantive subject knowledge (www.princes-ti.org.uk/ SubjectDays/), and there are also a range of commercially run courses, run by companies such as Keynote, SfE, Dragonfly, Lighthouse and others.

Ofsted (2011: 20) has pointed out that 'teachers' opportunities for continuing professional development in history have been limited', but if you use your initiative, there are still opportunities to improve your teaching, and to become part of history teacher networks, particularly if you make effective use of social media to keep up to date and in touch with other history teachers Twitter can be a useful and time-effective way of doing this, if used discerningly (see Chapter 9).

The combination of H/A membership and use of Facebook and Twitter history education links can alert you to other opportunities to share good practice and resources, such as regional seminars and conferences (London History Forum, Midlands History Forum etc.), local and regional history 'Teachmeets', where history teachers get together to quickly explain and share 'impact' resources (see Chapters 4 and 10), and other history consortia which exist or which have sprung into existence in recent years. There are still some 'county' networks, as well as seminars and workshops run by connected groups of schools, and initial teacher education mentor meetings often have a 'sharing good practice' element.

Doing a Masters Degree can improve your professional qualifications at the same time as developing your practice, and many ITE courses enable you to gain credits towards a Masters degree as part of your ITE work.

Electronic networks and resources provide useful advice and resources: the Times Educational Supplement (www.tes.co.uk/history-secondary-teaching-resources) and Guardian Education Teacher Network (http://teachers.theguardian.com/resources.aspx) have major resource collections which are free, subject to registration with the site. The School History site has an active and flourishing discussion forum, with strands of the forum, including 'Dropbox' collections, attracting thousands of posts and contributions (www.schoolhistory.co.uk/forum).

Exam boards and publishers also offer help and support to history teachers, as does Ofsted, with examples of good practice (see, for example, as one of the case studies of good practice www.ofsted.gov.uk/resources/good-practice-resource-meaningful-history-for-all-lampton-school-academy), resource packs for professional development (www.ofsted.gov.uk/resources/subject-professional-development-materials-history), and clear guidance on the criteria which are supposed to inform Ofsted inspection processes (see Ofsted website and www.uea.ac.uk/~m242/historypgce/welcome.htm). Whether all Ofsted inspectors have read these criteria is another issue, but it is difficult to accuse Her Majesty's inspectorate of not doing their best to be transparent about the 'rules of engagement' for inspection.

Task 12.4 *Finding out about history CPD opportunities*

Talk to the teachers you work with about their experience of history CPD; ask them what CPD experiences have been enjoyable and worthwhile, and which less so. Do a Google search on some of the commercial companies, awarding bodies and history organisations which offer CPD for history teachers (see list above) to get a feel for the range of courses which it is possible to enrol on. We would particularly recommend attending SHP and Historical Association conferences.

Finally, don't underestimate the potential of developing your own practice through an Action Research approach, which involves teachers researching their own practice and experimenting with different ways of doing things in a systematic and reflective way (for some definitions of Action research, go to www.uea.ac.uk/~m242/ddncl/welcome.html). A variant or strand of action research which is becoming increasingly influential worldwide is the practice of lessons study, where several teachers observe and/or record a lesson and collectively reflect on its strengths and weaknesses, and ways in which it might be improved (see Elliott, 2012 for a more developed explanation of this process). Lamb *et al.* (2012) describe a process of 'buddy peer review', whereby two colleagues (who could be student teachers or qualified teachers), agree to observe and video record one of their lessons, and then discuss their reflections on the lesson.

Summary and key points

Much of the enjoyment and fulfilment in teaching comes from the knowledge that you are continuing to become more accomplished and effective in various facets of teaching. Don't stop thinking about how to get better, and how to extend your range of teaching abilities. Be proactive in reading, observing, communicating with others, and looking out for valuable experiences.

Your ITE course is the first stage of your development as a history teacher, not the culminating point. Student teachers are not the only ones that sometimes 'plateau' in their development. A large measure of job satisfaction in teaching is derived from the satisfaction of doing the job well and getting better at it. You need to display initiative in your continuing professional development rather than simply waiting passively for professional advancement. Partly this should derive from your own sense of adventure in the classroom, partly from reading, and partly from advice, courses, conferences and guidance from other professionals. The challenge of becoming a comprehensively accomplished history teacher is a very difficult and demanding one, requiring a wide range of knowledge, skills and personal and professional qualities; the nature of this challenge helps to explain why the profession of the history teacher is such an interesting and (potentially) rewarding one.

Some history student teachers develop further than others in the course of their training. Some start well and seem to have the capacity for excellence at an early stage in the course, only to disappoint in terms of their subsequent development. Others start in a diffident and hesitant way but then make steady and sustained progress. The same variations in trajectory and progression continue after qualification. Even if you have been an outstandingly successful trainee, there are still many ways in which you can improve as a history teacher. There are two different questions which might be asked of student teachers. One relates to how far into their course it will be before those involved in their supervision and training feel confident that they meet all the Standards for QTS and can be 'passed' to go into teaching. The other is the question of the extent to which the history teacher will continue to develop towards being an inspirational and exceptional teacher, rather than a competent one. The latter question is perhaps the more important one.

Further reading

The conferences of the Historical Association, and the Schools Council History conference are important events in terms of keeping up to date with your subject and keeping abreast of the ideas of leading practitioners, official bodies and recent research into school history. In addition to keynote addresses, a wide choice of workshops, 'drop-in' ICT demonstrations, and publisher's exhibitions, it is generally exhilarating and enjoyable to meet with and talk to fellow history teachers in such a propitious and congenial environment. The conferences demonstrate that it is possible for in-service experience to be useful and enjoyable at the same time.

The main professional journal for history teachers is *Teaching History*, published four times a year by the Historical Association. As noted in Chapter 1, anyone going into history teaching should regard it as essential reading. Recent improvements to the Historical Association's website, including the archiving of past issues, the monthly newsletter, and reports on recent projects and innovations have made membership of the Historical Association even more essential.

In addition to the two recent collections edited by Davies and Harris *et al.* noted in Chapter 1, the forthcoming *Handbook of research in historical culture and history education* (Carretero *et al.*, in press), will provide valuable insights from many of the world's leading researchers in history education.

The internet address for the Historical Association is http://history.org.uk and for The Schools History Project website is www.schoolshistoryproject. org.uk/index.php.

Some recent texts on the teaching of history are more 'light' and 'user friendly' than others; they are not all easy reading, but as Lawlor (1987) has noted, many things in life – at school and later – including the acquisition of knowledge, require effort and concentration. The initial teacher education process, with its taut schedules, frenetic pace and constant demands, does not lend itself to discursive reading, but after qualification, you should at least have some time over the summer break to read some of the important and influential books which have shaped opinion on what school history should be, how it relates to academic history, and now it might best be taught.

And remember, both in your course of training, and in your NQT year, it is hard becoming an expert and inspirational teacher, accomplished at all aspects of the job. Teaching is not 'just common sense' it requires the development of a wide range of complex and sophisticated skills which take time to acquire (Elliott, 2009; Haydn, 2012). Laura Mcinerney, who was awarded the TeachFirst Excellence award at the end of her NQT year describes the challenges and difficulties of her NQT year, and the importance of just keeping going, doing your best:

> Like most new teachers, throughout that first year I endured a never-ending monotony of poor behaviour leading to little learning in my classroom. As a consequence I regularly cried my entire trip home on public transport – a journey that took the best part of an hour... By the end of the next year I was awarded the TeachFirst Excellence Award and the students in my classroom received the best results in the school. What caused the transformation? Trust me, it wasn't glamorous; it was just down to sheer hard work... First, what it didn't involve. It had nothing to do with innate teaching ability... The first time I ever taught – and a lot of the subsequent times too – were complete and utter disasters.... Really, it was terrible. **Hence whenever teachers recount their first awful weeks at school I feel fairly confident in telling them that the way you start out is not an indication of anything** (our emphasis).... Just one thing repeated over and over again in my head got me through: Is life really worse for me than it is for these kids? The answer, always, was 'no'. What I saw students going through in their lives, and yet still getting up every day and getting into school (and a school that was at times very chaotic), was truly humbling. Children whose parents neglected them. Children who were bullied by other children because they didn't look right. Children in mixed race relationships who had people spit on them in the street. Children who'd left countries where they had seen family members killed in front of their eyes. Children who cared for sick parents. Children who had no parents. All of them, children. All of them still getting on with it.
>
> In comparison what was I really complaining about? That I didn't know how to do something? That when they took all the hurt inside them and threw it out at me that it

pissed me off? Well, I would think to myself – even through tears and gritted teeth – I can take it

But, honestly, know that keeping going is about 90% of the difference. Keep turning up, keep thinking about learning, and keep pushing relentlessly toward it. After all, it's only what we expect from our pupils.

Good luck.

(This is an edited version from a blog post by Laura Mcinerney. The full post is online at http://bit.ly/1o6P2Uu)

Further reading

Chapter 24 of Harris R., Burn, K. and Woolley, M. (2014) Professional development for history teachers, *The guided reader to teaching and learning history*, London: David Fulton: 279–95.

Michael Fordham's blog, Clio et cetera, is also a useful resource: http://clioetcetera.com/author/mfordham/

References

Calderhead, J. (1994) The reform of initial teacher education and research on learning to teach: contrasting ideas, in P. John and P. Lucas (eds) *Partnership in progress*, Sheffield, University of Sheffield Department of Education. Capel, S., Leask, M. and Turner, T. (eds) (2013) *Learning to Teach in Secondary School: A companion to school experience*, 6th edition, London: Routledge.

Carretero, M., Berger, S. and Grever, M. (eds) (in press), *Handbook of Research in Historical Culture and History Education*.

DfE (2012) Teachers' Standards, London: DfE.

Elliott, J. (1991) *Action Research for Educational Change*, Buckingham: Open University Press.

Elliott, J. (2007) *Reflecting Where the Action is*, London: Routledge.

Elliott, J. (2012) Developing a science of teaching through lesson study, *International Journal for Lesson and Learning Studies*, 2 (1): 108–25.

Elliott, J.G. (2009) The nature of teacher authority and teacher expertise, *Support for Learning*, 24 (4): 197–203.

Haydn, T. (2012) 'Complex and sophisticated skills', in T. Haydn, *Managing Pupil Behaviour: Improving the classroom atmosphere*, London: Routledge: 152–77.

Lamb, P., Lane, K. and Aldous, D. (2012) Enhancing the spaces of reflection: a buddy peer-review process within physical education initial teacher education, *European Physical Education Review*, 19 (1): 21–38.

Lawlor, S. (1987) 'Correct core', in B. Moon, P. Murphy and J. Raynor (eds), *Policies for the Curriculum*, Buckingham: Open University Press.

MacDonald, B. (1984) 'Teacher education and curriculum reform – some English errors', paper presented at the Symposium *Theory and practice of teacher education*, Madrid, Ministry of Education, February.

Ofsted (2006) *Annual report of Her Majesty's Chief Inspector of schools, 2005-6*, London: Ofsted. TDA.

Ofsted (2011) *History for all*, London: Ofsted.

TTA (1996) *Qualities Desirable in Subject Mentors*, London: TTA.

Index

Figures in **bold** indicate the main section where this is dealt with in the book.

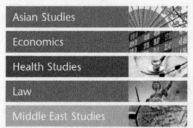